GOD AND THE ILLEGAL ALIEN

Today in the United States, millions of men, women, and children are considered "illegal aliens" under federal law. While the presence of these migrants runs against the law, many arrive in response to U.S. demand for cheap labor and stay to contribute to community life. This book asks where such migrants stand within God's world and how authorities can govern immigration with Christian ethics. The author tracks the emergence of the concept of the illegal alien in federal U.S. law while exploring Christian ways of understanding belonging, government, and relationships with neighbors. This is a thought-provoking book that provides a fresh response to the difficult issue of illegal immigration in the United States through the context of Christian theology.

ROBERT W. HEIMBURGER is Associate Chaplain with the Oxford Pastorate, Associate Researcher at the Fundación Universitaria Seminario Bíblico de Colombia, and Editor of IFES Word & World.

LAW AND CHRISTIANITY

Series Editor:

John Witte, Jr., *Emory University*

Editorial Board:

Nigel Biggar, *University of Oxford*
Marta Cartabia, *Italian Constitutional Court / University of Milan*
Sarah Coakley, *University of Cambridge*
Norman Doe, *Cardiff University*
Brian Ferme, *Marcianum, Venice*
Richard W. Garnett, *University of Notre Dame*
Robert P. George, *Princeton University*
Mary Ann Glendon, *Harvard University*
Kent Greenawalt, *Columbia University*
Robin Griffith-Jones, *the Temple, the Inns of Court*
R.H. Helmholz, *University of Chicago*
Mark Hill, *the Inns of Court / Cardiff University*
Wolfgang Huber, *Bishop Emeritus, United Protestant Church of Germany /
Universities of Heidelberg, Berlin, and Stellenbosch*
Michael W. McConnell, *Stanford University*
John McGuckin, *Columbia University*
Mark A. Noll, *University of Notre Dame*
Michael Welker, *University of Heidelberg*

The Law and Christianity series publishes cutting-edge work on Catholic, Protestant, and Orthodox Christian contributions to public, private, penal, and procedural law and legal theory. The series aims to promote deep Christian reflection by leading scholars on the fundamentals of law and politics, to build further ecumenical legal understanding across Christian denominations, and to link and amplify the diverse and sometimes isolated Christian legal voices and visions at work in the academy. Works collected by the series include groundbreaking monographs, historical and thematic anthologies, and translations by leading scholars around the globe.

Books in the series:

Under Caesar's Sword: How Christians Respond to Persecution edited by Daniel Philpott and Timothy Samuel Shah

God and the Illegal Alien Robert W. Heimburger

Christianity and Family Law John Witte, Jr. and Gary S. Hauk

(continued after Index)

God and the Illegal Alien

UNITED STATES IMMIGRATION LAW
AND A THEOLOGY OF POLITICS

ROBERT W. HEIMBURGER

CAMBRIDGE
UNIVERSITY PRESS

CAMBRIDGE
UNIVERSITY PRESS

University Printing House, Cambridge CB2 8BS, United Kingdom

One Liberty Plaza, 20th Floor, New York, NY 10006, USA

477 Williamstown Road, Port Melbourne, VIC 3207, Australia

314-321, 3rd Floor, Plot 3, Splendor Forum, Jasola District Centre, New Delhi - 110025, India

79 Anson Road, #06-04/06, Singapore 079906

Cambridge University Press is part of the University of Cambridge.

It furthers the University's mission by disseminating knowledge in the pursuit of education, learning and research at the highest international levels of excellence.

www.cambridge.org
Information on this title: www.cambridge.org/9781316629833
DOI: 10.1017/9781316817131

First published 2018
First paperback edition 2018

A catalogue record for this publication is available from the British Library

Library of Congress Cataloging in Publication data
NAMES: Heimburger, Robert W. (Robert Whitaker), 1979– author.
TITLE: God and the illegal alien : United States immigration law and a theology of politics / Robert W. Heimburger.
DESCRIPTION: Cambridge [UK] ; New York : Cambridge University Press, 2018. | Series: Law and christianity | Includes bibliographical references and index.
IDENTIFIERS: LCCN 2017034622 | ISBN 9781107176621 (hardback) | ISBN 9781316629833 (paperback)
SUBJECTS: LCSH: Illegal aliens–United States. | Emigration and immigration law–United States. | Emigration and immigration–Religious aspects–Christianity. | Political theology–United States. | Religion and state–United States. | Christianity and law. | Illegal aliens–Government policy–United States.
CLASSIFICATION: LCC KF4819 .H45 2017 | DDC 342.7308/2–dc23 LC record available at https://lccn.loc.gov/2017034622

ISBN 978-1-107-17662-1 Hardback
ISBN 978-1-316-62983-3 Paperback

For Douglas Corbett Heimburger
and Elizabeth Holloway Heimburger

Contents

Acknowledgments

As supervisors of the doctoral thesis at the University of Oxford that became this book, Bernd Wannenwetsch shaped my early thinking on the theology of politics, and Nigel Biggar honed my argument, pressing me on to completion. They served as wise and committed guides, though any errors are my responsibility. Examiners Eric Gregory and Joshua Hordern read the work carefully and provided valuable comments, while assessors John Perry, Dave Leal, and Matthew Kirkpatrick helped the work develop.

Funding came through the Sir Halley Stewart Fund and the Las Casas Institute at Blackfriars Hall, Oxford. There, Francis Davis provided early inspiration to take up this topic. At Blackfriars, Richard Finn O.P., Michael Oborne, and Richard Conrad O.P. encouraged me along the way, and the Moderators of the Hall along with Timothy Radcliffe O.P. afforded me a Junior Research Scholarship and space to turn the thesis into a book. Additional funding came from the Hensley Henson Fund through the Faculty of Theology and Religion.

Friendship and conversation with migrants drove this work forward, and among those were my students at the Shakespeare School in the Bronx, co-workers in landscaping in Birmingham, Alabama, and detainees at Campsfield House Immigration Detention Centre near Oxford. In Arizona and Sonora, Borderlinks provided a formative experience of the complexities of life along the Mexico–United States border on a trip led by Stevie Demarest and Tito Bojórquez where I spoke with "Miguel Villanueva" and others.

The Political Theology Reading Group at the Las Casas Institute shaped my thinking and writing as we read and talked together across three years. Among them, Joel Harrison helped to refine my legal arguments and my theology, Matt Anderson commented on my written work, and Mike Laffin and Brian Williams responded to presentations. I am grateful to the other members of the group, including Libby Longino, Peter Eckley, Päivi Neuvonen, Angela Wu Howard, Alex Sidhu, Emilie Noteboom, Arabella Milbank, Lexi Eikelboom, Nathan Pinkoski, Richard McCallum, and Sam Burgess.

Opportunities to air early versions of the work came at conferences and seminars in Edinburgh, Cambridge, Oxford, Sibiu, Chicago, Nottingham, and San Francisco. At these, comments by Victor Lee Anderson, James Souter, and Chris Jones were helpful, and Susanna Snyder and Joseph Wolyniak were especially encouraging. Of great value were responses to public presentations in Nashville, Oxford, Bristol, and Stanford.

Friends and colleagues gave their time to read drafts, including Philip Lorish, who kept me looking for God's work through government, along with David Robinson, Aron Mujumdar, David van Dusen, Ilsup Ahn, Therese Feiler, Ben Paulus, Ed Brooks, Matthew Moretz, and Jonathan Knoche. Others provided important insights in conversation: Stephanie Silverman, "Charles Adams," Lisa Lorish, Luke Bretherton, Jonathan Price, Oliver O'Donovan, Bob Barsky, Guido de Graaff, Victor Carmona, Matthew Soerens, Steve Meili, Vishal Mangalwadi, Casey Strine, Christopher Hays, Will Kynes, Alejandro Olayo Méndez S.J., James Hanvey S.J., Stuart Ramsay, Thomas Crockett and Tim Johnson at Rep. Spencer Bachus' office, Jenny Yang, Gordon McConville, Debbie and Scott Pennington, Mark and Marian Wilson, Joe Martin, Susan and Dem Ward, Betsy Heimburger, Corb and Carol Heimburger, and many more.

Librarians at Blackfriars Library, the Bodleian Library, and the Heard Library at Vanderbilt University made resources available for this project. Trinity College Bristol and Justin Stratis provided a welcoming place to write away from home. Through the last stages, Jonathan Brant, Michael Lamb, and others with the Oxford Character Project, and Tim Adams and others at I.F.E.S. helped bring the work to completion. At Cambridge University Press, Rebecca Jackaman, series editor John Witte, Jr., John Berger, Brianda Reyes, Claudia Bona-Cohen, Chloé Harries, Sindhujaa Ayyappan, Kevin Hughes, Paris West, Sian Welch, and others were a pleasure to work with. Comments from two anonymous readers strengthened the book.

My wife, Lizzie, has been a constant support, conversation partner, and source of laughter over the years that this project has developed. Our sons, were born during the years of writing, bringing me great joy. My parents-in-law, Jenny and Peter, assisted with childcare when I needed to be away from home. This work is dedicated to my parents, Doug and Beth, who supported me through the process of writing this book and were among its most eager readers. I thank each of these people, and I thank God for them.

Explanatory Note on the Cover Image
Ferdinand Hodler, *The Good Samaritan*, c. 1881. ©2017 Kunsthaus Zürich, Loan of the Gottfried Keller Foundation, Bundesamt für Kultur, Bern.
This image was chosen to reflect the mercy those deemed "illegal aliens" show to those who have permission to live in the United States.

Note to the Reader

It seems best to translate a crucial term from the Hebrew Bible, the גֵּר, gēr, as "migrant," "immigrant," or "displaced person," and other terms, נֵכָר, nēḵār, and נָכְרִי, noḵrî, as "foreigner," "stranger," or "outsider." The introduction describes how M. Daniel Carroll R. and James K. Hoffmeier handle these terms (pp. 5–10). On the gēr, Frank Anthony Spina is largely correct to define גֵּרִים, gērîm, as those outside of their original social setting who depend on a new group for their wellbeing.[1] Spina thinks that the term "immigrant" ably captures the way the gēr settles in a place after emerging from some degree of social conflict, and he prefers it to the "resident alien" or the "sojourner," which focuses on the present settlement of the person. As support, he cites three meanings of the related verb גּוּר, gûr, which can mean "to sojourn," "to stir up strife, create confusion, quarrel," or "to dread, be afraid."[2] He reckons that the use of gēr combines these meanings, as one who comes to settle in a new place, escaping from strife and experiencing fear.[3] When Spina uses the term "immigrant," he thinks of the gēr as someone from outside the community but not necessarily from outside of the nation of Israel, and so on Spina's own grounds, "migrant" or "displaced person" are better terms than "immigrant." Mark Awabdy agrees with Spina in translating gēr as "immigrant," arguing that the term indicates living outside the boundaries of one's place of origin, whether that person comes from within Israel or without Israel.[4] Since the term

---

[1] Frank Anthony Spina, "Israelites as Gērîm, 'Sojourners,' in Social and Historical Context," in *The Word of the Lord Shall Go Forth: Essays in Honor of David Noel Freedman in Celebration of His Sixtieth Birthday*, ed. Carol L. Meyers and Michael Patrick O'Connor (Winona Lake, Ind.: Eisenbrauns, 1983), 323. Material on the gēr appears in earlier form in Robert W. Heimburger, "Migration through the Eyes of Faith: God's People, National Lands, and Universities," *IFES Word & World*, no. 1 (May 2016): 6n4, used here by permission.

[2] Spina, "Israelites as Gērîm," 325.

[3] Ibid., 325–27.

[4] *Immigrants and Innovative Law: Deuteronomy's Theological and Social Vision for the Gēr* (Tübingen: Mohr Siebeck, 2014), 1–5.

"immigrant" tends to connote someone whose origin is outside of the political community where they currently reside, the suggestions of Spina and Awabdy that the *gēr* includes the internal migrant suggests that the best way to translate *gēr* is as "migrant."

The scholarly literature suggests other interpretations of the *gēr*. Christoph Bultmann traces a trajectory, proposing that in Deuteronomic law (chs. 12–26), the *gēr* was someone who did not own land and came from outside of the community, though perhaps still within Israel. By the time of the Holiness Code of Leviticus 17–26, he thinks that the *gēr* is a social class of Israelites, a group without land or family. Eventually, he sees the *gēr* as describing a circumcised convert who can partake in the Passover in Exodus 12:43–49, while the *nokrî* cannot partake.[5] Christiana van Houten also draws a trajectory, understanding *gērîm* in Deuteronomy as non-Israelites and *gērîm* as converts in those redactions of the Priestly Laws that she takes to arise after Israel's exile.[6] José E. Ramírez Kidd mentions another view, that the *gērîm* were immigrants fleeing from the northern kingdom after the fall of Samaria in 721 B.C.[7] Spina counters views like Bultmann's and van Houten's by arguing that the understanding of the *gēr* as a migrant cannot have arisen during Israel's exile, since the exile is only once spoken of as sojourning, in Ezra 1:4. Neither could the idea of Israel as *gērîm* have arisen during the settlement of Canaan, he argues, since there would be no reason for a settled people to begin imagining themselves as the children of migrants. Spina points to biblical passages that frame the patriarchs as *gērîm* prior to Israel, arguing that neither during the exile nor during the settlement would Israel have reason to introduce sojourning into earlier stories where it had not occurred.[8] Spina concludes that the account of Israel as *gērîm* in Egypt arose before Israel settled in Canaan. Thus, he thinks the Old Testament texts present a historically accurate memory of an experience as immigrants in Egypt.[9] Spina's case is convincing.

Despite their differences, all these authors agree that the *gēr* is a vulnerable outsider who might provoke conflict. Spina, with the more traditional interpretation, is open to the *gērîm* coming from outside Israel, not only from outside the clan or

---

[5] *Der Fremde im antiken Juda: eine Untersuchung zum sozialen Typenbegriff gēr und seinem Bedeutungswandel in der alttestamentlichen Gesetzgebung* (Göttingen: Vandenhoeck & Ruprecht, 1992), 34–119, 175–90, 200–207.

[6] *The Alien in Israelite Law* (Sheffield: J.S.O.T. Press, 1991), 106–8, 155–57.

[7] *Alterity and Identity in Israel: The Gēr in the Old Testament* (Berlin: De Gruyter, 1999), 5–6. See also D. Kellerman, who points out that the gēr stands between the native אֶזְרָח,'ezrah, and the foreigner, the nokrî, "גּוּר gûr; גֵּר gēr; גֵּרוּת gērûth; מְגוּרִים meghûrîm," in *The Theological Dictionary of the Old Testament*, ed. G. Johannes Botterweck and Helmer Ringgren, trans. J. T. Willis, vol. 2 (Grand Rapids, Mich.: Eerdmans, 1975), 439–49.

[8] Spina, "Israelites as Gērîm," 321–22. Among accounts of the patriarchs, Spina cites passages of sojourning among the Philistines, in Sodom, on an earlier visit to Egypt, with Laban, in Canaan and in Hebron: Genesis 12:10, 19:9, 20:1, 21:34, 23:4, 26:3, 32:4, and 35:27; Exodus 6:4; and Psalm 105:12.

[9] Ibid., 329.

tribe. "Migrant" and "displaced person" thus emerge as fitting translations for this person who might come from within or without the nation's boundaries. The *noḵrî* and the *nēḵār*, on the other hand, cannot or do not join themselves to Israel, and they are foreign visitors rather than migrants or resident aliens. These are others, the ones outside the family, strangers, foreigners, or simply foreign countries.[10]

---

[10] B. Lang and Helmer Ringgren, "נכר nkr; נֵכָר nēḵār; נָכְרִי noḵrî," in *The Theological Dictionary of the Old Testament*, ed. G. Johannes Botterweck, Helmer Ringgren and Heinz-Josef Fabry, trans. David E. Green, rev. edn., vol. 9 (Grand Rapids, Mich.: Eerdmans, 1998), 425–26; Ludwig Köhler and Walter Baumgartner, *The Hebrew and Aramaic Lexicon of the Old Testament* (*K.B.*), trans. M. E. J. Richardson (Leiden: Brill, 1994), 700.

Abbreviations

C.B.P.	United States Customs and Border Protection
C.D.	Karl Barth, *Church Dogmatics*
E.N.	Aristotle, *Nicomachean Ethics*
I.C.E.	United States Immigration and Customs Enforcement
I.B.P.	Grotius, Hugo. *De Iure Belli ac Pacis: In quibus ius naturae & Gentium: item iuris publici praecipua explicantur.* Ed. 2a emendatior & multis locis auctior. Amsterdam: Guilielmum Blaeuw, 1631
I.G.	O'Donovan, Oliver and Joan Lockwood O'Donovan, eds. *From Irenaeus to Grotius: A Sourcebook in Christian Political Thought 100–1625.* Grand Rapids, Mich.: Eerdmans, 1999
K.B.	Köhler, Ludwig and Walter Baumgartner. *The Hebrew and Aramaic Lexicon of the Old Testament.* Translated by M. E. J. Richardson. 5 vols. Leiden: Brill, 1994
K.D.	Karl Barth, *Kirchliche Dogmatik*
L.W.	Luther, Martin. *Luther's Works.* 55 vols. American edn. St. Louis: Concordia, 1955–1986
O.L.D.	Glare, P. G. W., ed. *Oxford Latin Dictionary.* Oxford: Clarendon Press, 1982
W.A.	Luther, Martin. *D. Martin Luthers Werke: Kritische Gesamtausgabe.* Weimar: Hermann Böhlaus Nachfolger, 1883–1929

Legal Citations

H.B.	House Bill
H.R.	United States House of Representatives Bill

I.N.A.	Immigration and Nationality Act of 1952, with Amendments
Stat., as in 1 Stat. 103	United States Statutes at Large
S.	United States Senate Bill
S.B.	Senate Bill
U.S., as in 130 U.S. 581	United States Reports
U.S.C.	United States Code

Bibles and Bible Translations

A.V.	Authorized Version, a.k.a. King James Version
E.S.V.	English Standard Version
N.A.S.B.	New American Standard Bible (Update)
N.I.V.	New International Version (2011, unless otherwise noted)
N.J.B.	New Jerusalem Bible
N.R.S.V.	New Revised Standard Version
R.S.V.	Revised Standard Version
T.N.I.V.	Today's New International Version

Permissions

The author and publisher gratefully acknowledge the permission granted to reproduce the copyright material in this book.

the National Council of the Churches of Christ in the United States of America. Used by permission. All rights reserved.

Scripture quotations marked R.S.V. are from the *Revised Standard Version of the Bible*, copyright ©1946, 1952, and 1971 the Division of Christian Education of the National Council of the Churches of Christ in the United States of America. Used by permission. All rights reserved.

Every effort has been made to trace copyright holders and to obtain their permission for the use of copyright material. The publisher apologizes for any errors or omissions in the above list and would be grateful if notified of any corrections that should be incorporated in future reprints or editions of this book.

Introduction

When I met Miguel Villanueva in the Mexican border town of Nogales, he had just been removed from the United States. He talked to me in fluent English as he ate breakfast at the Kino Border Initiative, a Roman Catholic shelter for migrants. After a prayer by a Jesuit priest, Miguel told me that at age fifteen, he had left his home in Mexico, where jobs were scarce and those that were available hardly paid enough to buy clothes, food, and fuel. Miguel and his brother headed north to the United States, settling in a Midwestern city. There he met a woman he came to call his wife, and together they had a daughter, now aged three. Lately, Miguel had worked two jobs waiting tables, one at a Mexican restaurant and another at an American breakfast restaurant.[1]

The trouble was that Miguel didn't have papers. He had entered the United States illegally, without permission from U.S. immigration authorities. Miguel's common law wife had permanent residency, and his daughter was a U.S. citizen because she was born on U.S. soil. Though Miguel lacked proper documentation, he managed to live in the Midwest for six years without being caught or deported. He tried registering for high school, but the school officials asked him for a Social Security number and identification, which he did not have. But just recently, at age twenty-one, Miguel was caught driving without a license, and the police handed him over to the immigration authorities. He was given the option of paying bail and waiting for a court date, where he might be sentenced to a few months in jail. Instead, he decided to return to Mexico, and the officials sent him to a Texas border town where he crossed into Mexico. After returning to see his mother – his father had died years before – Miguel made his way north to rejoin his wife and daughter. In decades past someone like him would have attempted a crossing at one of the larger border cities,

---

[1] To protect the subject's identity, his name has been changed and his places of residence have not been revealed. Given these conditions, the subject gave oral and written permission to let his story be used.

from Tijuana to San Diego or from Ciudad Juárez to El Paso, but now these cities had well-guarded crossing points, and high walls stretched along the U.S.-Mexico border for miles into the countryside. Avoiding the cities, Miguel crossed through the desert that stretches from the Mexican state of Sonora to the U.S. state of Arizona, a way that has led to death for many thousands of border crossers since 2000. Though he did not tell me so, Miguel probably paid someone called a *coyote* to help him across the border. He joined a group to walk on foot through an unfortified section of the border, making his way under a hot, dry sun through a mountainous landscape of snakes and scorpions, prickly cactuses, and flash floods in the summer monsoon season. After three days, the U.S. Border Patrol found Miguel, and when he could not produce travel documents, they took him into custody. As part of the Operation Streamline program, Miguel was tried along with dozens of others for illegal entry or reentry. He pled guilty to avoid a sentence of a year or two if he fought the charge. The judge gave him a month and a half in prison, telling him that if he was caught again he could be charged with a felony and spend years in prison. After serving his time in a jail in Arizona, Miguel was transported across the border to Nogales, Sonora, and left there.

At the Kino Border Initiative, Miguel ate his breakfast eagerly. I asked him what his plans were. "I'll go back to see my mother for a little while." "But you want to get back to your family, don't you?" I said, and he told me, "Yes, I'll try to get back to them. Can I go back to Tucson with you today?" "No, I'm sorry," I responded, pondering what it would be like to hide him in the fifteen-passenger van that would take me back to the United States that day. "When are you coming back here?" he asked. "I don't know," I said.

Rev. Charles Adams pastors an evangelical church in a small city in the American South.[2] He told me that a family like Miguel's comes to worship at his church. The parents lack the documents that would allow them to stay in the United States legally, and while in the United States they have had three children. Like Miguel's daughter, these children are U.S. citizens because every person born in the United States is a citizen. If the parents were to follow the law, they would have to move with their children to a country their children have never lived in, likely to a place where opportunities to make a living and support their children are few. Pastor Charles said that his church members do not feel it is appropriate to hire the parents to work for them, something that would be against the law. He said that the church has occasionally helped the family with personal needs, like taking them to see a lawyer, who was not able to help them find a way out of their dilemma. When I contacted Charles a few years later, he told me that the family was still at his church, and their son was to be baptized that week. The parents were working and paying Social Security taxes, but lawyers told them there is nothing they can do but

---

[2]   The name of the pastor has been changed and the location of his church hidden to protect his identity and the identity of the family. Under these conditions, the subject gave written permission for the use of his story.

wait, staying with their three U.S. citizen children, but staying without legal status. Charles refrained from telling me anything more, and his reticence indicated the bind he is in as the family's pastor and as a citizen who wishes to uphold the law.

Spencer Bachus served as a Republican member of the U.S. House of Representatives from 1993 to 2015, representing much of the Birmingham, Alabama, metropolitan area.[3] A regular churchgoer, Bachus attends Hunter Street Baptist Church in the Southern Baptist Convention.[4] During his last term in Congress, he served on the House Judiciary Committee, the committee that must approve proposals to alter immigration laws before the entire House has a chance to vote on the laws. On most issues, Bachus tended to side with the more conservative end of his party, but he broke rank with his peers on immigration issues. Up for debate in 2013 was a series of proposals for reform, many gaining support from conservative Republicans in the House. While his fellows supported an increase in funds and agents committed to border security and an increase in visas for highly skilled workers, few of them supported an additional proposal, a pathway to citizenship for those illegally present in the United States. Bachus' conservative colleagues rejected this pathway as a concession to lawbreakers who should be deported from the country.

Bachus saw things differently, and he said that his Christian faith guided his judgment. When a constituent asked about immigration reform at a meeting in Gardendale, Alabama, Bachus spoke highly of recent immigrants, saying that nearly all of them came to the United States for the same reason present citizens' ancestors immigrated, to seek a better life. He pointed out that nearly all immigrants who lack legal status live with family members who are U.S. citizens. In many cases, enforcing immigration laws would mean dividing families. Said Bachus, "Y'all may think I'm copping out, but with my Christian faith, it's hard for me to say that I'm going to divide these families up." He related stories of constituents, a Guatemalan national who grew up in the United States and did not speak Spanish removed to Guatemala at age eighteen, a widow of a U.S. veteran threatened with deportation to the Philippines, and a fast-food manager who depended on undocumented workers to clean his store overnight. Bachus gave his prescription: "Bring them into our system. Give them legal status. They will pay worker's compensation. They will pay Social Security. They'll work hard." If nothing is done, Bachus said, these men and women will continue to work in the shadows and undermine legal residents' wages. He concluded: "I'll tell you this, as your Congressman, I am not going to separate families or send them back."[5]

---

[3] "Bachus, Spencer T., III - Biographical Information," *Biographical Directory of the United States Congress*, accessed April 20, 2016, http://bioguide.congress.gov/scripts/biodisplay.pl?index=B000013.

[4] "Chairman Spencer Bachus," *House Committee on Financial Services*, accessed April 20, 2016, http://financialservices.house.gov/about/chairman.htm.

[5] Rep. Spencer Bachus III, "Speech to Constituents" (Gardendale Civic Center, Gardendale, Ala., August 21, 2013), www.dropbox.com/sh/lwo6835cvqrzofc/-xwvCTxas9; Greg Sargent, "A Conservative Christian in a Deep Red District Makes Case for Immigration Reform,"

More than eleven million men, women, and children are estimated to live in the United States without authorization, amounting to a little over three out of every hundred residents.[6] Those who remain in the United States live what Leo Chavez calls "shadowed lives," avoiding contact with government agencies while working without permission, going to college with little prospects for jobs afterwards, driving without a license, or witnessing crimes they are afraid to report.[7] Many experience life in the United States as what a character in a song by the band Los Tigres del Norte calls a *jaula de oro*, a golden cage, his prison. "I hardly ever leave the house / Well, I'm afraid they'll find me / and they can deport me," he sings.[8] Those like Miguel Villanueva who are prevented from returning to the United States leave behind a spouse or children whom they will rarely or never see. Some like Charles Adams' congregants who remain in the United States without permission feel torn between following the law and supporting their U.S.-born children. In churches like Adams', those who lack legal residency may be baptized and communing members, but their fellow churchgoers are hesitant to give them work. Those already established in the United States are unsure how to love their "illegal" neighbors. Lawmakers like Spencer Bachus want to prevent illegal immigration, but they find that their worship of Jesus Christ makes them unwilling to support enforcing the law if it means removing one member of a family to another country. In these stories and many more, following federal law stands at odds with the chance to make a decent living, the care of children and the unity of the family, the communion of the church, and friendship between neighbors.

Washington Post, August 23, 2013, www.washingtonpost.com/blogs/plum-line/wp/2013/08/23/a-conservative-christian-in-a-deep-red-district-makes-case-for-immigration-reform/.

[6] Jeffrey S. Passel and D'Vera Cohn, "Overall Number of U.S. Unauthorized Immigrants Holds Steady Since 2009" (Washington, D.C.: Pew Research Center, September 20, 2016), 3, www.pewhispanic.org/2016/09/20/overall-number-of-u-s-unauthorized-immigrants-holds-steady-since-2009/, estimate that 11.1 million people lived in the United States without authorization in 2014. These can only be estimates, since unauthorized immigrants meet with success so long as they avoid detection. The same report estimated that in 2014, the median length of time that unauthorized immigrants had lived in the United States was 13.6 years. Passel et al. arrive at their figures through what is called the "residual method," subtracting a government estimate of legal residents from the total foreign-born population measured in a survey, ibid., 22–24, 29–30. Their 2016 report bases its figures for 2014 on estimates of the total U.S. population from the American Community Survey, which lists the U.S. population in 2014 as 318,857,056. 11.1 million is 3.14 percent of this total, or a little over three per hundred residents, ibid., 8, 22; U.S. Census, "American Community Survey Demographic and Housing Estimates: 2014 1-Year Estimates" (U.S. Census Bureau, 2014), https://factfinder.census.gov/faces/tableservices/jsf/pages/productview.xhtml?pid=ACS_14_1YR_DP05&prodType=table.

[7] Leo R. Chavez, *Shadowed Lives: Undocumented Immigrants in American Society* (Fort Worth: Harcourt Brace Jovanovich, 1992).

[8] *Casi no salgo a la calle / Pues tengo miedo de que me hallen / y me pueden deportar / . . . Aunque la jaula sea de oro, / no deja de ser prisión*, Los Tigres del Norte, *Jaula de Oro*, Jaula de Oro (Fonovisa, 1984). Translation author's.

CHRISTIAN VOICES ON ILLEGAL IMMIGRATION

What response does Christian theological ethics offer to illegal immigration in the United States? For someone who is unlawfully present like Miguel, for a church like Pastor Charles' where some members lack legal status, for a lawmaker like Congressman Bachus seeking to be wise and faithful, what counsel does the Christian faith provide? Amid a battle over language, how can this sort of migration be spoken of with truth and charity? What guidance does the faith offer to those who are considering migrating or have already immigrated without legal authorization? Before God, how can governments judge justly and churches act faithfully?

These questions need answers. Among theologians, discussion has begun, but more needs to be said to provide a robust response to illegal immigration. This will become clear through a review of works that have come out of two significant Christian communities in the United States. Evangelical Protestants form the first community, represented here by Daniel Carroll and James Hoffmeier. Roman Catholics form the second, represented here by Magisterial teaching since the late nineteenth century. Recent academic monographs in Christian ethics have begun to contribute to these discussions, as the third section will show. The impasses and the gaps in these discussions provide the occasion for this book.

Evangelical Biblical Scholars on Illegal Immigration

Where can Christian wisdom on illegal immigration be found? One of the larger Christian communities in the United States, evangelical Protestants, tends to look to the Bible. Two Old Testament scholars represent this tradition as they seek to present how the Bible deals with migration, reading it in an American context and writing short books for a general but intelligent audience. These are M. Daniel Carroll Rodas, author of *Christians at the Border*, and James K. Hoffmeier, author of *The Immigration Crisis*. Both scholars are clear that due to God's character and the identity of God's people, immigrants deserve respect, love, and just treatment.[9] They also agree that the Old Testament attests to borders, border controls, and practices of granting permission to cross borders in the Ancient Near East.[10] But Carroll and Hoffmeier interpret Old Testament legislation about migrants differently, and from the New Testament they draw out opposing views on how Christians ought to interact with civil law. As a result, their counsel on illegal immigration differs.

---

[9] M. Daniel Carroll R., *Christians at the Border: Immigration, the Church, and the Bible*, 2nd edn. (Grand Rapids, Mich.: Brazos Press, 2013), 77–78, 87, 91, 94–100; James K. Hoffmeier, *The Immigration Crisis: Immigrants, Aliens, and the Bible* (Wheaton, Ill.: Crossway, 2009), 73, 75–76, 79, 120–21.

[10] Carroll R., *Christians at the Border*, 2013, 83–85; Hoffmeier, *The Immigration Crisis*, 32–34, 38–39, 57.

One aim of this book is to continue the unfinished discussion between Carroll and Hoffmeier, and so their discussion deserves attention.

The two scholars differ first in the way they read Old Testament legal codes about migrants. Looking to terms for migrants and foreigners in the Hebrew Scriptures, Daniel Carroll writes that the adjectives נָכְרִי, *nokrî*, and זָר, *zār*, apply to foreigners who may be newcomers to Israel but remain unassimilated, while the noun תּוֹשָׁב, *tôšāḇ*, seems to indicate one who relies on Israel for her sustenance. The more notable word is *gēr*, sojourner or migrant, and the term to which the laws about just treatment apply.[11] Sojourners were the ones the law says to love and to treat justly. These people without kin and land, who lacked ways to provide for themselves, were guaranteed protection in Israelite households and farms, at the temple, and at the city gate, where elders would issue judgments.[12] Unique among Ancient Near Eastern laws, these laws flowed from two sources, says Carroll: First, Deuteronomy and the Psalms present God as one who loves the sojourner, so that the one who does justice to the foreigner imitates God.[13] Second, the presence of immigrants reminded Israel that they had been sojourners enslaved in Egypt but rescued by a God who provided them with their land. "[T]he arrival and presence of sojourners," Carroll intimates, "were not a threat to Israel's national identity; rather, their presence was fundamental to its very meaning."[14] Since justice for the immigrant distinguished Israel's law from the laws of its neighbors and since it is described as a character trait of God himself, Carroll thinks that justice for the sojourner applies today. He says that like in ancient Israel, immigrants do not threaten American identity; rather, they remind the United States of her identity as a nation of immigrants.[15]

James Hoffmeier takes a different stance on the Old Testament terms for foreigners. Hoffmeier thinks these terms can be specified more fully, writing that the *nokrî* and the *zār* could be enemy invaders, squatters, people passing through, or workers residing for a limited time. Hoffmeier considers the *gēr* to be a foreigner who has been offered hospitality by a host, legally allowed to enter, protected by a sponsor, and when coupled with the term *tôšāḇ*, residing for a time.[16] Even the *gēr*, he says, could not invite family members to join him in his new land, except in the case of a spouse.[17] Hoffmeier finds a distinction between a foreigner and a resident alien, one passing through or staying temporarily and one who has been invited to stay for a while.[18] He infers that the *gēr* has "followed legal procedures to obtain

---

[11] Carroll R., *Christians at the Border*, 2013, 85–87.

[12] Ibid., 88–89.

[13] Ibid., 77–78, 87, 91; see Deut. 10:17–19; Ps. 146:6–9.

[14] Carroll R., *Christians at the Border*, 2013; see Exodus 22:21; 23:9; Leviticus 19:34; Deut. 5:15; 10:19; 16:12; 24:18, 22; 26:5–10.

[15] Carroll R., *Christians at the Border*, 2013, 96–98.

[16] *The Immigration Crisis*, 50.

[17] Ibid., 51.

[18] Ibid., 48–52, 57.

recognized standing as a resident alien," and he concludes that the laws concerning justice toward the foreigner only apply to the legal resident alien, not to the outright foreigner.[19]

When in the Old Testament, God commands and invites God's people to love the sojourner as God does, Hoffmeier thinks that this sojourner corresponds to the legal immigrant in contemporary America, while other types of foreigners correspond to illegal immigrants today.[20] Many of the recommendations that Hoffmeier draws out of the Old Testament, including equal treatment under the law and equal social benefits as citizens, apply in his opinion only to the legal immigrant.[21] Carroll disagrees: He thinks that the distinctions between terms for foreigners and migrants in the Old Testament do not correspond to distinctions between legal and illegal immigrants today. The Scriptures do not describe processes for securing legal residence or monitoring passage across borders, says Carroll: instead, they encourage a "surprising openness" to migrants.[22] Writing a more extended response in a review of Hoffmeier's book, Carroll ties this alleged misreading of Old Testament terms to a troubled starting place. Hoffmeier, says Carroll, starts his discussion with questions about borders and legal status, and this tone continues throughout his discussion. Carroll, on the other hand, begins by describing human beings as valuable and made in the image of God, and this starting point informs his treatment of immigration.[23]

Not only do Carroll and Hoffmeier differ on their views of Old Testament laws about migration, but they differ about what the New Testament says about Christian responsibility before civil government. On this subject, the two authors carry out a dialogue between the first edition of Carroll's book, Hoffmeier's book, and Carroll's second edition. In his first edition, Daniel Carroll deals with the place of government by qualifying the well-known passage from Romans 13:1–7 that begins, "Let every person be subject to the governing authorities. For there is no authority except from God, and those that exist have been instituted by God."[24] Carroll says that many quote this passage and bring discussions of illegal immigration to a quick end with the simple answer that Christians must follow the law.[25] Instead, Carroll chooses to place Paul's instruction about the governing authorities within a broader framework. He begins with Christ as a refugee and Christians as aliens and strangers, and he points to the Lord's Supper and the cross as situating hospitality at the center

[19] Ibid., 52.
[20] Ibid., 48–52.
[21] Ibid., 76, 89, 96.
[22] Carroll R., *Christians at the Border*, 2013, 94.
[23] M. Daniel Carroll R., "Review: James K. Hoffmeier, The Immigration Crisis: Immigrants, Aliens, and the Bible," *Denver Journal* 13 (2010), www.denverseminary.edu/article/the-immigration-crisis-immigrants-aliens-and-the-bible/.
[24] Romans 13:1 (E.S.V.)
[25] M. Daniel Carroll R., *Christians at the Border: Immigration, the Church, and the Bible* (Grand Rapids, Mich.: Baker Academic, 2008), 131.

of the work of God.[26] Next, Carroll refers to the context of the Romans 13 passage in Romans 12, where the Apostle Paul tells his readers not to be shaped by the "pattern of this world" but to love and serve their enemies.[27] He says that this must serve as the backdrop for a reading of Romans 13, which he does not quote. In the United States, national leaders agree that immigration law must be reformed, Carroll notes, adding that in a democracy, citizens are permitted to seek reform. Many "undocumented immigrants," he says, are Christians, and the Hispanic evangelicals and Pentecostals that he knows take Romans 13 seriously, recognizing that they violate the law, but recognizing the law's "contradictions and inequities" as well. He concludes by asking his readers to approach present U.S. laws "self-consciously *as Christians.*"[28]

Hoffmeier answers Carroll, framing his consideration of church and state issues by saying that because believers belong to the kingdom of God, they are dual citizens and aliens in the world. He draws on passages from the gospels that point to obedience to civil authority before alighting on Romans 13:1–7. This passage, he says, requires Christians to submit to civil laws while also holding Christian citizenship.[29] He calls Carroll's treatment of the passage "dismissive," and he writes that Carroll's use of other material in Scripture ignores the weightiness of immigration "crime."[30] Hoffmeier says that Carroll's reluctance about following U.S. immigration laws is only justified if those laws are "inherently unjust."[31] But with reference to the longstanding precedent from the Old Testament of laws concerning the border crossing and residence of immigrants, Hoffmeier writes, "I see nothing in Scripture that would abrogate current immigration laws."[32] He criticizes Carroll for failing to distinguish legal and illegal immigrants and to promote adherence to the law. Hoffmeier concludes that while churches are right to respond to people's basic needs regardless of their immigration status, they should remind everyone of their responsibility to follow the law. This might include assisting those who are unlawfully present to gain legal status.[33]

In the second edition of his book, Carroll reacts to Hoffmeier, arguing that before a higher authority, Christians cannot endorse immigration laws as they now stand. He says that it is not enough to say that the United States holds to the rule of law and to end the discussion on immigration law by saying it must be followed. Instead, there is an opportunity to discuss whether the law is "good (in relationship to Christian commitments) and practical and efficient (for the national benefit)."[34]

---

[26] Ibid., 130.
[27] Ibid., 133; Romans 12:1–2, 19–21.
[28] Carroll R., *Christians at the Border*, 2008, 133–34, emphasis Carroll's.
[29] *The Immigration Crisis*, 139, 141, 144.
[30] Ibid., 144–45.
[31] Ibid., 145; see also 140–42, 146–47.
[32] Ibid., 146.
[33] Ibid., 150–52.
[34] Carroll R., *Christians at the Border*, 2013, 124.

Immigration law fails on both counts, he says. Carroll makes clear that he is not calling for widespread civil disobedience, but simply calling for Christians to reflect as Christians on immigration law, seeking change. Romans 13, he says, does not require the Christian to obey the governing authorities but rather to submit, and this signals limits on supporting what a government says.[35] When Hoffmeier says he finds nothing in Scripture that would go against current immigration laws, and when he says that laws must be inherently unjust for a Christian to resist them, Carroll disagrees. He says that "Christians must respond to a higher authority, the Lord of the church, and to a higher law and set of values."[36]

For Daniel Carroll and James Hoffmeier, differing views on immigrants and differing views of civil authority produce differing views about illegal immigration. Their shared method of looking to the Bible as a whole to provide guidance about a current problem for Christian living produces different answers. Carroll thinks that the high valuation of migrants in the Scriptures should lead Christians to a nuanced response to U.S. immigration law, one that seeks better laws while siding with those who are present in the country without legal permission. Carroll does not spell out what legal reform would look like. Hoffmeier, on the other hand, thinks that U.S. immigration laws are not so unjust that Christians should oppose them.

Carroll's comprehensive treatment of the biblical witness points in the right direction, and his work is sensitive to lives of migrants and the circumstances surrounding them in the United States today. Hoffmeier brings to the discussion an awareness of the conventions surrounding lands and borders in the Ancient Near East, and many of his judgments are sound. Still, he draws too close a correspondence between distinctions in ancient Hebrew and distinctions in contemporary United States. His stories of migration to the United States, many drawn from his experience, do not demonstrate an acquaintance with the dire circumstances that send many to the United States. When it comes to factors that pull and push migrants to the United States without legal permission, Hoffmeier fails to take them seriously. He does not mention poverty or violence in a sending country, a desire for family reunion, or U.S. industries' dependence on low-paid undocumented labor. His statement that he finds nothing unjust about U.S. immigration laws shows a lack of knowledge of those laws, as Carroll notes. These are laws that provide no legal pathway to immigrate for many of the women and men whose labor U.S. employers require.[37] Hoffmeier's focus on following the law does not enable his readers to consider the ways that the life of the people of God might run counter to the

---

[35] Ibid., 123–26.

[36] Ibid., 125, citing Matthew 28:18; Ephesians 1:20–23; Philippians 2:9–11; Colossians 1:15–18; and Revelation 1:17–18. See Carroll R., *Christians at the Border*, 2013, 122n23, to confirm that Carroll is responding to Hoffmeier.

[37] Carroll R., "Review: Hoffmeier, The Immigration Crisis."

ways of a nation-state as it polices immigration. He does not leave room for U.S. immigration law to be exposed as the product of principalities and powers opposed to the reign of the Christ.

The disagreement between these evangelical biblical scholars reveals a need for two areas of inquiry if there is to be a more robust account of Christian living and witness in the face of illegal immigration. First, the discussion needs an attentive reading of the American legal tradition to see what about current immigration law can be affirmed and what needs reform. And while Carroll and Hoffmeier provide a basic biblical theology of migration, their discussion needs a more thorough theological account of civil authority.

Catholic Social Teaching on Illegal Immigration

The discussion of illegal immigration takes a different turn among Roman Catholics. On a visit to Mexico in 2016, Pope Francis prayed before a large cross set up in Ciudad Juárez to commemorate those who had died crossing the border into the United States. Proceeding to celebrate mass before a crowd gathered on both sides of the border, he spoke of the horror of forced migration, where poverty, violence, drug trafficking, and crime sends so many across hostile landscapes in search of a better life. He called his hearers to ask for open hearts to hear God's call "in the suffering faces of countless men and women."[38] At the time of the visit, Donald Trump was a candidate for the Republican nomination for U.S. president. At a press conference, a journalist told Francis that Trump had promised to build a wall between the United States and Mexico and deport eleven million illegal immigrants, a move that would separate families. Asked what he thought, Francis responded, "A person who thinks only of building walls, wherever it may be, and not of building bridges, is not Christian. This is not in the Gospel."[39] In what he did and said, Francis spoke out of the tradition of Catholic Social Teaching. What follows notes this tradition's valuable teaching on migration as promulgated by the Magisterium of the Roman Catholic Church, along the way indicating points where more needs to be said.

---

[38] Francis, "Homily" (Holy Mass, Apostolic Journey to Mexico, Ciudad Juárez Fairgrounds, February 17, 2016), https://w2.vatican.va/content/francesco/en/homilies/2016/documents/papa-francesco_20160217_omelia-messico-ciudad-jaurez.html; Jim Yardley and Azam Ahmed, "Pope Francis Wades Into U.S. Immigration Morass With Border Trip," *The New York Times*, February 17, 2016, www.nytimes.com/2016/02/18/world/americas/pope-francis-ciudad-juarez.html?emc=edit_ee_20160218&nl=todaysheadlines-europe&nlid=56985746.

[39] Francis, "Press Conference" (Apostolic Journey to Mexico, Flight from Mexico to Rome, February 17, 2016), https://w2.vatican.va/content/francesco/en/speeches/2016/february/documents/papa-francesco_20160217_messico-conferenza-stampa.html; "Conferencia de prensa" (Viaje apostólico a México, Vuelo de México a Roma, February 17, 2016), https://w2.vatican.va/content/francesco/es/speeches/2016/february/documents/papa-francesco_20160217_messico-conferenza-stampa.html.

In the 1891 encyclical letter *Rerum Novarum*, the touchstone of modern Catholic Social Teaching, Pope Leo XIII draws on natural law, the law of nations, and the Scriptures to argue that human beings are older than the state, and their right to provide for their lives comes before the state. He says that as human beings cultivate the soil, they transform the soil, and they rightly possess the fruits of their labor. Likewise, a man possesses property to provide for his family.[40] This family he calls a "true society," governed by the father, and it has "at least equal rights with the State in the choice and pursuit of the things needful to its preservation and its just liberty."[41] After defining the society and the economy of the household as primary, Leo XIII enumerates the duties of the state in safeguarding a community, but he does not mention the power to control migration, nor does he speak about migration for work. Still, his account of a right of the head of the family to provide for its needs, a right prior to the right of the state, is the seed that germinates and flowers in the teaching of more recent popes on migration.

In the 1961 encyclical *Mater et Magistra*, Pope John XXIII speaks of a right of families to migrate. He builds on Pope Pius XII's 1941 teaching that a father needs a "healthy liberty ... in order to fulfill the duties assigned him by the Creator regarding the physical, spiritual, and religious welfare of the family." John claims, "It is in this that the right of families to migrate is rooted."[42] Two years later, in *Pacem in Terris*, John mentions the "right to emigrate" among human rights. Just as every human being has freedom of movement within a country, he says, so "when there are just reasons in favor of it, he must be permitted to emigrate to other countries and take up residence there." John states that a human being is not only a citizen of one country but a member of the human family and a citizen of the world community.[43] Catholic Social Teaching in the early 1960s thus envisions migration as a matter of the right of the head of a family to provide for the rest of the family, a right that precedes and trumps the authority of the state.

Is there more: a right to migrate? The Second Vatican Council's pastoral constitution *Gaudium et Spes* says "yes" in the briefest of ways, interjecting "the personal right of migration" into a section on the duty of citizens to contribute to their community.[44] Pope John Paul II takes these claims further in a 1999 address,

---

[40] Leo XIII, *Rerum Novarum: Encyclical on Capital and Labor*, 1891, secs. 7, 12, www.vatican.va/holy_father/leo_xiii/encyclicals/documents/hf_l-xiii_enc_15051891_rerum-novarum_en.html.

[41] Ibid., secs. 12, 13.

[42] Pius XII, *Acta Apostolicae Sedis* 33 (1941), 202, quoted in John XXIII, *Mater et Magistra: Encyclical on Christianity and Social Progress*, 1961, sec. 45, http://w2.vatican.va/content/john-xxiii/en/encyclicals/documents/hf_j-xxiii_enc_15051961_mater.html.

[43] John XXIII, *Pacem in Terris: Encyclical on Establishing Universal Peace in Truth, Justice, Charity, and Liberty*, 1963, sec. 25, http://w2.vatican.va/content/john-xxiii/en/encyclicals/documents/hf_j-xxiii_enc_11041963_pacem.html.

[44] The Fathers of the Second Vatican Council and Paul VI, *Gaudium et Spes: Pastoral Constitution on the Church in the Modern Word*, 1965, sec. 65, www.vatican.va/archive/hist_councils/ii_vatican_council/documents/vat-ii_cons_19651207_gaudium-et-spes_en.html; Benedict XVI, "Message for the World Day of Migrants and Refugees (2013)," October 12, 2012,

citing the resolution of a Synod of Bishops as he speaks in Mexico City to the "Church in America," one America made up of many nations. John Paul says that the Church in America must be an advocate and defender of what the Bishops have affirmed at the Synod, "the natural right of individual persons to move freely within their own nation and from one nation to another."[45] Here, the head of the largest Christian church, present in nearly every nation on earth, says that the transnational Church in America must defend the legal priority of individuals to migrate, and it must defend "human dignity, even in cases of non-legal immigration."[46] Other recent documents do not emphasize what John Paul II seems to represent, a right not only to emigrate but to immigrate, but these documents do not rescind this right and are comfortable with a muted affirmation of a right to migrate.[47]

Alongside a right to emigrate and perhaps a right to migrate, Catholic Social Teaching provides a cluster of related affirmations. They describe migration as a matter of pastoral care, so that the ministries of a church of territorial parishes need to be reorganized to better serve migrants.[48] Foreigners are understood as human persons worthy of welcome, a welcome that extends in part from Christian charity, from the love of members of the universal Church.[49] Welcome also extends

---

https://w2.vatican.va/content/benedict-xvi/en/messages/migration/documents/hf_ben-xvi_mes_
20121012_world-migrants-day.html, cites this passage from *Gaudium et Spes*.

[45] *El derecho natural de cada persona a moverse libremente dentro de su propia nación y de una nación a otra*, John Paul II, *Ecclesia in America: Exhortación apostólica postsinodal sobre el encuentro con Jesucristo vivo, camino para la conversión, la comunión y la solidaridad en América*, 1999, sec. 65, www.vatican.va/holy_father/john_paul_ii/apost_exhortations/docu ments/hf_jp-ii_exh_22011999_ecclesia-in-america_sp.html; John Paul II, *Ecclesia in America: Post-Synodal Apostolic Exhortation on the on the Encounter with the Living Jesus Christ: The Way to Conversion, Communion and Solidarity in America*, 1999, sec. 65, www.vatican .va/holy_father/john_paul_ii/apost_exhortations/documents/hf_jp-ii_exh_22011999_ecclesia-in-america_en.html.

[46] *Ecclesia in America*, 1999, sec. 65.

[47] So, for example, Michael A. Blume S.V.D. focuses on a right to emigrate but then quotes John Paul II in *Ecclesia in America* as he affirms a natural right of individual persons to move freely from one nation to another, *Migration and the Social Doctrine of the Church* (Pontifical Council for the Pastoral Care of Migrants and Itinerant People, 2002), www.vatican.va/roman_curia/pontifical_councils/migrants/pom2002_88_90/rc_pc_migrants_ pom88-89_blume.htm. Benedict XVI mentions "the right of persons to migrate" without limiting that right, though in passing he says that "every state has the right to regulate migration," "Message for the World Day of Migrants and Refugees (2013)."

[48] *Ethnografica Studia*, *Acta Apostolicae Sedis* 6 (1914): 182–86; *Magni Semper*, *Acta Apostolicae Sedis* 11 (1919): 39–43; Pius XII, *Exsul Familia*, *Acta Apostolicae Sedis* 44 (1952): 649–704; Pontifical Council for the Pastoral Care of Migrants and Itinerant People, *Erga Migrantes Caritas Christi: The Love of Christ towards Migrants* (London: Catholic Truth Society, 2004).

[49] Paul VI, *Populorum Progressio: Encyclical on the Development of Peoples*, 1967, secs. 67, 69, http://w2.vatican.va/content/paul-vi/en/encyclicals/documents/hf_p-vi_enc_26031967_popu lorum.html.

from human solidarity, the notion that all human beings are part of one family, and that together they are responsible for the "universal common good."[50] Closely tied is an affirmation in Catholic Social Teaching that all created things have a common destiny, serving the good of every human being, so that any property, whether land or material good, is placed in the hands of individuals and families so that they might promote the welfare of all human beings.[51] Though government regulation is not thought to be capable of extending genuine fraternity between strangers, regulation has a particular role to play, protecting migrant laborers so that they receive the same pay and work in the same conditions as those who have not migrated.[52] Public authorities along with local people should endeavor not to treat them as tools but as persons, says the tradition, helping them to live with their families in decent housing.[53] At the same time, some of the documents of Catholic Social Teaching affirm that states have the right to restrict migration. These affirmations do not receive a full explanation, but they appear to be rooted in the duty of state officials to uphold "the good of their community, rightly understood."[54]

Applied to the United States, the documents of Catholic Social Teaching confirm that women, men, and children moving to the United States to provide for their families should not be considered "illegal," for they are exercising a right prior to any right of the state. Following the stronger claim from John Paul II and the bishops of an individual right to movement, more can be said: Individuals have rights to move greater than the rights of the U.S. government, except for very limited, unspecified cases. Instead of intimidating and troubling those who have broken its immigration laws, the government should endeavor to protect them from workplace exploitation. Parish churches in the United States are to care for migrants, and people across the country should welcome migrants into their community and treat them with dignity, even when they have not immigrated legally. The United States finds itself addressed as part of a larger America by a larger Roman Catholic Church, speaking from nature and revelation about the value of the human person and the family economy

---

[50] Ibid., sec. 67; *Gaudium et Spes*, sec. 84.

[51] *Populorum Progressio*, secs. 22–24; *Gaudium et Spes*, sec. 69.

[52] *Gaudium et Spes*, sec. 66; John Paul II, *Laborem Exercens: Encyclical on Human Work*, 1981, sec. 23, http://w2.vatican.va/content/john-paul-ii/en/encyclicals/documents/hf_jp-ii_enc_14091981_laborem-exercens.html.

[53] *Gaudium et Spes*, sec. 66.

[54] *Pacem in Terris*, sec. 106; see also Benedict XVI, "Message for the World Day of Migrants and Refugees (2013)." *Erga Migrantes Caritas Christi* states that "the Second Vatican Council recognized the right of the public authorities, in a particular context, to regulate the flow of migration." However, the passage cited from *Gaudium et Spes* is ambiguous: "Governments undoubtedly have rights and duties ... regarding the migration of country-dwellers to the cities," *Gaudium et Spes*, sec. 87. These rights and duties could consist in protection for those migrants rather than regulation of their movement; the passage does not elaborate.

in a way that relativizes claims that states may determine their immigration policies as they like.[55]

Catholic Social Teaching provides a needed warning that the priorities of the nation are not all that matter. Within God's design of this world, the social encyclicals and conciliar documents claim, the economy of the family and the dignity of the human person deserve respect. This tradition also provides a reminder of the Church as a charitable society and the human family as a fraternal reality. Together these affirmations speak powerfully on behalf of migrants, and those who heed Catholic Social Teaching will be well equipped to know when civil laws compromise other features of the created world.

Still, in three ways, Catholic Social Teaching on immigration is problematic and incomplete. First, the brief, accessible documents of the tradition do not engage in a close reading of American legal thought that might indicate what goods immigration law seeks to preserve, nor do they have space for such a reading. Second, as Catholic Social Teaching shifts from affirming migration for someone who needs to support their family to affirming in a muted way that right of any individual to migrate, the tradition is impoverished. Instead of supporting women and men who move out of service and love for their neighbors, a Synod of Bishops along with John Paul II have shown support for individuals' decisions to move, and later documents in Catholic Social Teaching do not oppose this right of the individual to migrate. This move from exalting love and service for neighbors to exalting individual choice is a move from a distinctively Catholic and Christian account of migration to an account of migration proper to liberalism. Third, the tradition has a low estimation of the predominant form of civil authority today, the territorial state, as well as the nations or peoples that often correspond to those territories. A more robust doctrine of creation could allow Christian theology to shed light on territorial government and peoples as contributing to the flourishing of human beings. In sum, legal history and an enhanced theology of politics will refine the insights of evangelical and Catholic traditions. This will lead to better counsel for the likes of Miguel Villanueva, Charles Adams, and Spencer Bachus.

Scholarly Works on Christian Ethics and Illegal Immigration

These discussions among evangelicals and Roman Catholics make plain the complexity of responding faithfully to illegal immigration. A response requires fresh explorations of theological themes from personhood and family to nationhood, from church to land to earthly government. Still, only a few theologians have written

---

[55] See also Conferencia del Episcopado Mexicano and United States Conference of Catholic Bishops, *Strangers No Longer: Together on the Journey of Hope: A Pastoral Letter Concerning Migration from the Catholic Bishops of Mexico and the United States* (Washington, D.C.: United States Conference of Catholic Bishops, 2003).

academic monographs on illegal immigration in the United States. In Christian ethics, there appear to be only three: Dana W. Wilbanks, *Re-Creating America*; Kristin E. Heyer, *Kinship Across Borders*; and Ilsup Ahn, *Religious Ethics and Migration*.[56] To name these three is to leave aside monographs and edited volumes that contribute to a discussion on migration within other subdisciplines of theology and religious studies, works in Latino/a theology and spirituality,[57] biblical studies,[58] theological journalism,[59] and the social sciences of religion.[60] It is also to leave aside

---

[56] Dana W. Wilbanks, *Re-Creating America: The Ethics of U.S. Immigration and Refugee Policy in a Christian Perspective* (Nashville: Abingdon Press, 1996); Kristin E. Heyer, *Kinship Across Borders: A Christian Ethic of Immigration* (Washington, D.C.: Georgetown University Press, 2012); Ilsup Ahn, *Religious Ethics and Migration: Doing Justice to Undocumented Workers* (New York: Routledge, 2014).

[57] A few of the monographs and edited volumes on the subject include Virgilio P. Elizondo, *The Future Is Mestizo: Life Where Cultures Meet* (New York: Crossroad, 1992); Virgilio P. Elizondo, *Galilean Journey: The Mexican-American Promise*, 2nd rev. edn. (Maryknoll, N.Y.: Orbis Books, 2000); Orlando O. Espín, ed., *Building Bridges, Doing Justice: Constructing a Latino/a Ecumenical Theology* (Maryknoll, N.Y.: Orbis Books, 2009); Orlando O. Espín, ed., *The Wiley Blackwell Companion to Latino/a Theology*, (Chichester, West Sussex: Wiley Blackwell, 2015); Justo L. González, *Santa Biblia: The Bible Through Hispanic Eyes* (Nashville: Abingdon Press, 1996); Ada María Isasi-Díaz, *Mujerista Theology: A Theology for the Twenty-First Century* (Maryknoll, N.Y.: Orbis Books, 1996); Carmen Nanko-Fernández, *Theologizing En Espanglish: Context, Community, and Ministry* (Maryknoll, N.Y.: Orbis Books, 2010); Alvin Padilla et al., eds., *Hispanic Christian Thought at the Dawn of the 21st Century: Apuntes in Honor of Justo L. González* (Nashville: Abingdon Press, 2005); María Pilar Aquino, Daisy L. Machado, and Jeanette Rodríguez, eds., *A Reader in Latina Feminist Theology: Religion and Justice* (Austin, Tex.: University of Texas Press, 2002); Fernando F. Segovia, *Interpreting Beyond Borders* (Sheffield: Sheffield Academic Press, 2000); Fernando F. Segovia, *Decolonizing Biblical Studies: A View from the Margins* (Maryknoll, N.Y.: Orbis Books, 2000).

[58] Examples include John J. Ahn, *Exile as Forced Migrations: A Sociological, Literary, and Theological Approach on the Displacement and Resettlement of the Southern Kingdom of Judah*, Beihefte zur Zeitschrift für die alttestamentliche Wissenschaft 417 (Berlin: De Gruyter, 2011); Mark A. Awabdy, *Immigrants and Innovative Law: Deuteronomy's Theological and Social Vision for the Gēr* (Tübingen: Mohr Siebeck, 2014); Christoph Bultmann, *Der Fremde im antiken Juda: eine Untersuchung zum sozialen Typenbegriff gēr und seinem Bedeutungswandel in der alttestamentlichen Gesetzgebung* (Göttingen: Vandenhoeck & Ruprecht, 1992); Gregory Lee Cuéllar, *Voices of Marginality: Exile and Return in Second Isaiah 40–55 and the Mexican Immigrant Experience*, 2nd edn. (New York: Peter Lang, 2008); Christiana van Houten, *The Alien in Israelite Law* (Sheffield: J.S.O.T. Press, 1991); Ched Myers' chapters in Ched Myers and Matthew Colwell, *Our God Is Undocumented: Biblical Faith and Immigrant Justice* (Maryknoll, N.Y.: Orbis Books, 2012); José E. Ramírez Kidd, *Alterity and Identity in Israel: The Gēr in the Old Testament* (Berlin: De Gruyter, 1999); Jean-Pierre Ruiz, *Readings from the Edges: The Bible and People on the Move* (Maryknoll, N.Y.: Orbis Books, 2011).

[59] These include Matthew Colwell's contributions to Myers and Colwell, *Our God Is Undocumented*; Ananda Rose, *Showdown in the Sonoran Desert: Religion, Law, and the Immigration Controversy* (New York: Oxford University Press, 2012); Miguel A. De La Torre, *Trails of Hope and Terror: Testimonies on Immigration* (Maryknoll, N.Y.: Orbis Books, 2009).

[60] A selection includes Jacqueline Maria Hagan, *Migration Miracle: Faith, Hope, and the Undocumented Journey* (Cambridge, Mass.: Harvard University Press, 2008); Pierrette Hondagneu-Sotelo, *God's Heart Has No Borders: How Religious Activists Are Working for Immigrant Rights* (Berkeley: University of California Press, 2008); Leah Sarat, *Fire in the Canyon: Religion, Migration, and the Mexican Dream* (New York: New York University Press,

works that link migration and theology but do not deal with the Christian ethics of illegal immigration in the United States.[61] The works by Wilbanks, Heyer, and Ahn move theological discussions about illegal immigration forward in significant ways. All three advance the discussions' awareness of the legal framework that makes possible the "alien unlawfully present in the United States." Dana Wilbanks'

2013); Grace Yukich, *One Family Under God: Immigration Politics and Progressive Religion in America* (New York: Oxford University Press, 2013).

[61] Monographs and edited volumes include Sarah Azaransky, ed., *Religion and Politics in America's Borderlands* (Lanham, Md.: Lexington Books, 2013); M. Daniel Carroll R. and Leopoldo A. Sánchez M., eds., *Immigrant Neighbors Among Us: Immigration Across Theological Traditions* (Eugene, Ore.: Pickwick, 2015); Gemma Tulud Cruz, *An Intercultural Theology of Migration: Pilgrims in the Wilderness* (Leiden: Brill, 2010); Gemma Tulud Cruz, *Toward a Theology of Migration: Social Justice and Religious Experience* (Basingstoke: Palgrave Macmillan, 2014); Athena Gorospe et al., eds., *God at the Borders: Globalization, Migration, and Diaspora*, A.T.S. Theological Forum (Manila: O.M.F. Literature and Asian Theological Seminary, 2015); Daniel G. Groody, *Border of Death, Valley of Life: An Immigrant Journey of Heart and Spirit*, (Lanham, Md.: Rowman & Littlefield, 2002); Daniel G. Groody and Gioacchino Campese, eds., *A Promised Land, a Perilous Journey: Theological Perspectives on Migration* (Notre Dame: University of Notre Dame Press, 2008); Jehu Hanciles, *Beyond Christendom: Globalization, African Migration, and the Transformation of the West* (Maryknoll, N.Y.: Orbis Books, 2008); David Hollenbach S.J., ed., *Refugee Rights: Ethics, Advocacy, and Africa* (Washington, D.C.: Georgetown University Press, 2008); David Hollenbach S.J., ed., *Driven from Home: Protecting the Rights of Forced Migrants* (Washington, D.C.: Georgetown University Press, 2010); Fleur S. Houston, *You Shall Love the Stranger as Yourself: The Bible, Refugees, and Asylum* (London: Routledge, 2015); VanThanh Nguyen and John Prior, eds., *God's People on the Move: Biblical and Global Perspectives on Migration and Mission*, 2014; Elaine Padilla and Peter C. Phan, eds., *Contemporary Issues of Migration and Theology*, (Basingstoke: Palgrave Macmillan, 2013); Elaine Padilla and Peter C. Phan, eds., *Theology of Migration in the Abrahamic Religions*, (Basingstoke: Palgrave Macmillan, 2014); Luis Pantoja, Jr., Sadiri Joy B. Tira, and Enoch Wan, *Scattered: The Filipino Global Presence* (Manila: Lifechange Publishing, 2004); Christine D. Pohl, *Making Room: Recovering Hospitality as a Christian Tradition* (Grand Rapids, Mich.: Eerdmans, 1999); Susanna Snyder, *Asylum-Seeking, Migration, and Church* (Farnham, Surrey: Ashgate, 2012); Paul Woods, *Theologizing Migration: Otherness and Liminality in East Asia* (Oxford: Regnum Books International, 2015). Nell Becker Sweeden mentions unauthorized immigration, but the book does not examine legality and illegality at any length, focusing instead on church, U.S. Latino/a theology, and ecclesial practices, *Church on the Way: Hospitality and Migration* (Eugene, Ore.: Pickwick, 2015), 3. Gioacchino Campese deals with the Mexico-United States border in one chapter of *Hacia una teología desde la realidad de las migraciones: método y desafíos* (Guadalajara: Cátedra Eusebio Francisco Kino SJ, 2008); this chapter is also included in Groody and Campese, *A Promised Land, a Perilous Journey*. Among book chapters and articles, one deserves special mention for its rich reflections on refugees and a theology of politics, Luke Bretherton, "National: Christian Cosmopolitanism, Refugees, and the Politics of Proximity," in *Christianity and Contemporary Politics: The Conditions and Possibilities of Faithful Witness* (Oxford: Wiley-Blackwell, 2010), 126–74; see by the same author, *Hospitality as Holiness: Christian Witness Amid Moral Diversity* (Aldershot: Ashgate, 2006). Peter C. Meilaender presents a theory of immigration within what he calls an "Augustinian liberalism," but he deals very little with Augustine, and his book is a work of political philosophy rather than theology, *Toward a Theory of Immigration* (Basingstoke: Palgrave, 2001), 6, 100.

Re-Creating America briefly explains the legal context from which the alien unlawfully present emerges. Kristin E. Heyer's *Kinship Across Borders* argues from resources in a wide range of disciplines including the social sciences, history, and law, and the book explores the current social context of immigration. Ilsup Ahn's *Religious Ethics and Migration* deals at more length than Wilbanks and Heyer with recent immigration legislation and court cases, presenting accounts of the North American Free Trade Agreement (N.A.F.T.A.), Arizona's Employer Sanctions Law, and Arizona Senate Bill 1070 that attempted to allow police officers to check immigration status.[62] Ahn provides a more extended history of one aspect of U.S. immigration law when he deals with the racism ingrained in this body of law.[63]

Wilbanks, Heyer, and Ahn also contribute richer theological accounts to discussions on illegal immigration. In the half of his book that deals with immigration policy, Dana Wilbanks considers notions of nationhood and sovereignty, affirming and questioning each. Wilbanks also suggests a principle of proximity that would direct justice toward those nearby. For him, this implies that immigration admissions should favor immigrants with ties, whether geographic, historical, or cultural.[64] His conclusions are built on brief citations from Scripture, theologians, and philosophers, and he reaches conclusions that accord with the conclusions of this work.[65] Kristin Heyer reflects on what it is to be human, on the social nature of sin, the family, global solidarity, and subversive hospitality. On a theology of politics, Heyer's *Kinship Across Borders* deals briefly with borders and the rule of law, suggesting that undocumented immigration is not the main thing that undermines U.S. immigration laws. Rather, those laws' disregard for human rights is the main thing that undermines them. On borders, Heyer criticizes the viewpoint "that international borders are more deserving of protection than are the humans who cross them."[66]

Ilsup Ahn links philosophy with theology as he meditates on justice, debt forgiveness, religious freedom, universal solidarity, democracy, compassion, racism, and the inclusion of the other. His work concentrates on justice for undocumented workers. He argues for forgiving what he describes as an invisible debt that those who immigrate without permission owe settled communities. At the forefront of Ahn's account are the structural injustices that force many to migrate illegally, and for him this is an occasion for new kinds of hospitality and for a restorative justice that seeks the wellbeing of the undocumented. As he commends forgiveness, hospitality, and a compassion that might run counter to the civil law, he builds an account of the church's own political life with and for migrants.

[62] Ahn, *Religious Ethics and Migration*, 44–51, 112–16, 89–91.
[63] Ibid., 137–42, 144–48.
[64] Wilbanks, *Re-Creating America*, 160–62.
[65] Ibid., 82–92, 109–23.
[66] Heyer, *Kinship Across Borders*, 137, 139.

These contributions take the discussion in Christian ethics forward. Still, that discussion needs more. First, it needs a more sustained attention to legal history. Citizens and legal residents are asking how to relate in a just and loving way to immigrants who lack legal status: Is it right to distinguish citizens from noncitizens and to treat them differently? Is the government's control of immigration legitimate, and should we respect it? To answer these questions, the discussion in Christian ethics needs a greater awareness of the assumptions the law takes for granted today and where they arise in history. For instance, where does the basic distinction between an alien and a citizen come from? Where did the assumption that a nation-state has sovereignty over the whereabouts of noncitizens come from?

Second, while the works of Wilbanks, Heyer, and Ahn begin to get into a theological account of political life, a few topics need more attention: Are nations part of the order that God creates, sustains, and brings to fulfillment? Can civil authorities be said to be sovereign, to possess exclusive authority over a territory? Can Wilbanks' principle of proximity be understood more fully as a way of loving our neighbors?

THE TASK AHEAD: A HISTORY OF LAW AND A THEOLOGY OF POLITICS

Evangelical biblical scholarship, Catholic Social Teaching, and monographs in Christian ethics advance an understanding of how Christians should act as migrants and respond to migrants, but there are gaps in the conversation, especially when it comes to illegal immigration. Alongside other kinds of migrants, those who are unlawfully present are particularly troubled because by immigrating they have contravened the authority of the law. As they go on living, they must continue to reckon with their relationship to civil authority. Those who relate to these immigrants must also face questions about where they stand in relationship to this law, whether in obedience, tension, or defiance. If Christians are to know how to act as immigrants who already lack legal status, and if Christians are to know how to respond to those immigrants, they need a better understanding of legal history: How did the illegal alien come to be? They also need a better theological account of politics: How ought the civil law's contentions about nationality, sovereignty, and justice to be evaluated in light of the revelation of Jesus Christ?

The first step in this project is legal history. There is a need to understand the moral judgments that have formed immigration law and made it possible for so many to be aliens unlawfully present in the United States of America. To avoid understanding immigration law as monolithic or unchanging, what follows presents close readings of the cases and legislation that have made what immigration law is today. This is a search for roots, for the historical origins of the concepts at work in each stage of legal history. This legal history does not consider refugee law with its separate set of guidelines about how those fleeing persecution may enter the United States. Knowledge of legal history then guides a search for theological concepts that fit the phenomenon of illegal immigration.

The second step of the project is a theology of politics. Such a theology emerges in response to U.S. law and its concepts of aliens, territorial government, and justice in immigration admissions. In search of a better developed political theology, this book asks what role these might play in the history of God's dealings with God's beloved creation. The search for answers leads to careful readings of relevant passages of Scripture in conversation with trusted interpreters.

This project rests on the work of other theologians as they commend and value migrants. A God who migrates with God's people, Israel and the church as a migrant people, the migrant as a bringer of blessing and good news, love and justice for and from migrants as at the core of God's being and the being of God's people: other works describe these themes clearly and ably. This work deals with specific questions about civil law and authority as they concern the migrant. Along the way, the book seeks to remind the church of its purpose and to remind civil authorities of their purpose, each given by God. The aim is to submit human guarding of communities and lands to the guarding of God. Much of the book pares back over-confident assertions of political authority over immigration, pointing to Christ as judge.

The work is a humble contribution to theology as it has been practiced for many years. It seeks to understand God and God's works at a time and place, as so many residents of the United States of America are considered unlawfully present. The work interprets the history of U.S. immigration law and responds to the assumptions of that body of law with theological accounts of nationality, government, and justice. As such, it can be described as a work in the theology of politics or a work in theological ethics. The theological contributions flow out of readings of Scripture alongside scholarly interpreters. Those interpreters are often Reformational, with Martin Luther, Karl Barth, and Oliver O'Donovan at the forefront. Still, a Roman Catholic author (Leo XIII) and a philosopher (Aristotle) make significant contributions.

Along the way, this work seeks to bring new insights to the history of U.S. immigration law, telling a distinctive story that focuses on how the illegal alien has come to be. While drawing primarily on the texts of cases and legislation, the account of U.S. legal history is indebted to more comprehensive histories by Daniel Tichenor and Aristide Zolberg, though this work organizes its telling of history differently. Tichenor's eight historical phases center on detailed accounts of the human actors involved in shaping policy and legislation, and Zolberg's nine historical phases circle around images of a front door, a side door, and a back door. The history of one period of immigration law by Mae Ngai provides inspiration through its more philosophical analysis, an analysis that draws out the paradoxes of U.S. law and political life with its "impossible subjects."[67] In response, this work focuses on three monumental shifts, three conceptual innovations borne out by legal texts and the circumstances that surround them. These are the alien, the alien unlawfully present, and the alien unlawfully present from a neighboring country.

The book does not interact with recent literature on philosophy and immigration. Recent works by the likes of Joseph Carens, Matthew Gibney, Bonnie Honig, Will Kymlicka, Peter Meilaender, David Miller, Yael Tamir, and Michael Walzer have great value, but here law is taken as a primary interlocutor rather than philosophy. This work resists the assumption that philosophy must be theology's primary interlocutor, looking instead to case law and legislation as a site of argumentation about immigration.

—

A quest to grasp the history of the illegal alien and discern a fitting theology of politics proceeds in three parts. Part I asks where the legal concept of the *alien* came from and looks for an alternative to that concept. Chapter 1 looks at how U.S. law from the start distinguished the alien from the citizen as its basic division of persons. A search for the origins of the alien leads back into the common law of England, showing how the alien emerged in the late medieval and early modern periods as a standalone concept. Doubts about the appropriateness of understanding those from far away as aliens prompt a turn to Christian theology for an alternative set of concepts. Chapter 2 interacts with Karl Barth's reading of Scripture, situating relationships with those from other countries within God's creation of the world, God's providential care for it, and the destiny of the many peoples in God's people, Israel and the church. Paul's communication with the Corinthians about being sent out as an apostle provides an example of the likeness that God's people have with what the common law considers unlike or alien. Part I achieves a critical account of the *alien* in legal history and points toward an alternative way of imagining the migrant drawn from Christian theology.

Part II asks how some aliens came to be classed as illegal. A reading of American legal history in Chapter 3 demonstrates when and how the authority of the federal government over immigration was articulated and established. As it turns out, Congressional legislation banned Chinese immigration in the late nineteenth century, and Supreme Court cases upheld that legislation, articulating a notion of sovereignty. A claim of a sovereign right to exclude and expel aliens, a right accountable only to the will of the people, is described in this work alongside its early modern forebears. Concerns over the unlimited nature of authority over immigration incite a turn to theology in search of an alternative. Chapter 4 asks,

---

[67] Daniel J. Tichenor, *Dividing Lines: The Politics of Immigration Control in America* (Princeton: Princeton University Press, 2002); Aristide R. Zolberg, *A Nation by Design: Immigration Policy in the Fashioning of America* (Cambridge, Mass.: Harvard University Press, 2006); Mae M. Ngai, *Impossible Subjects: Illegal Aliens and the Making of Modern America* (Princeton: Princeton University Press, 2004).

where do guarded places emerge in the Christian narrative of creation, fall, and redemption, and what is their destiny? Readings from Genesis and Revelation led by Martin Luther, Jacques Ellul, and Oliver O'Donovan qualify the value of guarding places during the world. A better sense of the responsibilities and limits that God's judgment places on guarding materializes through Luther's readings of two psalms. Does this account extend to the guarding of territories larger than cities? A reading from Deuteronomy suggests that a divine overlord oversees peoples as they possess lands and as they are dispossessed if they fail to respond to that overlord. How is guarding exercised rightly, and what kind of wrong is committed by those who go against that authority? Resources from Leo XIII and William Blackstone point toward answers. The chapter concludes with seven cases of offenses against U.S. immigration law, arguing that punishment of these offenses needs to be pared back. Part II reveals the troublesome notions on which the making of *illegal* aliens depends, and it indicates the limits that God's ongoing judgment places on those who protect territories.

Parts I and II produce a better grasp of the *alien* and the *illegal* alien, but it is not yet obvious how so many millions of men and women living in the United States today could be classed as aliens unlawfully present. Part III asks how it came about that those from *neighboring* countries could become aliens unlawfully present in the United States. Chapter 5 begins with a 1960s move by Congress to try to get rid of discrimination in immigration admissions, leading to a system that gave each nation equal standing. Mexico received the same treatment, but Mexican nationals kept migrating to the United States in higher numbers, now illegally rather than legally. This process made possible the growing community of immigrants now present in the United States without legal status and open to exploitation. This conundrum motivates a turn to theology and philosophy. In Chapter 6, immigration quotas and the opposition to discrimination make sense as applications of the notions of justice explored by Aristotle and Hugo Grotius. Examination of their twofold picture of justice results in recommendations of policies that better fit undocumented workers, especially those from Mexico. Prompted by aspirations of the United States to be a good neighbor in its foreign policy, a reading of the Parable of the Good Samaritan in the Gospel of Luke provides an approach to human encounters with neighbors, and the parable pushes against labels that enable U.S. citizens to turn a blind eye to a whole class of their neighbors. A reading of the parable suggests ways of becoming neighbors across divides of legality and ethnicity along with ways that the United States might become a neighbor. Part III shows how those from neighboring countries became illegal aliens through an unneighborly opposition to discrimination, and it sketches practices of justice and love that restore relationships with neighbors deemed illegal.

The conclusion draws together the fruits of this inquiry, and it indicates further areas for exploration for a theological response to the alien unlawfully present in the United States.

The Immigrant as Alien?

1

How the Alien Emerged

Allegiance, English Law, and Federal Immigration Law

What is a Christian response to the alien who is unlawfully present in the United States of America according to federal law? To discover the answer, Part I will explore what it means to be an alien. Where does the concept of the alien come from, and how does federal law conceive of an alien? Is the alien a type that belongs to nature, to the created order? Is regarding someone as an alien consistent with the freedom enjoyed by those within the law of Christ?

Chapter 1 will explore how the alien came to be a type of person who can be excluded from U.S. territory under federal law. This term will be seen to emerge from the English common law, first through the seminal case of *Calvin v. Smith* from 1608. This case gives evidence of the increasing isolation of the "alien" as qualifying terms disappear, and it shows how the alien is thought to be the consequence of a natural relationship of a subject to a sovereign. Second, medieval English law will reveal that the opposition of alien to subject was a new thing in about the year 1400. This means that the alien is not a fixed or eternal type of person but something that is up for negotiation. Chapter 2 will turn to sources from the Christian tradition to discover an alternative way of imagining those who come from afar.

THE ALIEN AS A CONSTITUTIVE CONCEPT OF
FEDERAL U.S. IMMIGRATION LAW

Where do the origins of federal U.S. immigration law lie? Historians disagree. Roger Daniels begins his story, "In the beginning Congress created the Chinese Exclusion Act," referring to the 1882 federal statute that banned the entry of Chinese persons into the United States.[1] Daniel Tichenor begins with the failure of nativist groups to

---

[1] Roger Daniels, *Guarding the Golden Door: American Immigration Policy and Immigrants Since 1882* (New York: Hill and Wang, 2004), 3; Daniels is speaking of An act to execute certain treaty stipulations relating to Chinese, 22 Stat. 58 (1882).

achieve restrictions on European immigration in the first hundred years of the American republic.[2] Aristide Zolberg identifies an earlier origin, arguing that "from the moment they managed their own affairs, well before political independence, Americans were determined to select who might join them, and they have remained so ever since."[3] To defend his claim he cites practices that went on in the colonial era: the killing of Native Americans, the importation of Africans as slaves, the recruitment of certain Europeans, and the deterrence of convicts and paupers.[4] This chapter locates an earlier origin, the origins of the concept that makes possible U.S. laws that restrict immigration. In 1790, the Congress of the newly formed United States passed a law regarding naturalization, breaking with the British language of "subjects" to speak of "citizens."[5] The law provided a "uniform rule" by which a newcomer could become a U.S. citizen. While these shifts represented a revolution, this revolution did not touch another basic concept: the law retained the concept of the "alien" from the laws of England. To understand the alien unlawfully present, this abiding concept deserves attention. Noting that the alien arises in a certain period and that the alien is not an eternal concept enables the reader to hold this concept at some distance and to search out true concepts in the light of Christ.

Today, the term "alien" is the basic building block of U.S. immigration law. The last significant overhaul of federal immigration law from 1996 uses the term "alien" or "aliens" some twelve hundred times in the course of 179 pages. This alien is the object of the Act, the item to admit or exclude, to remove if unlawfully present, whose forced importation is forbidden, whose employment is regulated, and whose benefits are restricted. But what does "alien" mean? This 1996 Act looks back to the Immigration and Nationality Act of 1952 for its definitions of terms like "alien" and "immigrant."[6] The 1952 Act defines the alien as "any person not a citizen or national of the United States," and it goes on to define an immigrant as any sort of alien that does not fall within certain "classes of nonimmigrant aliens," including foreign diplomats, tourists, businesspeople and students.[7] In contrast, the picture of an immigrant that emerges is an alien who comes to settle and stay. In these 1952 definitions, "immigrants" are a subset of aliens, the general term for one who belongs to another political community.

[2]   Daniel J. Tichenor, *Dividing Lines: The Politics of Immigration Control in America* (Princeton: Princeton University Press, 2002), 46–86.

[3]   Aristide R. Zolberg, *A Nation by Design: Immigration Policy in the Fashioning of America* (Cambridge, Mass.: Harvard University Press, 2006), 1.

[4]   Ibid., 1–2, 26.

[5]   An Act to establish an uniform Rule of Naturalization, 1 Stat. 103 (1790). This work's quotations and titles from historical sources maintain original spellings and capitalizations. To keep the pages uncluttered, the work does not note deviations from current usage such as "an uniform Rule" with [sic].

[6]   An Act: Making omnibus consolidated appropriations for the fiscal year ending September 30, 1997, and for other purposes, Pub. L. No. 104–208, 110 Stat. 3009–546 (1996).

[7]   An Act: To revise the laws relating to immigration, naturalization, and nationality; and for other purposes, Pub. L. No. 82–414, 66 Stat. 163 (1952), 166–69.

The founding documents of the United States of America prepared the way for the coming of the alien. The Declaration of Independence of 1776 protested that the British king had prevented the passage of "Laws for Naturalization of Foreigners" and the passage of other laws "to encourage their migration hither."[8] Some colonies sought to speed up the process of making subjects into aliens, as if they had been born, *natus*, in their current country. Colonies also passed Acts to ban the importation of slaves, to keep out paupers and convicts, and to give tax exemptions to settlers, but the crown blocked those Acts, interested in part in keeping valued subjects from leaving Britain. Once the new republic was freed from the oversight of London, its 1789 Constitution authorized Congress to "establish an uniform rule of Naturalization."[9] Only one other time does migration appear in the Constitution, when it forbade Congress from prohibiting "the Migration and Importation of such persons as any of the States now existing shall think proper to admit" until 1808.[10] In the Declaration of Independence and the Constitution, the breakaway colonists sought the power to promote the "migration" and increase the "population" of the new states. There are "foreigners" and "persons," but the founding documents do not yet use the term "alien."

The first appearance of the alien in federal U.S. law comes in Congress' first year, 1790. The United States Congress used its power to "establish an uniform rule of Naturalization," declaring

> That any alien, being a free white person, who shall have resided within the limits and under the jurisdiction of the United States for the term of two years, may be admitted to become a citizen thereof, on application to any common law court of record[11]

One who was naturalized no longer became a subject of the king but a citizen of the United States. According to R. R. Palmer, this was the first time that the English term "citizen" appeared in the law of a national government, indicating the republican aspiration that each person would share in ruling and being ruled.[12] Naturalization no longer required a legislative act; there was now a regular pattern by which those born elsewhere could become like those born within the limits and

[8] William Blackstone, *Commentaries on the Laws of England*, vol. 1 (Oxford: Clarendon Press, 1765), bk. 1, chaps. 10, 362, 363, from the Lillian Goldman Library at the Yale Law School, "The Avalon Project: Documents in Law, History, and Diplomacy," 2008, http://avalon.law .yale.edu/default.asp; Zolberg, *A Nation by Design*, 25–26.

[9] U.S. Const. art. I, § 8, cl. 4.

[10] U.S. Const. art. I, § 9, cl. 1.

[11] 1 Stat. 103.

[12] R. R. Palmer, *The Age of the Democratic Revolution: A Political History of Europe and America, 1760–1800*, vol. 1 (Princeton: Princeton University Press, 1959), 224. Palmer, 1:223, cites John Adams' draft of the Massachusetts Constitution from 1780 as the first appearance of the "citizen" (Adams, *Works*, 1851, IV, 219), and he speculates that the term may have come to John Adams from Jean-Jacques Rousseau's *Du Contrat social* of 1762, ch. 6, book 1, which Adams read as early as 1765.

the jurisdiction of the United States. Despite the revolutionary move to call the member of the political community a citizen, the American citizen was produced out of the same material as the English subject. That material was the alien.

In the years after 1790, the process of naturalization was revised.[13] Still, the alien remained as the contrast figure to the citizen, and the alien remains so until the present. Though largely static over more than two centuries, the alien has appeared with some variation in sense and application in U.S. law. An anomaly in the law occurred in 1798, when in response to upheaval in France and Ireland, Congress passed two Acts to give the President power to bring about the removal of certain aliens, whether through command or by force. Among these were "such aliens as he shall judge dangerous to the peace and safety to the United States"[14] as well as "alien enemies," defined as "natives, citizens, denizens, or subjects of the hostile nation."[15] These Acts were not renewed, but the Acts indicated what it meant to be an alien. After this, for most of the nineteenth century the alien appeared only in naturalization law, not in immigration law.[16] The alien was the kind of person who could be made a citizen, but there was no talk of aliens as persons who move into the United States, whether to visit or to settle. The rare federal laws that governed the movement of persons into the United States used other terms. Acts concerning shipping spoke of "passengers" who might become "inhabitants," and other Acts used the term "emigrant" with an "e."[17] Among these was an 1864 Act that sought to encourage "immigration" during the Civil War.[18] A later Act from 1882 used the term "immigrant" alongside the "passenger not a citizen of the United States."[19]

Alongside legislation concerning "passengers" and "emigrants," laws restricted emigration from China before "aliens" were restricted from entering the country. The first Act of this kind, from 1862, restricted the forced migration of "coolies,"

[13] See An act to establish an uniform rule of naturalization; and to repeal the act heretofore passed on that subject, 1 Stat. 414 (1795); An act to establish an uniform rule of naturalization; and to repeal the acts heretofore passed on that subject, 2 Stat. 153 (1802).

[14] An Act concerning Aliens, 1 Stat. 570 (1798), 571.

[15] An Act respecting Alien Enemies, 1 Stat. 577 (1798).

[16] See 1 Stat. 103; 1 Stat. 414; An Act supplementary to and to amend the act, intituled "An act to establish an uniform rule of naturalization; and to repeal the act heretofore passed on that subject," 1 Stat. 566 (1798); 2 Stat. 153; An Act in addition to the act intituled, "An act to establish an uniform rule of naturalization; and to repeal the acts heretofore passed on that subject," 2 Stat. 292 (1804); An Act supplementary to the acts heretofore passed on the subject of an uniform rule of naturalization, 3 Stat. 53 (1813); An Act relative to evidence in cases of naturalization, 3 Stat. 258 (1816); An Act in further addition to "An act to establish an uniform rule of naturalization; and to repeal the acts heretofore passed on that subject," 4 Stat. 69 (1824); An Act to amend the acts concerning naturalization, 4 Stat. 310 (1828); An Act to amend the Naturalization Acts and to punish Crimes against the same, and for other Purposes, 16 Stat. 254 (1870).

[17] An act regulating passenger ships and vessels, 3 Stat. 488 (1819), 488, 489; An act to regulate the Carriage of Passengers in Merchant Vessels, 9 Stat. 127 (1847), 127, 128; An Act to Regulate the Carriage of Passengers in Steamships and other Vessels, 10 Stat. 715 (1855), 716–21.

[18] An Act to encourage Immigration, 13 Stat. 385 (1864), 386.

[19] An act to regulate Immigration, 22 Stat. 214 (1882).

"Chinese subjects" who were brought as "servants" or "apprentices," but the Act did not forbid "voluntary emigration."[20] This changed two decades later in a series of laws. An Act of 1882 forbade all "Chinese laborers" from "coming . . . to the United States" and remaining there. These persons were not eligible for citizenship.[21] Two years later, Congress restricted the "coming" of "all subjects of China and Chinese, whether subjects of China or any other foreign power."[22] These laws moved from restricting Chinese laborers to positing a Chinese race stretching beyond the Chinese empire. This new class of "Chinese" spanned the divide between immigration law and naturalization law: "Chinese" were excluded from entering the United States, and if already present, they were excluded from becoming citizens. Still, up to this point in U.S. law, an alien was the sort of person who might become a citizen, while those who moved into U.S. territory were "passengers," "emigrants," "immigrants," or "Chinese."[23]

Just around this time, an innovation in the language of federal immigration law spanned the same divide that the term "Chinese" had spanned. For the first time, the term "alien" was used not only in the context of becoming a citizen, but in the context of moving into U.S. territory. An 1875 law, known as the Page Law, sought to ensure that "immigration" into the United States was "free and voluntary," forbidding the importation not only of coolies but specifically of "immigrants" who have agreed to serve "a term of service within the United States, for lewd and immoral purposes."[24] The law also forbade the importation of persons convicted of a felony in some other country and sent to the United States as punishment. While it might seem right for lawmakers to prohibit the importation of prostitutes and convicted felons into the United States, by doing so they introduced a new phrase into federal law that would make it possible to forbid other groups from entering. Part of the mechanism by which the law forbade sex trafficking and the transportation of convicts was by stating that "it shall be unlawful for aliens of the following classes to immigrate into the United States."[25] Here, the alien was no longer simply a noncitizen who could be made a citizen, but a potential member of a "class," and a class that could be forbidden from "immigrat[ing] into the United States" with no attention given to the particularities of the person and her case.

This innovation in the language of federal law, the notion of classes of aliens, facilitated the development of immigration laws that parceled aliens into certain types to be excluded. The next step happened in 1891, when a law declared

---

[20] An Act to prohibit the "Coolie Trade" by American Citizens in American Vessels, 12 Stat. 340 (1862), 340, 341.
[21] 22 Stat. 58, 59.
[22] An Act to amend an act entitled "An act to execute certain treaty stipulations relating to Chinese approved May sixth eighteen hundred and eighty-two," 23 Stat. 115 (1884), 115, 118.
[23] For more on Chinese exclusion, see Chapter 3.
[24] An act supplementary to the acts in relation to immigration, 18 Stat. 477 (1875).
[25] Ibid.

"that the following classes of aliens shall be excluded from admission into the United States," going on to name

> all idiots, insane persons, paupers or persons likely to become a public charge, persons suffering from a loathsome or a dangerous contagious disease, persons who have been convicted of a felony or other infamous crime or misdemeanor involving moral turpitude, polygamists, and also any person whose ticket or passage is paid for with the money of another or who is assisted by others to come[26]

A 1917 law used the same formula to introduce a much longer list of classes of aliens, excluding, among others, "anarchists" and persons originating from a triangle stretching from Arabia and Afghanistan to Asiatic Russia and the East Indies.[27]

And who was an alien, briefly stated? Federal law first defined the alien indirectly in 1798 as "natives, citizens, denizens, or subjects of [another] nation." The first direct definition comes in 1917 in the same law that generated a lengthy list of excluded "classes of aliens," where the alien is defined as "any person not a native-born or naturalized citizen of the United States."[28] The definition quoted from 1952, the one that would be assumed in 1996, is similar: an alien is "any person not a citizen or national of the United States."[29]

The alien had now bridged the gap: aliens were not only the stuff new citizens were made of, but they were the stuff that was excluded from entry into American territory. Naturalization law and immigration law were merged at the federal level around this term "alien." Though the powers of the federal government over the alien had been expanded, the understanding of what defined an alien stayed relatively constant over the course of two centuries of federal law. Lawmakers assumed that an alien, someone who was not a citizen, was a normal part of the universe.

A recent presentation by a federal agent testified to the consensus that the alien is real. Richard Crocker, Deputy Special Agent in Charge of United States Immigration and Customs Enforcement (I.C.E.) in Southern Arizona, discussed his work with a community group in Tucson. As well as explaining his efforts to deter the smuggling of drugs, weapons, and human beings across the United States–Mexico border, Crocker described his efforts to prevent the movement of "aliens" across the border. He only occasionally used the term "economic migrant," but he spoke again and again about aliens being smuggled, about aliens walking through difficult desert routes to cross the border, about drop houses for aliens, and about the removal of 392,000 illegal aliens by I.C.E. in 2010. The alien was a basic feature of his job, and as he spoke about aliens, he encouraged his hearers, "Trust me ... I'm just talking

[26] An act in amendment to the various acts relative to immigration and the importation of aliens under contract or agreement to perform labor, 26 Stat. 1084 (1891), 1084.

[27] An Act: To regulate the immigration of aliens to, and the residence of aliens in, the United States, Pub. L. No. 64–301, 39 Stat. 874 (1917), 875–76.

[28] 39 Stat. 874, 874.

[29] 66 Stat. 163, 166.

about reality." For this agent, the world he worked in included aliens as plainly as it included deserts, rivers, mountains and drugs.[30]

THE ALIEN AS DEFINED IN COMMON LAW: *CALVIN V. SMITH* (1608)

Across the history of U.S. federal law, then, American lawmakers were consistent in defining the alien, though its use shifted from naturalization statutes to immigration statutes. While the United States rejected the English notion of subjecthood and replaced it with a notion of citizenship, the contrast term for both the subject and the citizen remained the alien. The law of England, the common law that American lawmakers and judges took as precedent, is the source of the alien. One case in the common law lent federal U.S. law its practice of giving citizenship to anyone born on U.S. soil, and along the way this case gave the notion of the alien its classic definition.[31] This was the 1608 case of *Calvin v. Smith*, better known as *Calvin's Case* or *The Case of the Postnati*. The most influential account of the case comes from the Report of Sir Edward Coke, who was at the time the chief justice of the Court of Common Pleas.[32] As one step of investigating the origins of U.S. immigration law and questioning what the law assumes, what follows will reveal what the alien was in this pivotal case and why.

The Alien as One Outside the Allegiance of the King

This was the matter at hand: at the death of Queen Elizabeth I in 1603, the crown of England had descended to her relative King James VI of Scotland, who became

[30] Richard Crocker and Rudy Bustamante, Community Relations Officer, "Immigration and Customs Enforcement in Southern Arizona" (Borderlinks, Tucson, Ariz., July 28, 2011).

[31] Calvin's Case is cited in federal U.S. law as the source of the rule that every person born within U.S. territory is a citizen, United States v. Wong Kim Ark, 169 U.S. 649 (1898). See Chapter 3, pp. 85–6. on U.S. v. Wong Kim Ark. See also Polly J. Price, "Natural Law and Birthright Citizenship in Calvin's Case (1608)," *Yale Journal of Law & the Humanities* 9, no. 1 (1997): 73–74. In an earlier case, Justice Story's minority opinion cites Calvin's Case as an authority and later claims that "nothing is better settled at common law than the doctrine that the children even of aliens born in a country . . . are subjects by birth," John Inglis v. Trustees of the Sailor's Snug Harbor, 28 U.S. 99 (1830).

[32] Sir Edward Coke, Calvin v. Smith, 77 *Eng. Rep.* 377 (1608); Allen D. Boyer, ed., "Introduction," in *Law, Liberty, and Parliament: Selected Essays on the Writings of Sir Edward Coke* (Indianapolis: Liberty Fund, 2004), viii. References are drawn from this edition: Sir Edward Coke, "Calvin's Case, or the Case of the Postnati," in *Selected Writings of Sir Edward Coke*, ed. Steve Sheppard, vol. 1, 3 vols. (Indianapolis: Liberty Fund, 2003), http://oll.libertyfund.org/title/911/106337. Coke's Report, Moore's Report on the case, and two prominent speeches on the case by Lord Francis Bacon and Thomas Egerton, Lord Chancellor Ellesmere, are included in William Cobbett et al., eds., *Cobbett's Complete Collection of State Trials and Proceedings for High Treason and Other Crimes and Misdemeanors from the Earliest Period to the Present Time*, vol. 2 (London: R. Bagshaw, 1809), 559–657.

King James I of England. After James' accession to the English throne, a man named Robert Calvin was born in Edinburgh, Scotland. Calvin was due to inherit property in Shoreditch, Middlesex, England, but Englishmen Richard and Nicholas Smith had taken control of the land, claiming that as a Scotsman, Calvin was not able to inherit land in England. That was how inheritance worked for the *antenati*, those born under the old arrangement when England and Scotland were two separate kingdoms and James was king only of Scotland. In the old system, a "subject born" of the King of Scotland could inherit property in Scotland but not in England, where the same person was an "alien born." But how did inheritance work for the *postnati*, for those born after James' accession as King of England? Could Robert Calvin lawfully inherit the land in Shoreditch?[33]

The Smiths claimed that though James now ruled over both England and Scotland, the two remained separate kingdoms, with separate allegiances and separate laws.[34] Thus, ran the argument, Robert Calvin remained an alien born: "Every subject that is *alienae gentis (id est) alienae ligeantiae, est alienigena*," or translated, "Every subject that is of an alien people, i.e., of an alien ligeance, is alien born."[35] As an alien born, Robert Calvin was not eligible to inherit the land at Shoreditch. But the Lord Chancellor and twelve of the fourteen judges assembled ruled "that the Plaintiff was no alien," and that the land was rightfully his.[36] The majority in the case ruled that Calvin could not be an enemy or merely an alien friend of the king. Instead, he was born under the ligeance and obedience, within the power and protection of the King of Scotland, who was also the King of England. This relationship happens according to the law of nature, and it cannot be altered. Since Calvin was not an alien to the one who was king of both kingdoms, he could not be an alien to the subjects of England. Thus, not being an alien, Calvin could inherit the property at Shoreditch.[37]

These arguments indicate the conceptual space that surrounded the term "alien," centered on the notion of *ligeantia* or ligeance from the Anglo-French of the medieval law courts. Every person is a subject, the thinking goes, born into the ligeance of a sovereign. In this ligeance, this bond, the subject offers obedience in return for protection; the subjects obey and serve the king, who maintains and defends his subjects.[38] In his Report, Coke offers other ways of describing ligeance, saying that "they that are born under the obedience, power, faith, ligealty, or ligeance of the King, are natural subjects, and no aliens."[39] In another work, Coke

---

[33] Coke, "Calvin's Case," 2a.
[34] It would not be until a century later that England and Scotland would be made the United Kingdom of Great Britain through the Act of Union of 1707.
[35] Coke, "Calvin's Case," 3a. Translation author's, here and throughout the interpretation of Coke.
[36] Ibid., preface, 3b.
[37] Ibid., 24b–25b.
[38] Ibid., 4b–5a.
[39] Ibid., 5b.

describes ligeance as "the highest and greatest obligation of dutie and obedience that can be. Ligeance," he says, "is the true and faithful obedience of a liegeman or subject to his liege lord, or soveraigne."[40] The term "allegiance" has replaced the term "ligeance" in contemporary English.[41]

Ligeance takes a number of forms, says Coke, describing four: (1) Natural ligeance is due from someone born in the dominion of the king and considered a *subditus natus*, "subject born." (2) Acquired ligeance is granted by king or Parliament so that one becomes a *subditus datus*, a "subject given" or "made." (3) Local ligeance comes about when, for example, a "Frenchman" or "Portugal born" enters the protection of the King of England as an alien friend, and this person's children become subjects if they are born in England. (4) Legal ligeance is something which all free and noble men swear by oath, promising truth and faith to the king and his heirs, "life and member, and terrene honour" to defend the king against any ill.[42]

In this account of the reasoning of the majority in *Calvin's Case*, subjects are defined as natural, born into the ligeance of the king, or else made by grant. The "alien born" fits within this setting as one who is not a subject of the king. Coke defines the alien: "An Alien is a subject that is born out of the ligeance of the king, and under the ligeance of another, and can have no real or personal action for or concerning land"[43] Now, how can an alien still be a subject? In Coke's *Report*, "subject" is a basic term for an individual in his or her capacity as a political being, more common than the words "man" or "person." Even an alien is still a subject of some king.

Having defined the alien, Coke maps out types of subjects and aliens:

> Every man is either *Alienigena*, an *Alien* born, or *subditus*, a subject born. Every Alien is either a friend that is in league, &c., or an enemy that is in open war. &c. Every Alien enemy is either *pro tempore*, temporary for a time, or *perpetuus*, perpetual, or *specialiter permissus*, permitted especially. Every subject is either *natus*, born, or *datus*, given or made.[44]

---

[40] Edward Coke, *The First Part of the Institutes of the Laws of England, or, a Commentary upon Littleton* (*Coke on Littleton*), ed. Francis Hargrave, Charles Butler, and Charles Butler, 18th edn., corrected, vol. 1 (London: J. & W. T. Clarke, R. Pheney, and S. Brooke, 1823), 129a, sec. 198.

[41] See "Ligeance, N.," *Oxford English Dictionary Online* (Oxford University Press), accessed January 24, 2017, www.oed.com/view/Entry/108166; "Allegiance, N.," *Oxford English Dictionary Online* (Oxford University Press), accessed January 24, 2017, www.oed.com/view/Entry/5213#eid6946301.

[42] Coke, "Calvin's Case," 5a–7a.

[43] Ibid., 16a.

[44] Ibid., 17a. Coke explains that all of Christendom is in league with the king, and the subjects of these lands are alien friends, who can trade and own goods but not land. Aliens may enter into a temporary war and become alien enemies *pro tempore*. Perpetual enemies include "the devils," *infideli*, *Judaei*, and "Pagans." Specially permitted enemies may be allowed into the Realm for a time. No alien enemy may trade or own anything in the Realm (ibid., 17a–b).

The two categories of subject and alien include every human being. There is no man or subject in between, no one without a sovereign, no one with partial or dual ligeances. Those who are alien born may come as friends, and they often do. They may show the king a temporary ligeance, a local ligeance, when they pass through or reside in his lands. But even if they come as friends, they have not sworn to defend the king with their life and give him all earthly honor as have the noblemen of England. So long as they are alien, they remain obedient to another sovereign. They may come as enemies to undermine the realm and even to kill the king.

The Alien as a Consequence of the Law of Nature

Coke accounts for the distinction between subjects and aliens in relation not only to the positive developments of the common law but also to the natural law. Does he think that aliens occur naturally or only arise as a consequence of the law of nature? To answer this requires an examination of Coke's argument about government and the alien, an argument that can be organized as follows:

[1] "The Law of Nature is that which God at the time of creation of the nature of man infused into his heart, for his preservation and direction; and this is *lex aeterna*, the Moral Law, called also the Law of Nature."[45]

[2] "For whatsoever is necessary and profitable for the preservation of the society of man, is due by the Law of Nature:

[3] But Magistracy and Government are necessary and profitable for the Preservation of the society of man;

therefore [4] Magistracy and Government are of Nature."[46]

Corresponding to government is the obedience of the subject:

[5] "By this Law of Nature is the Faith, Ligeance, and Obedience of the Subject due to his Sovereign or Superiour."[47]

The one born outside of the bond between a particular sovereign and his subjects is the alien, in a passage already quoted:

[6] "An Alien is a subject that is born out of the ligeance of the king, and under the ligeance of another, and can have no real or personal action for or concerning land"[48]

---

[45] Coke, "Calvin's Case," 12b.
[46] Ibid., 13a.
[47] Ibid.
[48] Ibid., 16a.

In [1], Coke draws his initial account of natural law both from the Bible and from reason: The people of God, Coke says, were governed by the law of nature even before Moses wrote the law, and as the Apostle Paul writes in the Letter to the Romans, those who do not have the law still follow the law.[49] The law of nature and the law of God are the same for all. Coke mentions Aristotle, Bracton, and Fortescue as authorities who agree on this picture of natural law. Fortescue and Virgil, he says, also attest to a "natural equity" by which kings judged before judicial and municipal laws were made.[50]

Against this backdrop of the law of nature comes Coke's argument in [2]–[5] that the obedience of a subject to a superior is by nature. Coke says that the natural law does not only preserve individual women and men but also preserves the society of human beings; indeed, anything that preserves human society is by the law of nature. Magistracy and government achieve this end of preservation, and thus they are by nature, as are the faith, ligeance, and obedience that correspond to them. Coke cites a few authorities to establish this argument. In the Law of Moses, he says that the command to honor one's father extends to honoring the father of the fatherland, the *pater patriate*.[51] Similarly, Coke argues that just as everyone is born as son or daughter of a father, a state that cannot be changed by law, he also says that everyone is born into the protection of the king as *pater patriae*, a relationship that is indelible and immutable.[52] Coke also thinks that Paul's Letter to the Romans refers to government by nature when it says, "Let every soul be subject to the higher authorities."[53] Coke also says that Aristotle in the *Politics* proves "that to command and to Obey is of Nature."[54]

Out of this picture flows Coke's proposition [6]: those outside of this particular bond of ligeance and magistracy are aliens. In saying this, Coke introduces new concepts and assumptions: propositions [2]–[4] speak of magistracy and government as a general principle. Proposition [5] moves to identify one person who is sovereign and superior. However, in proposition [6], Coke has shifted to a world of multiple dominions and sovereigns. He does not explain this shift. Does he think that the existence of multiple sovereigns is part of the natural law? Not quite. He argues that the law of nature is "parcel of the Laws, as well of England, as of all other nations."[55] For him, the law of nature is discerned in a world where England is one of "several & distinct kingdoms."[56] So, while he thinks that government is by nature, he does not say that the existence of several kingdoms is also by nature. Coke takes

---

[49] Exodus 18:13–27 precedes Ex. 24:4; Romans 2:14–16.

[50] Coke, "Calvin's Case," 12b–13a.

[51] Ex. 20:12. Coke, "Calvin's Case," 12b.

[52] *Indelebilis et immutabilis*, ibid., 13b–14a.

[53] *Omnis anima potestatibus sublimioribus subdita sit*, Romans 13:1, in ibid., 12b.

[54] Ibid., 13a; Aristotle, *Politics*, trans. H. Rackham, rev. edn., Loeb Classical Library 264 (Cambridge, Mass.: Harvard University Press, 1944), 1254a14–1255b15, 1254b19–23.

[55] Coke, "Calvin's Case," 14a.

[56] Ibid., 15a.

plurality for granted, but he does not give it greater force by saying that there are many kingdoms by nature. When Coke goes on to define the alien in proposition [6], he also does not say directly that the subject-alien relationship is by nature. So, for Coke government is natural, the plurality of governments is taken as fact, and the existence of some who are alien comes as a consequence.

The Alien as Suspicious

In Coke's Report on *Calvin's Case*, the alien is defined as one outside of the relationship of a subject to the sovereign of this dominion, and the alien comes as a result of this natural relationship. At this time, around 1608, how would Coke's contemporaries hear the term "alien"? Today the term "alien" conjures up extra-terrestrial life forms, perhaps threatening or monstrous. When the law describes a human being as an alien, that term appears to modern ears to accentuate that person's strangeness. Before the use from about 1929 onward of "alien" to mean a being not from this planet, would the term "alien" have been a more pleasant term for someone? Would it have indicated a milder form of strangeness than "alien" does today?[57]

Two sources provide evidence about what sort of connotation "alien" might have had before its use in science fiction. The first is the Authorized Version of the Bible, or the King James Version, bearing the name of the same king whose accession to the English throne provided the occasion for *Calvin's Case*. This English translation of the Bible from 1611 uses the word "stranger" to translate the Hebrew word גֵּר, *gēr*. This word refers to someone who moves from another place to take up residence, someone who can eat the Passover meal if, as a male, he and all males in his household are circumcised. The *gēr*, the "stranger," is thus one who can be joined to Israel, more akin to an immigrant than a foreign visitor.[58] The Authorized Version only occasionally uses the word "alien," and that word is used to translate נָכְרִי, *nokrî*, and נֵכָר, *nēḵār*, the Hebrew words for one who comes from afar but does not remain in Israel or attach herself to the people of Israel. At times, the Authorized Version translates *nokrî* and *nēḵār* as "foreigner."[59] The translators of

---

[57] The *Oxford English Dictionary* lists the first instances of "alien" to mean "extra-terrestrial" as 1929 for the adjective and 1931 for the noun, while the phrase "alien life form" first appears in 1937, "Alien, Adj. and N.," *Oxford English Dictionary Online* (Oxford: Oxford University Press, September 2012), www.oed.com/view/Entry/4988.

[58] On the *gēr*, see the Note to the Reader.

[59] Deuteronomy 14:21 gives instruction on what to do with a dead animal: it can be given charitably to what the A.V. calls the "stranger," or it can be sold to an "alien." Here the stranger is at the margins of Jewish society, while the alien is outside. Four Old Testament passages use "alien" in poetic couplets where "stranger" translates זָר, *zār*, in the first line and "alien" translates *nokrî* or *nēḵār* in the second line. In these passages, the speaker bemoans the misfortune of becoming an "alien" unto members of his household (Job 19:15; Psalm 69:8), laments the seizure of Israel's houses by 'aliens' (Lamentations 5:2) or foretells that "aliens" will plow and dress vines for Zion (Isaiah 61:5). Only one passage translates *gēr*

the Authorized Version carry forward this pattern into the New Testament, where "alien" appears twice, referring to those separated from the people of Israel or to enemies in battle.[60] In the verb form, the Authorized Version uses "alienated" in Ezekiel for a term meaning to turn away in disgust with connotations of a tear, a split, or a crack.[61] In the Pauline epistles, someone may be "alienated" from the life of God or "alienated and enemies" of Christ because of "wicked works."[62] In sum, the Authorized Version of the Bible uses "stranger" as a milder term for someone not from here, while "alien" stresses the strangeness of the person more powerfully, sometimes indicating tragic separation or violent conflict.

A second source indicates that the term "alien" held a consistent meaning through to the nineteenth century, prior to the aliens of science fiction. *Silas Marner*, Mary Ann Evans' 1861 novel written under the name George Eliot, describes how peasants perceived weavers who came from the city to ply their trade. These "pallid undersized men," writes Eliot, "by the side of the brawny country-folk looked like the remnants of a disinherited race." To weathered, strong country people, these weavers were "alien-looking men." They suspected that weaving might take place with the help of the "Evil One," and "superstition clung easily round" them: "No one knew where wandering men had their homes or their origin; and how was a man to be explained unless you at least knew somebody who knew his father and mother?" Even one who came and settled would continue to be "viewed with a remnant of distrust," allowing for no surprise if after a long time of benign conduct the tradesman was found to commit a crime.[63] Skill and cleverness were in themselves "suspicious," since their source was hidden and thus seemed a kind of "conjuring." The passage concludes: "In this way it came to pass that those scattered linen-weavers – emigrants from the town into the country – were to the last regarded as aliens by their rustic neighbors"[64] That Eliot chooses "alien" and not "foreigner," "stranger," or some other word is significant. The unfamiliar origins, the strange physical characteristics, and the obscure expertise of the tradesmen cause the locals

---

as "alien," Exodus 18:3, out of keeping with general practice in the A.V. On *nēḵār* and *noḵrî*, see the Note to the Reader.

[60] In Ephesians 2:12, the A.V. translates ἀπηλλοτριωμένοι, *apēllotriōmenoi*, a passive participial form of ἀπαλλοτριόω, *apallotrioō*, as "being aliens" in the phrase "being aliens from the commonwealth of Israel." In Hebrews 11:34, the A.V. translates παρεμβολὰς ἔκλιναν ἀλλοτρίων, *parembolas eklinan allotriōn*, as "turned to flight the armies of the aliens."

[61] In Ezekiel 23:17, 18, 22, 28, the A.V. uses "alienate" and "alienated" to translate forms of the related verbs יָקַע‎, *yq'* and נָקַע‎, *nq'* which mean "to turn away in disgust." Cognates in similar languages also mean splitting, tearing, cracking, and breaking, Ludwig Köhler and Walter Baumgartner, *The Hebrew and Aramaic Lexicon of the Old Testament* (K.B.), trans. M. E. J. Richardson (Leiden: Brill, 1994), 431, 722.

[62] In both Ephesians 4:18 and Colossians 1:21, the word "alienated" is used to translate passive participial forms of *apallotrioō* as in Ephesians 2:12. See note 60.

[63] George Eliot, *Silas Marner* (London: Penguin, 1994), 9.

[64] Ibid., 10.

to respond to them with distrust, even associating them with occult powers, and it is as aliens that Eliot describes this assessment of the newcomers by the peasants.

While the term "alien" continued to apply to human beings through the nineteenth century, "alien" appears to be the strongest English term short of "enemy" for someone from far away. It is not surprising, then, that science-fiction writers adopted the term "alien" for extra-terrestrials. When Coke's report describes the alien as born elsewhere, under another ruler, and within another sovereignty, that term to the original readers would have emphasized the strangeness of a person and given them license to suspect the person of hostility to the king. Coke's definition of the subject thus depends on circumscribing a foreign, perhaps hostile other – the alien – as a contrast term.

THE ALIEN AS A NEW LEGAL CONCEPT IN MEDIEVAL ENGLAND

The alien that the common law hands on to federal U.S. law is someone who lies outside of the bond between a subject and a sovereign. As defined in the seventeenth century, the alien was not from another planet, but still strange and worthy of suspicion. This person had not promised to put their life and body on the line to protect the king from harm. But this is not all there is to say about the alien. A careful reading of *Calvin's Case* reveals that the alien is a new legal concept that arose in the centuries preceding the case, a concept with a beginning and a development. If this is the case, then the laws that human beings live by do not have to include aliens, and the world they live in does not have to include aliens. What does Coke reveal, and is this suggestion of the alien's novelty borne out by the evidence from prior centuries?

Calvin's Case and the Making of the Alien

As Coke tries to demonstrate that the conception of the alien in *Calvin's Case* is well established in the law that precedes it, he begins with the common law, citing authorities that attest to a similar notion of an alien. Despite his presentation of them as authorities in agreement, the oldest authorities disagree with Coke. Coke says that after the Danish king Canute conquered England in the eleventh century, the peers and nobles of England sought to persuade Canute to reduce the numbers of troops he stationed in England. They did this by proposing a law to guarantee that if someone who was not an Englishman was killed, the killer would be held to account and punished. Coke explains, "This law was penned *Quicunque occiderit Francigenam, &c.* not excluding other aliens, but putting *Francigena*, a Frenchman for example, that others must be like unto him, in owing several ligeance to a several Sovereign."[65] Coke writes that in the

---

[65] Coke, "Calvin's Case," 16b. Coke cites Bracton lib. 3. Tract. 2. Cap. 15. Fol. 134.

same context, the legal authorities Bracton and Fleta "describ[e] an alien [as] *ad fidem Regis Franciae*," or "owing faith to the King of France."[66] Later in the same century from the laws of William the Conqueror, Coke cites a law defining the privileges of *omnis Francigena*, all French born, saying that *Francigena* was "there put for example as before is said, to expresse what manner of person *alienigena* should be."[67]

Coke's examples indicate that in a prior period, the law employed the terms *Francigena* or *ad fidem Regis Franciae* but no more general term for someone who was not an English subject. A Danish subject could qualify under laws that Coke quotes as referring to *Francigena* without being called *alienigena* or "alien." When Coke thinks that he can replace *Francigena* with *alienigena* to translate the law into its current use and application, he fails to recognize a key difference. While the older laws used the name for someone from one foreign realm, *Francigena*, Coke took for granted general terms for "subjects" from any other realm, the terms *alienigena*, "alien born," and "alien." Interpreting these texts is a complicated task, intertwined with the shifts in legal language that the conquest of England by the Norman French brought about. Still, what is clear from Coke is that the alien or the alien born did not dominate laws about those from far away.

In *Calvin's Case*, these terms *alienigena*, "alien born," and "alien" are available in common law as terms for the class of those who are not subjects of the king. Still, two of these three terms retain a helpful suffix, *-gena* or "born," a reminder that these are aliens only in a restricted sense – only in the sense that they are born in a land that is alien and other. But Coke also uses the term "alien" on its own, and this term becomes available to future generations of judges and lawmakers. By the time of the American founding, the term "alien" is the primary term used for someone who is not a citizen, not "French born" with its specificity or "alien born" with its helpful suffix. The era of *Calvin's Case* bequeaths to the United States of America the notion of an alien as summing up a type of person.

Coke's survey of the common law thus reveals two shifts. The first is a shift from naming a person by their place of origin with terms like "French born" to positing a general type of person called "alien born." The second is a shift from the qualified term "alien born" to the standalone "alien." Over time, the law yields a sharper definition of those from other lands as aliens – no longer as ones from France or from alien lands, but as aliens plain and simple. From English law to U.S. law, those with attachment to other domains are no longer described with qualifying terms. Those from far away are made aliens, alienated and isolated.

---

[66] Coke, "Calvin's Case," 16b. Coke writes that the law also stated that if someone was found slain, the person had to be proved to be "an Englishman," or else "he should be taken for an alien." Coke says that this law of "Englesherie" continued until it was abolished in 14 Edw. 3. Cap. 4.

[67] Coke, "Calvin's Case," 17a.

The Novelty of the Alien in Medieval Law

The alien emerges as a new thing in medieval England. This is what *Calvin's Case* reveals: that sometime in the more than half millennium between Kings Canute and James, the alien arose as an isolated term in English law. Besides this case that defines the alien, is there more evidence that the alien was once a new thing, discovered or fabricated?

Histories of English law agree that the concept of the alien is not a fixed notion in English law. But the histories disagree about whether the alien was always present as a concept that receded and emerged again or a genuinely new thing at some point in history. In his history of early English law, Frederic William Maitland assumes that the distinction between a foreigner and a nonforeigner is a given in law, yet a distinction of diminished importance for a couple of centuries. In his view, when the foreigner William conquered England in 1066 and became its king, there was little sense in distinguishing foreigners from nonforeigners.[68] In Maitland's estimation, laws distinguishing foreigners and English returned from 1259: "It is, we believe, in the loss of Normandy that our law of aliens finds its starting point."[69] After this point, French subjects who made claims to land in English courts were refused a hearing. But, says Maitland, "a claimant of land is met, not by the simple 'You are an alien,' but by the far more elaborate 'You are within the power of the king of France and resident in France'"[70]

Here, Maitland's evidence weakens his case. While this is a law against those outside the faith and allegiance of the King of England, the practice in courts is to name those within the power of France without using a general term like "alien." Strictly speaking, this is not a law about aliens as a blanket category.

But there is a further reason to object to Maitland's thesis, as legal scholar Keechang Kim demonstrates. Kim disputes the influential opinion of Maitland through extensive textual evidence. He points to a way out of the assumption that human beings have always distinguished foreigners from themselves in law, even if that distinction rises and falls in its importance. Instead, Kim demonstrates that in English law, the alien was a new concept, appearing around the year 1400. For centuries, English law held to the Roman pattern, that the main distinction between persons in law was between free and unfree. Somewhere around 1400, this distinction receded in importance, and a distinction between subject and alien rose to take

---

[68] Frederick Pollock and Frederic William Maitland, *The History of English Law before the Time of Edward I*, vol. 1 (Cambridge: Cambridge University Press, 1895), 443.

[69] Ibid., 1:444.

[70] Ibid., 1:445. Maitland cites Henry de Bracton, *Bracton's Note Book: A Collection of Cases Decided in the King's Courts during the Reign of Henry the Third*, ed. Frederic William Maitland (London: C. J. Clay & Sons, 1887), 110, 1396. In the preface to *The History of English Law*, Pollock acknowledges that Maitland did the far greater share of the writing, and Keechang Kim attributes this work to Maitland alone, *Aliens in Medieval Law: The Origins of Modern Citizenship* (Cambridge: Cambridge University Press, 2000), x, 12.

its place. No longer was it the unfree person who could not file suit in a court, but it was the alien who could not file suit. The subject-alien distinction became the primary distinction between persons in law, says Kim. Kim does not explain why the subject-alien distinction grew in importance, but he claims it was part of what produced the modern state. When distinctions between who is in and who is out became primary in law, then allegiance to the king was primary.[71] If Kim's account is right, this pattern remains today in federal U.S. law, with the citizen replacing the subject. Today, the principal factor that determines legal rights is whether someone is an alien or a citizen.

What is Kim's evidence? He points to the claim from Coke's Report on *Calvin's Case*, mentioned above: "Every man is either *Alienigena*, an *Alien* born, or *subditus*, a subject born" (1608).[72] A few centuries before, the authority on English law Henry de Bracton says something entirely different: "The first and shortest classification of persons is that all men are either free or unfree" (ca. 1220–50).[73] Bracton mimics the judgment of Roman lawyer Gaius, passed on to common law through Justinian: "The primary division of the law of persons is this, that all men are either free or slaves" (ca. 130–180).[74] The shift from Bracton to Coke becomes apparent among authorities in English law when John Fortescue opposes a law that considers servitude normal, standing instead for the freedom that God has given human nature (ca. 1468–70).[75] In the same work, Fortescue describes political rule as involving a man governing a community in the way that a head regulates the body. This body, which he calls a mystical body or *corpus misticum*, is bound together by law.[76] Kim thinks that Fortescue shows how a new distinction will limit how far equality extends if the unfree are no longer excluded: equality can be limited only to one political community, tied together by laws in a mystical body.[77] Echoes of the

---

[71] Kim, *Aliens in Medieval Law*.

[72] Coke, "Calvin's Case," 17a.

[73] *Est autem prima divisio personarum haec et brevissima, quod omnes homines aut liberi sunt aut serui*, Henry de Bracton, *De legibus et consuetudinibus Angliæ*, ed. George E. Woodbine, vol. 2 (New Haven: Yale University Press; London: Humphrey Milford; Oxford: Oxford University Press, 1922), 29; Kim, *Aliens in Medieval Law*, 1. English translation modified by the author from that included in Henry de Bracton, *On the Laws and Customs of England*, ed. George E. Woodbine, trans. Samuel E. Thorne, vol. 2 (Cambridge, Mass.: The Belknap Press of Harvard University Press, 1968), 29.

[74] *Et quidem summa diuisio de iure personarum haec est, quod omnes homines aut liberi sunt aut serui*, Gaius, *The Institutes of Gaius and Rules of Ulpian: The Former from Studemund's Apograph of the Verona Codex*, ed. and trans. James Muirhead (Edinburgh: T. & T. Clark, 1880), I, 8.

[75] John Fortescue, "In Praise of the Laws of England," in *On the Laws and Governance of England*, ed. Shelley Lockwood, trans. S. B. Chrimes (Cambridge: Cambridge University Press, 1997), chap. 42; Kim, *Aliens in Medieval Law*, 5.

[76] Fortescue, "In Praise of the Laws of England," chap. 13; the Latin is found in John Fortescue, *De Laudibus Legum Anglie*, trans. S. B. Chrimes (Cambridge: Cambridge University Press, 1942), chap. 13.

[77] Kim, *Aliens in Medieval Law*, 5.

shift from the free-unfree distinction to the subject-alien distinction appear just a little earlier in Thomas Littleton (ca. 1450–60). There, among the kinds of persons who cannot bring lawsuits are aliens, those who are outside the ligeance of the lord, the king.[78]

When did the monumental shift from free-unfree to subject-alien happen? Kim claims that the new distinction between subject and alien was ensconced by about 1400. Where before, merchants could trade so long as they could demonstrate they were free, now it mattered whether they were born subjects or born aliens. While a customs document from Norwich from around 1340 awarded access to traders based on whether they were free rather than unfree, the letters patent of John Swart from 1397 allowed him to trade only if he paid homage to the king and left the society of the alien born.[79] Around the same time, shifts happened regarding who could become the minister of a church, says Kim. While before this time, foreigners were not excluded from being the clerk of a benefice, in a statute of 1383 an alien could be punished for purchasing, possessing, or occupying a church benefice.[80] In a parallel change in 1413, the houses of foreign religious orders in England could be seized by the realm regardless of whether England was at war with their country of origin.[81] The linchpin in the rise of alien status came in a statute about whether someone born abroad could inherit land in England, argues Kim. Cases in 1343 and 1350 considered whether children born abroad to English subjects could inherit land. It was already clear that if the king's child was born abroad, that child would inherit the monarchy. These cases clarified the circumstances for subjects of the king who bear children abroad, perhaps because they are in the king's service as soldiers. The decision was that these children, though born outside the allegiance of the king, are subjects of the king if their parents are of the faith and allegiance of the king.[82] Thus, they can claim an inheritance in England. Notice the logical sleight of hand: a child can be born outside the allegiance of the king while her parents – including her mother – are of the allegiance of the king. This is based on a double meaning of "ligeance" or allegiance: the child is born outside the allegiance of the

---

[78] Coke, *Coke on Littleton*, 1:129a (sec. 198); Kim, *Aliens in Medieval Law*, 6–7.

[79] Kim, *Aliens in Medieval Law*, 34, 53, 58.

[80] Statute 7 Richard II c. 12 (1383), in Kim, *Aliens in Medieval Law*, 83.

[81] *Rotuli Parliamentorum*, IV, 13 (1413), 22 (1414), in Kim, *Aliens in Medieval Law*, 99.

[82] *Touz les enfantz heriters, qi serront neez desore dehors la ligeance le Roi, des queux enfantz les piere et miere au temps du nestre sont et serront a la foi et de la ligeance du Roi Dengleterre, eient et enjoient meismes les benefice et avantage daver et porter heritage deinz la dite ligeance, come les autres heriters avantditz, en temps avenir.* "All Children Inheritors, which from henceforth shall be born without the Ligeance of the King, whose Fathers and Mothers at the Time of their Birth be and shall be at the Faith and Ligeance of the King of England, shall have and enjoy the same Benefits and Advantages, to have and bear the Inheritance within the same Ligeance, as the other Inheritors aforesaid in Time to come," French and English translation from *De natis ultra mare* (1351), *The Statutes of the Realm*, vol. 1 (London: George Eyre and Andrew Strahan, 1810), 310; Kim, *Aliens in Medieval Law*, 117, 210.

king in the sense of being outside of the king's lands, but the mother giving birth is of that allegiance because she is bound to the king by faithfulness and obedience.[83] This statute in question, *De natis ultra mare* (1351), based decisions in personal law and decisions about inheritance on subject status. This was the legacy of the statute: a person's loyalties determined their legal privileges and advantages. Someone's status before the king as a faithful subject made all the difference for legal proceedings on matters like holding property, trading, and ministering. Alien status was now a reason to take away a host of legal rights.[84]

Is Kim right that the alien was only distinguished from the subject as the primary division between persons in law in about 1400? The preceding evidence is just a sample of what Kim draws out, and the evidence is strong. His rereading of the medieval law has received commendation from reviewers and fellow scholars, and he appears to be right. However, on another point Kim goes beyond the evidence. He claims in a few places that faith and allegiance were tied in this period to a growing notion of the political community as a mystical body, a *corpus mysticum*, but he does not present evidence of this tie. His only source on the mystical body is the Fortescue passage mentioned above, where Fortescue does not speak of faith and allegiance.[85] But Kim's point drawn out here, that the alien is a new legal concept arising in about 1400, is worth accepting.

It is only possible to notice that the alien is a new legal concept when an assumption is left behind. That is the assumption that law starts with insiders and outsiders, with us and them. It is the assumption that the most important thing about law is how it binds a political community together, causing the law to apply first to those within the political community and only in a limited way to those outside. Coke's Report on *Calvin's Case* displays this assumption, that there simply are aliens and subjects, and that they are of chief importance when determining inheritance. Kim argues that Coke and others import the assumption that national membership is the most important thing in law into their readings of past laws. Kim invites his readers to examine the evidence and consider the possibility that a person's status as a subject or an alien was not at the center of the law of persons. Human societies always distinguish outsiders from themselves, Kim clarifies, but he does not think that these distinctions have always been paramount in law or even present in law. On the contrary: in the common law, before 1400 being an outsider made little difference for legal matters between persons.[86]

As the alien emerges as a given in law, so do new ways of characterizing political rule. It is all important to be a subject of some sovereign, and to be a subject involves bearing faith and allegiance to that sovereign. The alien-subject distinction

---

[83] Kim, *Aliens in Medieval Law*, 139–41.
[84] Ibid., 143–44.
[85] Ibid., 5–6, 142, 144, 171, 176, 178, 195, 210; see p. 41.
[86] Ibid., 205–6.

begins to take over common life, determining who can do things and who cannot, who has privileges and who cannot.

—

This chapter scrutinized the concept that makes federal U.S. immigration law possible. That concept is the alien, someone described in English common law as outside the faith and allegiance of the king. The term "alien" is increasingly isolated in legal language, becoming a standalone item for U.S. law to use, and it carries an overtone of suspicion. Though in later common law and in U.S. law the distinction of the alien from the subject or citizen is the primary distinction between persons, it was not always so. Only about six hundred years ago did the subject-alien distinction replace the distinction between free and unfree. Since this shift, a person's allegiance has made all the difference for activities like trading, inheriting, ministering, and going to court. The alien, someone to be distrusted, is the by-product of this strengthening of bonds between subject and sovereign.

Aliens have not always been a central preoccupation of law. There are other ways that common life can be ordered and that human beings can relate to authority. In the next chapter, attention to the world that God loves and to the community that is Christ's body will point to a more salutary way of living. This way does not produce aliens to be distrusted. Instead, it draws near to those far away out of fellow humanity and love.

2

Coming Near to Distant Neighbors in God's World

The concept of the alien makes United States immigration law possible. The previous chapter examined this concept and found that U.S. law defines the alien as someone who may become a citizen and someone whose entrance into U.S. territory may be restricted. This concept was defined in English common law, in *Calvin's Case*, as someone who is not the subject of a given sovereign. In that case, the alien was in the process of emerging as a standalone concept no longer modified by other terms: a person worthy of suspicion. Earlier sources revealed that distinguishing aliens from subjects was not a central concern of the law before 1400. This means that human beings can order their common life without identifying aliens to be excluded and disenfranchised. Other ways of ordering life are possible.

How else can a relationship with those from far away be understood and practiced? In this chapter, renewed ways of relating with migrants and foreigners arise from the Christian Scriptures, read alongside trusted interpreters. Two questions guide this search: First, how are those from far away situated within God's work of bringing God's world to its fulfillment? Karl Barth's reckoning with nationhood from Genesis to Ephesians points to an answer. Second, how are those from far away situated within the church? The Apostle Paul's account of his migration as a missionary in 1 Corinthians 9, read with Brian Brock and Bernd Wannenwetsch, provides a picture of the church in relation to migrants.

THE ONES NEARBY AND THE ONES FAR AWAY:
BARTH'S BIBLICAL THEOLOGY OF THE PEOPLES

How do those from far away fit into the world that God creates and preserves? One way of answering that question is to examine the role of nations across the narratives of the Bible. A noteworthy account of peoples in Scripture comes from the twentieth-century Reformed theologian Karl Barth in a section of the *Church Dogmatics* entitled *Die Nahen und die Fernen*, translated as "Near and Distant

Neighbors."[1] Barth's attentive exegesis of key biblical passages, his careful assessment of national belonging, and his guarding of nationhood from distortion commend his writing.[2] Barth is known for his opposition to natural law arguments, and he might seem too easy a figure to oppose to Edward Coke. Yet a reading of "Near and Distant Neighbors" along with the surrounding writing in Barth's ethics of creation shows that Barth was confident in describing how God has made the world and in characterizing human life within one nation and within all humanity.[3]

Just as Coke's definition of the alien in *Calvin's Case* arose in a context, Barth's ways of describing those from other countries arose in a context. In one sense, that context is the *Church Dogmatics*, a bold exploration of the Word of God that formed Barth's life work from the 1930s until his death in 1968. The section that merits attention falls within Barth's teaching on creation, where he says that the command of God directs persons toward their fellow human beings, to "affirm, honor, and enjoy" them.[4] Barth writes that certain kinds of relationships belong to humanity as created by God: Every human being is male or female and incomplete without the other, and everyone is a child and possibly a parent. But are there further spheres of human relationships that belong to creation? Are human beings necessarily given a *Volk*, a people or a nation to be a part of, and a wider sphere of humanity to be a part of?[5]

As Barth explores this question, he reveals his historical context, an occasion of the utmost urgency. Writing just after the Second World War, Barth wants to rectify the errors of the *"völkische Bewegung,"* the "nationalist movement" in German Protestant theology that aided and abetted the disastrous nationalism of the Third Reich just a few years prior.[6] He decries the invention by "sentimental or wicked fools" of a theology and ethics that sees the *Volk* as God's chief gift to humanity.[7] The likes of Paul Althaus, Emmanuel Hirsch, and Friedrich Gogarten understood

---

[1] Karl Barth, *Die kirchliche Dogmatik (K.D.)*, vol. III/4, *Die Lehre von der Schöpfung* (Zürich: Theologischer Verlag Zürich, 1980), 320–66, originally published in 1951; Karl Barth, *Church Dogmatics (C.D.)*, ed. G. W. Bromiley and T. F. Torrance, trans. A. T. Mackay et al., vol. III/4, *The Doctrine of Creation* (Edinburgh: T. & T. Clark, 1961), 285–323. Carys Moseley, in *Nations and Nationalism in the Theology of Karl Barth* (Oxford: Oxford University Press, 2013), 201, argues that this 1951 statement by Barth represents his mature thought on nations and nationalism and something he did not modify before his death in 1968.

[2] Two contemporary theologians interpret peoplehood in ways that closely echo Barth. Nigel Biggar makes his debt to Barth clear in "The Value of Limited Loyalty: Christianity, the Nation, and Territorial Boundaries," in *Boundaries and Justice: Diverse Ethical Perspectives*, ed. David Miller and Sohail H. Hashmi (Princeton: Princeton University Press, 2001), 38–54. Oliver O'Donovan's debt to Barth remains implicit in *The Ways of Judgment* (Grand Rapids, Mich.: Eerdmans, 2005), 149–57.

[3] See Emil Brunner and Karl Barth, *Natural Theology: Comprising "Nature and Grace" by Emil Brunner and the Reply "No!" by Karl Barth*, trans. Peter Fraenkel (London: Geoffrey Bles, The Centenary Press, 1946); Stanley Hauerwas, *With the Grain of the Universe: The Church's Witness and Natural Theology* (London: S.C.M. Press, 2002).

[4] *C.D.*, III/4:116.

[5] Ibid., III/4:286.

[6] *K.D.*, III/4:347; *C.D.*, III/4:307.

[7] *C.D.*, III/4:292, 307–8.

the life of the nation as the basic revelation of God's ways, the foundational God-given imperative that government rather than the Church is equipped to illuminate. The church was tasked with upholding the nation and supporting the preservation of a healthy race, which in the hands of the National Socialists soon led to the murder of those considered weak or degenerate.[8] Barth says this is a movement without precedent in theology and "one of the most curious and tragic events in the whole history of Protestant theology."[9] With this behind him, Barth's writing returns to the question of the role of the people and all humanity in creation, pruning away over-confident assertions about nationhood yet not discarding what might be true about the people, the nation, as the setting in which a person hears the command of God.[10]

Barth offers two suggestions about how human beings relate to those whom federal U.S. law calls "aliens." In Barth's terms, he is concerned about how God's command frees the hearer for relationship. First, Barth writes that the members of other peoples are always fellow human beings. A human being is always a fellow human being, he says; a *Mensch* is always a *Mitmensch*, an "I" encountering, relating to, and partnering with a "You." For Barth, this basic truth about humanity becomes clear through an understanding of how the human being relates to God: The human being is determined to be the covenant partner of God, and likewise human beings are brought into partnership with other human beings. For Barth, this truth also becomes clear when God is seen as triune rather than solitary, so that human beings made in God's image are not solitary but freed in fellowship.[11] When Barth moves to consider the members of other peoples, he says that they can be called *Fremden*, "foreigners" in Harold Knight's translation, but they are "only partial and relative foreigners" because they are fellow human beings.[12] If the German term *Fremde* means one who is foreign, strange, or other, then it coincides with the English term "alien," or at least with the milder term "foreigner."

So, from the beginning Barth opposes the notion that some human beings are simply alien or plainly foreign. Barth does not base this stance against considering others to be alien on a claim that everyone shares a common humanity, some common substance or nature. Instead, he says that someone is human to the extent to which she partners with other human beings: that she moves out toward her fellow human beings. Barth suggests, then, that before God the Creator, the

---

[8] Ibid., III/4:308–9. See Timothy Gorringe, *Karl Barth: Against Hegemony* (Oxford: Oxford University Press, 1999), 118; Arthur C. Cochrane, *The Church's Confession Under Hitler* (Philadelphia: Westminster Press, 1962).

[9] *C.D.*, III/4:305.

[10] Ibid., III/4:287.

[11] Ibid., III/4:116–17; *K.D.*, III/4:127–28. For Barth's fuller account of humanity as fellow-humanity, see *C.D.*, ed. Geoffrey W. Bromiley and T. F. Torrance, trans. Harold Knight et al., vol. III/2, *The Doctrine of Creation* (Edinburgh: T. & T. Clark, 1960), sec. 45, especially 247, 285.

[12] *C.D.*, III/4:286; *K.D.*, III/4:322. See also *C.D.*, III/4:287, 290.

members of other peoples are only relatively alien because they are fellow human beings, partnering human beings.

There is a second reason that distinctions between what Coke calls subjects and aliens cannot be static or final, according to Barth. He develops a distinctive kind of speech to explain the relationship between a nation and other nations, between a people and all humanity. He speaks in terms of *die Nahen und die Fernen*, which Harold Knight's 1961 translation renders as "near and distant neighbors." Knight's translation represents a gloss on Barth; Barth does not mention the *Nächster*, the next or proximate one that is not there by choice, the standard term in German Bibles for the Greek πλησίον, *plēsion*, translated "neighbor" in English Bibles. Nor does Barth mention the *Nachbar*, the German term for the neighbor that is chosen, except when he discusses the *Nachbarvolk*, the neighboring people, which will receive attention below. *Die Nahen und die Fernen* simply means "the nearby ones and the distant ones," "the ones close by and the ones far away," without drawing out the associations that the "neighbor" carries in Christian theology. In the end, Knight's gloss "near and distant neighbors" proves a helpful way of tying together Barth's insights, as will become clear from a careful reading of Barth on his own terms. Another of Knight's translations is worth resisting: He renders Barth's *Volk* as "people," "nation," and "race," but Barth uses *Volk* to mean a people or a nation, not to speak of a biological human type, a "race."[13] With these German terms better defined, the next step is to turn to Barth's distinctive understanding of peoples.

Where does the command of God meet human beings to free them for fellowship, asks Barth? It meets them where they are, among those nearby, among their people, determined sometimes by blood relationships, by history, by language, by customs, or by location. The command of God also meets human beings where they are among those far away, among the peoples of the world. God makes each place where someone lives holy, among those nearby and those far away, and here he commands human beings to obey. There is no autonomous law that holds in the national or international spheres, but there too God is Lord and Deliverer, says Barth.[14] Human beings live within a people and among all humanity, but is nationality an essential feature of how they are created? Is someone always called to honor, promote, and protect the people they are a part of? No, Barth says. In an earlier work, the 1928 *Ethics*, Barth had placed nationhood within a discussion of calling, so that someone could be called to loyalty to their people. Here in 1951, Barth writes otherwise: The people is not an order of creation, but instead an ordinance.[15] Nationhood is a sphere of obedience, a sphere in which the command of God meets a person, and no more. The eternal God rules over all of history, but some of God's gifts God only gives for a time, and the people is among those.[16]

---

[13] Moseley is right to reject the translation of *Volk* as "race," *Nations and Nationalism*, 178.

[14] *C.D.*, III/4:287.

[15] *Ethics*, ed. Dietrich Braun, trans. Geoffrey W. Bromiley (Edinburgh: T. & T. Clark, 1981), 191, 193. See Moseley, *Nations and Nationalism*, 177.

[16] Barth, *C.D.*, III/4:301, 305.

While the confrontation between man and woman and parent and child is unalterable, Barth says, the confrontation between the near and the distant is not fixed or permanent. The peoples are a "fatherly" gift of God to preserve humanity from harm, but they are neither original nor final.[17]

This case for the near ones and the distant ones as temporary dispositions of God arises from Barth's reading of the peoples or nations in the biblical narrative.[18] Barth remarks that the peoples do not arise in the creation accounts of Genesis 1 and 2, nor do they appear in the account of the fall and its aftermath for a united humanity in Genesis 3–9.[19] Instead, the peoples arise after God has made a covenant with Noah and every living creature in Genesis 8:20—9:17, when God promises to preserve them from total destruction.[20] The peoples first appear in what Barth reads as synchronous accounts in Genesis 10:1–32 and 11:1–9. The first account presents a separation into peoples, lands, and languages as an obedient response to God's command to multiply and fill the earth, while the second account presents the dispersion of separate peoples as a divine judgment. In Barth's reading of this second account, while humanity has one language, it gathers to build a tower at Babel where it will make a name for itself rather than calling on God's name, where it will offer sacrifices under its own power. The sinfulness of the one humanity grows, and the unity it achieved through force and ideology threatens to destroy it. God comes down to scatter the peoples and their languages to preserve them from self-destruction.[21] God's judgment is severe, since human beings now live in a world with geographical borders and separate histories. They dwell in an antithesis of near and distant, where there can be little cooperation across borders, where there remains a "great homesickness."[22] Still, God does not leave them without hope.

A plurality of peoples has arisen both as a response to the divine command and as divine judgment. The many peoples form the scene on which the main story of Scripture takes place from Genesis 12 onward. In Barth's reading, God forms a unique people, Israel, who lies now at the center of history with the other peoples at the periphery. Israel is only a people so long as it remembers that God has brought it together, and it is made to summon the peoples to worship God. Barth says that it is the Jews and not others who sing Psalm 100:

Make a joyful noise unto the Lord, all ye lands.

Serve the Lord with gladness; come before his presence with singing.

Know ye that the Lord he is God: it is he that hath made us, and not we ourselves; we are his people, and the sheep of his pasture.[23]

---

[17] Ibid., III/4:324.
[18] This appears in small type in ibid., III/4:309–23.
[19] Ibid., III/4:309, 311.
[20] Ibid., III/4:315.
[21] Ibid., III/4:312–18.
[22] Ibid., III/4:317.
[23] Ibid., III/4:318–19. Ps. 100:1–3, A.V.

For Barth, God does a work within Israel at Pentecost. There the followers of Jesus are filled with the Holy Spirit and enabled to speak the languages of the known world, "telling . . . the mighty works of God."[24] God enables disciples from Galilee, the margins of Israel, to speak the languages of the Jewish diaspora, while the Acts passage does not mention Jerusalem, Israel's metropolis. The Holy Spirit breaks Israel out of its old confines and makes possible a new Israel, an Israel which will include the speakers of a multitude of languages, writes Barth. It is a work of the Holy Spirit, not of a human being, to build this bridge from those nearby to those far away. The Spirit enables the witnesses of Christ to move out to those far away.[25] Moving beyond Barth, it is good to resist seeing Pentecost as a reversal of the tower of Babel. The work of the Holy Spirit is not to unify the peoples of the world under one language. Rather, the Spirit enables a new Israel to form, speaking the one Word about the risen Christ in many languages.

"But now in Christ Jesus you who once were far off have been brought near by the blood of Christ. For he himself is our peace, who has made us both one and has broken down in his flesh the dividing wall of hostility." Barth concludes his reading of Scripture with this passage from the Letter to the Ephesians (2:13–14). It is here that the provenance of Barth's central terms becomes clear. The destiny of the far ones and the near ones is disclosed: their end is to come near in the blood of Christ, where the walls of hostility are broken down.[26] This is not simply a move toward the universal: The nations are not headed toward the unified humanity present at creation, nor are their members to become cosmopolitans.[27] Rather, the destiny of the peoples is that they will be included in that very particular people made by God, Israel. In Barth's striking phrase, "It is not any other people, nor the totality of others, but the Jews who are the universal horizon of each and all peoples."[28] It is as part of Israel that the nations find their end.

---

[24] Acts 2:11, E.S.V. here and unless otherwise noted.

[25] *C.D.*, III/4:320–22.

[26] Ibid., III/4:323.

[27] Ibid., III/4:293, 312. While Barth rejects cosmopolitanism, theologian Luke Bretherton argues for a "Christian cosmopolitanism" in *Christianity and Contemporary Politics: The Conditions and Possibilities of Faithful Witness* (Oxford: Wiley-Blackwell, 2010), 129–37. Barth and Bretherton are not strongly opposed, however. Bretherton argues against a rationalist cosmopolitanism that sees national memberships as dissolving into a united humanity. Instead, he proposes a Christian cosmopolitanism in which national communities have value, nations seek an international common good within a commonwealth of nations, and nations find their *telos* in the communion of human beings with God. Bretherton calls this end the "city of God" (134), and he states that Christian universality is more properly called "catholicity" (136), a reference to the church in its wholeness. Barth on the other hand avoids talk of world citizenship or cosmopolitanism in favor of what he sees as the end of nations: inclusion in the people of Israel, the people made by God.

[28] *C.D.*, III/4:319. *Kein anderes Volk und auch nicht die Völker in ihrer Gesamtheit, sondern sie, die Juden, sind der universale Horizont aller Völker und jedes einzelnen Volkes,* *K.D.*, III/4:361.

In Barth's writing, the reading of Scripture on the peoples follows a general treatment of the peoples, but this general treatment only makes sense at the end of Barth's writing on the Bible when the origin and end of the peoples becomes clear. It appears that for Barth, the nature and purpose of peoples and nations only makes sense once God's purpose for them is clear.

Human beings really are among peoples with their languages, their shared places, and their histories, Barth says in his general treatment of peoples. And those who hear God's command ought to be committed to each of these, to learn their national speech and use it well, to have a proper patriotism about their country, and to take responsibility within history. But to be really among one's people, says Barth, is to make use of language, place, and history in an outward-looking manner. The command of God moves its hearers to use speech rightly, to seek to communicate not only with those who speak the same dialect or national language, but to seek fellowship with those who speak foreign languages.[29]

Locality, too, is best understood as a place to look out from, Barth argues. Human beings are in a place with all the others who look out from that place, and that place will stick with someone invisibly even if they pass on to another place.[30] At the borders of a locality there is a neighboring people, a *Nachbarvolk*, to whom one must reach out.[31] Barth writes, "One's own people in its location cannot and must not be a wall but a door. Whether it be widely opened or not, and even perhaps shut again, it must never be barred, let alone blocked up."[32] Arguing that distinctions between near ones and distant ones are fluid, Barth continues:

> We have seen that, although this does not mean the removal of boundaries, it certainly means the overthrow of barriers and a certain coming and going, a common mind and mutual intercourse, a certain measure of co-operation and the establishment of genuine societies across the frontiers.[33]

As human beings stand within their people's history, too, they are to look out toward the history of all peoples as it finds its center in Jesus Christ.[34] Not when someone makes their language a prison, not when they bar their borders, not when they act only to further their nation's history, but when they move outward are they most faithful to their people. Barth announces, "The one who is really in his own people, among those near to him, is always on the way to those more distant, to other peoples."[35]

---

[29] C.D., III/4:289–91, 294–98.
[30] Ibid., III/4:290–92.
[31] Ibid., III/4:293; K.D., III/4:330.
[32] C.D., III/4:294.
[33] Ibid., III/4:300. *Wir sahen ja: da brauchen zwar die Grenzsteine nicht ausgerissen zu werden, da gehen aber die Schlagbäume auf*, K.D., III/4:339.
[34] C.D., III/4:297.
[35] Ibid., III/4:294.

Human beings must begin with those nearby, Barth says, but they are really on the way to those who are far off. The command of God meets human beings on the way, as pilgrims.[36] Someone does not find their essence only in their people or among all humanity; rather, each person is involved in a centrifugal motion; they are set on a path, moving out from near to far.[37] Someone's place within one people rather than another is "reversible." It is "fluid" and hard to define even if someone is not Alsatian, and it is ultimately "removable."[38] While human beings remain man and woman, parent and child, Barth suggests that when it comes to being a Chicagoan or an American or a Mexican, a person puts on "pilgrim's clothing," and they might put it off again.[39] One's location is simply one place to exercise natural fellow-humanity. Barth concludes:

> Since the confrontation of near and distant neighbors is reversible, fluid, and removable, this means that it is not original or final. It is not a natural and necessary confrontation. It is a fact. It is thus self-evidently according to the will of God and under his lordship.[40]

Here it becomes clear that Knight's mistranslation of *die Nahen and die Fernen* as "near and distant neighbors" is a fitting interpretive move. Barth thinks that a person is freed by the divine command to come near to those nearby and to those far away. If someone's basic stance toward the members of their people is to grow in loyal and responsible partnership with them, then it is right to call them "neighbors," potentially or actually. If someone's basic stance toward the members of other peoples is to seek fellowship with them, then it is also right to call them "neighbors." Someone who hears the Word of God is freed to name, view, and treat those nearby and those far away as neighbors. They may be near or they may be far, but they are near neighbors or distant neighbors.

This picture of the nearby ones and the distant ones has an unexpected similarity with Coke's subjects and aliens. Coke was content to call government and allegiance natural without saying the same about distinctions between subjects and aliens, treating those distinctions as not so much natural as factual. Barth explicitly proposes that the distinctions between peoples are mere facts, occasions for being freed by God, but not natural distinctions. Still, Barth goes beyond Coke when he touches on the question of the foreigner or the alien. Coke's legal writing sets up clear distinctions between subjects and aliens, allowing for an alien to become a subject through a process of naturalization. But in Barth's theological writing, the terms themselves are not to be left alone but to be directed toward a coming near in Christ.

---

[36] Ibid., III/4:302.
[37] Ibid., III/4:291.
[38] Ibid., III/4:299–302.
[39] Ibid., III/4:302.
[40] Ibid.

Barth's masterful teaching holds together large swaths of biblical material without muting distinct voices as they attest to God's initiative with and for the nations. His work resists the temptation to overvalue the people, chastened as he is by the errors of Protestants under the Nazis, and yet Barth does not throw out the biblical witness on this subject but lets it come to light. His compelling picture offers a framework for situating those from far away within the activity of God, a Christian alternative to the stark terms of federal U.S. law.

That picture goes like this: Human beings rightly exercise their place within their people when they are not content to let those far away remain alien, when they seek fellowship and partnership with those far away. Indeed, every human being wears pilgrim's clothing. Migrants are not fundamentally different or alien to those who are more settled among a people; all travel on the pilgrim's way. This way leads to a drawing near in the body of Christ, a coming near as the peoples are grafted into Israel, the people that God has made. This bridging process is made possible through the Holy Spirit. During this coming together, migrants remain fellow human beings and neighbors. Extending Barth's terms, migrants can be called distant neighbors coming near. As they hear God's Word, those who are more settled are freed to come near to these neighbors.

THE MIGRANT MISSIONARY AND THE APOSTOLIC CHURCH: BROCK AND WANNENWETSCH ON 1 CORINTHIANS 9

Having seen how those from far away might be situated within the world that God provides for and brings to completion, there remains more to ask about God's community: How are those from far away situated in the church? Is there something about God's renewed people that alters how its members regard those from other lands?

The theme of the people of God as a migrant people appears regularly in the Scriptures and in the theologians of the church.[41] One angle on this theme comes in

---

[41] For example, in Leviticus, Yhwh addresses Israel as former migrants in the land of Egypt and migrants with Yhwh (19:34; 25:23, etc.). The Letter to the Hebrews those who lived by faith as visiting foreigners (*xenoi, parepidēmoi*) on earth for whom God has prepared a city (*polis*) (11:13, 16). The First Epistle of Peter addresses Christians as settled migrants (*paroikoi*) and visiting foreigners (*parepidēmoi*) made into God's household economy (*oikos*) (2:11; 4:16, 17), following the interpretation of John H. Elliott, *A Home for the Homeless: A Sociological Exegesis of 1 Peter, Its Situation and Strategy* (Philadelphia: Fortress Press, 1981), 25, 47, 194–204; *1 Peter: A New Translation with Introduction and Commentary*, Anchor Bible 37B (New York: Doubleday, 2000), 101, 312, 458–61.

In the early church, the Epistle of Diognetus describes Christians as living like settled migrants (*paroikoi*), acting fully as citizens (*politai*) but submitting like aliens or foreigners (*xenoi*), "The Epistle to Diognetus," in *Early Christian Writings: The Apostolic Fathers*, ed. Andrew Louth, trans. Maxwell Staniforth and Andrew Louth (Harmondsworth: Penguin, 1987), sec. 5. Augustine narrates the sojourning of the heavenly city among the earthly city,

the First Letter to the Corinthians, chapter 9. In this passage, the Apostle Paul writes that he has been sent out "to become all things to all people" as he preaches the good news, migrating, being forced to migrate, and becoming like those he goes to. What follows will explore what it is to be a migrant missionary in conversation with a commentary on 1 Corinthians by contemporary moral theologians Brian Brock and Bernd Wannenwetsch.[42] The migrant missionary connects to the church's nature as apostolic, as sent out. This reading of 1 Corinthians 9 will demonstrate a special solidarity between the missionary church and her fellow migrants, a solidarity that resists calling migrants "aliens." In a setting where the term "alien" prevails, the solidarity between church and migrants draws the church to join her fellow migrants under the banner of "alien."

In chapter 9 of this letter, Paul writes to the Corinthians, "Am I not free? Am I not an apostle?"[43] Paul addresses Corinthian expectations that he would receive remuneration for his work preaching the gospel, that he would be wined and dined. This would be right, he says, since workers are due their wages, whether in the temple or as evangelists (9:3–12). But Paul travels as a single man, makes tents (Acts 18:2–4), and does not accept payment for his preaching. Brock and Wannenwetsch suggest that he does this not in a heroic renunciation of material goods, but so that nothing will get in the way of the good news of Christ (9:12b).[44] As an apostle, he is one sent out; a necessity is placed upon him, a commission is laid upon him, and he is under compulsion to preach the gospel (9:16–17). He wants nothing to get in the way of his sharing in the "spiritual" reward fitting the gospel (9:11): in a reward intrinsic to the act of preaching the gospel, and in sharing with the Corinthians in the outworking of the gospel (9:23). In a reading from Brock and Wannenwetsch that follows early church commentators, only one person receives the prize (9:24), the risen Christ. Paul shares in that prize as the resurrection takes hold among the Corinthians.[45]

The City of God against the Pagans, ed. and trans. R. W. Dyson (Cambridge: Cambridge University Press, 1998), esp. chs. 14, 15, and 19.

In the twentieth century, Karl Bath claims that "the earthly Church stands over against the earthly State as a sojourning (*paroikia*) and not as a State within the State, or even as a State above the State," rendering the Church "an establishment among strangers," a "foreign community" that preaches justification, *Church and State*, trans. G. Ronald Howe (London: Student Christian Movement Press, 1939), 45–46. The Second Vatican Council likewise declares that "the pilgrim church is missionary by her very nature, since it is from the mission of the Son and the mission of the Holy Spirit that she draws her origin, in accordance with the decree of God the Father," Second Vatican Council, *Ad Gentes: Decree on the Mission Activity of the Church*, 1965, sec. 2.

[42] Brian Brock and Bernd Wannenwetsch, *The Malady of the Christian Body: A Theological Exposition of Paul's First Letter to the Corinthians*, vol. 1 (Eugene, Ore.: Cascade, 2016), 190–225. 1 Corinthians is the first letter from Paul to the Corinthians in the canon, though probably the second letter he sent: He mentions an earlier letter in 1 Cor. 5:9.

[43] ἀπόστολος, *apostolos*, 9:2.

[44] Brock and Wannenwetsch, *The Malady of the Christian Body*, 1:190–211.

[45] Ibid., 1:213–14, 223. See 1 Cor. 15.

Paul reveals what his freedom in the gospel enables:

¹⁹ For being free from all things,
    I have enslaved myself to all,
        that I might win more of them.

    ²⁰ I became
        to the Jews, as a Jew,
            in order to win Jews;
        to those under the law, as one under the law,
                though not being myself under the law,
        that I might win those under the law;

    ²¹   to those outside the law, as one outside the law,
                  not being outside the law of God but within the law of
        Christ,
        that I might win those outside the law;

    ²² I became
        to the weak, weak,
            that I might win the weak;
        to all people
    I have become all things,
        that by all means I might save some.

²³ All things I do for the sake of the gospel,
    that I may become a fellow partaker of it.⁴⁶

As one sent out, Paul is free from all things that would get in the way of the gospel –
here, free from honorariums, from lavish hospitality. According to Brock and
Wannenwetsch, there should be no "though" in v. 19, as in the N.R.S.V. and
E.S.V., "for though I am free from all." It is not that Paul deserves praise for con-
ceding to enslavement despite his privileges. Rather, he is freed in such a way that he
can make himself a slave to all people, so that he might win more of them over to
participating in Christ's victory over death.⁴⁷ In his freedom, a movement begins that
follows a pattern in these verses: "I became to the Jews, as a Jew ... to those under
the law as one under the law ... to those outside the law as one outside the law ... to
the weak, weak." The movement begins with the necessity that has been laid upon
him as an apostle in previous verses (9:16–17). In response, Paul undergoes a process
of becoming. The verb here for becoming indicates that he participates in this
process of transformation, actively involved in the process laid out before him,
against Brock and Wannenwetsch's emphasis on a more passive way of becoming.⁴⁸

---

⁴⁶ Translation and diagram author's.
⁴⁷ Brock and Wannenwetsch, *The Malady of the Christian Body*, 1:215.
⁴⁸ On the middle voice of the verb ἐγενόμην, *egenomēn*, translated above as "I became," Brock
   and Wannenwetsch are wrong to claim that the middle voice lies between the passive and the
   active and thus cannot be rendered in English, ibid., 1:216–17. They read the phrase as

What does Paul become? To the Jews, he becomes not exactly a Jew, but as a Jew, like a Jew.[49] Other New Testament passages describe Paul as a practicing Jew before his encounter with Christ on the Road to Damascus.[50] Yet now in Jesus Christ he is no longer subject to "the law," to the Law of Moses that orders each realm of the life of the Jews (see 9:9). Paul's side comments explain: though outside of the Law of Moses, he does not lie outside of the law of God. He is under the law of Christ – literally, he has been "en-lawed" (ἔννομος, *ennomos*) in Christ.[51] Though commentators Barrett and Conzelmann kick against this unusual use of the word *nomos*, there is no reason to resist accepting a "law of Christ" as the way of Christ's death, burial, and resurrection, a way that both compels Paul and frees him.[52] Under this law, Paul moves, he is moved, out into different social practices and new sets of rules. He is concerned with preaching to the descendants of Abraham, the people to whom Yhwh has revealed himself, and he returns to their ways and norms so that they might recognize Jesus as the promised Messiah. He does not assume that it will be easy to become "a Jew" completely while en-lawed in Christ, but instead he recognizes that legal and cultural barriers are significant. Paul approximates their ways; he becomes "like a Jew," "as one under the law," respecting the significance of the boundaries that mark off Jews from himself and from other groups. His purpose remains to win and to gain Jews. Not "the Jews"; there is no definite article here. Brock and Wannenwetsch point out that Paul's aim is to win Jews, some Jews, leaving room for the Spirit to move among individuals.[53]

The Apostle Paul begins with the Jews, but the flow of the passage moves outward. To those without the Law of Moses, those beyond the way of the Torah, Paul becomes like one outside the law. He accommodates himself to the ways of the

---

indicating that as Paul becomes a missionary, his self is actively engaged in a process of becoming, but that process is passive in the sense that it is laid out in advance by larger forces. In contrast, Greek grammarians tend to understand the middle voice as indicating something simpler than Brock and Wannenwetsch do, that the subject is involved in the process that the verb indicates. Having no active form, the word *ginomai* in the middle voice indicates that the process of becoming involves the subject who becomes. Thus 1 Cor. 9:20 means that Paul acts as a Jew, and his self is involved in this change of his nature. One must look to other points in the passage to see signs that Paul responds in a more passive way to a role or office given to him (9:1, 16, 17). See James Hope Moulton, *A Grammar of New Testament Greek*, vol. 3 (Edinburgh: T. & T. Clark, 1976), 54; Daniel B. Wallace, *Greek Grammar Beyond the Basics: An Exegetical Syntax of the New Testament with Scripture, Subject, and Greek Word Indexes* (Grand Rapids, Mich.: Zondervan, 1996), 414.

[49] ὡς Ἰουδαῖος, *hōs Ioudaios*, 9:20; Brock and Wannenwetsch, *The Malady of the Christian Body*, 1:94.

[50] See Philippians 3:5, Romans 11:1, 2 Corinthians 11:22, Acts 9:1ff.

[51] Brock and Wannenwetsch, *The Malady of the Christian Body*, 1:220.

[52] C. K. Barrett, *A Commentary on the First Epistle to the Corinthians* (London: Adam & Charles Black, 1968), 214; see also 199; Hans Conzelmann, *1 Corinthians: A Commentary on the First Epistle to the Corinthians*, ed. George W. MacRae, trans. James W. Leitch (Philadelphia: Fortress Press, 1975), 159–61.

[53] *The Malady of the Christian Body*, 1:216.

Gentiles, of non-Jews, bearing the good news to peoples beyond Judea.[54] Paul's move from those under the law to those outside the law is centrifugal, directed outward under the transcending direction and the freeing peace of the rule of Christ. His journey to Corinth and his activities there bear out this movement from those under the law to those outside the law. The account of his first visit to Corinth in the Acts of the Apostles shows Paul reasoning with Jews and Greeks (18:1–17). Some of them believe and are baptized, and others oppose him and bring charges against him before the Roman proconsul. This very letter, the First Letter to the Corinthians, bears out Paul's accommodation to become like the Corinthians, say Brock and Wannenwetsch.[55] He will not approve incest (chapter 5) or their use of civic courts to judge disputes between them (chapter 6), but he takes great care to address what concerns and troubles them. Paul takes up their questions about whether to eat food offered to idols (chapters 8 and 10), he sets them straight about what place marriage has for believers (chapter 7), and he opposes the ways that some get drunk while others go hungry when they gather to celebrate the supper of the Lord (11:17–34).

Following this first set of becomings is another: "I became to the weak, weak . . . to all people I have become all things." Paul's stance is not just to become like the weak in the way he has become like the Jews, like those under the law, and like those outside the law. He really becomes weak. His approach as apostle, as missionary, is not to come in strength or to condescend for just a while. This is not the sort of missionary who might point out his rights and then accept the attention that his heroic sacrifice brings, the sort that a misunderstanding of the earlier part of chapter 9 would invite. Paul empties himself. He does not hold onto a national or legal identity; his Jewish origin is not controlling. He opens himself, accepting a flexibility, meeting others in a weak state, embodying what Brock and Wannenwetsch say "encapsulates the core of Christian existence as a life of dependence on grace."[56] He does not steel himself for an inflexible encounter, a power play, but comes as a weak man to those who are weak. He does not take the time to mention a mission to the powerful, to the movers and shakers; he does not meet them with power. He is ready to encounter those who are simple and humble. He is ready to be attacked and imprisoned by the recipients, or even to be shaped by them.

The movement culminates: "To all people I have become all things, that by all means I might save some." Paul is not concerned to exercise his power or authority.[57] He is moved out by the power of the gospel to every sort of people, taking whatever form is needed, using any and all means. He does not expect to win

---

[54] This flow outward parallels the account of Jesus' final promise and charge to his disciples in the Acts of the Apostles: "You will be my witnesses in Jerusalem and in all Judea and Samaria, and to the end of the earth" (Acts 1:8b).

[55] *The Malady of the Christian Body*, 1:221.

[56] Ibid., 1:220.

[57] ἐξουσία, *exousia*, 9:4–6, 12, 18.

all, but hopes that "some" are gained for the rule of Christ. As he is moved out by the gospel, his hope is that he might be made, he might become, a fellow partaker of it.[58] Here, most modern translations read, "so that I might share in its blessings," as if Paul gets to share in the dividends the gospel pays.[59] The Authorized Version presents a stricter reading of the Greek: "that I might be partaker thereof with you." This reading is liberating: Paul's hope is to share with the Corinthians and with the recipients of the gospel in that very gospel. Brock and Wannenwetsch indicate that his hope is not in the gospel's results or payback; his hope is in the gospel itself, as individuals from all nations come to share in Christ's death and resurrection.[60]

In a different work, Bernd Wannenwetsch describes Paul's movement as the "migration" of the missionary.[61] The pattern is this: The apostle, the missionary, both acts and is acted upon, deciding to move and being moved. This may be a movement to a new place, to another neighborhood, or to another land with new laws. It may be a movement into a new social setting, with new ways of communicating, new ways of doing business, new food or attire. This movement happens under allegiance to God in human flesh, died and risen, an allegiance that precedes and moderates other allegiances, loyalties, and belongings. This allegiance moves the missionary to take on a temporary and local allegiance, to use the term from *Calvin's Case*, becoming like a local and abiding by the rules of that place up to a point. That approximation of local life leaves space to exercise moral judgment through the law of Christ, avoiding those new ways that run counter to the resurrection life. The move into local customs recognizes some distance, seeing that the integrity of the new society will not allow for quick transitions. The missionary is in a profound state of weakness, open to intellectual and cultural encounter and transformation. If this is not the case, that missionary has accepted some compromise that does not fit the gospel: The missionary has claimed rights, seeking glory as a hero, or the missionary has grasped the gospel as his or her own, assuming full understanding of its significance, and meeting hearers in triumph and domination. The one fully set free by the living Christ will not fall into futile efforts at self-directed achievement: The Pauline missionary arrives, willing, flexible, and vulnerable. This is the migrant missionary, the alien apostle.

In Christian worship, those gathered confess in the ancient words of the creed, "We believe in one holy catholic and apostolic church."[62] The church acts out its apostolicity not only by relying on the teaching of the apostles who were

---

[58] ἵνα συγκοινωνὸς αὐτοῦ γένωμαι, *hina sugkoinōnos autou genōmai*, 9:23.

[59] The R.S.V., the N.R.S.V., the E.S.V., the N.A.S.B., the N.I.V., and Today's New International Version go in this direction.

[60] *The Malady of the Christian Body*, 1:195, 208, 209, 210, 223.

[61] Bernd Wannenwetsch, "'Becoming All Things to All People': The Migration of the Gospel and the Kenotic Travelling of the Migrant Missionary" (Societas Ethica, Sibiu, Romania, August 24, 2012).

[62] πιστεύομεν... εἰς μίαν ἁγίαν καθολικὴν καὶ ἀποστολικὴν ἐκκλησίαν, *pisteuomen ... eis mian hagian katholikēn kai apostolikēn ekklēsian*, the Nicene-Constantinopolitan Creed of 381, J. N. D. Kelly, *Early Christian Creeds*, 3rd edn. (London: Longman, 1972), 297–98.

eyewitnesses of Jesus and handing on that teaching. The church is also apostolic because it is sent out, commanded by the authority of the gospel, freed through the death and resurrection of Christ. It is apostolic so long as it is missionary, sent to become as Japanese to the Japanese, as Brazilian to the Brazilians, as American to the Americans, in order to win some. The church's confession of its divinely given character depends on a freeing obedience to the law of Christ, becoming weak, becoming all things to all people. Within the church are individuals who are sent out like Paul as migrants crossing cultural or natural divides. Yet everyone in the church is arrested by the good news and sent out to those who are different from themselves.

The Spirit who sends out the church and ensures its apostolicity makes possible a new solidarity with migrants. Stronger than the solidarity that Catholic Social Teaching emphasizes between every human being, missionaries bear a solidarity with migrants.[63] The people of God are given a more specific solidarity with the migrant, a concern for the wellbeing of the migrant and a desire to be blessed by the migrant. This solidarity means that the simple and unqualified term "alien" is not a true term for a believer to use for a migrant since the migrant is not fundamentally different from the believer, not "other" from the one forced to migrate.

The freedom of the migrant church enables a transformed relationship with migrants, who indeed are fellow migrants. Along her missionary journey, the church encounters men, women, and children who are also on a journey. Like her, these migrants may have entered new countries and new societies, freely, under compulsion or both. They might answer to some loyalty beyond their country like the missionary. They may be weak, lacking local knowledge, friends, or family like those sent out by the good news. These fellow human beings may be hungry or homeless, or they may be detained or imprisoned, like the apostolic church. These encounters with fellow migrants play a part in saving the church by reminding her of her missionary character. Meetings with fellow migrants dislodge the church from a disobedient settling into place, particularly if that settling requires her to classify certain migrants as aliens in contrast to her own existence. Encounters with fellow migrants awaken the church to freedom, freedom to be on the move within the law of Christ.[64]

The missionary freedom of those in Christ places them in tension with the ways of nation-states like the United States that restrict and punish acts of migration. Will the migrant people of God uphold laws that regard migrants as aliens? Will they serve in branches of government that enforce immigration laws predicated on the existence of aliens? When the terms of the law stimulate broader habits of treating

---

[63] See pp. 10–14.

[64] Mark Griffin and Theron Walker make a similar argument, *Living on the Borders: What the Church Can Learn from Ethnic Immigrant Cultures* (Grand Rapids, Mich.: Brazos Press, 2004). On a life lived between Mexico and the United States, see Sandra Cisneros' novel *Caramelo: Or Puro Cuento* (New York: Alfred A. Knopf, 2002). On Hispanic culture as a borderland culture, see Gloria Anzaldúa, *Borderlands/La Frontera: The New Mestiza* (San Francisco: Aunt Lute, 1987); Virgilio P. Elizondo, *Galilean Journey: The Mexican-American Promise* (Maryknoll, N.Y.: Orbis Books, 1983).

those from far away as aliens, will God's missionaries go along? Will those within the law of Christ do business in ways that treat migrants as simply foreign? When migrant neighbors are forced into greater alienation, when migrants are made more vulnerable, will God's people remember their weakness as missionaries and resist the spirit of the age? Will God's migrant people resist calling their fellow migrants "aliens"? Or when the language of the "alien" is firmly entrenched, will God's people gladly identify themselves as fellow aliens? Will the church resist alienation or accept that she is an alien church? Those who follow the risen Christ as migrants have a new freedom to bring to these vexing questions: a freedom like Paul's to become weak.[65]

The freedom of the people of God as migrants and toward migrants is revealed in ordinary ways. Around the world, members of one political community worship alongside nonmembers. Churches send out missionaries to become like foreigners, to become weak. The freedom of the people of God as migrants and toward migrants also comes in extraordinary ways. In the Sanctuary Movement in the 1980s, when the federal U.S. government did not give refugee status to men and women fleeing civil conflicts in Guatemala and El Salvador, churches and synagogues in the United States protected them in their places of worship. One of the movement's leaders, Jim Corbett, a Quaker, describes their work not as civil disobedience but as "civil initiative," upholding the law when the government did not. He describes sanctuary as community with the violated within a transnational church.[66] Eight members of the movement were successfully prosecuted for felonies including conspiracy, bringing an illegal alien into the United States, and harboring and transporting illegal aliens.[67] But as movement leader and Presbyterian minister John Fife tells the story, the first person to be prosecuted, a School Sister of St. Francis named Darlene Nicgorski, said that she would not stop smuggling unless the judge locked her up. Responding to this dare, the judge said he would give her probation, but she could do what she wanted.[68] The movement was eventually vindicated before the law. The group won a civil case, and thousands of those who entered the United States illegally were given refugee status.[69] Ordinary and extraordinary, such is the politics of the church.

---

[65] On the church as a colony of resident aliens after Christendom, see Stanley Hauerwas and William H. Willimon, *Resident Aliens: Life in the Christian Colony* (Nashville: Abingdon Press, 1989), 12.

[66] Jim Corbett, *The Sanctuary Church* (Wallingford, Pa.: Pendle Hill Publications, 1986), 13, 17; see also 6, 22–23, 27.

[67] United States v. Aguilar, 883 F.2d 662 (9th Cir. 1989); Ann Crittenden, *Sanctuary: A Story of American Conscience and the Law in Collision* (New York: Weidenfeld & Nicolson, 1988), 323.

[68] John Fife, "The Sanctuary Movement" (Borderlinks, Tucson, Ariz., July 28, 2011). Crittenden does not mention this anecdote about Nicgorski, giving no reason why U.S. District Court Judge Earl H. Carroll only sentenced Sanctuary Movement members to probation, *Sanctuary*, 335, 337–38.

[69] Fife, "The Sanctuary Movement."

As a response to the ascendancy of the alien in common law and United States law, what did this chapter discover from Christian theology? Viewing nationhood within a broad biblical narrative, it became clear that to understand those far away as alien is not a truthful way of describing them as a fatherly God watches over the world and as the good news of the Lord Jesus goes out in the power of the Spirit. Following the nations through the Scriptures, distinctions between peoples come not at the beginning but farther into human history as both a blessing and a judgment. These distinctions are fluid, not fixed. Life as part of a people is an occasion from which to enjoy a rich life as creatures, a life that is oriented toward other peoples. To be authentically within a people is to reach out to those from afar, a movement fulfilled as the Holy Spirit draws together those nearby and those far off within the one people of God. The end of the peoples is to be drawn into fellowship with the people that God has made, Israel. Reflecting further on God's people, it became clear that one of its key figures is the missionary, who migrates and adapts to local customs in the service of the good news that Christ has defeated death. As a church that includes missionaries and is missionary herself, the people of God have a special solidarity with other kinds of migrants. These migrants serve the church by reminding her that she is a community of sojourners. She is a people en-lawed in Christ, becoming like the members of the many peoples of the world so that they might share in the fruits of the gospel.

Now, one might object that it is acceptable for the alien to remain as a category in written law since it helps divide those who are on the inside of a political community from those on the outside. Perhaps the fact that Part I is so concerned with what it means to call someone alien is a symptom of a certain American disease, the politicization of all of life. In a modern democracy like the United States, the objection goes, its members gather not around a monarch or some other symbol but around the law and its terms, and so Americans take on the category of the alien as their own. It is this politicization of life, rather than the concept of the alien, that deserves resistance.[70]

This objection highlights the degree to which law infiltrates American life. Living under the category of the alien makes plain how far the law stretches: Someone who is considered an alien is subject to legal restrictions not only at the border and the voting booth but also at the workplace, the bank, the hospital, in court, and on the road. Once this alien does not have a legal right to remain in the United States, any of these places becomes a venue for arrest leading to detention and removal from the country. If federal agents act on good evidence, even the home may be a place for such an arrest. The case of the alien proves that status before the law makes all the difference for ordinary life in the United States. The question about the politicization of American life suggests a few ways forward. One is to limit the domain over which laws about alien status holds sway, working within federal law to pare back that law's purview. A second is to change the law,

---

[70] Thanks to Matthew Lee Anderson for raising this objection.

still working within federal law. A third is to celebrate a common life where designations of aliens and citizens do not apply.

But these options are not mutually opposed, and one does not have to choose between limiting the law's scope, changing the law, or living within a different community with its own law. Could it be possible to work to alter the law and limit its scope while enjoying life among a new community? As Karl Barth quoted from Ephesians, "But now in Christ Jesus you who once were far off have been brought near by the blood of Christ. For he himself is our peace, who has made us both one and has broken down in his flesh the dividing wall of hostility."[71] Among this people there is freedom.

In summary, when it seems obvious that there are aliens in the world, when the world becomes divided between those within one allegiance and those outside of that allegiance, worthy of suspicion, then this way of living does not reflect how God's world and God's church are. A closed, starkly defined territorial state is not humanity's final belonging, though a modest, thankful approach to earthly political community is appropriate now, as Part II will indicate. Final belonging lies not in this nation now but in that gathering of every nation and tongue to worship the true Sovereign.

---

[71] Eph. 2:13–14; Barth, *C.D.*, III/4:323.

The Alien as Unlawfully Present?

3

How Aliens Became Illegal

Sovereignty, Chinese Migration, and Federal Immigration Law

How did it become possible for an alien to be considered illegal under federal United States law? Part I discovered the origin of the alien in late medieval English common law and then developed another way of understanding those who come from other countries in Christian theology. Part II will examine how the alien became unlawfully present in U.S. law, evaluating that turn through dialogues with Scripture and theology. This chapter will begin by describing the terrain, naming the terms the law uses for this sort of alien and the kinds of persons who can be excluded under federal legislation. A survey of immigration law from across U.S. history will clarify what kinds of aliens are banned from being present in United States territory and why they are banned. Second, the chapter will reckon with the arguments in case law that established the federal government's authority to dictate who could be present in the United States. This discovery will focus on a series of intriguing nineteenth-century Supreme Court judgments relating to Chinese immigrants. Third, the chapter will place the Supreme Court's judgment within an intellectual tradition reaching to Vattel and Hobbes in preceding centuries. This study will prepare the way for a theological evaluation in Chapter 4 of the legal notions that make it possible to be an alien who is unlawfully present in the United States.

ALIEN ILLEGALITY: TERMINOLOGY AND EXCLUSION IN FEDERAL LEGISLATION

What are the Terms of Federal Legislation?

Part I showed that the alien has a stable meaning across the history of federal law, though there are shifts in how legislation uses the term. In contrast, terms surrounding those women and men who are present in the United States without legal permission have only recently begun to stabilize in federal law. "Illegal aliens" and their ilk are a comparatively new thing. It has been possible to be present in the country without permission under federal law since 1808, but before 1986, there were hardly any references to these persons in Congressional legislation. An 1891 Act speaks of "aliens who may unlawfully come to the United States," but it does not envision them staying long, ordering that they should "be immediately sent back on the vessel by which they were brought in."[1] Significant immigration Acts from 1921, 1924, 1952, and 1965 speak of those who are "lawfully admitted," but the Acts have no term for those who are not legally admitted or who overstay their leave.[2] The 1952 Act mentions those who have entered improperly within a section more concerned to identify "deportable aliens" who become dangerous to the United States after entering.[3] Only in 1986 does federal law register a preoccupation with those who do not have permission to be in the country.[4] The Immigration Reform and Control Act of 1986 announces its first priority in Title I: "Control of Illegal Immigration."[5] Here, the term "illegal immigration" makes its first appearance in major Congressional legislation, emerging as a problem that demands a response. Two other terms also appear for the first time: the "illegal alien" and the "unauthorized alien." The Act speaks of illegal aliens only when it addresses those convicted of a felony, while it speaks of unauthorized aliens only when it deals with those who are unauthorized to work.[6] Of these terms, only the unauthorized alien receives a definition: This is an alien without the lawful admission for permanent residence that would authorize employment, or otherwise without authorization to be employed.[7] In this Act, there is still no broad term for a range of cases where someone is in the United States illegally.

The next major immigration Act announces its priority in its title: the Illegal Immigration Reform and Immigrant Responsibility Act of 1996. In this Act, the "illegal immigrant" makes its first appearance in a significant immigration Act, here in the context of felons to incarcerate.[8] The "unauthorized alien" again appears

---

[1] An act in amendment to the various acts relative to immigration and the importation of aliens under contract or agreement to perform labor, 26 Stat. 1084 (1891), 1086.

[2] An Act: To limit the immigration of aliens into the United States, Pub. L. No. 67–5, 42 Stat. 5 (1921), 5; An Act: To limit the immigration of aliens into the United States, and for other purposes, Pub. L. No. 68–139, 43 Stat. 153 (1924), 154, 155, 164; more than thirty times in An Act: To revise the laws relating to immigration, naturalization, and nationality; and for other purposes, Pub. L. No. 82–414, 66 Stat. 163 (1952), 166, 169, etc.; An Act: To amend the Immigration and Nationality Act, and for other purposes, Pub. L. No. 89–236, 79 Stat. 911 (1965), 911, 913, 915 (twice), 916, 918.

[3] 66 Stat. 163, 204.

[4] See pp. 149–51, 158–63 for the story of how the Acts of 1965 and 1976 made possible the growing numbers that made deportable aliens a subject for lawmaking in 1986.

[5] An Act: To amend the Immigration and Nationality Act to revise and reform the immigration laws, and for other purposes, Pub. L. No. 99–603, 100 Stat. 3359 (1986), 3359.

[6] The illegal alien appears in 100 Stat. 3359, 3443, and the unauthorized alien appears in 100 Stat. 3359, 3360, 3361, 3364, 3366, 3367, 3368, 3369, 3370, 3381, 3416, 3441.

[7] 100 Stat. 3359, 3368.

[8] An Act: Making omnibus consolidated appropriations for the fiscal year ending September 30, 1997, and for other purposes, Pub. L. No. 104–208, 110 Stat. 3009–546 (1996), 3009–631.

primarily within discussions of work, but the "illegal alien" admits of a wider range of uses, appearing not only in the case of felons but also as the name for those who can be harbored, apprehended near the border, and forbidden to have driver's licenses.[9] Along with the expanded use of the illegal alien, a new type of alien appears in the 1996 Act, "the alien unlawfully present in the United States."[10] Occasionally, this figure is reduced to the "alien unlawfully present," but the phrase "in the United States" usually remains, and often "alien" is broken away from its qualifying terms as part of a lengthier phrase, as in "an alien who was unlawfully present in the United States."[11] What it means to be unlawfully present is defined here:

> An alien is deemed to be unlawfully present in the United States if the alien is present in the United States after the expiration of the period of stay authorized by the Attorney General or is present in the United States without being admitted or paroled.[12]

This type includes two sorts of aliens, those who overstay visas and those who enter without permission. The alien who is unlawfully present in the United States proves to be the primary category of alien that runs afoul of the law, appearing more often than the illegal alien in the 1996 Act.

As of the time of writing, no comprehensive immigration legislation has passed since the 1986 and 1996 Acts, but there have been many efforts to reform the law. Looking at two representative reform efforts, two pieces of state legislation from 2010 and 2011 and a Bill that passed the U.S. Senate but not the House of Representatives in 2013, the alien unlawfully present in the United States appears to lead the field as the term for someone who lacks permission to be in the country. In these pieces of legislation, the illegal alien only occasionally appears, and the illegal immigrant disappears altogether.[13] These bills deal with unauthorized aliens when they address employment on its own, but they speak of aliens unlawfully present in the United States when they deal with those who lack permission to be in the country.[14]

---

[9] The unauthorized alien or aliens appear in 110 Stat 3009–546, 3009–565, 648, 660, and the illegal alien or aliens appear approximately nine times in 110 Stat. 3009–546, 3009–567, 631, 634, 651, 671.

[10] Forms of the alien unlawfully present appear approximately twelve times in 110 Stat. 3009–546, 3009–575, 576, 577, 586, 631, 641, 720, and unlawful presence appears approximately six times in 110 Stat. 3009–546, 3009–576, 577, 578.

[11] 110 Stat. 3009–546, 3009–576.

[12] 110 Stat. 3009–546, 3009–576; Immigration and Nationality Act (I.N.A.) § 212(a)(9)(B)(ii).

[13] The illegal alien appears in the Support Our Law Enforcement and Safe Neighborhoods Act, Arizona Senate Bill (S.B.) 1070 (2010), 2, 6; Beason-Hammon Alabama Taxpayer and Citizen Protection Act, Alabama House Bill (H.B.) 56 (2011), 1, 3, 51, 52; and not at all in the Border Security, Economic Opportunity, and Immigration Modernization Act, U.S. Senate Bill S. 744 (2013).

[14] The unauthorized alien appears approximately fifty times in Arizona S.B. 1070, 5, 6, 7, etc.; over twenty five times in Alabama H.B. 56, 1, 2, 10, etc.; and over fifteen times in U.S. Senate Bill S. 744, 151, 250, 263, etc. The alien unlawfully present appears approximately five times in

This survey of the terminology of the law signals that only in the 1980s did the law identify the issue dealt with in this work as "illegal immigration," and only in the 1990s has it begun to use two newly defined terms to qualify the object of this study, the "unauthorized alien" and the "alien unlawfully present in the United States." While Chapter 1 saw the English and American legal tradition narrow in on a concise term for the nonmember of the body politic, the alien, this case involves a different tendency toward multiple, more sophisticated terms. The defined term that is available for use in the most contexts, the alien unlawfully present in the United States, is unlike the simple term alien: It takes some time to say, it keeps its qualifying phrase, and it is often broken apart in the course of a sentence. This is a move that resists defining some persons as simply and essentially illegal.[15] Then again, the illegal alien continues to appear in Congressional legislation, though it lacks a strict definition.

Still, current discourses beyond the texts of legislation tend to depend on tersely stated essences, with a notable exception. Federal law enforcement agencies tend to speak of the illegal alien rather than the alien unlawfully present in the United States.[16] In popular discourse and in the press, those who wish to emphasize the illegality of the person's presence tend to use the terms "illegal immigrant," "illegal alien," or simply "illegal," while those wanting to focus attention away from illegality or ease immigration restrictions tend to use the term "undocumented worker." In 2013, a source that provides other news media outlets with reporting took a turn that parallels to the designations of the federal law: The stylebook of the Associated Press was updated to forbid speaking of persons as illegal, allowing actions alone to be deemed illegal, so that reporters could speak of "living in the country illegally" but not call someone an illegal immigrant.[17]

Support Our Law Enforcement and Safe Neighborhoods Act, 1, 5; over twenty times in Alabama H.B. 56, 1, 2, 8, etc.; and twice in U.S. Senate Bill S. 744, 209, 441.

[15] As incisive as it is, Mae M. Ngai's history of immigration law and policy fails to notice this more complicated picture of federal law, instead assuming that the illegal alien is the primary term for outsiders without permission to be in the United States, *Impossible Subjects: Illegal Aliens and the Making of Modern America* (Princeton: Princeton University Press, 2004), xix.

[16] Websites for the U.S. Department of Homeland Security, Immigrations and Customs Enforcement, and Customs and Border Protection emphasize enforcing and administering immigration laws, with only occasional mentions of "illegal aliens" and "inadmissible persons," "Snapshot: A Summary of C.B.P. Facts and Figures," *CBP.gov*, January 31, 2014, www.cbp .gov/linkhandler/cgov/about/accomplish/cbp_snapshot_2014.ctt/cbp_snapshot_2014.pdf; and "criminals aliens," "Criminal Alien Program," *I.C.E.*, accessed March 5, 2014, www.ice.gov/ criminal-alien-program/; "Enforce and Administer Our Immigration Laws," *Homeland Security*, accessed March 5, 2014, www.dhs.gov/administer-immigration-laws. In a public presentation, an official tended to talk about illegal aliens, though he also mentioned "economic migrants," Richard Crocker, Deputy Special Agent in Charge, I.C.E., Southern Arizona and Rudy Bustamante, Community Relations Officer, "Immigration and Customs Enforcement in Southern Arizona" (Borderlinks, Tucson, Ariz., July 28, 2011). See pp. 25–31.

[17] Paul Colford, "'Illegal Immigrant' No More," *The Associated Press: The Definitive Source*, accessed April 3, 2013, http://blog.ap.org/2013/04/02/illegal-immigrant-no-more/.

This work develops a theological response to how the federal U.S. law defines and constructs the lives of those who lack permission to be in the country. Its concern is not primarily about what the law calls "the unauthorized alien," since the authorization in question is authorization to work. Rather, it is concerned with those who are on U.S. lands but not allowed to be there. Since 1996, the law has used the lengthier term, the "alien unlawfully present in the United States." This work attempts to reflect this salutary turn in the law, speaking of aliens who are unlawfully present in the United States, though now and again the work will use the simpler term that remains in law and law enforcement, the "illegal alien."

Who is Excluded under Federal Legislation?

To become an alien unlawfully present in the United States requires breaking a ban on entry or continued presence. What sorts of persons have been excluded from admission by federal legislation over the course of American history? What follows is a brief survey of the first restrictions of different types of aliens, without noting points when some of those restrictions were removed.

The very first men and women excluded from admission did not come to the United States of their own volition. After the trade in human slaves was outlawed in 1808, about fifty thousand slaves were smuggled into the United States between then and the end of slaveholding in 1865, and these were the first aliens who were present in the United States without legal permission.[18] The Page Act of 1875 required that no one could enter the United States from "China, Japan, or another Oriental country" if they were brought to serve as prostitutes, if they came to be servants without their consent, or if their sentences for felonies were reduced on the condition that they leave their home countries.[19] The Chinese Exclusion Act of 1882 forbade Chinese laborers from coming into the United States, and related court cases described this as a measure to prevent the growth of a settlement of foreigners who would not assimilate into American society.[20] Later in the same year, the Act to Regulate Immigration forbade "any convict, lunatic, idiot, or any person unable to take care of himself or herself without becoming a public charge" from landing at U.S. ports.[21] In an effort to protect jobs for United States citizens, the Foran Act of 1885 discouraged the entry of aliens under a contract to perform labor by forbidding and annulling

---

[18] Roger Daniels, *Guarding the Golden Door: American Immigration Policy and Immigrants since 1882* (New York: Hill and Wang, 2004), 6; An Act to prohibit the importation of Slaves into any port or place within the jurisdiction of the United States, from and after the first day of January, in the year of our Lord one thousand eight hundred and eight, 2 Stat. 426 (1807).

[19] An act supplementary to the acts in relation to immigration, 18 Stat. 477 (1875), 477.

[20] An act to execute certain treaty stipulations relating to Chinese, 22 Stat. 58 (1882). See pp. 72–8.

[21] An act to regulate Immigration, 22 Stat. 214 (1882), 214.

such contracts.[22] In 1891, Congress added to the banned list polygamists, those with a "dangerous contagious disease," those who had committed a crime "involving moral turpitude," and those whose ticket had been paid by another.[23] An Act of 1903 expanded bans on those who were diseased and impoverished and added anarchists and those opposed to organized government to the list. The Act issued a general ban on prostitutes beyond those coming from Asia, and it banned those who attempted to bring women into the country for prostitution.[24] In 1917, Congress further expanded bans on disease and mental illness, and it banned admission from a region stretching from Afghanistan to the Pacific, except for Japan and the Philippines. The Act also required that immigrants be able to read in English or some other language.[25] One of the more significant later laws to continue this trajectory, the Immigration and Nationality Act of 1952, added new categories of aliens to be excluded from admission such as alcoholics, drug addicts, and drug traffickers; communists; those convicted of two or more offenses, even if they did not involve moral turpitude; and "aliens coming to the United States to engage in any immoral sexual act," targeting homosexuals.[26] Though many of these restrictions have been removed, amendments to the Immigration and Nationality Act since 1952 have added to reasons for exclusion certain kinds of transnational crimes like money laundering and the trafficking of persons and political acts related to Nazi persecution, violations of religious freedom, and terrorist activity, among others.[27]

These qualitative restrictions served three aims. The first aim was to protect women and men from being brought to the United States against their will to work, so that from 1808 onward, newcomers would do so freely, by their own consent. The second aim was to bar men and women who were *unhealthy* from entering the country. Those who would infect the United States with contagious diseases, who would sap its resources because they were unable to work, who would sully its public morals – these would compromise the health of the American people. The laws had a third aim: to bar those who were *healthy* from entering the country.

---

[22] An act to prohibit the importation and migration of foreigners and aliens under contract or agreement to perform labor in the United States, its Territories, and the District of Columbia, 23 Stat. 322 (1885), 332.

[23] 26 Stat. 1084, 1084.

[24] An Act: To regulate the immigration of aliens into the United States, Pub. L. No. 57–162, 32 Stat. 1213 (1903), 1214. In the Gentleman's Agreement, Executive Order no. 589 (1907), the United States made a diplomatic agreement with Japan under which Japan agreed to limit emigration by denying passports to laborers; cited in Ngai, *Impossible Subjects*, 39, 39n61. This was not legislated, and so it is not listed here.

[25] An Act: To regulate the immigration of aliens to, and the residence of aliens in, the United States, Pub. L. No. 64–301, 39 Stat. 874 (1917), 875–77; Ngai, *Impossible Subjects*, 37, 37n51 defines the "Asiatic barred zone."

[26] 66 Stat. 163, 182–85.

[27] I.N.A. § 212.

Congress barred from admission those immigrants who formed an enclave that might threaten the integrity and power of the body politic because of its virility. The Chinese community, separate from the European stock of U.S. citizens, was seen as *a state within a state*, a healthy community threatening the nation that dominated the territory stretching from the Atlantic to the Pacific. The first threat was a lack of freedom unbecoming to American ideals; the second threat was a contagion that would make the American people diseased; and the third threat was a virile counter-society that would oppose U.S. control over territory.[28]

A kind of restriction on immigration started in 1921, when Congress added numerical limits on the rest of the Eastern Hemisphere to the absolute limits already in place for much of Asia.[29] These so-called emergency quotas preceded the full-blown quota system of the Johnson-Reed Act of 1924, which eventually reduced admissions from other countries in proportion to the contribution those countries made to the citizenry in 1920. The Act exempted the wives and children of citizens along with students from these quotas, but it placed numerical limits on everyone coming from the Eastern Hemisphere even if they were healthy, self-supporting, and peaceable.[30] The Act's effect was to allow continued immigration from Northern and Western Europe while limiting immigration from the rest of Europe, Africa, the Middle East, and the South Pacific. The Hart-Celler Act of 1965 followed, and while expanding categories of immigrants not subject to numerical limits, it initiated a movement toward numerical limits for every country.[31] The system of preferences for the first time included the Western Hemisphere in its scope, and by 1976 every country from Canada to Chile was subject to the same quotas as countries in the Eastern Hemisphere.[32] Though the Johnson-Reed Act produced a lull in numbers of immigrants and the Hart-Cellar Act allowed for a great increase in numbers, Hart-Cellar reproduced the basic pattern of Johnson-Reed. This was that in addition to qualitative screening of candidates for immigration, screening would be quantitative: each year, only so many newcomers would be allowed in from each country in the world.[33]

The second era of restrictions from 1921 onward changed the game. These restrictions set most of those who wanted to migrate to the United States under a system of numerical quotas. Bans on those threatening the body politic remained: bans on the unfree, the unhealthy, and the healthy. A growing pattern of bans on immigrants who would not assimilate, on people groups thought to be incompatible

---

[28] Bernd Wannenwetsch suggested the idea that immigration restrictions represent responses to healthy and unhealthy threats.

[29] 42 Stat. 5, 5.

[30] 43 Stat. 153, 155, 159.

[31] 79. Stat. 911, 911–14.

[32] 79. Stat. 911, 921; An Act: To amend the Immigration and Nationality Act, and for other purposes, Pub. L. No. 94–571, 90 Stat. 2703 (1976), 2704.

[33] See pp. 158–63 for further discussion of the 1965 response to the 1924 Act.

with American society, ended up producing a new scheme from 1965 onward. The assumption stuck that immigration from other countries needed to be numerically limited, regardless of what a newcomer might bring to the United States. In this setting, categories emerged of immigrants with special privileges, especially family members and useful workers. But soon an all-embracing bureaucracy came into place, and lawmakers came to assume that the federal government needed to apply numbers to the human persons who could emigrate from each country in the world, as Mae Ngai argues.[34] The architecture of the system implied that not only the poor, the sick, or the criminal would compromise the United States, but simply too many newcomers from a particular country would prove a threat.

Whether on qualitative or quantitative grounds, each person who disobeyed these restrictions became an alien unlawfully present in the United States. This new figure became a basic feature of federal immigration law and a significant form of life. The illegal alien, the illegal immigrant, the alien unlawfully present, became a new sort of member of American society – and yet not a member in the eyes of the law. Today, more than eleven million women and men live life as aliens unlawfully present, or about three or four out of every hundred people living in the United States.[35]

THE RIGHT TO EXCLUDE AND EXPEL ALIENS: THE SUPREME COURT AND CHINESE IMMIGRANTS, 1812–1898

Congress progressively restricted immigration into the United States, but it was not always assumed that the federal government had such a power. The authority to govern immigration was not explicitly given to the federal government in the United States Constitution, and so it remained to the courts to look to reason and legal precedent to establish this authority. The key move that set in place the right of the federal government to restrict immigration came in legal challenges to the Chinese Exclusion Acts of 1882 and following. In two cases, the Supreme Court established the right to exclude and expel aliens as a basic feature of national sovereignty. These cases followed on from a noteworthy precedent dealing with immigrants like imported goods, and alongside these cases came a stream of cases establishing the rights of Chinese already in the country. This is the story that follows: the story of how the Supreme Court established immigration authority as a matter of sovereignty.

---

[34] Ngai, *Impossible Subjects*, 227–28.

[35] 11.1 million people are estimated to live in the United States without authorization as of 2014, Jeffrey S. Passel and D'Vera Cohn, "Overall Number of U.S. Unauthorized Immigrants Holds Steady Since 2009" (Washington, D.C.: Pew Research Center, September 20, 2016), www.pewhispanic.org/2016/09/20/overall-number-of-u-s-unauthorized-immigrants-holds-steady-since-2009/. See p. 4 note 6.

Chae Chan Ping v. United States *Affirms the Right to Exclude Aliens*

The first step along the way to establishing federal sovereignty over immigration came when the United States Supreme Court ruled on taxes for ship passengers. In the Passenger Cases of 1849, the Court responded to New York and Massachusetts, two states that had placed taxes on passengers arriving from other countries.[36] The Court ruled that the power to place a tax on persons entering the United States was reserved to the federal government and not within the scope of state authority. It ruled that just as the U.S. Constitution gave Congress the power "to regulate Commerce with foreign Nations" (art. 1, sec. 8), so only Congress could levy taxes on ship passengers. An analogy was made: Just as goods arriving by ship from another country can be taxed by the federal government, so persons arriving by ship from another country can be taxed by the federal government. At a stage when most persons and goods entered the United States by water rather than by land or air, the Court judged that commercial goods and human persons both counted as objects of commerce. The Passenger Cases represented a first step toward establishing federal authority over immigration, but while in them the Court looked only to the Constitution to make its case, in the cases that followed, the Court made arguments about powers that accrue to any sovereign state.

The Supreme Court firmly established federal sovereignty over immigration when it took up a case from the new state of California. Just after 1848, as explorers struck gold, as the United States wrested control of western lands from Mexico, and as the building of the trans-continental railway demanded laborers, Chinese immigrants began arriving in California.[37] The following decades saw the city of San Francisco, the state of California, and the U.S. federal government enact a series of laws meant to impede Chinese immigration and restrict those Chinese already present. By 1882, Congress passed An Act to Execute Certain Treaty Stipulations Relating to Chinese, announcing that "in the opinion of the Government of the United States the coming of Chinese laborers to this country endangers the good order of certain localities within the territory thereof."[38] Better known as the Chinese Exclusion Act, the Act forbade any new Chinese laborers from

---

[36] Passenger Cases: George Smith v. William Turner, Health Commissioner of the Port of New York; James Norris v. The City of Boston, 48 U.S. 283 (1849). The Court confirmed this decision in Henderson v. Mayor of City of New York, 92 U.S. 259 (1875); Chy Lung v. Freeman, 92 U.S. 275 (1875); and in the Head Money Cases: Edye and Another v. Robinson, Collector; Cunard Steamship Company v. Same; Same v. Same, 112 U.S. 580 (1884).

[37] See pp. 165–6 on the Treaty of Guadalupe Hidalgo that transferred Alta California from Mexico to the United States. Gold was discovered in California at Sutter's Mill just nine days before the treaty was signed. The transcontinental rail line was built jointly by the Central Pacific and the Union Pacific between 1863 and 1869.

[38] 22 Stat. 58.

coming to the United States or remaining in the United States, and it barred all Chinese from U.S. citizenship.

In the case of *Chae Chan Ping v. United States* (1889), the Supreme Court upheld the policy of Chinese exclusion.[39] Chae Chan Ping arrived in California in 1875 and resided there without gaining citizenship until 1887, when he left by ship for a year-long visit to China. Upon leaving, Ping took with him a certificate guaranteeing that he could reenter California, a certificate provided for in 1882 and 1884 Congressional legislation.[40] On September 7, 1888, Ping boarded the steamer Belgic, bound for San Francisco from Hong Kong. On October 1 of that year, Congress passed an Act annulling the sort of certificate Ping held.[41] The Belgic arrived in the port of San Francisco on October 8, and Ping was held on board the steamer because his certificate was now invalid. In effect, a long-time resident of California, a Chinese man who did not become an American citizen and in the latter years of his residency was ineligible for citizenship, departed from the United States with a certificate promising him the right to reenter, only to have that certificate annulled while on board a ship returning to the United States.

Hired by Chinese community organizations who rallied around Ping, Ping's lawyers mounted an argument against Ping's detention aboard the Belgic and his exclusion from American territory.[42] They argued that Ping's detention was a punishment given out without a ruling from a court or judicial officer and a deprivation of Ping's liberty without due process, against Ping's inalienable possession of liberty as a man, a liberty guaranteed by the Constitution.[43] Ping's detention came as the result of an exercise of power that the people of the United States had not delegated to Congress or any other branch of government, the lawyers argued: the power to prohibit entry into U.S. territory.[44] They also said that the 1888 law that annulled certificates like Ping's was an *ex post facto* law that wrongfully applied the punishment of detention and banishment to those who had acted lawfully.[45] What was more, Ping had entered the United States under the terms of a treaty with China, and after living there he had established a right of residence that gave him a right to return to the United States.[46] Indeed, the United States had made a contract

---

[39] Chae Chan Ping v. United States, 130 U.S. 581 (1889). The Supreme Court had considered two prior cases that tested the 1882 law, Chew Heong v. United States, 112 U.S. 536 (1884); United States v. Jung Ah Lung, 124 U.S. 621 (1887).

[40] 22 Stat. 58; An Act to amend an act entitled "An act to execute certain treaty stipulations relating to Chinese approved May sixth eighteen hundred and eighty-two," 23 Stat. 115 (1884).

[41] An Act a supplement to an act entitled "An act to execute certain treaty stipulations relating to Chinese," approved the sixth day of May eighteen hundred and eighty-two, 25 Stat. 504 (1888).

[42] Gabriel J. Chin, "Chae Chan Ping and Fong Yue Ting: The Origins of Plenary Power," in *Immigration Stories*, ed. David A. Martin and Peter H. Schuck (New York: Foundation Press and Thomson/West, 2005), 9.

[43] *Chae Chan Ping*, 130 U.S. at 584; U.S. Const. amends. 5, 14.

[44] *Chae Chan Ping*, 130 U.S. at 585.

[45] 130 U.S. at 589, U.S. Const. art. I, §§ 9, 10.

[46] *Chae Chan Ping*, 130 U.S. at 585–86; Additional Articles to the Treaty between the United States and China, June 18, 1858, 16 Stat. 739 (1868).

under the 1882 and 1884 Acts, allowing Ping to leave and return with a certificate in hand, an offer the United States made in good faith. Ping kept his side of the contract, but the United States did not, acting in bad faith by annulling the certificates of resident aliens in 1888.[47] Not only was Ping's detention on board the Belgic a retrospective punishment carried out without due process by a government that had no such power, but it also represented a breach of contract against a man who had a right to return to the United States.

Despite the arguments of Ping's counsel, the Supreme Court upheld the exclusion of Chae Chan Ping from United States territory. Justice Stephen J. Field wrote the opinion of the Court and explained its judgment as follows: The Burlingame Treaty of 1868 had recognized "the inherent and inalienable right of man to change his home and allegiance" along with the "mutual advantage of the free migration and emigration of [American] citizens and [Chinese] subjects respectively from the one country to the other."[48] Yet, Justice Field argued, laws passed since 1868 to restrict Chinese immigration in contravention of the treaty were justified because "a limitation to the immigration of certain classes from China was essential to the peace of the community on the Pacific coast, and possibly to the preservation of our civilization there."[49]

Justice Field explained: Chinese immigrants came to California to work in the gold mines, but soon their numbers grew, and they began to work as tradesmen and artisans. The Chinese worked hard and lived frugally, and in business they undercut their competition from U.S. citizens, evoking "irritation" and "open conflicts."[50] "The differences of race added greatly to the difficulties of the situation," Justice Field wrote. "They remained strangers in the land," he said, living together and holding on to the habits and customs of their country. "It seemed impossible for them to assimilate with our people," Justice Field stated. As the numbers of Chinese grew, Americans began to worry that "the crowded millions" of China would soon "overrun" the West Coast. Justice Field wrote that the 1878 constitutional convention of California had petitioned Congress to act to limit Chinese immigration, describing the situation as dire. The convention complained that the presence of Chinese had "a baneful effect. . .upon public morals," a reference to concerns about Chinese prostitutes and opium dens.[51] The convention went on, in Justice Field's words, to judge that Chinese

> immigration was in numbers approaching the character of an Oriental invasion, and was a menace to our civilization; . . . that they retained the habits and customs of their own country, and in fact constituted a Chinese settlement within the state, without any interest in our country or its institutions.[52]

---

[47] *Chae Chan Ping*, 130 U.S. at 586–89.
[48] Additional Articles to the Treaty between the United States and China, June 18, 1858, 740.
[49] *Chae Chan Ping*, 130 U.S. at 594.
[50] 130 U.S. at 594–95.
[51] 130 U.S. at 595.
[52] 130 U.S. at 595–96.

To the perceived threat that the Chinese posed to "material interests," "public morals," and the people of America, the Court ruled that Congress was justified in progressively limiting Chinese immigration.[53] This threat justified Congress in going against its treaty with China, in restricting entry, and in annulling reentry certificates.[54]

Justice Field's opinion went beyond these prudential considerations to provide a general justification for the right of a nation to exclude aliens. This argument has two prongs, and the first appears here:

> That the government of the United States, through the action of the legislative department, can exclude aliens from its territory is a proposition which we do not think open to controversy. Jurisdiction over its own territory to that extent is an incident of every independent nation. It is a part of its independence. If it could not exclude aliens it would be to that extent subject to the control of another power.[55]

Justice Field's argument was that for a nation to be independent and free from the control of another nation, it must maintain exclusive rule over its lands. To establish precedent for this assertion, Justice Field quoted from Chief Justice Marshall's opinion from the 1812 case of *The Schooner Exchange v. McFaddon & Others*:

> The jurisdiction of the nation within its own territory is necessarily exclusive and absolute. It is susceptible of no limitation not imposed by itself. Any restriction upon it, deriving validity from an external source, would imply a diminution of its sovereignty to the extent of the restriction, and an investment of that sovereignty to the same extent in that power which could impose such restriction.

> All exceptions, therefore, to the full and complete power of a nation within its own territories, must be traced up to the consent of the nation itself. They can flow from no other legitimate source.[56]

What it means to be independent and sovereign is to issue binding judgments within a territory, judgments that no other authority may make – this much was clear in the Court opinion from the *Exchange*. Also clear from the *Exchange* was that only the nation can consent to an abridgement of control over its territory. Justice Field seized this terse definition of sovereignty and grafted in an argument about the exclusion of aliens: a basic feature of sovereignty, jurisdiction over territory, implies the right to decide who will enter that territory. Hence, an independent and sovereign nation by definition can exclude those who are not its citizens or its subjects. As a nation has "exclusive and absolute" jurisdiction over its territory, as it has

---

[53] 130 U.S. at 594–96.

[54] 130 U.S. at 600.

[55] 130 U.S. at 603–4.

[56] The Schooner Exchange v. McFaddon & Others, 11 U.S. 116 (1812); *Chae Chan Ping*, 130 U.S. at 604. Justice Field also cites dispatches of U.S. diplomats stretching back to 1852 which claim that it is basic power of a sovereign nation to exclude aliens, 130 U.S. at 606–9.

"full and complete power ... within its own territories," it also has exclusive, absolute, full, and complete power to turn away aliens from its territory.

Justice Field's argument had a second prong:

> To preserve its independence, and give security against foreign aggression and encroachment is the highest duty of every nation, and to attain these ends nearly all other considerations are to be subordinated. It matters not in what form such aggression and encroachment come, whether from the foreign nation acting in its national character, or from vast hordes of its people crowding in upon us.[57]

Justice Field argued that another dimension of a nation's independence is to provide security against attack, and this is its first and greatest purpose. But Justice Field was not content to affirm that a sovereign nation is responsible to defend itself from an organized military attack by another nation. Large numbers of private citizens moving into a territory also count as "aggression and encroachment." When the legislative branch of the United States determines "foreigners of a different race ... who will not assimilate with us to be dangerous to its peace and security," Congress has the authority to exclude such foreigners.[58] Justice Field said that it does not matter that the United States is not at war with the nation whose subjects the foreigners are. Large numbers of nonassimilating foreigners can be repelled during times of peace. Justice Field concluded that if foreigners resident in the United States are dissatisfied about how they are treated, their government should complain directly to the executive head of the United States. It seems that diplomacy – or war – is the only check on the power of a government to defend its peace and security from attack by aliens.[59]

Justice Field expressed his case for the power to exclude as a general argument that would apply to any nation. Yet his account of Chinese immigration to the United States provides an insight into what he thinks state power over immigration is meant to protect. Justice Field implied that it is the government's role to maintain peace and to protect the economic interests of its citizens. He also indicated that it is the government's role to protect a civilization and to prevent the tarnishing of public morals. He assumed that if immigrants come and settle somewhere, it is their duty to take on the customs and ways of living of their new country, and to take interest in that country and its institutions. Justice Field saw race as a complicating factor in this assimilation, though he did not imply that racial differences make integration impossible.[60] He did not envision a society composed of multiple and separate

---

[57] 130 U.S. at 606.

[58] 130 U.S. at 606.

[59] 130 U.S. at 606.

[60] Justice Field mentions "race" at significant junctures in his argument: as a complicating factor in the peaceful cooperation of the peoples of California, and as a feature of those foreigners who in not assimilating threaten the "peace and security" of the country, 130 U.S. at 595, 606. One might read his opinion less charitably, arguing that in using the word "race" Justice Field employs a rhetorical fiction designed to protect a "white" America. One might, on the other

ethnic groups, but neither did he oppose immigration altogether; he merely required that immigrants join in the customs of their new country and take an interest in that country. Taken as a whole, the Court opinion appears to claim that the sovereign powers of government serve to protect the common life of a nation. The Justice seemed concerned that a society be unified by shared practices, by common institutions, and by mutual concern.

In justifying the exclusion of aliens, *Chae Chan Ping v. United States* supplied the conceptual framework for an immigration policy as such. Justice Field's opinion for the Court described how national sovereignty implies the power to exclude an immigrant, who for his purposes embodies the threatening power of another nation. The power to exclude made possible the general policies on immigration that Congress would institute in the twentieth century. A byproduct of these policies is that those who defy them are aliens unlawfully present in the United States. Yet along with providing a framework for an immigration policy, and one which would make possible the illegal alien, Justice Field's opinion revealed what state power over movement across borders was thought to protect: the unity and common life of a society.

Fong Yue Ting v. United States *Establishes the Right* to Expel Aliens Despite Strong Dissent

In the case of *Chae Chan Ping v. United States*, the Supreme Court was unanimous: The power to exclude aliens was given in the notion of national sovereignty.[61] But just four years later, another new assertion about a sovereign nation's power over aliens caused uproar in the Court. In 1893, *Fong Yue Ting v. United States* resolved a battle over further restrictions placed on Chinese immigrants. Justice Horace Gray, writing for the five justices in the majority, wrote that along with the power to *exclude* aliens came the power to *expel* aliens. The four dissenting justices wrote heated statements objecting to this move from turning foreigners away at the border to removing them from within the confines of the United States. Indeed, one of these opinions opposing the power to expel aliens came from Justice Stephen Field, the very justice who had written the Court opinion affirming the power to exclude aliens in *Chae Chan Ping v. United States*. In what follows, an examination of opinions in *Fong Yue Ting v. United States* will demonstrate that as the notion of federal sovereignty over aliens developed, it rested on an articulation of national self-preservation as paramount. At the same time, that

---

hand, see "race" as a feature of the conceptual world Justice Field inhabits, and one that does not preoccupy him as much as assimilation into a united society.

[61] Justice Gray writes in his opinion that Chae Chan Ping v. United States was a unanimous judgment of the court, Fong Yue Ting v. United States, Wong Quan v. United States, Lee Joe v. United States, 149 U.S. 698 (1893).

sovereign authority was contested in the name of a right of domicile, a fair trial, and limits to powers that could turn despotic.

In 1893, three cases involving Chinese immigrants came before the Supreme Court just as a new law came into effect. After the 1882, 1884, and 1888 Acts progressively tightened the restrictions on the Chinese, the Geary Act of 1892 added a new twist: Chinese men and women were deemed to be in the United States illegally unless they were able to prove otherwise. Chinese immigrants were required to apply for a certificate of residence from the government, a sort of internal passport that would demonstrate that they were present prior to the 1882 Exclusion Act and thus entitled to stay in the United States. Without such proof, any "Chinese person or person of Chinese descent" would "be removed from the United States to China."[62] After the passage of the Geary Act, as an act of civil disobedience, about nine tenths of the Chinese community in the United States resisted registering for a certificate.[63] The Chinese had been given a year to register, and as soon as that year was up, three cases came before the Court. The three Chinese men in question were residents of New York, and they had been in the United States since before the first Exclusion Act. When New York marshals found that Fong Yue Ting, Wong Quan, and Lee Joe lacked certificates, they arrested the three men and threatened them with deportation. The first two had not registered for a certificate, and the third had attempted to register, but his application was refused because he failed to comply with one of the conditions of the Geary Act: He needed "at least one credible white witness" to testify that he had been a resident of the United States in 1892.[64] Top lawyers were again brought in to articulate the case of the Chinese, arguing that those invited by the federal government to come to the United States gained a right of residence that could not be taken away. To take away that residence by ordering the deportation of Chinese women and men without certificates would be an exercise of power that had not been given to Congress, and it would represent a dangerous expansion of governmental power. But the Court judged that it was within the authority of the federal government to expel and deport these three men, and the conceptual move required to justify that authority deserves attention.

Chae Chan Ping v. United States had established the right of the government to exclude foreigners, to bar them from entering the country. What was in question in *Fong Yue Ting v. United States* was whether the government could expel foreigners who were living within its borders by its consent. Justice Gray's opinion dealt more extensively than Justice Field's with cases and authorities in federal and international law. Along with reiterating the power to exclude aliens that the Court had upheld in *Chae Chan Ping v. United States*, Justice Gray repeated a statement he had made in an intervening case, *Nishimura Ekiu v. United States*:

[62] An act to prohibit the coming of Chinese persons into the United States, 27 Stat. 25 (1892).
[63] Daniels, *Guarding the Golden Door*, 21.
[64] 27 Stat. 25, 26; *Fong Yue Ting*, 149 U.S. at 702–4.

It is an accepted maxim of international law, that every sovereign nation has the power, as inherent in sovereignty, and *essential to self-preservation*, to forbid the entrance of foreigners within its dominions, or to admit them only in such cases and upon such conditions as it may see fit to prescribe.[65]

Here, Justice Gray made clear that authority over immigration serves to defend the continuing life of a society, which is oriented toward its own preservation. To back up this national self-interest, he drew on the scholar of international law Emer de Vattel, who had stated in the previous century,

Every nation has the right to refuse to admit a foreigner into the country, when he cannot enter without putting the nation in evident danger, or doing it a manifest injury. *What it owes to itself, the care of its own safety*, gives it this right, and in virtue of its natural liberty, it belongs to the nation to judge whether its circumstances will or will not justify the admission of the foreigner.[66]

Having established that the right to exclude aliens rests on self-care and self-preservation, Justice Gray cited a series of authorities in international law who recognized a right to expel foreigners. Among these was Théodore Ortolan, who claimed that a government always reserves "the right to compel foreigners who are found within its territory to go away, by having them taken to the frontier," as foreigners are only present in its territory by "pure permission."[67]

In what is the central conceptual innovation of his judgment, Justice Gray said that the power to exclude aliens and the power to expel aliens are so closely tied that they are two aspects of a single power: "The power to exclude aliens and the power to expel them rest upon one foundation, are derived from one source, are supported by the same reasons, and are in truth but parts of one and the same power."[68] The same sorts of goals that Justice Field offered in the case of *Chae Chan Ping v. United States* are scattered through Justice Gray's opinion: protecting the sole power of the nation over its territory, keeping it secure against attack, and maintaining its health. Justice Gray offered a summary of these two powers wrapped up in one:

---

[65] Nishimura Ekiu v. United States, 142 U.S. 651 (1891), emphasis author's.

[66] Emer de Vattel, *The Law of Nations*, bk. 1, sec. 230, as quoted in 149 U.S. at 707, emphasis author's. See pp. 88–94.

[67] *Règles internationales et diplomatie de la mer*, 4th édn. (Paris: Henri Plon, 1864), lib. 2, c. 14, 297; cited in 149 U.S. at 708. Justice Gray also cites U.S. Secretary of State Fish from 1869 in Francis Wharton, ed., A *Digest of the International Law of the United States: Taken from Documents Issued by Presidents and Secretaries of State, and from Decisions of Federal Courts and Opinions of Attorneys-General*, 2nd. edn. (Washington: Government Printing Office, 1887), sec. 206; Robert Phillimore, *Commentaries Upon International Law*, 3rd edn., vol. 1 (London: Butterworths, 1879), c. 10, sec. 220; Ludwig von Bar, *International Law: Private and Criminal*, trans. G. R. Gillespie (Edinburgh: W. Green, 1883), 708 note, 711; citations in 149 U.S. at 707–8.

[68] *Fong Yue Ting*, 149 U.S. at 713.

The right to exclude or to expel all aliens, or any class of aliens, absolutely or upon certain conditions, in war or in peace, [is] an inherent and inalienable right of every sovereign and independent nation, essential to its safety, its independence, and its welfare.[69]

It is worth noting that in uniting exclusion and expulsion, Justice Gray called them both *powers* and *rights*. These powers do not just touch individual aliens but *all* aliens or *any class* of aliens. Both are non-negotiable aspects of what it means to be a nation that is sovereign, independent, safe, and well. That nation is interested in what is *its own* to possess.

Having established a unity of the powers to exclude and expel aliens, Justice Gray located those powers as Congress' to regulate and the President's to execute, as with other matters of international relations. It is not for the courts, then, to pass judgment on the exclusion and expulsion of foreigners.[70] Indeed, as the Court affirmed in *Nishimura Ekiu v. United States*, one officer from the executive branch of the government could judge exclusively about the cases of exclusion or expulsion, that person's decision counts as due process of law in keeping with the Fourteenth Amendment to the Constitution, and foreigners have no right to trial before a court when they are threatened with deportation.[71] Also, to the charge that expulsion represents a type of cruel and unusual punishment forbidden by the Eighth Amendment to the Constitution, Justice Gray argued that expulsion is merely a way of enforcing conditions that are within the government's proper exercise of authority to place on aliens.[72]

Now that Justice Gray had established the absolute and inalienable powers of the United States as a sovereign nation over the location of aliens, he said that those powers were limited in other ways. He affirmed that aliens are still owed a range of protections under the law, among them the rights to person and property. Despite the civil rights they have once inside the country, as aliens they gain no rights before immigration authorities. Even those who came to live in the United States legally and intend to continue to reside in the United States do not over time gain a right to remain:

It appears to be impossible to hold that a Chinese laborer acquired, under any of the treaties or acts of Congress, any right, as a denizen or otherwise, to be and remain in this country, except by the license, permission and sufferance of Congress, to be withdrawn whenever, in its opinion, the public welfare might require it.[73]

In sum, Justice Gray affirms that noncitizens benefit from certain legal rights and responsibilities, but before the raw power of the immigration authorities,

[69] 149 U.S. at 711.
[70] 149 U.S. at 711–12.
[71] *Nishimura Ekiu*, 142 U.S. at 660.
[72] *Fong Yue Ting*, 149 U.S. at 730.
[73] 149 U.S. at 723–24.

noncitizens have no one to appeal to once a single immigration officer makes a judgment about their case. The Court had affirmed in *Chae Chan Ping v. United States* that while civil rights and responsibilities hold within national territory, at the border of that territory, the sovereign power of the nation holds absolute sway over aliens wishing to enter. In *Fong Yue Ting v. United States*, the Court allows the powerful arm of immigration authorities to reach within national territory, plucking up the aliens it chooses and banishing them from its territory. The 1889 decision had envisaged bare federal power as operating at the borders, while the 1893 decision authorized that power to operate within the country's interior.

—

The four dissenters raised a vociferous protest against Justice Gray's conceptual innovation of uniting the power to exclude aliens with the power to expel aliens. Justice David Josiah Brewer, Chief Justice Melville Fuller, and the same Justice Field who had penned the opinion justifying the power to exclude aliens each wrote to object to the power to expel aliens. The dissenters drew upon international law, the U.S. Constitution, and a notion of the appropriate limits of federal power to frame their arguments. They argued that someone invited to settle in the United States gained a right of domicile and benefited from a limitation on the powers of government over those domiciled. The dissenters reasoned that persons who move to a new place and set up an abode with an intention to stay gain a right to domicile, strengthened when they pay taxes, give allegiance, and obey the laws of their new country. Following the common law precedent, Fong Yue Ting, Wong Quan, and Lee Joe possessed the status of denizens, between aliens and citizens.[74]

Since they owed temporary obedience to the Constitution, these denizens deserved to receive its guarantees, including freedom from "unreasonable searches and seizures" and from "cruel and unusual punishment."[75] They also deserved the constitutional "right of a speedy and public trial, by an impartial jury," along with the guarantee that they would not "be deprived of life, liberty, or property, without due process of law."[76] Chinese residents deserved "equal protection of the laws" accorded to everyone within U.S. territorial jurisdiction in the Fourteenth Amendment, a protection extended to people "without regard to any differences of race, of color, or of nationality" just a few years before in the case of *Yick Wo v. Hopkins*.[77] As denizens, these persons differ from citizens only in that they lack voting privileges

---

[74] 149 U.S. at 735–36, citing Emer de Vattel, *The Law of Nations: Or Principles of the Law of Nature Applied to the Conduct of Nations and Sovereigns*, bk. 1, sec. 218; Phillimore, *Commentaries Upon International Law*, vol. 1, chaps. 18, 347; Wharton, *International Digest*, sec. 198.

[75] *Fong Yue Ting*, 149 U.S. at 739, 740, 749, 759, 760; U.S. Const. amends. 4, 8.

[76] 149 U.S. at 698, 739, 741, 749, 754, 761; U.S. Const. amends. 5, 6.

[77] *Yick Wo*, 118 U.S. 356 (1886); quoted by Justice Brewer in 149 U.S. at 739.

and cannot hold public office. Justice Field said that this was right for "men having our common humanity,"[78] and he expressed this pride:

> It is certainly something in which a citizen of the United States may feel a generous pride that the government of his country extends protection to all persons within its jurisdiction, and that every blow aimed at any of them, however humble, come from what quarter it may, is "caught upon the broad shield of our blessed Constitution and our equal laws."[79]

The dissenters argued that while the power to exclude holds legitimately at the borders, the power to expel domiciled foreigners is a novelty, claimed only in the "barbarous" Alien Act of 1798.[80] This expulsion was certainly cruel and unusual punishment, in the words of Justice Field:

> As to its cruelty, nothing can exceed a forcible deportation from a country of one's residence, and the breaking up of all the relations of friendship, family and business there contracted. The laborer may be seized at a distance from his home, his family and his business, without permission to visit his home, see his family, or complete unfinished business.[81]

Lawful punishment requires a trial and the due process of law, but instead, these resident aliens had their cases decided by a single individual.[82] This power was "dangerous and despotic," in the warning of Justice Field, who said that deportation without a fair trial by jury "establishe[s] a pure, simple, undisguised despotism and tyranny with respect to foreigners resident in the country by its consent."[83]

Another of the dissenters, Justice Brewer, took aim at Justice Gray's analysis of sovereignty in a tightly argued passage:

> It is said that the power here is inherent in sovereignty. This doctrine of powers inherent in sovereignty is one both indefinite and dangerous. Where are the limits to such powers to be found, and by whom are they to be pronounced? Is it within legislative capacity to declare the limits? If so, then the mere assertion of an inherent power creates it, and despotism exists. May the courts establish the boundaries? Whence do they obtain the authority for this? Shall they look to the practices of other nations to ascertain the limits? The governments of other nations have elastic powers – ours is fixed and bounded by a written constitution. The expulsion of a race may be within the inherent powers of a despotism. History, before the adoption of this Constitution, was not destitute of examples of the

---

[78] *Fong Yue Ting*, 149 U.S. at 754. This reference to a "common humanity" that necessitates legal protections appears to be unique in this court case, though a lawyer for Chae Chan Ping made recourse to what was owed "men, as men," 130 U.S. at 584.

[79] *Ho Ah Kow v. Nunan*, 5 Sawyer 552 (C.C.D. California 1879); cited in *Fong Yue Ting*, 149 U.S. at 755.

[80] An Act concerning Aliens, 1 Stat. 570 (1798); *Fong Yue Ting*, 149 U.S. at 746–47.

[81] 149 U.S. at 759.

[82] 149 U.S. at 749.

[83] 149 U.S. at 750, 755.

exercise of such a power, and its framers were familiar with history, and wisely, as it seems to me, they gave to this government no general power to banish.[84]

According to Justice Brewer, the notion of sovereignty required to justify the expulsion of a lawfully admitted alien is an unlimited and dangerous sort, where the sovereign body merely asserts what its powers are. This despotism needed the limits of the Constitution.

Writing the opinion for the Supreme Court in *Fong Yue Ting v. United States*, Justice Gray had proposed a new power to expel aliens that he saw as one and the same as the power to exclude aliens. His argument made plain that this rested on the powers of a sovereign nation to preserve itself, its safety, and its welfare. The dissenting minority displayed outrage at what they saw as a despotic power to remove aliens from the country who had gained a right of residence or domicile. Especially those permitted and, in their words, "invited" to make a home in the United States deserved the protections of the Constitution, including a fair trial and a protection from cruel and unusual punishment.[85] Yet as they objected to expulsion, these dissenters did not object to the move made just four years prior in *Chae Chan Ping v. United States*. As the ship came into port, as the train arrived at the border, as someone walked across that border, in the entire Court's opinion the inherent powers of sovereignty held: It was fully within the rights of that government to exclude the alien, to turn away the foreigner at the point of entry.

Yick Wo v. Hopkins *and* United States v. Wong Kim Ark
Expand Rights for Aliens Lawfully Admitted

Alongside the Chae Chan Ping-Fong Yue Ting stream of cases ran the Yick Wo-Wong Kim Ark stream. On first glance, this second stream seems opposed to the first, since just as the powers to exclude and expel aliens were being established, these cases established that aliens were owed many of the rights owed to citizens. The cases extended guarantees awarded to former slaves and their descendants in the Fourteenth Amendment to the Constitution in 1868. A few years before *Chae Chan Ping v. United States*, the Supreme Court ruled in *Yick Wo v. Hopkins* (1886) that the city of San Francisco could not deny permits to Chinese-owned laundries while granting permits to laundries owned by those with European heritage. The Court cited the provisions of the Fourteenth Amendment of the Constitution of due process of law and equal protection of the laws, arguing that "these provisions are universal in their application, to all persons within the territorial jurisdiction, without regard to any differences of race, or color, or of nationality; and the equal protection of the laws is a pledge of the protection of equal laws."[86] Every branch of

---

[84] 149 U.S. at 737.
[85] 149 U.S. at 737.
[86] *Yick Wo*, 118 U.S. at 369.

government, even local authorities, had to apply laws equally. The Court said that the sovereign powers of government were circumscribed by laws, which applied in the same way to every person in its jurisdiction.[87]

In the following years, 1889 and 1893, the Supreme Court affirmed that aliens had no rights before the sovereign powers to exclude and expel them, but just a few years later, the Court extended a further right to aliens already present in U.S. territory. Wong Kim Ark had been born in San Francisco in 1873 to parents who were subjects of the Chinese emperor. He left the United States for a temporary visit to China in 1894, and when he returned in 1895, he was denied permission to land because he was judged not to be a citizen of the United States. While the port authorities judged that Wong Kim Ark "has been at all times, by reason of his race, language, color and dress, a Chinese person," the Supreme Court called on another provision of the Fourteenth Amendment: "All persons born or naturalized in the United States, and subject to the jurisdiction thereof, are citizens of the United States."[88] Writing the Court opinion, Justice Gray argued that this provision guarantees citizenship not only to the children of slaves but also to the children of aliens. Since federal law had not clarified the issue, Justice Gray ruled that the law followed not the civil law pattern of *ius sanguinis*, where the citizenship of a child followed its parent, but the English common law pattern of *ius soli*. As birth within the dominions of the king made one a subject at birth, so birth within U.S. jurisdiction made one a citizen. Wong Kim Ark was a citizen.[89] Aliens born outside of the United States were subject to the sovereign powers of exclusion and deportation, but their children, born on U.S. soil, were citizens who could come and go from the United States as they pleased.

Within a decade and a half, the Supreme Court affirmed significant civil rights for aliens, yet at the same time it affirmed the powers of government to exclude and deport aliens. Though these two streams seem to clash, in fact they complement one another. *Yick Wo v. Hopkins* and *United States v. Wong Kim Ark* were moves to define the American polity as enveloping everyone within a territory: moves to apply the law to everyone within U.S. lands and to extend membership to everyone born in those lands. *Chae Chan Ping v. United States* and *Fong Yue Ting v. United States* strengthened the borders around U.S. territory, justifying government as it turned aliens away at its boundaries and reached within its lands to expel unwanted aliens. Extensions of legal protections to everyone within a territory coincided with a strong enunciation of territorial sovereignty. The two streams are closely related: Government is increasingly defined as the power of law over a territory. Along with this conceptual confluence comes a practical agreement between the two streams: As everyone in the United States receives greater

---

[87] 118 U.S. at 370.
[88] United States v. Wong Kim Ark, 169 U.S. 649 (1898).
[89] 169 U.S. at 666–67, 675, 688, 694, 705.

legal protections, the law grows to fend off newcomers. A hard crust protects privileges newly extended to everyone in the interior.[90]

—

In the nineteenth century, the Supreme Court articulated a vision of goods held in common: peace, safety, economic wellbeing, democratic participation, sexual propriety, freedom from slavery and from drug addiction, and social and racial unity. Within the country, aliens were increasingly enabled to share in at least some of those goods as their rights and privileges expanded. Yet, if the people judged that prospective immigrants would compromise those goods, or if the nation judged that present immigrants detract from what is held in common, by their consent the federal government was given a tool that it still possesses in the early twenty-first century: the right to expel and exclude aliens, later interpreted as the "plenary power doctrine."[91] So far as the people of the United States are independent from other authorities, it is up to them to judge when what they share is threatened, and when a threat is identified, their powers over aliens are practically unlimited. By their consent, the legislature can draw up laws to expel and exclude aliens, and the executive branch can exclude and expel aliens even if just one of its agents judges it right. The courts have little or no hold on what Congress and executive agencies do. In the early twenty-first century, plenary power is restricted only minimally: Before expulsion, aliens are promised a hearing, they may have legal counsel present for the hearing though that counsel is not supplied, and they may not be held beyond six months if no other country will receive them.[92] Beyond those holds, powers to exclude and expel are not limited: The federal government retains sole control over immigration, and only very rarely do complaints about immigration authority reach the courts. The door is open for the federal government to claim extensive

---

[90] Kieran Oberman calls this the "coconut consensus," "What Is Wrong with Permanent Alienage?" (Oxford, October 29, 2012), http://podcasts.ox.ac.uk/what-wrong-permanent-alienage.

[91] Chin, "Chae Chan Ping and Fong Yue Ting," 7; Daniel J. Tichenor, *Dividing Lines: The Politics of Immigration Control in America* (Princeton: Princeton University Press, 2002), 109. See also Gabriel J. Chin, "Is There a Plenary Power Doctrine? A Tentative Apology and Prediction for Our Strange but Unexceptional Constitutional Immigration Law," *Georgetown Immigration Law Journal* 14 (2000): 257–87, which casts doubt on whether a plenary power doctrine exists, arguing that discrimination based on race, belief, and sexual preference in immigration law were consistent with discrimination in domestic law at the time of the court decisions.

[92] The Immigration and Nationality Act outlines the procedures for a removal hearing: An alien must be given notice of the charges and of the time and place of the hearing, the alien may be represented by legal counsel at no expense to the government, the alien will have opportunity to examine the evidence and cross-examine witnesses, and deportation can only be served if it is based on "reasonable, substantial, and probative evidence," 66 Stat. 163, 209–210, § 242(b). In Zadvydas v. Davis, 533 U.S. 678 (2001), the Court ruled that an alien may not be held for more than six months under a deportation order if no other country will accept that person. Steve Meili pointed out these limits on plenary power.

powers, to break faith with Chae Chan Ping and not honor the certificate guaranteeing reentry to a long-term resident, and to expel Fong Yue Ting, Wong Quan, and Lee Joe because of their failure to secure certificates of residence. The door is open for the government in the mid-twentieth century to imprison the alien wife of an American veteran or to imprison a legal resident of twenty-five years based on confidential evidence.[93] The door is open in the early twenty-first century for the government to remove an unlawfully present alien and take her children into state custody or to remove a young adult brought to the United States illegally as a child. The sharp edge of the sovereign powers over aliens remains nearly unlimited.

In the cases considered here, there are hints that sovereignty over immigration is to be limited by notions of justice. For instance, when Justice Field outlines "sovereign powers" in *Chae Chan Ping v. United States*, he states that these are "restricted in their exercise only by the Constitution itself and considerations of public policy and justice which control, more or less, the conduct of all civilized nations."[94] This statement allows for a reading of the cases that emphasizes the moral goods to which the people must refer if they are to remain "civilized" in their exercise of sovereign power. Yet the stress of the arguments of the Court in *Chae Chan Ping v. United States* and *Fong Yue Ting v. United States* lies on uncompromised sovereignty for the purpose of self-preservation. While other moral considerations may be at play, national independence trumps these in frequent cases of detention and expulsion. In contrast to other sorts of federal law, only very few limits are placed on immigration law, its scope and its authority. There is little evidence that anything beyond the existence of the nation-state matters. *Ius* or Right, human rights, the good of other nations, and the judgment of God seem to place no hold on federal authority over the bodies of aliens. If the people signal through their representatives that they wish to exclude an alien from entering U.S. territory or if the legislature decides to expel an alien already within U.S. territory, it may do so. Indeed, power over immigration seems to prove the independence of the nation; it demonstrates that no other power rules the land. Insofar as power over immigration is a sign of sovereignty, it does not need any other justification.

These cases leave a legacy, then. They bequeath to U.S. immigration law a notion of sovereignty that is disconnected from some wider moral field, some outside considerations of justice. Here it is right to heed the warnings of the dissenters in *Fong Yue Ting v. United States*, who said that the assertion of the right to expel aliens "contains within it the germs of the assertion of an unlimited and arbitrary power," one leading to "despotism and tyranny."[95]

---

[93] United States ex rel. Knauff v. Shaughnessy, 338 U.S. 537 (1950); Shaughnessy v. United States ex rel. Mezei, 345 U.S. 206 (1953); in Tichenor, *Dividing Lines*, 200.

[94] *Chae Chan Ping*, 130 U.S. at 604.

[95] *Fong Yue Ting*, 149 U.S. at 755, 763.

SOVEREIGNTY OVER IMMIGRATION IN INTELLECTUAL HISTORY:
SELF-INTEREST IN VATTEL AND HOBBES AGAINST GROTIUS

What tradition of thought did the Supreme Court draw upon when it said that absolute authority over immigration is simply part of what it means to be a sovereign nation and when it said that this authority depends on the consent of the nation and no other substantial considerations? The Court opinion in *Chae Chan Ping v. United States* did little to connect to a juridical tradition: Justice Field reasoned from sovereign authority to the right to expel aliens, he demonstrated the agreement of the Court in other judgments, and he cited examples of diplomatic communications that accorded with his view. In his opinion on *Fong Yue Ting v. United States*, however, Justice Gray turned to leading authorities on the law of nations to find agreement with his argument for the right of a nation to exclude or expel aliens. He cited Emer de Vattel, Théodore Ortolan, Robert Phillimore, and Ludwig von Bar, and while Ortolan, Phillimore, and Bar wrote not long before *Fong Yue Ting v. United States*, Vattel wrote in the previous century.[96] Vattel's *Le Droit des Gens* (1758) was perhaps the most prominent work on the law of nations in the eighteenth century, and it exerted great influence over American jurisprudence through the nineteenth. The work is also a link to an earlier tradition, drawing on Christian Wolff, Samuel Pufendorf, Thomas Hobbes, and Hugo Grotius.[97] Of these, what follows will consider Hobbes and Grotius from the seventeenth century in connection with Vattel. Though Vattel refers to Grotius more often than to Hobbes, Vattel sides with Hobbes in placing self-interest as primary in the law of nature. In contrast, Grotius' mature work posits a desire for society as the wellspring of natural right, and he alleges that those who start with self-love think there is no such thing as justice. Vattel and Hobbes will cast the nation as aiding the foreigner only when their self-preservation is not compromised, notions that pave the way for the late nineteenth-century judgments of the United States Supreme Court.

In his opinion in *Fong Yue Ting v. United States*, Justice Gray used a quotation from Emer de Vattel to justify a nation's exclusion of a foreigner to protect against

---

[96] 149 U.S. at 707–9. The first edition of Ortolan appeared in 1845, and Justice Gray cites from the 1864 edition, *Règles internationales et diplomatie de la mer*. Phillimore first appeared in 1854–1861, and Justice Gray cites from the 1879 edition, *Commentaries Upon International Law*. Bar was published in German as *Das internationale Privat- und Strafrecht* (Hannover: Hahn'sche Hofbuchhandlung, 1862); Gray cites from the 1883 English translation, *International Law*. Vattel appeared in French as *Le Droit des Gens, ou, Principes de la Loi naturelle appliqués à la conduite et aux affaires des Nations et des Souverains*, 2 vols. (London, 1758), and the work appeared in English translation in various editions from 1760 onward. This section draws upon the Liberty Fund edition, *The Law of Nations*, ed. Béla Kapossy and Richard Whatmore (Indianapolis: Liberty Fund, 2008), a representation of *The Law of Nations: Or Principles of the Law of Nature Applied to the Conduct of Nations and Sovereigns* (London: G. G. and J. Robinson, 1797).

[97] As an indication of the importance of Vattel for American understandings of the law of nations, Chief Justice Marshall cites Vattel and only other one other authority, Cornelius van Bynkershoek, in the *Exchange*, 11 U.S. at 143, 144; Vattel, *The Law of Nations*, bk. 4, sec. 92.

danger or injury. Justice Gray extracted a phrase justifying a nation's right to refuse to admit a foreigner out of a passage that sets out the opposite aim, to encourage nations to receive foreigners in need. Still, the Justice's quotation captures something that runs through Vattel's treatise: self-interest is prior to mutual aid, both for individuals and for nations. In the passage, the jurist from Neuchâtel, born under Prussian rule but made an advisor to the elector of Saxony, writes that nations should respond to the imperfect right of those driven from home by giving them a place to stay, temporarily or permanently.[98] The proto-historical rise of property and national domain does not take away the right given by nature and nature's author to every person, the "right to dwell somewhere on earth."[99] But Vattel offers an abundance of provisos: If the nation has reason to believe that the exile may cause damage to it by consuming its scarce resources, spreading disease, tarnishing manners, or disturbing the peace, that nation can – indeed, it must – ban the foreigner from entering its domain.[100] Still, this prudential reasoning should not hold onto "unnecessary suspicion and jealousy," and it should be tempered by "charity and commiseration."[101] Even for those who fall into an unhappy state by their own fault, Vattel reminds his readers that all human beings should love one other.[102]

Vattel's handling of the case of admitting exiles is an instance of a pattern of reasoning that continues throughout his lengthy treatise. For the individual as for the nation, Vattel announces a duty of mutual aid, since no one can fulfill their needs without others. His strong case for universal human society rests on something still stronger: This society enables a person to achieve her own preservation and the perfection of her nature.[103] Likewise with nations: "Each individual nation is bound to contribute every thing in her power to the happiness and perfection of all the others."[104] But such a claim does not stand on its own. Right away, Vattel qualifies it: "The duties that we owe to ourselves [are] unquestionably paramount to those we owe to others."[105] This is because whether individual or collective, a moral being no longer exists if it does not fulfill its obligations to itself: *"To preserve and to perfect his own nature,* is the sum of all duties to himself," says Vattel.[106] And though the nation differs from the individual in some ways, it still is duty-bound to do what the individual is bound to do according to the law of nature, "to fulfill the duties of humanity toward strangers."[107] Not only is an individual due a place to live, but so is

---

[98] *The Law of Nations,* bk. 1, sec. 230.
[99] Ibid., bk. 1, sec. 229. *Le droit d'habiter quelque part sur la terre, Le Droit des Gens.*
[100] *The Law of Nations,* bk. 1, sec. 231. *Nation, Le Droit des Gens.*
[101] *The Law of Nations,* bk. 1, sec. 231. *La charité & le commisération, Le Droit des Gens.*
[102] *The Law of Nations,* bk. 1, sec. 231. *Tous les hommes doivent s'aimer, Le Droit des Gens.*
[103] *The Law of Nations,* Prelim. sec. 10.
[104] Ibid., Prelim. sec. 13. *Bonheur & perfection, Le Droit des Gens.*
[105] *The Law of Nations,* Prelim. sec. 14.
[106] Ibid., bk. 1, sec. 14, emphasis Vattel's. *Se conserver & se perfectioner, c'est le somme de tous devoirs envers soi-même, Le Droit des Gens.*
[107] *The Law of Nations,* Prelim. sec. 11.

a whole nation, says Vattel in a separate passage: "If a people are driven from the place of their abode, they have a right to seek a retreat."[108] But immediately, Vattel offers a way out: The country to which the beleaguered nation comes can dismiss new arrivals if it does not have enough by which to preserve itself.[109]

When Justice Gray uses Vattel, then, he does not responsibly represent the flow of the argument, but his misquotation grabs onto something rooted firmly in Vattel. Vattel agrees with the Roman-Christian legal synthesis that the earth is given to human beings in common, and that the duties and rights of humanity hold even after they join sovereign bodies.[110] Here Vattel seems to maintain a sense of Right that guides the treatment of foreigners by the sovereign state and its members. But he does not speak of Right in a strong sense; for him, everything boils down to the preservation and perfection of self. Vattel speaks of love that tempers suspicion toward foreigners, and he even claims that nations ought to love one another.[111] Despite this, Vattel argues that the nation is the final judge of what it ought to do. The nation alone decides whether aiding another will help it achieve its development or will compromise its continuing existence and its development. Vattel says that as a being naturally in possession of liberty and independence, "it exclusively belongs to each nation to form her own judgment of what her conscience prescribes to her – of what she can or cannot do, – of what it is proper or improper for her to do."[112] This is a precursor to the assertions that Justice Field draws from Chief Justice Marshall that "all exceptions. . .to the full and complete power of a nation within its own territories, must be traced up to the consent of the nation itself."[113] For Vattel as for these Supreme Court justices of the nineteenth century, the nation is judge of when it can assist others. Also like the justices, Vattel says that the rights of domain and empire that are intrinsic to a nation's hold over land mean that the sovereign may forbid the entrance of foreigners "according as he may think it advantageous to the state."[114] His reference to virtue and love restrains the excesses of a state seeking its own advantage, but it does not stop the state seeking its own advantage. The basic right, the basic law that moves the world, is to preserve self.

Standing before Vattel, seventeenth-century philosopher Thomas Hobbes does not treat immigration at any length in his masterwork *Leviathan* (1651).[115] He does not offer casuistry in international law of the sort found in Vattel, but what he

---

[108] Ibid., bk. 2, sec. 125. *Peuple. . .retraite, Le Droit des Gens.*

[109] Vattel, *The Law of Nations,* bk. 2, sec. 125. *Pays, Le Droit des Gens.*

[110] Vattel, *The Law of Nations,* bk. 2, sec. 203.

[111] Ibid., bk. 2, sec. 11.

[112] Ibid., Prelim. sec. 16.

[113] *The Exchange,* 11 U.S. at 136; *Chae Chan Ping,* 130 U.S. at 604.

[114] *The Law of Nations,* bk. 2, sec. 94. . . .*Selon qu'il le trouve convenable au bien de l'Etat. . . .Droits de Domaine & d'Empire, Le Droit des Gens.*

[115] Thomas Hobbes, *Leviathan, Or, The Matter, Form, and Power of a Common-Wealth Ecclesiastical and Civil* (London: Printed for Andrew Crooke, 1651). The page numbers here come from the bracketed numbers in *Leviathan,* ed. Richard Tuck, rev. student edn. (Cambridge: Cambridge University Press, 1996). These are drawn from the large-paper 1651 London edition

does offer is an account of the genesis of civil authority that would set the terms of philosophical debate for generations to come, an account that lends a certain interpretation of immigration. In *Leviathan*, Hobbes claims that by nature, human beings have equal faculties, and they equally desire certain ends. If someone gains, builds, or cultivates a "convenient Seat," a pleasant bit of land or homestead, then another will come as "Invader," to take what the first owns, perhaps taking their life or liberty as well. "Competition," "Diffidence," and "Glory" cause human beings to quarrel, leaving them without desire to keep company.[116] "Hereby it is manifest," writes Hobbes, "that during the time men live without a common Power to keep them all in awe, they are in that condition which is called Warre; and such a warre, as is of every man, against every man."[117] In such a setting, without a "common Power," there is "no Law" and therefore "no Injustice."[118]

Hobbes describes in the subsequent chapters how human beings grow tired of such a miserable state, wanting to defend themselves and the work of their hands from the threats of others. The "Fundamentall Law of Nature, ... to seek Peace, and follow it," compels them to make a new arrangement, yet that arrangement must go through and not around "the summe of the Right of Nature," which, according to Hobbes, is "by all means we can, to defend our selves."[119] A desire for peace reigns, and that peace cannot be other than complete self-defense. So, a great multitude gathers to achieve peace and to defend themselves from "the invasion of Forraigners," says Hobbes. The multitude achieves unity by placing all their power and strength on one person, or one assembly of persons, reducing their will to one will and allowing that man or assembly to bear their person.[120] They make a "Covenant of every man with every man," giving up their "Right of Governing" themselves to a new person, an "Artificiall person."[121] The one that carries this person is "Soveraigne," and everyone else is "his Subject."[122] The multitude united in one person is "a COMMON-WEALTH, in latine CIVITAS ... that great LEVIA-THAN, or rather ... that *Mortall God*, to which wee owe under the *Immortal God*, our peace and defence."[123] Thus Hobbes thinks the war of every man against every man ends within a commonwealth, but the same war continues on at its borders:

> Yet in all times, Kings, and Persons of Soveraigne authority, because of their Independency, are in continuall jealousies, and in the state and posture of Gladi-ators; having their weapons pointing, and their eyes fixed on one another; that is,

from the Cambridge University Library, *Syn* 3.65.1. The quotations here from *Leviathan* reflect the spelling, capitalization, and italics of Tuck's edition.

[116] Hobbes, *Leviathan*, 1996, 60–61.
[117] Ibid., 62.
[118] Ibid., 63.
[119] Ibid., 64.
[120] Ibid., 87.
[121] Ibid., 80, 87.
[122] Ibid., 88.
[123] Ibid., 87.

their Forts, Garrisons, and Guns upon the Frontiers of their Kingdomes; and continuall Spyes upon their neighbours, which is a posture of War.[124]

Hobbes says little more in *Leviathan* about immigrants and international relations. Indeed, some say there is reason to think that his views on international relations would be very different from the protean picture in this work if it had dealt with the law of nations.[125] Still, imagining where immigrants fall in the picture from *Leviathan*, immigrants cross militarized borderlands. No Right guides the treatment of immigrants by sovereign nations because Right can only operate within those sovereign nations. How sovereigns respond to immigrants will flow out of their *raison d'être*, to defend against foreign invasion. Immigrants will be dealt with in the nexus of competition, diffidence, and glory that Hobbes has described. The sovereign is first tasked with defending those it represents, seeking their peace, allowing them to hold on to their property, and maintaining their life and liberty. The immigrant can only be understood within this framework, as threat or benefit, but not as a creature bearing witness to some external Right or as messenger of some divine word.

In the same century as Hobbes lies a figure whose work Vattel often draws on but who posits another source for justice – and alleges that the likes of Hobbes and Vattel have given up believing in justice. In his early work *De Indis* (1603/1604), not published in full until 1868, well after Vattel, jurist Hugo Grotius resembles Hobbes and Vattel in theological attire. He claims that in the way that God has fashioned creation, "love, whose primary force and action are directed to self-interest, is the first principle of the whole natural order."[126] The regard of self, he says, can be seen not only in human beings but in animals and inanimate objects, "being a manifestation of that true and divinely inspired self-love which is laudable in every phase of creation."[127] The regard for self produces two laws of nature: "It shall be permissible to defend [one's own] life and to shun that which threatens to prove injurious; secondly, that It shall be permissible to acquire for oneself, and to retain, those things which are useful for life."[128] But human beings are also made to regard others and seek their welfare, even loving them, says Grotius. This is the starting point of

---

[124] Ibid., 63.

[125] So argues Michael C. Williams, "Hobbes and International Relations: A Reconsideration," *International Organization* 50, no. 2 (1996): 213–36.

[126] Hugo Grotius, *Commentary on the Law of Prize and Booty*, ed. Martine Julia van Ittersum and Gwladys L. Williams (Indianapolis: Liberty Fund, 2006), 5'; based on Hugo Grotius, *De Iure Praedae Commentarius: Commentary on the Law of Prize and Booty*, ed. Gwladys L. Williams and Walter H. Zeydel, 2 vols. (Oxford: Clarendon Press, 1950); Oliver O'Donovan, "The Justice of Assignment and Subjective Rights in Grotius," in *Bonds of Imperfection: Christian Politics, Past and Present*, ed. Oliver O'Donovan and Joan Lockwood O'Donovan (Grand Rapids, Mich.: Eerdmans, 2004), 175.

[127] Grotius, *The Law of Prize and Booty*, 5'a.

[128] Ibid., 6.

"justice properly so called," justice that concerns the good of others.[129] In this early work, then, love motivates justice, and the first love is love of self. Love for others follows on from this, and justice proceeds with this love for others.

By the time he writes his mature work *De Iure Belli ac Pacis* (1625), Grotius starts in a different place. His previous commitment to self-preservation only appears as a foil, in the person of Carneades as represented in Cicero's *De Re Publica*.[130] Carneades argues that there is no natural Right, since Right changes according to custom and time, and since with other animals, human beings by nature pursue their own interests. Carneades says according to Grotius, "either there was no such thing as justice, or such justice as existed was pure folly, for concern for others' welfare damaged one's own."[131] Grotius responds that this teaching cannot be accepted, either for human beings or for some other animals. Human behavior is distinguished by a "desire for society" or "community," for "peaceable society with members of the same species, organized appropriately to human rational capacities."[132] This inclination to society is fixed in human nature, and this, not self-interest, is "the mother of natural Right."[133] Out of humankind's social nature, then, flow other kinds of right, a stricter sense of right in giving and taking, and wider sense of right in wise judgment.[134] Human beings have their social nature by the free will of God (*ex libera Dei voluntate*), and their inclinations are helped by interest (*utilitas*), says Grotius.[135]

In Grotius' mature account of natural Right or justice, then, a desire for society is the feature of human nature on which everything else builds. Vattel resembles Grotius in giving mutual aid a strong role, but by choosing the preservation of self as his starting point, he resembles Hobbes. When Hobbes begins his account of the Right of nature with self-defense, he manifests the dark side of self-preservation. When the Supreme Court judgments that established the sovereign right to exclude and expel aliens quoted from Vattel, then they were more indebted to Hobbes' primary assertion of self than to Grotius' primary assertion of community. The

---

[129] Ibid., 6.

[130] Carneades' words are known through a lost section of Cicero known now, as to Grotius, through Lactantius, *Divinae institutiones* 5. See O'Donovan, "The Justice of Assignment and Subjective Rights in Grotius," 187n52.

[131] *De Iure Belli ac Pacis: In quibus ius naturae & Gentium: item iuris publici praecipua explicantur (I.B.P.)*, Ed. 2a emendatior & multis locis auctior (Amsterdam: Guilielmum Blaeuw, 1631), Prol.5; in Oliver O'Donovan and Joan Lockwood O'Donovan, eds., *From Irenaeus to Grotius: A Sourcebook in Christian Political Thought* 100–1625 *(I.G.)* (Grand Rapids, Mich.: Eerdmans, 1999), 792–93. For more on the text of I.B.P., see p. 182 note 20.

[132] *Inter haec autem quae homini sunt propria, est appetitus societas, id est communitatis, non qualiscunque, sed tranquillae & pro sui intellectus modo ordinatae cum his qui sunt generis,* I.B.P., Prol.6, in I.G., 793.

[133] I.B.P., Prol.16, in I.G., 795.

[134] I.B.P., Prol.8–9, in I.G., 793–94. On these types of justice, which Grotius calls expletive and attributive, see pp. 182–5.

[135] I.B.P., Prol.12, 16, in I.G., 794, 795.

intellectual lineage from Justices Field and Gray through Vattel to Hobbes casts the sovereign nation as fundamentally committed to its own life, to preserving itself and defending itself from threat. Though in Justice Field's account, like in Vattel's, the nation can weigh substantial goods in deciding what it owes a foreigner as it seeks to preserve its own society, in the end, the nation does that weighing. External notions of justice do not have a hold on a nation that decides it is not in its interests to admit or assist a foreigner. Grotius believes that this thinking leads to a dead end: If relationships with foreigners are predicated on self-interest, then there is no Right to speak of; there is no justice to speak of. There is only deficient self-love. In the Paris of 1651, where Hobbes writes, much the same framework holds as in the Washington of 1889. The sovereign state reigns paramount over immigrants, and there is no Right beyond the judgment of the nation.[136]

—

This chapter explained that in the first century of the American republic, the federal government did not have a general authority over immigration. This authority came into place as Congress responded to what it saw as the threat of nonassimilating Chinese immigrants by excluding new Chinese arrivals and expelling some of those already present. In challenges to those laws, the Supreme Court justified this new federal power primarily on philosophical grounds, arguing that the right to exclude and expel aliens rested on the sovereignty, self-preservation, and self-defense of the nation. In U.S. immigration law, only the consent of the nation constrains this authority over the whereabouts of aliens. No standard of Right beyond what the nation judges is right for itself holds when it comes to immigration. This does not bode well for immigrants, who are left as pawns within the self-interested logic of the federal government.

---

[136] The genealogy of a politics sanctioned only by the people and insulated from divine and natural Right extends beyond Hobbes to Marsilius of Padua, *Defensor pacis*, 1324.

4

The Humble Guard

Governing Immigration Under God

Is this a world without universal Right, where governments fend off threatening foreigners to preserve their own sphere of justice? No: Each nation stands judged by God in Christ. In a world created and upheld, judged and restored by the living God, not only those from far away but also the guarding of places takes on a different light. Should those who see the guarding of places as subject to Christ's judgment oppose the government of immigration altogether? Or, do God's plans for the world allow for some human authority over immigration? Reading Scripture with Martin Luther and other trustworthy theological interpreters in this chapter, the guarding of places will emerge as a good for this age, limited by the judgment of God. Readings from a pope and a lawyer will clarify what immigration authorities rightly do and what sort of wrong those who break immigration laws commit. Applied to seven cases of immigration-related offenses, these resources will suggest a more modest approach to punishment than federal United States courts currently take.

KEEPING PLACES, GUARDING PLACES: LUTHER, ELLUL, AND O'DONOVAN ON GENESIS 2–4 AND REVELATION 21–22

Does the guarding of places properly belong within God's saving purposes? If so, where does guarding come from, and where is it destined? The following section will seek answers in biblical accounts of the world's beginnings and its endings. Three trusted interpreters will draw out insights from the Book of Genesis, chapters 2 to 4, and the Book of Revelation, chapters 21 and 22: sixteenth-century reformer Martin Luther, twentieth-century sociologist and biblical interpreter Jacques Ellul, and contemporary moral theologian Oliver O'Donovan.

The Kept Garden

Human life began in a defined place. This is what the creation narrative that begins in Genesis 2:4 says, Luther states in the lectures on what he considers the first book of Moses. "And the LORD God (Yhwh Elohim) planted a garden in Eden, in the east, and there the LORD put the earthling whom the LORD had formed" (Gen. 2:8).[1] יְהוָה אֱלֹהִים, *Yhwh Ĕlōhîm*, defined a place, planting a garden not called Paradise but a garden with the proper name עֵדֶן, *Ēden*. This place was "from where things start," or from where the sun comes up, an indicator of location in the east.[2] And there God placed the אָדָם, the *'ādām*, the one that God had formed from the dust of the ground, in whom God breathed the breath of life.[3] God placed the earthling not in all of nature, but in "a particular and limited bit of nature," Jacques Ellul stresses.[4]

The passage continues: "The LORD God (Yhwh Elohim) took the earthling and put them in the garden of Eden to till it and keep it" (2:15). This place came with a twofold task. The first was עבד, *'bd*, to till, to toil, to work the ground, to cultivate the garden.[5] The second task was שמר, *šmr*, a term with a meaning that can include to keep, to preserve, to watch over, to keep watch, to guard, or to spy out.[6] In what sense would the earthling keep or guard the garden? Luther imagines a sort of protecting tied to the earthling's relation to the animals. In the passage, Yhwh Elohim brought every beast and bird to the earthling. For Luther, the earthling in innocence and righteousness knew the nature of each animal and was enabled to choose a name

---

[1] The subject of the sentence is named in the first instance (Yhwh Elohim), but the verb simply assumes a subject in the following instances. Genesis 2 translations here and in what follows are by the author.

[2] Martin Luther, Lectures on Genesis Chapters 1–5 (1535/1538), trans. George V. Schick, American edn., Luther's Works (L.W.) 1 (St. Louis: Concordia, 1958), 87–88; מִקֶּדֶם, *miqqedem*, Ludwig Köhler and Walter Baumgartner, *The Hebrew and Aramaic Lexicon of the Old Testament* (K.B.), trans. M. E. J. Richardson (Leiden: Brill, 1994), 1070.

[3] שָׁם, *šām*, "there," K.B., 1546. *'ādām* is translated "earthling" because of its connection with אֲדָמָה, *'ădāmâ*, the dust, earth, or ground from which the being was made (Gen. 2:7). *'ādām* does not appear to function as the proper name "Adam" until Gen. 5:1–5. Compare K.B., 14–15.

[4] Jacques Ellul, *The Meaning of the City*, trans. Dennis Pardee (Grand Rapids, Mich.: Eerdmans, 1970), 173. *Dieu crée l'homme dans un jardin, au milieu du monde. Il lui donne comme milieu de vie, comme cadre et comme moyen d'expression, cette nature particulière et fermée qui n'est pas toute la nature*, Jacques Ellul, *Sans feu ni lieu: signification biblique de la grande ville*, 2nd edn. (Paris: Table Ronde, 2003), 308.

[5] K.B., 773; Helmer Ringgren, U. Rüterswörden, and H. Simian-Yofre, "עָבַד *'ābad*; עֶבֶד *'ebed*; עֲבֹדָה *'ăbōdâ*," in *The Theological Dictionary of the Old Testament*, ed. G. Johannes Botterweck, Helmer Ringgren, and Heinz-Josef Fabry, trans. Douglas W. Stott, vol. 10 (Grand Rapids, Mich.: Eerdmans, 1999), 383.

[6] שמר is also the word for keeping covenant, keeping faith, and keeping festival, K.B., 1582; F. García López, "שָׁמַר *šāmar*; אַשְׁמֻרָה/אַשְׁמֹרֶת *'ašmûrâ/'ašmōret*; מִשְׁמָר *mišmār*; שָׁמְרָה *šōmrâ*; שְׁמֻרָה *š°murâ*; שִׁמֻּרִים *šimmurîm*; שֶׁמֶר *šemer*," in *The Theological Dictionary of the Old Testament*, ed. G. Johannes Botterweck, Helmer Ringgren, and Heinz-Josef Fabry, trans. David E. Green, vol. 15 (Grand Rapids, Mich.: Eerdmans, 2006), 279–305.

that fit the animal's nature. This naming was an indication of the earthling's rule over the animals.[7] The earthling's naming extended farther, writes Luther: "Therefore by one single word he was able to compel lions, bears, boars, tigers, and whatever else there is among the more outstanding animals to carry out whatever suited their nature."[8] In Luther's understanding, when God placed the earthling in the garden with the twofold task of tilling and keeping it,[9] the kind of protection that the first human being offered would have been very different: "By one single word, even by a nod, the earthling would have put bears and lions to flight."[10] The garden needed guarding against animals, not against fellow human beings, and that was best done not with a wall but with a word. This is one way of imagining the kept garden.

The Guarded Garden and the Guarded City

Yet a little further into the Genesis account, the earthling was banished from the garden. The earthling had been told to eat from any tree of the garden, but not from the tree of the knowledge of good and evil (2:16–17). Yet the *'āḏām* did what God forbade, breaking the command. So that the earthling might not eat from the tree of life, Yhwh Elohim sent out the earthling from the garden with the task of tilling (עבד, *'ḇḏ*) the ground, the ground from which the creature was taken (3:23). And to the east of the Garden of Eden, God placed the cherubim, and a sword to keep (שמר, *šmr*) the way to the tree of life (3:24). The same two verbs that defined the earthling's task in the garden reappear: The earthling had the task of עבד, *'ḇḏ*, tilling the ground beyond the garden, but the task of שמר, *šmr*, the task of guarding the garden, was left to the cherubim. As a response to the breaking of the command, then, God banished the earthling from this defined place, expelling the first human beings. God delegated the keeping of the garden to an angelic creature who had to prevent the earthling from entering it. With the coming of sin, a place defined and kept became a place that was guarded against human creatures. The kept garden was now the guarded garden.

After the first man and woman were banished from the garden, what future was there in keeping places? For Luther, the task of keeping or guarding was transformed by sin. No longer do human beings guard just by fending off animals with a single word, but they have to fend off fellow human beings who are "thieves and murderers."[11] "For this reason we have walls, hedges, and other defenses," Luther writes, "and yet only with difficulty can you keep unharmed what you have raised with

---

[7] L.W. 1, 119; *innocentia et iusticia; dominium in omnes animantes*, Martin Luther, Genesisvorlesung (cap. 1–17) 1535/38, D. Martin Luthers Werke (W.A.): Kritische Gesamtausgabe 42 (Weimar: Hermann Böhlaus Nachfolger, 1911), 90.

[8] L.W. 1, 119; *uno verbo; quae naturae eius conveniebant*, W.A. 42, 90.

[9] *Ut operator et custodiret eum*, W.A. 42, 77.

[10] L.W. 1, 103.

[11] Ibid., 102. *Furibus et homicidis*, W.A. 42, 78.

much toil."[12] He goes on: "Indeed, we have protection today, but it is obviously awful. It requires swords, spears, cannons, walls, redoubts, and trenches; and yet we can scarcely be safe with our families."[13] In the spirit of Luther, today there are also guns, drones, boats, passports, surveillance cameras, detention centers, and long waits at airports, but many do not feel safe. Luther describes how tilling and keeping would have been carried out in play and with great delight, something seen in the zeal of the gardener. But there are only obscure and fleeting vestiges of this delight. Now, he says, tilling and keeping are difficult and sad words.[14] For Luther, then, sin disfigures keeping into something nearly bereft of joy, taken on as a necessity because other human beings come to steal and to murder, and even so, safety is hard to come by. The guarding of places involves fortifications; it involves setting one's land apart, in opposition to other pieces of land and other human beings. After the human rebellion against God, keeping becomes guarding.

A little farther in the Genesis narrative, Cain built a city. Luther and Ellul treat this episode from Genesis 4 with some care, but they do not make much of this as an instance of a guarded place. Luther reads Cain as a wanderer who founded the city to oppose the true church, gathering his own church through childbearing out of pride and a lust for ruling.[15] Still, Luther does not take the city as indicative of the general guarding of places. Ellul begins his *The Meaning of the City* with Cain who, unsatisfied with God's promise to avenge him after his death, went his own way to build a city, to guarantee his security and that of his family along with stable relationships with animals and things.[16] Yet Ellul does not read the city as solely a protected or fortified place, citing Chinese, Indian, and then medieval European cities, the last of which he understands as defined by their charter rather than by their wall.[17] Both Luther and Ellul follow Augustine's line of thought, though they do not refer to him, when he identifies Cain with the "City of man" and Abel with "the City of God." Augustine views Cain as a citizen of the world set against God's ways who founded a city, while Abel remained a pilgrim in this world on God's way, not founding a city.[18] All read Cain's work to build a city as an act of defiance.

But perhaps the city that Cain built is in fact a divine gift to protect Cain's life, Oliver O'Donovan suggests. While Luther and Ellul are not sure about the identity

---

[12] L.W. 1, 102. *Ideo muris, sepibus et aliis munitionibus opus est, et tamen aegre servari possunt, quae magno labore coluisti,* W.A. 42, 78.

[13] L.W. 1, 103. *Hodie habemus quidem defensionem, sed plane horribilem. Opus enim est ad eam gladiis, hastis, bombardis, muris, sepibus, fossis, et tamen vix possumus cum nostris in tuto esse,* W.A. 42, 78.

[14] L.W. 1, 102–3. *Operari et custodire sunt tristia et difficilia vocabula,* W.A. 42, 78.

[15] L.W. 1, 311, 314–15. *Superbiam ac dominandi libidinem,* W.A. 42, 229, 232.

[16] *The Meaning of the City,* 2, 5; *Sans feu ni lieu,* 28, 33.

[17] *The Meaning of the City,* 149–50; *Sans feu ni lieu,* 267.

[18] Augustine, *The City of God Against the Pagans,* ed. and trans. R. W. Dyson (Cambridge: Cambridge University Press, 1998), 15.1, 634–35.

of the mark of Cain, and while they read Cain's city as an act against divine purposes, O'Donovan thinks that the editor of Genesis 4 leaves the comment about the mark of Cain hanging. Soon after, Cain built a city (4:15, 17). Following this reading, Cain killed his brother Abel out of jealousy for the favor Yhwh had shown Abel, and when Yhwh asked Cain where his brother was, Cain responded, "I do not know; am I my brother's keeper?" (4:9) Cain disavowed keeping or guarding his brother, and the blood of Abel that Cain had spilled cried out from the ground to Yhwh. Yhwh sentenced Cain to being a wanderer, but Cain protested that anyone who finds him would kill him. Cain articulated the implications of murder in the face of natural justice: The horror of murder demands infinite retribution and opens the possibility of a never-ending feud.[19] Yhwh responded by promising that if Cain were killed, the killer would be avenged sevenfold. To fend off attackers, Yhwh placed a mark on Cain, or he appointed a sign for Cain.[20] Cain moved to the east and built a city, and O'Donovan makes it possible to read this city as the very warning mark from Yhwh. The city is thus what protected Cain's life, serving as a hold on vengeance. It was the guarded stopping place for this wanderer. Insofar as the city enclosed a governed community, the city replaced private vengeance with public judgment that is limited and provisional. O'Donovan thinks the story reveals that "the purpose of political life is to set a limit to the infinite reckonings of justice."[21] Even if other commentators are correct that the mark is not the city itself, there is good reason to read the building of the city as one of a number of positive developments in human civilization.[22]

Connected with the city as a hold on vengeance, in the Hebrew Scriptures, the guarded city is also a city of refuge. O'Donovan draws attention to the institution of the cities of refuge proposed around the time of the conquest of Canaan, where a manslayer could flee and await a decision about whether the killing was truly murder.[23] The success of this arrangement depends on a public authority, but to move a step farther, its success also depends on walls and weaponry. If the next-of-kin of the recently dead person can be successfully kept from killing the manslayer, what

---

[19] Oliver O'Donovan, *The Ways of Judgment* (Grand Rapids, Mich.: Eerdmans, 2005), 66.

[20] Most modern translations render the phrase from Gen. 4:15, וַיָּשֶׂם יְהוָה לְקַיִן אוֹת, "And the LORD put a mark on Cain," though the New American Standard Bible translates it, "And the LORD appointed a sign for Cain."

[21] O'Donovan, *The Ways of Judgment*, 27.

[22] Along with Luther and Ellul, none of the following commentaries equate the mark of Cain with the city: Bill T. Arnold, *Genesis*, New Cambridge Bible Commentary (Cambridge: Cambridge University Press, 2009), 80–81; Walter Brueggemann, *Genesis*, Interpretation (Atlanta: John Knox Press, 1982), 60, 63; Laurence A. Turner, *Genesis*, 2nd edn., Readings (Sheffield: Sheffield Phoenix Press, 2009), 30–32; Claus Westermann, *Genesis 1–11: A Commentary*, trans. John Scullion S.J. (London: S.P.C.K., 1984), 314, 322, 328. Westermann writes that cities are one of many good developments in human culture in Genesis 4:17–22, ibid., 343.

[23] O'Donovan, *The Ways of Judgment*, 25. See Num. 35:6–34; Deut. 4:41–43; 19:1–13; Josh. 20:1–9.

is needed are the stone walls and the iron swords of the city.[24] And this much can be found in the Genesis 4 narrative of Cain's descendants: Tubal-cain was the first to forge instruments of bronze and iron, and his brothers were the first to make music and herd livestock (4:20–22). Their father Lamech made a boast: Lamech has killed a man, but if Cain's revenge is sevenfold, then Lamech's is seventy-sevenfold (4:24). Cain's city provided the protection that enabled revenge on an attacker, but the bronze and iron of Tubal-cain would allow for weapons that can more powerfully repel attack and avenge bloodshed.

Against this account of the city as the way forward for the human community, is there another way forward? There might be a case to be made about Seth, Adam and Eve's new child to replace Abel (4:25). Could Seth provide a way forward for the people who trust God's promise to avoid the city, walls, and weapons? In the book of Genesis, Seth's line provided some witness to the life of those like Enoch who walked with God (Elohim, 5:22, 24). Still, the Genesis narrative does not say that Seth's line produces any kind of human culture, except perhaps the relief that Noah brings, which could have been wine (5:29; 9:21). It is hard to work out how Genesis would have its readers discover Augustine's City of God as something maintained in and by a separate family of Seth. More likely, the genealogy of Genesis 4:17–22 overlaps with the genealogy of Genesis 5:1–32, especially in the persons of Enoch and Lamech (4:17–18; 5:18, 25). Descended from this line is Noah, who with his wife is the parent of all human beings after the flood (5:28; 7:7, 21).[25] An alternative comes from Jabal, the descendent of Cain, who "was the father of the those who dwell in tents and have livestock" (4:20). In the Genesis 4:17–22 genealogy, even those who have known city life move on to tents. The nomadic life remains an option, though nomads might look to the city as a place of refuge in times of threat. Either way, there appears to be one human family, a mix of city-dwellers and tent-dwellers. The city remains as "that which protects" in the Hebrew, allowing for human life to continue.[26]

Despite the institution of the city, the justice it provides is provisional. The ground still cries out, as the Letter to the Hebrews says: "Abel ... still speaks." Only God's judgment against the world could put that voice to rest, says O'Donovan.[27] The sacrifices of the Jerusalem temple could not end the demand of Abel's blood, but the writer to the Hebrews points to the heavenly Jerusalem and to Jesus, "the mediator of a new covenant," whose "sprinkled blood ... speaks a better word than

---

[24] It is plain that עִיר, 'îr, or city, refers to a walled or fortified settlement, since it is placed in opposition to חָצֵר ḥāṣēr, the village with no wall about it, in Leviticus 25:29, 31. See also Num. 13:19; Deut. 3:5; 1 Sam. 6:18. E. Otto, "עִיר 'îr," in *The Theological Dictionary of the Old Testament*, ed. G. Johannes Botterweck, Helmer Ringgren, and Heinz-Josef Fabry, trans. David E. Green, vol. 11 (Grand Rapids, Mich.: Eerdmans, 1997), 54.

[25] Oliver O'Donovan suggested the lines of thought beyond *The Ways of Judgment* regarding weaponry and the one family in private communication.

[26] The Hebrew for city, עִיר 'îr, is likely derived from the verb * 'r, to protect, Otto, "עִיר 'îr," 54.

[27] Heb. 11:4; O'Donovan, *The Ways of Judgment*, 27.

the blood of Abel."[28] The sacrifice required to respond to the demand of cosmic justice has been given in the body of Jesus, yet it is a sacrifice that brings a new start rather than destruction. As the world awaits the consummation of that new life, the guarded city foreshadows the new city to come, the new place to come.

The guarded city points to the city to come in another way. O'Donovan offers an interpretation of the city that draws on a different passage of Augustine than Luther and Ellul draw on to interpret the city-builders as beholden to the City of Man. Augustine recalls that to grow the new city of Rome, Romulus declared that all who joined him would be given impunity from their past crimes. This protection from vengeance, Augustine says, anticipates the remission of sins to come in the eternal *patria*.[29] Augustine demonstrates, then, that the asylum that earthly cities grant ·foreshadows the asylum to come in the heavenly city, when the blood of Christ satisfies all demands for retribution and brings peace to the faithful. That city takes shape as the seventy-sevenfold vengeance of Lamech is overcome by the seventy-sevenfold forgiveness of Jesus (Matt. 18:21–22).

While it is right to modestly commend the guarding of places, guarding easily falls prey to the temptation of defiance and of confident self-seeking. As a reminder of this temptation, Jacques Ellul's voice needs to be heard. As Ellul tracks the city through the canon of Scripture, he turns from Cain to Nimrod, the mighty conqueror who stood before the Lord and built cities.[30] Yet Ellul insists that God's people Israel did not build cities at God's invitation. When God formed a people, the first thing they built was a pile of rubble as witness to God.[31] The people of Israel first learned to build cities while enslaved in Egypt, and they occupied cities in Canaan that they did not build.[32] The prophets told the people in exile to seek the welfare of the city, but nowhere, writes Ellul, were the people of God told to build a city.[33] The city is subject to the curse, and the prophets spoke against Babylon and her ilk, but the city was also subject to "temporal election," says Ellul: God chose and even used Babylon.[34] And as Ellul reads the Scriptures, even though humanity chose the city as a move away from the place God had made, God "adopted" the city. God took on this human work with its idolatry and vice and made it his own: God adopted Jerusalem as a city to bear witness to God's judgment and grace.[35] As Jesus Christ came, writes Ellul, he spoke only words of rejection and woe to

---

[28] Heb. 12:24.
[29] Oliver O'Donovan, "Romulus's City: The Republic without Justice in Augustine's Political Thought" (unpublished manuscript used with permission, 2009), 16; Augustine, *City of God*, 5.17; see also 1.34, 2.29.
[30] Ellul, *The Meaning of the City*, 12.
[31] Ibid., 23; Gen. 31:43–50.
[32] Ellul, *The Meaning of the City*, 25, 27.
[33] Ibid., 72, 74.
[34] Ibid., 85.
[35] Ibid., 102–6.

the cities.[36] He rejected the settled life, wandering and indeed dying outside of the city.[37] As a man, as king, and as the living God, Jesus replaced Jerusalem with its temple and its royal aspirations, and he rendered Jerusalem common, a city like any other city.[38] Yet at the end of time, says Ellul, God will provide a wholly new city. This reading allows for no illusion that the city is praised or that the guarding of places is lauded in Scripture. Even if it is right to accept that God provides guarded places, those who dwell there tend to defy God, and at best they witness to something better to come.

The Open City

The asylum of the city looks forward to what Jesus' sacrifice makes possible: a renewed place at the end of time, an open city. Ellul points out that in Ezekiel, the vision of the future is for a Jerusalem with a new temple, a new temple that the glory of Yhwh fills (Ezek. 40:1; 43:4).[39] But in the Revelation to John, the dwelling place of θεός, *Theos*, God, is in the whole city, where God will dwell with human beings, and where they will be God's peoples (Rev. 21:3).[40] There is no temple in this city, for the Lord God Almighty and the Lamb are the temple, giving light (21:22–23). The nations will walk by that light, John relays, and the kings of the earth will bring their glory into it (21:24). For Ellul, here the nations become the *peoples* of God, retaining their plurality, their "particularity, their individual riches," and they walk by the light of God and the Lamb.[41] This is the city that Ezekiel calls יְהוָה שָׁמָּה, *Yhwh Šāmmah*, "The Lord is there" (48:35).[42]

The Lord God Almighty and the Lamb, Christ, will make their dwelling in the new Jerusalem. The city John sees on a high mountain (21:10), a city with walls, great and high, with twelve gates (21:12). The prophets have been crying, "Open the gates!" (Isa. 26:2) and declare, "your gates shall be open continually; day and night they shall not be shut" (Isa. 60:11). And so it is with the new city: "its gates will never be shut by day," nor is there night in the city lit by God and the Lamb (21:25). Ellul makes two things of this: First, while elsewhere the prophets reveal that all of nature will be transformed, in the resurrection, human beings will live only in one place,

---

[36] Ibid., 113–17.

[37] Ibid., 120–23.

[38] Ibid., 135–39.

[39] Ellul notes that a new Jerusalem is recorded in a variety of books, canonical and noncanonical: Isaiah, Ezekiel, Daniel, Zechariah, Ezra, Enoch, Jubilees, the Twelve Patriarchs, Baruch, and on to the Apocalypse, or the Revelation of Jesus Christ According to John, ibid., 183, 185, 192–93.

[40] Ibid., 185.

[41] Ibid., 193; *Sans feu ni lieu*, 342. U.B.S. 4 chooses the reading of the plural λαοὶ, *laoi*, "peoples," giving it a [B], though the singular λαός, *laos*, "people," appears in some manuscripts. Barbara Aland et al., eds., *The Greek New Testament*, 4th rev. edn., 6th printing (Stuttgart: Deutsche Bibelgesellschaft; United Bible Societies, 2001), 4.

[42] *Šāmmah* is in the locative, and the phrase might be translated "The Lord is toward there."

just as they did in Eden – not in all the earth, but in a limited, particular place. Yet this time, they will live in the city, a human work that God takes on and makes in a new way, as Ellul sees it.[43] Living in the city, the peoples will leave nature "relatively autonomous."[44] Yet on the other hand, Jerusalem is "an open city."[45] Ellul says: "This city is first of all no longer 'against' someone. It is no longer the city of war, no longer the city of slavery, no longer the world of confusion."[46] The city is no longer defined in opposition to someone else; it is circumscribed but lacks a belligerent stance. What then does the wall mean? For Ellul, "this wall no longer has the meaning of a set of defenses, of a break between inside and outside. It is rather the sign of order, of harmony, of balance, of precision."[47] This is a city defined and distinguished, yet no longer defended against other human beings in a posture of war.[48]

The future of humanity belongs in a place, then – in one city, provided by God, marked out, full of the presence of God, where the tree of life grows with leaves for the nations' healing, and where a flowing river brings life. Possessing walls with gates left open, this is a place no longer guarded against threat, though it is kept in the sense of being defined and ordered.

—

A reading of Scriptures about the genesis and fulfillment of the world with trustworthy guides has led to some answers to the questions about the place of guarding in God's world. The keeping and guarding of places is not opposed to the unfolding reign of God in Christ. From the start, God created earthlings to live in a defined place and to keep that place. This is the kept garden. Because of their rebellion, God expelled the earthlings and set a guard on their first dwelling. This is the guarded garden. When killing began, the keeping of places turned into guarding, and cities were built to stop a cycle of vengeance. This is the guarded city. Perhaps those cities were a divine gift to preserve human life, though guarding presents a temptation to forget the God who enables guarding. Still, guarded cities point toward an end to guarding; asylum within city walls foreshadows the end of vengeance achieved through the shed blood of Christ. In the end, God will provide a new city with walls and open gates, no longer defended. This is the open city.

The narrative surrounding guarded places is wider in this biblical account than it is in Hobbes' genesis narrative, but at a key point, the stories coincide. Defended

---

[43] *The Meaning of the City*, 163.

[44] Ibid., 191; *Sans feu ni lieu*, 338.

[45] *The Meaning of the City*, 193.

[46] Ibid., 192. *La ville tout d'abord n'est plus une ville "contre" quelqu'un, Sans feu ni lieu*, 340.

[47] *The Meaning of the City*, 197; *Sans feu ni lieu*, 349.

[48] The ones "written in the Lamb's book of life" (Rev. 21:27) are included, though others are kept outside the city and burned, those without faith, who remain detestable, who are wrapped up in falsehood (21:8, 27). The open city is made possible by the elimination of those who do not trust in the Lamb.

walls protect against threats from outsiders in Hobbes just as they do in the biblical narrative, after Eden and before the new Jerusalem. Hobbes envisions borders as a place of war, where sovereigns brandish their weapons and maintain forts, where no law forbids killing. In Genesis, Lamech boasts of his ability to protect himself from vengeance after he murders a man, a boast based on the defenses of his city and its weapons. Despite some convergence in this era, in the Christian faith, God's gracious rule continues even at walls and border fences. To move beyond killing at the borders and discover some Right that holds even internationally will require attention to the authority that governs the city.

GUARDS UNDER GOD: LUTHER ON PSALMS 127 AND 82

The guarding of cities is a divine provision to protect human life, but who is supposed to guard the city, and how are they to guard it? In what follows, Martin Luther's interpretation of Psalms 82 and 127 will provide guidance for a theology of political authority regarding immigration. In the church's long conversation about God's designs for earthly politics, Luther finds in the Bible an affirmation of political life as governed directly by God, independently of church authority. Luther affirms that God guards political communities, establishes political authority, and tasks those in authority with duties to judge and to protect, duties that extend to immigrants.[49]

Unless God Guards the City

Luther stresses the first verse of Psalm 127:

> Unless the LORD builds the house,
> > those who build it labor in vain.
> Unless the LORD guards the city,
> > the guard keeps watch in vain.[50]

---

[49] Accounts of Luther's theology of politics are often drawn from his occasional works like "On Temporal Authority" and "Whether Soldiers, Too, Can Be Saved." This reading looks to his biblical commentaries for the heart of his political thought. There, a view of political authority emerges as something that makes sense precisely because God has established it out of love. This stands in contrast to a dominant view from Augustine that makes sense of political life in terms of human desires and loves, where "two cities, then, have been created by two loves: that is, the earthly by love of self extending even to contempt of God, and the heavenly by love of God extending to contempt of self," *City of God*, 14.28. Guides to this reading include the teaching of Bernd Wannenwetsch along with his "'For in Its Welfare You Will Find Your Welfare': Political Realism and the Limits of the Augustinian Framework," *Political Theology* 12, no. 3 (2011): 457–65; and Philip A. Lorish, "Subjected to the Spirit: An Investigation of Luther's Political Ethics" (M.Phil. Thesis, Faculty of Theology, University of Oxford, 2010).

[50] Author's translation, following the N.R.S.V. In the Hebrew:

אִם־יְהוָה‎ לֹא־יִבְנֶה בַיִת שָׁוְא עָמְלוּ בוֹנָיו בּוֹ
אִם־יְהוָה לֹא־יִשְׁמָר־עִיר שָׁוְא שָׁקַד שׁוֹמֵר:

In the previous section, Luther described the changing nature of keeping before and after the disfiguring effects of sin. At the start, the earthling *kept* the garden from injury by animals with a single word, but after Cain murdered Abel, his descendants *guarded* their cities against human beings who come to steal and murder. Psalm 127:1 connects the theme of keeping or guarding (שָׁמַר, *šmr*) with the city (עִיר, *'îr*). The actor here is "vigilant" or "watchful" over the city, and this is a step beyond the keeping of the garden toward the city that Cain first built, the city walled and ruled.[51] This is better expressed as guarding rather than keeping: "Unless the LORD (Yhwh) guards the city, / the guard keeps watch in vain."

On Luther's reading, too few of the nations of the world know the truth of this verse. Those in authority might possess reason, cleverness, courage, and prudence; they might grow in strength and wealth, building towers and walls while they put in place wise laws. They might obtain wisdom and virtue, yet they remain "blind" if they do not know God and his work.[52] God allows governments to rise for a time, even the great empires of Assyria, Babylon, Persia, Greece, and Rome. So long as they rise through human ingenuity and pride, they will fall: "The true watchman had ceased to uphold them," Luther writes.[53] If God keeps the city, should city dwellers leave their gates open and their cities undefended, allowing attackers to destroy and kill those who dwell within?[54] No, says Luther. The psalm does not teach that those who know God should give up guarding cities. Instead, the psalm militates "against arrogance and anxiety"[55] and offers instead a faith or trust that allows God to do the worrying.[56] "Bar the gates, defend the towers and walls, put on armor, and procure supplies," Luther says.[57] "In general, [those in authority] should proceed as if there were no God and they had to rescue themselves and manage their own affairs."[58] Guard even as though God were not guarding, he says, but watch out for the condition of the heart so that it does not become arrogant or worried. The one in authority "should regard all such preparation and equipment as being the work of our Lord God under

---

[51] שָׁקַד, *šāqaḏ*, "be vigilant" or "watchful," K.B., 1638.
[52] Martin Luther, "Exposition of Psalm 127, for the Christians at Riga in Livonia (1524)," trans. Walter I. Brandt, in *Christians in Society II*, ed. Walter I. Brandt, American edn., Luther's Works (L.W.) 45 (Philadelphia: Fortress Press, 1962), 328. *Sie Gott und seyn werck nicht kennet, Predigten und Schriften 1524*, D. Martin Luthers Werke (W.A.): Kritische Gesamtausgabe 15 (Weimar: Hermann Böhlaus Nachfolger, 1899), 370. In this chapter, the spelling and capitalization of the German follows Luther's Early New High German (*Frühneuhochdeutsch*) from the Weimar edition rather than modern High German.
[53] L.W. 45, 329. *Der rechte wechter auff hoeret zu bewaren*, W.A. 15, 371.
[54] L.W. 45, 331.
[55] Ibid., 332. *Wider die vermessenheyt und sorgfelltickeyt*, W.A. 15, 373.
[56] L.W. 45, 330. *Glauben*, W.A. 15, 371.
[57] L.W. 45, 331. *Thor zu schliessen, thuern und mauren bewaren, harnisch anlagen, vorrhad schaffen*, W.A. 15, 373.
[58] L.W. 45, 331. *Und sich eben stellen, alls were keyn Gott da und muesten sich selbs erretten und selbs regiren*, W.A. 15, 373.

a mask."[59] Again, Luther states that all in authority ought to watch over the city while at the same time, in faith, entrusting this watching to God, letting God care for the city. They should remember that their work preserves the city only if God acts to preserve the city.[60] For Luther, two actors participate in an analogous act: God and human ruler both guard. Knowing that God guards the city will allow rulers to do their proper business, Luther says, without either fearfulness or false pride.[61]

This verse and Luther's commentary on it prove illuminating. Once murder becomes a possibility in human history, it is right to guard the places where women and men live. Go ahead with watching and guarding cities, the psalm suggests, but know that that guarding depends on the guarding of God, who cares to watch over human life and fend off agents of death. Those who know this verse have this edge over the most reasonable, prudent, courageous, and wise of them all: They know that their watching is only successful if God deems it right to be successful. The knowledge that, in Luther's words, their work is the "mask" under which God works frees their heart from the twin tendencies of arrogance and worry, of overconfidence and of anxiety.

The Congregation of God

Knowing that God guards the city will in decisive ways alter the practices of the human guardians of cities. For a better understanding of God's direction of those who have authority over cities, Psalm 82 through Luther's eyes proves instructive. Luther translates the first verse along these lines:

> God stands in the congregation of God
> And is Judge among the gods.[62]

While some interpret this psalm as a vindication of the one God over the many when an early Hebrew monotheism emerges from an earlier polytheism, Luther sees the psalm in a different light. Since the psalmist charges the "gods" to judge justly (v. 2) and since God tells the "gods" they will die like princes (v. 7), Luther takes this psalm to deal with worldly authority (*weltliche oberkeit*) as distinguished from

---

[59] L.W. 45, 331. *Sondern soll all solch bereytschafft und ruestunge lassen unsers Herr Gottes mummerey seyn*, W.A. 15, 373.

[60] L.W. 45, 330; W.A. 15, 371–72.

[61] L.W. 45, 335. W.A. 15, 377.

[62] "Commentary on Psalm 82 (1530)," trans. C. M. Jacobs, in *Selected Psalms II*, American ed., Luther's Works (L.W.) 13 (St. Louis: Concordia, 1956), 41. The Hebrew reads: אֱלֹהִים נִצָּב בַּעֲדַת־אֵל בְּקֶרֶב אֱלֹהִים יִשְׁפֹּט׃. Luther translates this, *Gott stehet ynn der gemeine Gotes/ Und ist richter unter den Goettern*, *Psalmenauslegungen 1529/32*, D. Martin *Luthers Werke* (W.A.): *Kritische Gesamtausgabe* 31 (Weimar: Hermann Böhlaus Nachfolger, 1913), 189. Noting the words for deities, a word-for-word translation of the Hebrew runs like this: "Elohim stands in the congregation of El; / in the midst of the elohim, [Elohim] judges."

spiritual authority within the church, with what he also calls the worldly *regiment* or the worldly "estate" (*stand*).[63] His adjective *weltlich* ought to be translated "temporal" rather than "worldly," referring to an authority belonging to this time, this age between God's act of creation and the consummation of that creation in the new heavens and the new earth.[64]

Luther responds to what he sees as folly: "mad reason" declares that human communities have come about by accident when people live side-by-side, just like when murderers and robbers live side-by side.[65] But no – as the psalm says, each human community is the congregation of God:

> For He has made, and makes, all communities. He still brings them together, feeds them, lets them grow, blesses and preserves them, gives them fields and meadows, cattle, water, air, sun, and moon, and everything they have, even body and life, as it is written in the first chapter of Genesis.[66]

This phrase, "the congregation of God," comforts those who live in human communities, knowing that God continues to care for them, but the same phrase is a threatening word against "evil-willed" rulers.[67] If they do what they like, if they do wrong to the communities they are set over, they are mistreating what is God's own.[68]

Likewise, some say that government comes about by "human will."[69] But Luther says this is wrong; the psalmist calls those in authority "gods." They are "gods" in the sense that they are divinely established and preserved, writes Luther, and rule over

---

[63] L.W. 13, 42; W.A. 31, 190.

[64] This reading of Luther's psalm commentaries and Genesis commentaries reveals traces of two predominant themes of Luther's. Here, he distinguishes two regiments, two *regimente*, as well as two estates, two *stande*. The first is well known in the English-speaking world as the doctrine of the two kingdoms, but its importance is often overplayed over against the doctrine of the three estates of *ecclesia*, *economia*, and *politia*, says Oswald Bayer, *Martin Luther's Theology: A Contemporary Interpretation* (Grand Rapids, Mich.: Eerdmans, 2008), 124–25, 324–25.

[65] L.W. 13, 46. *Die tolle kluge vernunfft*, W.A. 31, 193. Here, *tol* does not mean "great" as the contemporary High German *toll* often means, but rather "mad" or "crazy." The Early New High German term *tol* means *wahnsinnig*, "mad, insane," *geisteskrank*, "mentally ill," *durcheinander*, "in a mess, mixed up," *unvernünftig*, "unreasonable," or *töricht*, "foolish." Thus this phrase means something like "stupidly clever reason," "foolish reason," or "mad reason," Ulrich Goebel, Anja Lobenstein-Reichmann, and Oskar Reichmann, eds., Frühneuhochdeutsches Wörterbuch, vol. 5: Lfg. 2 (Berlin: de Gruyter, 2014), 902, 904, 914; *Frühneuhochdeutsches Wörterbuch*, vol. 8 (Berlin: de Gruyter, 2013), 1156, 1157; *Langenscheidt Muret-Sanders Grosswörterbuch Englisch*, völlige Neubearbeitung, vol. 2 (Berlin: Langenscheidt, 2004), 283, 436, 1031, 1032, 1094, 1125, 1134, 1168, 1181.

[66] L.W. 13, 46; English translation modified based on W.A. 31, 193.

[67] L.W. 13, 47. *Mutwillig*, W.A. 31, 194. C. M. Jacobs translates *mutwillig* as "self-willed" here and *mutwille* as "self-will" at L.W. 13, 45, 60; W.A. 31, 192, 207. The translation draws out the connection of the German word to "will," but "evil-willed" or simply "bad-minded" better captures the corrupted boldness that the term implies. Thanks to Therese Feiler for guidance with the German.

[68] L.W. 13, 47; W.A. 31, 194.

[69] L.W. 13, 44. *Menschliche wille*, W.A. 31, 191.

a human community is not just an expression of human desire, but it is God's ordinance.[70] To maintain a peaceful life for the children of Adam, God establishes all authority and government office: "It is God's servant to you for good," Luther quotes from Paul's Letter to the Romans.[71] Without peace, human beings would be threatened by wrongdoing and violence, they would have no space to teach God's word or to rear children, and they would have no opportunity to till the land and fill it.[72] To preserve God's creatures, God sets up government, giving it "the sword and the laws"; God sets up authority, and God preserves it.[73] Luther says that this follows from the first chapter of Genesis, from God's establishing and caring for human communities,[74] and the same pattern continues in the New Testament: "Our rulers ... have been established anew, through Christ, by a special word."[75] For Luther, only "believers" know these truths: that communities and the authority that guards their peace come from God as Creator and through the word given by Christ.[76]

Where is God among human communities and temporal government? In Luther's understanding, God does not merely set them going and leave them to himself. No: "'He stands in His congregation,' for the congregation is also His; and 'He judges the gods,' for the rulers, too, are His."[77] God expects certain things of both the congregation and the rulers: that human communities obey the rulers and that the rulers give good judgment and protect the peace. Luther does not allow for popular revolt, stressing subjection, but he places the judgment of rulers in God's hands. If rulers do evil, God will judge and punish them; they will not escape God.[78] But again, where is God? "God stands in the congregation," and for Luther, God stands there through priests and preachers.[79] It is wrong to speak evil of rulers in private, but it is different for those who have been given "the duty of teaching, exhorting, rebuking, comforting, in a word, of preaching the Word of God."[80] It is

---

[70] L.W. 13, 44. *Ordnung*, W.A. 31, 191–92.

[71] Romans 13:4; L.W. 13, 44; W.A. 31, 192. The American edition translates Luther's Romans 13:4 with the word "minister," but Luther's *dienerin* corresponds more closely to the English "servant" and to the Greek διάκονός, *diakonos*. Later in Romans 13, Paul calls the authorities λειτουργοὶ...θεοῦ, *leitourgoi...theou*, or "ministers of God" (13:6).

[72] L.W. 13, 44–45; W.A. 31, 192.

[73] L.W. 13, 45. *Das schwerd und gesetze*, W.A. 31, 192.

[74] L.W. 13, 46; W.A. 31, 194.

[75] L.W. 13, 48. *Unser oeberkeit ... durch Christum von newen mit sonderlichem wort bestetigt sind*, W.A. 31, 195. Luther cites Jesus' teaching from Matthew's Gospel, "Give to Caesar what is Caesar's" (Matthew 22:21), along with instruction to be subject to rulers in Romans 13:1 and the First Letter of Peter 2:13; he says there are many more such passages.

[76] L.W. 13, 46. *Die gleubingen*, W.A. 31, 194.

[77] L.W. 13, 45–46. *Er stehet ynn seiner Gemeine, denn die Gemeine ist auch sein, wideruemb, Er richtet die Goetter, denn die oberkeit ist auch sein*, W.A. 31, 193.

[78] L.W. 13, 45; W.A. 31, 193.

[79] L.W. 13, 49; W.A. 31, 196.

[80] L.W. 13, 49–50. *Denn daselbst hat er seine Priester und Prediger bestellet, welchen er das ampt befolhen hat, das sie leren, vermanen, straffen, troesten und summa, das wort Gottes treiben sollen*, W.A. 31, 196–97.

the duty of the preacher to "stand in the congregation," to speak honestly and boldly before God and the community.[81] Preachers are right to "rebuke" rulers publicly as part of their office, and such rebuke, Luther says, is "not seditious."[82] In fact, it would be more seditious to remain silent; if preachers remain silent, they would bear responsibility for the growing anger of the people and the growing tyranny of the rulers, and God as judge might allow for rebellion.[83] So, God actively judges those in authority, and God calls them to account through God's preachers.

Luther's interpretation of Psalm 82, then, brings out an understanding of government that is opposed to the statements of the U.S. Supreme Court. While it might be right that certain rulers have supreme authority over a community, it is not right that those rulers are limited only by the consent of that community. For Luther, civil authority is not just an expression of popular will, against the American assumption that looks back to Hobbes and beyond him to Marsilius of Padua. It is not the people that bestow authority to some person or assembly, but it is God who first bestows that authority. The God who sets in place offices of authority continues to judge those who hold office. Those in power must answer to the God who preserves and sustains human communities and life on earth. For Luther, the one through whom government officials hear God's directives for them is the preacher, the proclaimer of God's Word.

Judge the Weak and Rescue the Oppressed

What responsibilities might those who govern immigration have before God? The next three verses of Psalm 82, read alongside Luther, reveal more:

> [2] "How long will you judge unjustly
> and show partiality to the wicked?
>
> [3] Judge the weak and the orphan;
> do justice to the afflicted and the destitute.
>
> [4] Rescue the oppressed and the needy;
> snatch them out of the hand of the wicked."[84]

These verses draw out the task of government as the task of *judging* (שׁפט, *šft*), which includes settling a case, arbitrating a dispute, deciding between right and wrong, or

---

[81] L.W. 13, 49; W.A. 31, 196.

[82] L.W. 13, 50. *Straffen; nicht auffrhuerissch*, W.A. 31, 197.

[83] L.W. 13, 50–51; W.A. 31, 197–98.

[84] Author's translation. Though "give justice" (R.S.V., N.R.S.V., E.S.V.) or "vindicate" (N.A.S.B.) communicates more simply in English, I maintain the command "judge" in v. 3 to reflect the singular Hebrew verb שְׁפטוּ, *šiftû*. Translations render the second half of v. 3, עָנִי וָרֵשׁ הַצְדִּיקוּ, alternatively as "do justice to the afflicted and destitute" (A.V., N.A.S.B.), "maintain the right" (R.S.V., N.R.S.V., and E.S.V.), or "be fair" (N.J.B.). Luther says that everyone in authority should have these verses painted on their walls, on their beds, over their tables, and on their clothes – imagine the sight! L.W. 13, 51; W.A. 31, 198.

praising and punishing.[85] This task of *judging* is the same task that Elohim carries out, recalling the mirrored activity of *guarding* in Psalm 127 that both Yhwh and the watchman carry out.[86] "Judge the weak and orphan," God commands the authorities God has established. Can judging amount to anything good? Yes, if the task of judgment means treating disputants fairly, not favoring the rich, the strong, or the powerful. Luther draws from this verse one of his virtues for rulers, "to help the poor, the orphans, and the widows to justice, and to further their cause."[87] Luther thinks this help is best achieved when a city is governed by good laws and customs so that relationships are ordered well and businesses are honest. He writes that it is a great thing to endow a hospital, but a much greater thing to turn a whole land into a hospital, where the land is so ordered by law that no one has to become a beggar.[88]

Luther takes the "orphan" of verse 3 as shorthand for the orphan and the widow, though the context of the Old Testament demands a further step to include the sojourner, the stranger, or the migrant. The widow, the orphan, and the migrant: This is the star trio of good government in the Old Testament; judgment is just if and only if the widow, the orphan, and the migrant are not mistreated.[89] These three were those left outside the Israelite household and thus without a source of food, shelter, and protection: the widow and the orphan without a head of household, and

[85] K.B., 1622–26.

[86] Luther draws from this verse the first virtue (*tugent*) of three for rulers: "The first [virtue] is that they can secure justice for those who fear God and repress those who are godless," L.W. 13, 52. *Die erst ist, das sie koennen recht schafffen den Gottfuerchtigen und steuren den Gottlosen,* W.A. 31, 199. Because he translates רְשָׁעִים, *rešā 'îm*, as *Gotlossen,* "godless," Luther reads verse 2 as "How long will you judge unjustly / and prefer the persons of the godless?" L.W. 13, 41. *Wie lange wolt yhr unrecht richten / Und der Gottlosen person furzihen?,* W.A. 31, 189. This leads him to say that the first virtue of rulers is to protect those who fear God and to suppress the teaching of heresy, L.W. 13, 52–53, 61–67; W.A. 31, 199–200, 207–13. It is better to translate *rešā 'îm* as "wicked" or "guilty," so that verse 2 asks how long the ruler will show partiality to the "wicked," K.B., 1295. In the Hebrew Scriptures, guilt is ultimately guilt before God, but it is better to interpret this verse as dealing with wrongdoing in general rather than wrong teaching about God. Still, it must be acknowledged that when Luther gives princes authority over the teaching of the churches, he allows princes room to do things that might work against him and his followers. When he allows princes to suppress teaching against the Creed and resolve conflicts between the "papists" (*die Papisten*) and "my Lutherans" (*meine Lutherisschen*), he is driven by a concern for right teaching and peace that may not work in his favor, L.W. 13, 62–63; W.A. 31, 209.

[87] L.W. 13, 53. *Die ander tugent, das sie den elenden, waisen und widwen zum recht helffen und yhre sachen foddern,* W.A. 31, 200.

[88] Luther charges those in authority to keep a close eye on financial transactions to prevent extortion, robbing, and cheating. Without this watchful care, those of the lowest social status will be oppressed, L.W. 13, 53–54; W.A. 31, 200.

[89] אַלְמָנָה, *almānâ,* "widow,"; יָתוֹם, *yāṭôm,* "fatherless," and גֵּר, *gēr,* "migrant." See the Note to the Reader for the decision to translate *gēr* as "migrant." For a contrary account of the laws that guard this trio, see Harold V. Bennett, *Injustice Made Legal: Deuteronomic Law and the Plight of Widows, Strangers, and Orphans in Ancient Israel* (Grand Rapids, Mich.: Eerdmans, 2002), ix, 11, 22, who draws on critical theory and social-scientific study of the Hebrew Bible to argue that the laws in Deuteronomy that appear to protect these three in fact serve to oppress them further.

the migrant without local ties. The trio first appears in the Book of the Covenant, the short law code of Exodus 20–23, where Yhwh commands Israel not to wrong or oppress the widow, the orphan, or the migrant.[90] Yhwh invokes Israel's history as migrants in the land of Egypt as reason not to oppress migrants among Israel (Ex. 22:21; 23:9). Also, Yhwh adds a warning: When these three on the margins are mistreated, they will cry out, and I will listen to them; I will avenge them by killing the oppressing Israelites and leaving their wives and children as widows and orphans (22:22–24).[91]

When Psalm 82 tells those in authority, "Judge the weak and the orphan; do justice to the afflicted and the destitute," the psalm carries forward this tradition. It implies that intrinsic to the right use of political authority is proper judgment of those who are most vulnerable. Among these is the migrant, the one from outside the community who comes to stay. Even when human authorities neglect this responsibility, God lends God's ear in a special way to the one from outside the community, as in Exodus 22. This marks God's ongoing activity as judge, regardless of whether government officials are faithful in shielding the migrant from harm.

"Rescue!" The imperative heralds verse 4. And rescue not just "the weak and the needy," as many English translations have it. The Hebrew terms include a dimension of oppression and powerlessness: "Rescue the oppressed and the needy."[92] The second half of the verse demands dramatic action: "Snatch them out of the hand of the wicked," take them away, extricate them from the clutches of wrongdoers.[93] In this verse Luther finds his third virtue of the ruler: to "protect and guard against violence and force. This," he says, "is called peacemaking."[94] While the last verse spoke of the law, this verse deals with the sword. It is right that rulers protect those who are helpless from the onslaught of the violent; those entrusted to the prince deserve to live in safety and peace. Luther thus orients the sword toward peace: Arms exist to maintain peace. Here, Luther concurs with the just war tradition: Do not begin a war or work for it; avoid it if at all possible.[95] Luther describes what peace

---

[90] The code follows the giving of the Ten Commandments in Ex. 20:1–21, stretching from 20:22 to 23:19, and concluding with a promise in 23:20–33 that Yhwh will clear space for Israel to live in Canaan.

[91] Yhwh repeats this warning when he forbids leaving a person to face the night without their cloak, again commanding the protection of the most vulnerable (22:26–27). The trio appears again in Psalm 146: Yhwh's reign is distinguished from that of the human princes by this: "Yhwh guards (שֹׁמֵר) the migrants; he upholds the widow and the fatherless" (146:9a, b, author's translation).

[92] The R.S.V., N.R.S.V., E.S.V., N.I.V., N.A.S.B., and N.J.B. translate v. 4a as "Rescue the weak and the needy." The first term, דַּל, *dal*, also means "powerless" or "oppressed," and the second, אֶבְיוֹן, *'ebyōn*, also means "oppressed," K.B., 5, 221–22. I translate the pair "the oppressed and the needy" to indicate the power relationship of oppression that the two connote.

[93] The verb is הַצִּילוּ, *haṣṣîlû*, Hiphil of נצל, *nṣl*, meaning "to tear from, . . . remove, withdraw, . . . pull out," K.B., 717.

[94] L.W. 13, 55. *Die dritte tugent ist, das sie koennen schuetzen und schirmen widder frevel und gewalt, das heisst frieden schaffen,* W.A. 31, 201.

[95] L.W. 13, 57; W.A. 31, 203–4.

brings: "It is from peace that we have our bodies and lives, wives and children, houses and homes, all our members – hands, feet, eyes – and all our health and liberty."[96] And for Luther it is not only arms but walls that guarantee the integrity of body and home: "within these walls of peace we sit secure."[97] Luther envisions a peaceful realm, a city or land armed at the edges so that within there might not be danger or fear. Without peace, life is "half a hell,"[98] he says, but a strong and peaceful city is a "heavenly stronghold."[99] He writes that the keeping of peace does not depend on monks and priests but on the divinely given work of the "gods," the authorities.[100] Protecting a realm of peace is a high, God-given task.

Protecting a place is not just an expression of the desires of the people to protect themselves, then. For Luther, that protection is something that comes from God, bestowed on certain office holders, who are given the unique task of holding the sword and protecting their subjects within walls. It is not the case, as in *Chae Chan Ping v. United States*, that the people judge for themselves what constitutes peace and good order, or that the people can do what they want when they judge that nonmembers threaten that peace and order. Rather, God establishes authority and directs it to protect the vulnerable. Following the logic of two of the Old Testament collections of laws in the spirit of Luther's interpretation, it is right to say that the vulnerable include those who come from far away to stay, migrants.

Arise, O God

Psalm 82 presents divine priorities for government: that authorities are to judge rightly, to shield the poor, and to protect the vulnerable against violent attack. But as the psalmist writes, the fact of the matter is different: The "gods," the rulers, do not carry out their duties, and so the foundations of the earth shake (82:5). These "gods" will die like any mortal; they will fall (82:7). The psalmist concludes by invoking Elohim:

> [8] Arise, O God, judge the earth!
> For it is You who possesses all the nations.[101]

---

[96] L.W. 13, 55; W.A. 31, 202.

[97] L.W. 13, 55. *Wir. . .sitzen sicher ynn dieser mauren des friedes*, W.A. 31, 202.

[98] L.W. 13, 55. *Eine halbe Helle*, W.A. 31, 202.

[99] L.W. 13, 56. *Da sihe nu, was fuer eine Keiserliche, ja himelissche burg ein solcher Fuerst bawen kan, seine unterthan zu schuetzen*, W.A. 31, 203.

[100] L.W. 13, 56; W.A. 31, 202–3.

[101] N.A.S.B. Luther translates verse 8b as *Denn du erbest unter allen heiden*, where *erbest* means "you inherit," W.A. 31, 189, 218. Other English translations render the word תִּנְחַל, *ṭinḥal*, in terms of inheritance. Norman C. Habel surveys the literature and decides that the verb נָחַל, *nāḥal*, and the noun נַחֲלָה, *naḥᵃlâ*, usually do not have to do with the allotment of land after death, but more simply with the division of property. The *naḥᵃlâ* thus is the "portion, share, entitlement, allotment, and rightful property," *The Land Is Mine: Six Biblical Land Ideologies* (Minneapolis: Fortress Press, 1995), 35.

In a sense, this verse reiterates what the whole psalm promises: that Elohim judges in an ongoing way, and the peoples beyond Israel belong to him. But Luther emphasizes a different sense of the verse, reading it as a prayer for a better future. Disenchanted with the failings of human governments, the psalmist "prays for another government and kingdom," according to Luther.[102] This God that the psalm names is Jesus Christ, Luther says, who alone is "overlord" of all the earth.[103] It is the kingdom of Christ that the psalmist looks for: "Over and above temporal righteousness, wisdom, and power, although they are godly work, there is need for another kingdom, in which there is another righteousness, wisdom, and power."[104]

—

In response to the strong claims that the federal U.S. government has plenary power over immigration, a reading of Psalms 127 and 82 guided by Martin Luther qualifies those claims. Psalm 127 makes plain that those who guard the city guard it under God, so that the power to guard is delegated rather than sovereign in some independent way. Psalm 82 declares that government is a divinely given task for this era, a task of judgment under God's judgment, a task of judgment that the interpreter of God's Word must call to account. The psalm draws attention to two virtues of those in authority under God: that they shield the powerless, even the migrant, from harm, and that they shield those under their authority with laws, sword, and walls. While commending these virtues, the psalmist speaks in a setting that resembles the setting of modern U.S. immigration law: Temporal authorities claim independent sovereignty to the neglect of their duties, and the earth quakes. This is a setting in which to follow the psalmist in verse 8 as he cries out to God, hoping for another kingdom that is revealed as Christ's.

What does this mean for the claims of the federal United States government to sovereignty? It means that God delegates governmental authority, and so government cannot be understood as sovereign in an ultimate sense. The guarding of places is limited to this era, and it is subject to the ongoing judgment of God. It serves some good for a people to be independent of the governance of other peoples, but independence is only one good among many. Government is tasked with preserving other goods as well: here, with Luther, protecting the helpless and oppressed. Immigrants, then, must not be understood as pawns in a game of sovereignty. The U.S. government has responsibilities to protect immigrants' wellbeing, responsibilities that are not trumped by the effort to maintain

---

[102] L.W. 13, 72. *Bittet er umb ein ander regiment und Reich*, W.A. 31, 218.

[103] L.W. 13, 72. *Oberherr*, W.A. 31, 218.

[104] Translation modified from L.W. 13, 72. *Also sehen wir, das uber die welltliche gerechtigkeit, weisheit, gewalt, obs wol auch Goettliche werck sind, noch ein ander Reich not ist, darin man eine andere gerechtigkeit, weisheit, gewalt finde*, W.A. 31, 218. C. M. Jacob's English translation misses the phrase *obs wol auch Goettliche werck sind*, "although they are godly work."

independent power. Authority over immigration is not plenary or unlimited as in U.S. law, nor is it a good in itself. The government of immigration must serve goods other than itself.

LANDS GRANTED AND TAKEN AWAY:
THEOLOGICAL INTERPRETERS ON DEUTERONOMY 2–3

Cities are a divine provision to preserve human life, and God oversees those who watch over cities. What, then, of larger tracts of land, aggregates of towns, pasture, farmland, wilderness, and waterways? Within divine plans to bless and save the world, do lands belong to peoples, and do they have some significance? Chapter 2 drew on Karl Barth's account of the nations within the wider biblical narrative of salvation. This section asks about national lands, drawing on a side story within the main story of God's love for Israel, Jesus, and the church.[105] Through the account of Israel's encounters with other nations on their journey from Egypt in Deuteronomy, chapters 2 and 3, and with the assistance of theologically attuned contemporary Hebrew Bible scholars, the answer to the question is a qualified "yes": National lands do have a place within the history of redemption, but with their possession comes requirements linked to their giver.[106]

Those who pray the Psalms perceive an aspect of the human condition that frames an account of national lands drawn from Deuteronomy:

> Hear my prayer, O LORD,
> and give ear to my cry;
> do not hold your peace at my tears!
> For I am a migrant with you,
> a resident, like all my fathers.[107]

Here, human beings are first human beings before God, creatures who can claim no rights against God. Yet out of love, God listens to those who address God and enables them to enter God's presence. They are newcomers, invited in to speak to God.[108]

---

[105] Theological discussions about bounded national lands often invoke brief phrases from the Song of Moses (Deut. 32:8–9) and Paul's speech at the Areopagus (Acts 17:26–27).

[106] I am grateful to J. G. McConville for suggesting I look at Deuteronomy 2–3 to help address these questions. An earlier, abbreviated version of this section appears in Robert W. Heimburger, "Migration through the Eyes of Faith: God's People, National Lands, and Universities," *IFES Word & World*, no. 1 (May 2016): 4–10, used with permission.

[107] "I am a *gēr* with you, a תּוֹשָׁב, *tôšāḇ*," Ps. 39:12, author's translation, modified from the E.S.V. *Tôšāḇ* remains ambiguous because of its infrequent use in the Hebrew Scriptures, but it seems to indicate someone who comes from outside the community to reside and settle, *K.B.*, 1712–13. Here it is translated "resident."

[108] On this theme, see Georges Chawkat Moucarry, "The Alien According to the Torah," trans. Joye Smith, *Themelios* 14 (1988): 17–20.

Elsewhere in the Psalms, it becomes clear that a similar pattern occurs for land. Human beings are guests in a world that is already God's: "The earth is the LORD's and everything in it, the world, and all who live in it."[109] On a narrower scale, the experience of Israel is not one of owning land. It is one of receiving land as a gift. In the Book of Deuteronomy, the land of Israel is more than just land. Again and again, it is "the land that the LORD (Yhwh) our God is giving us."[110] Elsewhere in the Pentateuch, limitations on the sale of land include this declaration: "The land is mine. For you are migrants and residents with me."[111] Land first belongs to Yhwh, Israel receives land as a gift from a divine landlord, and Israel remains a tenant on that land.

Do the other nations also receive land from God, or is Israel's experience unique? In Deuteronomy, an answer arises out of a message of a God who migrates with a migrant people. As God's people reach the River Jordan in sight of the land God is giving them after wandering in the wilderness for years, Moses reminds them of what has been happening since Yhwh brought their mothers and fathers up from Egypt. In his first speech, he tells them that on their journey to the land that Yhwh their God is giving them, "You have seen how the LORD your God carried you, as a man carries his son, all the way that you went until you came to this place" (1:31). Even though they did not trust in God, Moses says, "the LORD your God . . . went before you in the way to seek you out a place to pitch your tents, in fire by night and in the cloud by day, to show you by what way you should go" (1:32–33). This God migrated with the people, carrying them along the way and going ahead of them to show them the way.

In the same speech, Moses reminds Israel what Yhwh told them as they met other peoples on their way:

> ¹Then we turned and journeyed into the wilderness in the direction of the Red Sea, as the LORD told me. And for many days we traveled around Mount Seir. ²Then the LORD said to me, ³ "You have been traveling around this mountain country long enough. Turn northward ⁴and command the people, 'You are about to pass through the territory of your brothers, the people of Esau, who live in Seir; and they will be afraid of you. So be very careful. ⁵Do not contend with them, for I will not give you any of their land, no, not so much as for the sole of the foot to tread on, because I have given Mount Seir to Esau as a possession. ⁶You shall purchase food from them with money, that you may eat, and you shall also buy water from them with money, that you may drink. ⁷For the LORD your God has blessed you in all the work of your hands. He knows your going through this great wilderness. These forty years the LORD your God has been with you. You have lacked nothing.'" ⁸So we went on, away from our brothers, the people of Esau, who live in Seir, away from the Arabah road from Elath and Ezion-geber (2:1–8a).

---

[109] Ps. 24:1, N.I.V.
[110] Variations on this phrase occur in Deut. 1:20, 25; 2:29; 3:20; 4:1, 21; and beyond.
[111] *Gērîm* and *tôšābîm*, Leviticus 25:23b, author's translation.

In Moses' telling, the same pattern happened twice more after Israel passed the descendants of Esau, the Edomites.[112] As Israel approached Moab (2:8b-16) and then Ammon (2:16–25), Yhwh told Moses not to provoke these peoples to war, since Yhwh had already given the Moabites and the Ammonites territories as possessions. Along the way, the passage names peoples that preceded Esau, Moab, and Ammon in their territories. Regarding Esau, the preacher Moses recounts that Esau dispossessed the Horites, just as Israel dispossessed peoples in the land Yhwh gave them (2:12),[113] and Yhwh destroyed the Horites before Esau (2:22). After encountering three nations whose territories God did not give to Israel as a possession, the pattern shifted as they met Sihon, king of Heshbon (2:24–37), and Og, king of Bashan (3:1–7): Yhwh gave these lands to Israel to possess. Within a narrative focused on Israel, the passage displays a remarkable degree of attention to the lands and even the liberation of other nations.[114]

In the narrative, a phrase stands out: "You are about to pass through the territory of your brothers and sisters." As the people of Yhwh traveled toward the land that Yhwh was giving them, they passed through – or passed by – the lands and territories of other peoples. The word "territory," from the Hebrew גְּבוּל, *gᵉbûl*, can also be translated as "border," and so J. G. McConville translates the phrase from verse 4 as "You are about to cross the border of your brothers."[115] In the passage from Deuteronomy, river gorges marked many of the borders (2:13–14, 24, 36, 37; 3:8, 16, 17),[116] and the edges of other territories were marked by a sea (3:17), a mountain (3:9), and two cities (3:10). In the Ancient Near East, monarchical authority might have radiated from fortresses and cities, leaving boundaries fuzzy, but in this narrative many boundaries were clear.[117] In the parallel telling of Israel's encounter with Edom in the Book of Numbers, Moses sent messengers to the king of Edom, asking permission to pass through his territory (Num. 20:16–17, 21).[118] Later in

---

[112] Moses refers to the people with the familiar term of their ancestor Esau, the brother of Jacob/Israel. The children of Esau were otherwise known as Edom; see Gen. 32:3–4.

[113] The Hebrew text shifts here to express Israel's dispossession in the past tense.

[114] Gerhard von Rad remarks with surprise on Israel's attention to histories that do not affect its own, *Deuteronomy: A Commentary*, trans. Dorothea M. Barton (London: S.C.M., 1966), 43.

[115] Magnus Ottosson, "גְּבוּל gᵉbûl; גָּבַל gābal; גְּבוּלָה gᵉbûlâ," in *The Theological Dictionary of the Old Testament*, ed. G. Johannes Botterweck and Helmer Ringgren, trans. J. T. Willis, vol. 2 (Grand Rapids, Mich.: Eerdmans, 1975), 361–66; J. G. McConville, *Deuteronomy*, Apollos Old Testament Commentary 5 (Leicester, England: Apollos; Downers Grove, Ill.: InterVarsity Press, 2002), 77.

[116] What the E.S.V. renders as "brook" or "river," the N.R.S.V. renders "Wadi," and McConville explains that this is a river gorge, *Deuteronomy*, 84.

[117] Elsewhere in the Old Testament, the term *gᵉbûl* refers to the borders of national lands (e.g., 1 Kings 4:21, 1 Samuel 27:1). The term also applies to the limit of family lands, which Yhwh establishes to protect the vulnerable. See Deut. 19:14, 27:17; Proverbs 15:25; Job 24:1ff; 1 Kings 21.

[118] In Numbers 20:14–21, the king of Edom refused to allow Israel to pass through his territory. In the Deuteronomy passage, it is the Edomites who were afraid (2:4), and in the Septuagint, Israel went through Moab, but the Masoretic Text leaves the ending ambiguous, saying that the Israelites went away from their brothers (2:8a), McConville, *Deuteronomy*, 79, 83.

Deuteronomy, as God's people approached Heshbon, Moses sent messengers to ask if they could pass through, buying food and water, but God hardened King Sihon's spirit and gave the people possession of Heshbon (Deut. 2:24–37). Along with Moab and Ammon, then, Edom had a territory with borders, and on one telling, Israel had to ask Edom permission to pass through its land. In the narrative of Deuteronomy, nations other than Israel have territories and exercise control over passage through their borders.[119]

Another phrase stands out in the Deuteronomy narrative. As the people approached the Edomites, Yhwh told them, "Do not contend with them, for I will not give you any of their land, no, not so much as for the sole of the foot to tread on, because I have given Mount Seir to Esau as a possession" (2:5). Yhwh said the same about the lands of Moab (2:9) and Ammon (2:19): The people were not to fight them, because Yhwh had given them land as a possession. In a surprising way, the pattern that applied to Israel throughout Deuteronomy here applied to three other nations. What was this pattern, according to interpreters? McConville reads the book as a story of giving (נתַן, *nātan*): Yhwh gave the land and everything in it to Israel, and under the covenant that Yhwh established, Israel was to give in return. As an example, the people of Yhwh were to give freely to the poor, without their heart begrudging their brothers and sisters.[120] The way that Yhwh gave the land, the recipients were not free to do whatever they like with the land. They were subject to an agreement laid out in the book of Deuteronomy, a typical Ancient Near Eastern treaty in which an overlord granted the use of land to a vassal lord, according to Habel and Lohfink.[121] Israel was given the privilege of enjoying something belonging to another, writes Waltke,[122] and Israel remained responsible to this divine Other.

---

[119] James K. Hoffmeier is a rare theological writer on migration who highlights territories and borders in the Tanakh. He begins his biblical survey by drawing on the Edom episode to conclude that "nations could and did control their borders and determined who could pass through their land," *The Immigration Crisis: Immigrants, Aliens, and the Bible* (Wheaton, Ill.: Crossway, 2009), 33.

[120] Deut. 15:7-11; J. G. McConville, *Law and Theology in Deuteronomy*, Journal for the Study of the Old Testament Supplement Series 33 (Sheffield: J.S.O.T., 1984), 11–13.

[121] Habel, *The Land Is Mine*, 44. Deuteronomy includes statutes Israel must follow (12:2—26:15), a series of declarations (26:16–19), a ceremony of sacrifice (27:1–8), and a list of blessings and curses (27:9—28:68), Norbert Lohfink, "יָרַשׁ *yāraš*; יְרֵשָׁה *yᵉrēšâ*; יְרֻשָּׁה *yᵉruššâ*; מוֹרָשׁ *môrāš*; מוֹרָשָׁה *môrāšâ*," in *The Theological Dictionary of the Old Testament*, ed. G. Johannes Botterweck and Helmer Ringgren, trans. David E. Green, vol. 6 (Grand Rapids, Mich.: Eerdmans, 1990), 385. See also Moshe Weinfeld, who finds parallels between Deut. 1–4 and Hittite treaties, where overlords granted lands to vassals and limit them to their lands, *Deuteronomy and the Deuteronomic School* (Oxford: Clarendon Press, 1972), 72. Similar prohibitions on trespass extended to Sumerians and were basic to Ancient Near Eastern treaties, he claims, ibid., 61n3, 73.

[122] *An Old Testament Theology: An Exegetical, Canonical, and Thematic Approach* (Grand Rapids, Mich.: Zondervan, 2007), 537.

On Brueggemann's telling of the land grant, the land was given for Israel's "satiation."[123] Deuteronomy describes "a good land" flowing with water, full of wheat, barley, figs, and pomegranates, "a land in which you will eat bread without scarcity ... You shall eat and be full" (8:9-10). But the land served as a temptation, its abundance an opportunity to forget God.[124] The land also brought responsibilities. In Brueggemann's summary, Israel was (1) forbidden from making images of other gods, (2) was to carry on the Sabbath practices of freeing slaves and letting the land rest, and (3) was to maintain justice for those who lacked standing in the community.[125] These were those who have "no allotment or portion among you," and among these was the *gēr*, the migrant.[126] If God's people did not carry out these tasks of worship, Sabbath, and judgment, according to the preacher they would "soon utterly perish from the land."[127]

To hold on to her lands, then, God required Israel to judge the vulnerable outsider fairly. This requirement for possessing lands will reward closer attention since it relates to this work's inquiry into the governance of migration under God's government. Deuteronomy 10:12–22 develops the requirement of justice for the vulnerable as flowing out of Yhwh's activity toward Yhwh's people.[128] The passage calls Israel to walk in Yhwh's ways, reminding the people that although Yhwh owns all the heavens and the earth, Yhwh's heart is attached in love to Israel (vv. 12–15). In response, Moses tells Israel, "circumcise therefore the foreskin of your heart" (v. 16). What would it mean to have a heart set aside and purified after the fashion of a circumcision? Look at the way that Yhwh judges, the preacher suggests: "For the LORD your God is God of gods and Lord of lords, the great, the mighty, and the awesome God, who is not partial and takes no bribe" (v. 17). Yhwh's righteous judgment is distinguished by this: "The LORD executes judgment for the fatherless and the widow, and loves the migrant (*gēr*), giving them food and clothing."[129] The preacher might be expected to say that Yhwh executes judgment for the migrant, but he points to divine love. It is part of who this God is that God demonstrates love

---

[123] Walter Brueggemann, *The Land: Place as Gift, Promise, and Challenge in Biblical Faith*, 2nd edn. (Philadelphia: Fortress Press, 2002), 46.

[124] Ibid., 50.

[125] Ibid., 58–61.

[126] Deut. 14:27, author's translation. This verse deals specifically with the Levite, who was allotted no land. חֵלֶק, *ḥēleq* is best translated "allotment," and נַחֲלָה, *naḥᵃlâ*, "portion." See p. 112 note 101; K.B., 323. See the Note to the Reader for the decision to translate *gēr* as "migrant."

[127] Deut. 4:26; see also 11:17; 30:18.

[128] Mark Glanville sets this passage within the broader economy in Deuteronomy of God's generosity, the people's response of thanksgiving, and the people's ensuing "generosity, justice, and inclusion," "Immigration, Refugees, and the Old Testament," *Comment: Public Theology for the Common Good*, December 12, 2011, www.cardus.ca/comment/article/3015/immigration-refugees-and-the-old-testament/; see also his "The *Gēr* in Deuteronomy: An Ethic of Inclusivism?" (Ph.D. Thesis, Trinity College Bristol, forthcoming).

[129] V. 18, author's translation. See the Note to the Reader for the decision to translate *gēr* as "migrant."

for the outsider, the migrant. Moses calls the people to imitate not only Yhwh's judgment but also Yhwh's love: "You all shall love the migrant, for you were migrants in the land of Egypt."[130] The Hebrew verb translated "love" has a dual sense, and it can be read as a command as well as a statement about the future. So, "You all shall love the migrant" means both "I command you all to love the migrant" and "I promise, you all will love the migrant."[131] Such love demonstrates proper "fear" of Yhwh: right worship of the one who loved Israel first (v. 20). In response to Yhwh's giving, judging, and loving, Israel was commanded and enabled to love like Yhwh does, as a community showing love to the vulnerable person who has come from afar. This is one aspect of what was required if Israel was going to continue living in the land Yhwh was giving them.

This is the pattern of Yhwh's land grant to Israel, and something of the pattern applied to other nations in the early chapters of Deuteronomy. In the passage, Yhwh does not only own Canaan and grant it to Israel, but Yhwh granted another part of the earth to Edom as a "possession" (יְרֻשָּׁה, $y^eru\check{s}\check{s}\hat{a}$). This word also appears in forms of the verb יָרַשׁ $y\bar{a}ra\check{s}$, translated "possess" or "dispossess," and it receives a special use in the early chapters of Deuteronomy.[132] According to Lohfink, $y\bar{a}ra\check{s}$ means

---

[130] V. 19, author's translation.

[131] The verb here, וַאֲהַבְתֶּם, $va\,'^ahabtem$, is a *Vav* consecutive Qal perfect second-person masculine plural verb lacking a preceding verb. It can be read as indicating a command, as S. R. Driver judges, "you must love" the migrant, A Treatise on the Use of the Tenses in Hebrew, 3rd rev. edn. (Oxford: Clarendon Press, 1892), 141. Following Driver's interpretation of the *Vav* consecutive perfect as taking on the meaning of the imperfect, the word can also be read in its parallel sense as indicating the future, "you shall, you will, you are going to love" the migrant (140–41). Alternatively, if the punctuation at the end of vv. 17 and 18 is taken away, the *Vav* consecutive perfect follows the Qal imperfect verbs of v. 17 and the participles of v. 18. The *Vav* consecutive perfect following the imperfect denotes the future, according to J. Weingreen, permitting the translation "you will love" the migrant, A *Practical Grammar for Classical Hebrew*, 2nd edn. (Oxford: Clarendon Press, 1959), 91. In J. C. L. Gibson's more recent update of Davidson's Hebrew grammar, as a *Vav* consecutive perfect, $va\,'^ahabtem$ may begin an independent clause about the future following on from a prior statement, *Davidson's Introductory Hebrew Grammar: Syntax*, 4th edn. (Edinburgh: T. & T. Clark, 1994), 88. On this reading, "You will love" the migrant follows from the statement in v. 17 involving two imperfect verbs, that Yhwh does not prefer persons and does not take bribes, or it follows from the statements in v. 15 that Yhwh attached his heart in love to Israel's fathers and is choosing their offspring, with a perfect and a *Vav* consecutive imperfect verb. The love of the migrant is thus what will happen because of Yhwh's character as judge and Yhwh's covenant love with Israel. Alternatively, if the *Vav* consecutive perfect has a special relationship with the imperfect verbs of v. 17, the passage is either a future indicative, or it has a modal or contingent meaning (Gibson 92–93). The phrase would then mean either "you will love the migrant, it is sure," or "I want you to love the migrant," or "you are commanded to love the migrant." On these accounts, the meaning of the Hebrew is unclear, but the clues point to a multivalent meaning that combines a promise about loving the migrant with a command to love the migrant.

[132] Where much of the Hebrew Bible would use the noun $nah^al\hat{a}$ and the verb $n\bar{a}hal$ to speak of the division or allotment of lands and possessions, Deuteronomy 2–3 utilizes the distinctive vocabulary of $y^eru\check{s}\check{s}\hat{a}$ and $y\bar{a}ra\check{s}$. Like $nah^al\hat{a}$, $y^eru\check{s}\check{s}\hat{a}$ is sometimes translated as "inheritance," but it is better translated as "possession"; see p. 112 note 101.

to "take formal possession of real property acquired by virtue of certain rights."[133] On this telling, in Deuteronomy 2–3 Yhwh granted the land to a nation, and then the nation occupied that land. Indeed, in the enfolding story of Edom, Yhwh granted the land to Edom as a possession, Yhwh destroyed the Horites before Edom, and Edom dispossessed (יִירָשֻׁם) the Horites and settled in their place (2:5, 12, 22).

A clue about what it means to take possession came when God told Israel about the Edomites, "I will not give you any of their land, no, not so much as for the sole of the foot to tread on" (2:5b).[134] A later passage in Deuteronomy reiterates this pattern, when Yhwh promised to bless Israel if they kept his command by driving out nations before them so that they might dispossess (*yāraš*) these nations. "Every place which the sole of your foot treads shall be yours," Yhwh said through the preacher, going on to tell the people the extent of the territory (*gᵉḇûl*) they will receive (Deut. 11:24). These passages could reflect a ceremony of treading on the land to claim it as a possession, or they could mean something simpler: To possess a territory is to tread on it, to walk back and forth through it. Either way, in Deuteronomy not only Israel but also other nations possessed land by treading on it. When Yhwh forbade Israel from treading on the land of Edom, Yhwh declared the hill country of Seir to be Edom's to tread on with the sole of the foot, Edom's to possess.[135]

The Deuteronomy account suggests that Yhwh not only gives lands to possess but also to dispossess, with the same verb, *yāraš*, indicating both possession and dispossession. Yhwh's grant of land and destruction of the Horites enabled Edom to "dispossess" the Horites (2:12, 22), and the preacher presents variations on the theme: The Emim preceded the Moabites (2:10), the Ammonites "dispossessed" the Zamzummim (2:20–21), the Caphtorim "settled" in the place of the Avvim (2:23), and Israel "captured" the cities of Heshbon (2:34) and Bashan (3:4). There is reason to recoil from the hasty dispossessions in the narrative, where whole peoples died with the single word "destroy," where when Israel carried out the dispossession, Moses speaks of the ritual killing of every man, woman, and child (2:34, 3:6).[136] The passage

---

[133] Lohfink, "יָרַשׁ *yāraš*," 379.

[134] Lohfink suggests this line of thinking, and he cites the handing of a sandal to a new owner, ibid., 371, 379.

[135] What the E.S.V. calls Mount Seir, Weinfeld translates "the hill country" of Seir, *Deuteronomy 1–11: A New Translation with Introduction and Commentary*, Anchor Bible 5 (New York: Doubleday, 1991), 154.

[136] These passages depict the people of Yhwh as they ritually destroyed every human being in Heshbon and Bashan: "we devoted them to destruction" (וַנַּחֲרֵם, 2:34, 3:6). Elsewhere in Deuteronomy, Moses commands this practice when Yhwh gives nations over to the people of Israel (7:2). For a discussion of the questions these passages raise about divine goodness, contemporary, moral judgments, the nature of revelation, and the interpretation of Scripture, see Christian Hofreiter, "Genocide in Deuteronomy and Christian Interpretation," in *Interpreting Deuteronomy: Issues and Approaches*, ed. David G. Firth and Philip S. Johnston (Nottingham: Apollos, 2012), 240–62; "Reading Herem as Christian Scripture" (D.Phil. Thesis, Faculty of Theology and Religion, University of Oxford, 2014).

does not shy away from presenting a complete, bloody displacement of one nation by another. As God's chosen instrument, Israel itself faced widespread death in this passage, as Yhwh "destroy[ed]" the older generation that failed to trust Yhwh and take possession of the land (2:14–15; see 1:19–46). In the economy of Deuteronomy, dispossession happens for a reason: Yhwh did not allow injustice to go on forever in the lands granted to the nations. Moses makes clear that Israel's second generation will not gain land because of its צְדָקָה, *ṣ^edāqâ*, its blameless behavior, or the just judgments of its rulers, but because of the רֶשַׁע, *reša ʿ*, the wrong and injustice of the nations that preceded them in the land (9:4–5).[137] This is in keeping with the telling of the land promise in the Book of Genesis: Yhwh promised Abram the land, but Yhwh would not give Abram the land until his descendants sojourn in Egypt: "And they shall come back here in the fourth generation, for the iniquity of the Amorites is not yet complete" (Gen. 15:16). Yhwh refused to dispossess the Amorites from the land of Canaan in Abram's time because the Amorites' wrongdoing was not great enough. Yhwh holds back from judging.[138]

If Yhwh gives lands to the nations like Yhwh gives lands to other nations, and if Yhwh allows for the dispossession of lands like Yhwh does for Israel, could it be that some of the requirements Yhwh makes of Israel to keep their lands apply to other nations? If wrong and injustice disqualify any nation from possessing land, then the best indicators of what counts as wrong within the narrative of Deuteronomy are the statutes given to Israel in Deut. 12:2 to 26:15. Brueggemann's summary of Yhwh's treaty with Israel as forbidding idolatry, requiring the freeing practices of Sabbath, and urging good judgment for those on the margins of society provides a starting point. Still, on first glance it is difficult to know what standard Yhwh required other nations to uphold as possessors of land in Deuteronomy. Readings of the books of prophecy would give further indication about what Yhwh required of the Gentile nations. But there are hints in Deuteronomy: Moses' second speech can be read as suggesting that the other nations perished because they followed gods other than Yhwh (8:19–20). Perhaps injustice to outsiders is another reason that Yhwh would allow a nation to lose its land. A reading of Deuteronomy 10:12–22 demonstrated that right judgment for widows and orphans stands at the heart of divine justice. It also revealed that in Deuteronomy, reflecting Yhwh's love for migrants is at the center of what it means to be attuned to the God of the universe. Surely, this account of divine justice and love would not be displaced by some more generic version of justice required of other nations. It would not make sense for Yhwh to set aside Yhwh's unique ways when judging nations other than Israel for their injustice. It appears that not only justice for the vulnerable but also justice and love for migrants remain requirements for every nation. If a nation is to continue possessing its land, it cannot practice injustice toward migrants.

---

[137] *K.B.*, 1006, 1296.
[138] Thanks to Joe Martin for bringing this verse to my attention.

On the present interpretation, Deuteronomy 2–3 signals a pattern of God granting land to nations other than Israel, but an objection can be made: Only the close relatives of Israel received lands in these passages. God gave lands to the descendants of Esau, the brother of Jacob, also known as Israel (2:4; see Gen. 32:3; 35:10), and God gave lands to Moab and Ammon, descendants of Lot, the nephew of the patriarch Abraham (Deut. 2:9, 19; see Gen. 11:27; 19:37–38). But the one exception to this rule hints at a pattern larger than the granting of land to those nations that are related to Israel. Amid the litany of possessions and dispossessions, Moses says that "the Caphtorim, who came from Caphtor, destroyed [the Avvim] and settled in their place" (Deut. 2:23). Here, Yhwh is not named as the cause of this turn of events, but the mention of the Caphtorim comes within a passage steeped in Yhwh's action in causing possession and dispossession. The Caphtorim were a people who appear to be unrelated to Israel, and in the tables of the nations they are said to be descended from Egypt (Gen. 10:13; 1 Chron. 1:11).

In one of the very few other mentions of Caphtor in the Scriptures, a striking motif emerges from Amos 9:7 (N.R.S.V.):

> Are you not like the Ethiopians to me,
>   O people of Israel? says the LORD.

> Did I not bring Israel up from the land of Egypt,
>   and the Philistines from Caphtor and the Arameans from Kir?

The prophet Amos bears a message that strikes at Israel's pride. As the one master of the stars, who brings night and day, who commands the seas (Amos 5:8; 9:6), Yhwh poses rhetorical questions to Israel: Are the Ethiopians not like you to me, those people known for their different color of skin (Jeremiah 13:23)? When it comes to your perennial enemies, did I not bring them up like I brought you up from Egypt, the Philistines from Caphtor and the Syrians from Kir?[139] The Israelites to whom Amos speaks would rather answer "no" and consider themselves special, but Yhwh's answer is "yes." The prophet declares that just as Yhwh characteristically "brings up" (עלה, *'lh*) Israel out of Egypt, so Yhwh brings up other nations, even Israel's foes.[140] Beyond the granting of land to the other nations in Deuteronomy, according to Brueggemann the prophet Amos declares that Yhwh "performs exodus" for nations

---

[139] Deut. 2:23 describes the Caphtorim taking the place of the Avvim in Gaza. Both the Caphtorim in Deut. 2:23 and the Philistines in Amos 9:7 came from Caphtor, and they may be the same people, if Gen. 10:14 describes the Philistines coming from the place of the Casluhim. Gen. 10:14 may also be read as saying that the Philistines descended from the Casluhim people, who are listed as distinct from the Caphtorim, and in that case, the Philistines and Caphtorim might be two different peoples who came out of Caphtor. Then again, the accounts of peoples coming from Caphtor might not cohere.

[140] Walter Brueggemann interprets Amos this way, and he thinks that 9:7 stands apart from its immediate context, "'Exodus' in the Plural (Amos 9:7)," in *Many Voices, One God: Being Faithful in a Pluralistic World*, ed. Walter Brueggemann and George W. Stroup (Louisville, Ky.: Westminster John Knox Press, 1998), 20.

that bear no kinship with Israel.[141] Perhaps these nations, too, were subject to oppression and cried out to God, to Elohim. Perhaps God heard them and brought them up from the land of their oppressors, granting them land as a possession, as Brueggemann imagines.[142] Not only for Israel's relatives but also for those unrelated to it, writes Brueggemann, "there is more than one promised land assured to more than one people."[143]

—

Do something like national territories as well as guarded cities play a role in God's saving purposes? This is the question that prompted the present inquiry. Interpreted alongside theologically oriented biblical scholars, the comments from the fringes of Israel's story in Deuteronomy 2–3 indicate that national lands do play a role, in a carefully limited way. God migrated with a migrant people to the land God was giving them, carrying them and finding them a place to pitch their tents. Along the way, this people encountered other nations, and God's instructions to them demonstrate that God gives lands to other nations. The living God, the one revealed to Israel as Yhwh, rules all the earth, and lands are God's to give and take away. In this era after the expulsion from the Garden of Eden, God grants lands to peoples so that they might enjoy their fruits and flourish. These are lands often defined by borders, lands to possess and walk about in. The giving God requires a people to give in response, to avoid wrong and to seek just judgment, and if they do not, God will remove them from the land. Giving and giving in return, possession and dispossession: This is the rhythm of Deuteronomy 2–3 and the pattern for national lands during this age before that age when "the meek will possess the land."[144]

An observation arises from this account from Deuteronomy and linked passages. As peoples and nations possess lands, they are due a request when nonmembers want to cross their lands. Yet at the same time, part of the condition of keeping their land is that they judge rightly. The hallmark of God's just judgment, his governance, is justice for the one from far away and love for the migrant. It looks like nations may maintain their borders and admit or not admit outsiders, but this passage raises the possibility that if their legislatures, their courts, and their police do not treat migrants with justice, they may lose their lands. It looks like the United States of America might rightly allow a noncitizen to enter or turn them away. Still, the U.S. government risks losing control of its lands if it does not treat noncitizens with justice.

---

[141] Walter Brueggemann, *Deuteronomy*, Abingdon Old Testament Commentaries (Nashville: Abingdon Press, 2001), 38.

[142] Brueggemann, "'Exodus' in the Plural," 23–24.

[143] Brueggemann, *Deuteronomy*, 35.

[144] Ps. 37:11. Within a psalm built around the possessing of land, Ps. 37:11 declares that "the meek will possess (*yāraš*) the land," and the passage finds echoes in the Sermon on the Mount (Matthew 5:5), "Blessed are the meek, for they shall inherit the earth" (E.S.V.), or highlighting the Hebrew resonances, "Blessed are the meek, for they will possess the land."

In the language of Deuteronomy, the U.S. risks being destroyed and dispossessed. If the Border Patrol mistreats those at the borders, if the courts fail to give a fair hearing to those charged with immigration offenses, if laws fail to give legal standing to the wage laborers the American people depend upon, then God might end the U.S. government's possession of its current territories. The message of Deuteronomy 2–3 for this modern nation is double-edged: Possess this land and enjoy it, but another nation will soon displace you if you fail to follow God's ways and practice God's justice.

RESPONDING TO A THREAT OF HARM: LEO XIII AND IMMIGRATION AUTHORITY

Authority over territory is divinely granted, but this authority and the authority over immigration is checked by the requirements of the one Sovereign. What, then, do authorities rightly do when they restrict the whereabouts of noncitizens? A claim from Pope Leo XIII's encyclical *Rerum Novarum* points toward an answer, with elaboration from Oliver O'Donovan's *The Ways of Judgment*. Their arguments about public authority as responding to a threat of harm helps frame immigration authority in this way: *In most cases, authority over immigration responds to a threat of harm against what is held in common.* Leo and O'Donovan's arguments enable both the formulation of this rule and exceptions to the rule when immigration authority reacts to wrong or to a past act.

In his 1891 encyclical on capital and labor, Leo XIII deals with public authority, paralleling the findings in the preceding sections about guarding when he says that "rulers should ... anxiously safeguard the community and all its members." He reiterates the findings from the Psalms above when he writes that "the power to rule comes from God, and is, as it were, a participation in His, the highest of all sovereignties."[145] Next, Leo asserts this about civil authority:

> Whenever the general interest or any particular class suffers, or is threatened with harm, which can in no other way be met or prevented, the public authority must step in to deal with it ... The limits must be determined by the nature of the occasion which calls for the law's interference – the principle being that the law must not undertake more, nor proceed further, than is required for the remedy of the evil or the removal of the mischief.[146]

---

[145] *Rerum Novarum: Encyclical on Capital and Labor*, 1891, sec. 35, www.vatican.va/holy_father/leo_xiii/encyclicals/documents/hf_l-xiii_enc_15051891_rerum-novarum_en.html.

[146] Ibid., sec. 36. The Latin original reads, *Si quid igitur detrimenti allatum sit aut impendeat rebus communibus, aut singulorum ordinum rationibus, quod sanari aut prohiberi alia ratione non possit, obviam iri auctoritate publica necesse est... Quos fines eadem, quae legum poscit opem, causa determinat: videlicet non plura suscipienda legibus, nec ultra progrendiendum, quam incommodorum sanatio, vel periculi depulsio requirat*, Leo XIII, *Rerum Novarum: Litterae Encylicae de Conditione Opificum*, 1891, http://w2.vatican.va/content/leo-xiii/la/encyclicals/documents/hf_l-xiii_enc_15051891_rerum-novarum.html. P. 11 addresses the pivotal role of *Rerum Novarum* in Catholic Social Teaching on migration.

In the quotation above, Leo announces that the task of the public authority is to protect the *res communes* – communications, or common matters, things, possessions, or affairs – as well as to protect any particular grouping within the whole.[147] The public authority protects against *quid detrimenti*, any harm, damage, loss, or material diminishment, whether that harm is *allatum*, already brought, or *impendeat*, threatens or hangs over.[148] In the ellipsis between the sections quoted above, Leo indicates a number of common matters that the public authority protects: peace and order, justice, families, religious life, moral standards, and health. A different list of common possessions might well apply to the matter of immigration authority.[149]

Oliver O'Donovan elaborates upon Leo XIII's brief claim about public authority in *The Ways of Judgment* and in comments on that book. O'Donovan argues that Leo's claim stands within a long discussion about where government falls in the history of God's dealings with the world. In O'Donovan's telling, Church Fathers like John Chrysostom and Augustine saw the rule of one human being over another as coming after the fall of Adam, and they drew on images from the first eleven chapters of Genesis that contrast an innocent beginning with a world of wrongdoing and bloodshed. One significant alternative to this line of thinking came with Thomas Aquinas, who under the influence of Aristotle cast government as ordering human life in a way that would be helpful to human beings had they not sinned. In O'Donovan's narrative, some resolution of this tension came in the sixteenth century. As explained earlier in this chapter, the reformer Luther saw the first signs of government in the earthling's words for the animals, but he placed the guarding of places with walls and arms after the threat of murder entered the world. Likewise, the Dominican Francisco de Vitoria noted a shift toward something new when Cain and Nimrod build their city, a city needed to fend off violent attack.[150] Thus on O'Donovan's reading of the tradition, political life takes two forms: first, human beings share, gather together, and organize themselves because of how they are created; and second, one person rules another when human society is threatened by sin.[151] Thus when Leo XIII names "public authority" as defending against harm or a threat of harm against common matters, common matters that also have a

---

[147] *Oxford Latin Dictionary (O.L.D.)* (Oxford: Clarendon Press, 1982), 369–70, 1625–26.

[148] Ibid., 77–78, 532, 841–42. The translation here, from www.vatican.va, accurately follows the Latin original, while another translation diverges from the Latin in ways that are significant for this discussion, that of David J. O'Brien and Thomas A. Shannon, eds., *Catholic Social Thought: The Documentary Heritage* (Maryknoll, N.Y.: Orbis Books, 1992), 12–39. O'Brien and Shannon translate *detrimenti* as "evils," while the Vatican website translates it more accurately as "harm." O'Brien and Shannon wrongly translate *aut* as "of" in "the general interest *of* any particular class," while the Vatican translation translates the word as "or," so that it is *either* the general interest *or* any particular class that suffers or is threatened by harm, O.L.D., 219–20, 532.

[149] *Rerum Novarum*, 1891, sec. 36.

[150] Vitoria, *On Civil Power*, 4, q. 1, art. 2, sec. 4, in *Political Writings*, trans. Anthony Pagden and Jeremy Lawrance (Cambridge: Cambridge University Press, 1991), 9.

[151] O'Donovan, *The Ways of Judgment*, 59–60.

political character, he produces a sharp statement that is the fruit of a long-running conversation. On O'Donovan's reading, Leo's statement also responds to the threat of totalitarianism in the nineteenth century and the dangerous notion that civil authority dictates everything, that every sort of sociality has government at the top.[152]

What O'Donovan does not note is that Catholic Social Teaching since *Rerum Novarum* has moved to affirm a more positive role for political authority. As an example, Pope John XIII affirms in *Pacem in Terris* that "the attainment of the common good is the sole reason for the existence of civil authorities."[153] Still, O'Donovan is right to commend Leo's formulation of public authority since this formulation succeeds at integrating two insights from the Christian tradition about political life, sharing among creatures and rule among fallen creatures. Some of the Fathers understand politics as a result of the fall to the exclusion of a political life for creatures, and twentieth-century Catholic Social Teaching along with Aquinas perceive a positive role for authority as upholding common life, while tending to neglect its role as guarding against evil. Leo's statement in *Rerum Novarum*, however, conserves both views of political life, created and fallen.

What Leo articulates, O'Donovan calls "the reactive principle."[154] Human beings act freely and share in a common good, not because political authority has manufactured these things, but because it is in our nature to be social.[155] There is a sort of public activity that precedes the activity of civil government, an activity that seeks to develop social communications and pursue common goals. The role of political activity, however, is to react when the common good is harmed. For Leo, civil authority steps in to prevent harm to antecedently existing social relations. But Leo says more: Civil authority not only reacts to harm or injury that is actual, but also to a *threat* of harm. Political judgment, in O'Donovan's words, is "at once *reactive* to wrong and *proactive* to avert the threat of harm."[156] This qualification keeps Leo from libertarianism, says O'Donovan; government does not only respond to actual crimes and torts, but also to threats of future harm to the common good. If failure to act means that in years to come, what a people shares will experience harm, and if civil authority is best suited to the task, then that authority is right to fend off harm.[157] O'Donovan makes a final distinction, between wrong and harm: Civil authority protects against both wrong as a "moral relation" and harm as an "objective detriment."[158] Government acts rightly when it protects the common good against

[152] Ibid., 61; Oliver O'Donovan, "Judgment, Tradition, and Reason: A Response," *Political Theology* 9, no. 3 (2008): 397.

[153] John XXIII, *Pacem in Terris: Encyclical on Establishing Universal Peace in Truth, Justice, Charity, and Liberty*, 1963, sec. 54, http://w2.vatican.va/content/john-xxiii/en/encyclicals/docu ments/hf_j-xxiii_enc_11041963_pacem.html.

[154] O'Donovan, *The Ways of Judgment*, 59.

[155] Ibid., 55.

[156] Ibid., 62; emphasis O'Donovan.

[157] Ibid., 61; O'Donovan, "Judgment, Tradition, and Reason," 397.

[158] O'Donovan, *The Ways of Judgment*, 58.

acts that incur guilt as well as acts that diminish or hurt the common good, he says. The limits that Leo places on civil authority are worth heeding: Political activity must go no further than the matter in hand requires. Once that authority appropriately punishes the wrong or adequately averts the harm, it must stop.

Leo XIII's terse characterization of political authority represents a high point of Christian reflection on government. The notion that public authority responds to harm or a threat of harm appeals, avoiding the excesses of totalitarianism and libertarianism and authorizing the use of authority, but placing it within limits. His argument also helps make sense of immigration authority. It helps clarify the truth of what a government is doing when it restricts who can enter and who can live in its territory. It also helps clarify what government *rightly* does when it excludes or expels nonmembers.

The transition from Leo's view of public authority to a definition of immigration authority will proceed in three steps. First, Leo speaks of what is harmed, those things held in common. Some class or order within the community may also be the object of harm. What does this imply for authority over immigration? Civil authority can only be right to restrict immigration if by doing so it fends off some harm to what society shares or to some group within society. Immigration authority, like any civil authority, does not in the first instance make or manufacture society. Rather, human beings gather together and associate because of how they are created, while immigration authority acts to protect those gatherings against some danger. If those in government begin to see themselves as "making" society through immigration policy, then they arrogate to themselves a dangerous power. Now, immigration authority is unusual among civil powers: It has the power to shape the future membership of society, allowing some to come in and keeping others out. Recent scholarship recognizes this point: Aristide Zolberg's masterful history, *A Nation by Design: Immigration Policy in the Fashioning of America*, stresses the ways that immigration authority has shaped American society. Zolberg acknowledges at the start of his book that he draws this emphasis from Benedict Anderson's influential account of nations as *Imagined Communities*.[159] While it may take an act of imagination to be joined with others who are not present, and while immigration law shapes society as it shifts and grows, on balance, there are better reasons to think that immigration law does not constitute society at its start. Even in the United States, where most members are descended from migrants who arrived in the last four centuries, these migrants settled and gathered together before there were laws to restrict entry. Zolberg offers as early instances of immigration policy controls on transported convicts and paupers, but even so, these controls sought to protect new societies in North America from harm.[160] Moves to restrict entry and residence

---

[159] Aristide R. Zolberg, *A Nation by Design: Immigration Policy in the Fashioning of America* (Cambridge, Mass.: Harvard University Press, 2006), 1111; Benedict Anderson, *Imagined Communities: Reflections on the Origin and Spread of Nationalism* (London: Verso, 1983).

[160] *A Nation by Design*, 26, 35, 42.

constituted reactions to some harm or threat of harm against communal wellbeing. Authority over immigration thus exists only to serve *what is held in common*, protecting what is common but not making a society in the first place.

Of course, there is some ambiguity in the phrase *res communes*, what is held in common, the common things. Is this only what is common to one nation-state or to one region with shared immigration controls? *Res communes* may also refer to what is common to all human beings. Here, Catholic Social Teaching suggests the "universal destination of earthly goods," the teaching that the things of this world are given to humankind as a whole so that the possessions of one person or group are intended to benefit everyone.[161] Immigration authority that protects what a nation shares in service to what all share will have a different outlook. Those who exercise its authority could consider how certain immigration restrictions affect not only their country but also the members of another country, perhaps a next-door neighbor or a country beset by famine or war.

In the second step that makes possible a definition of immigration authority, Leo distinguishes some harm that is already brought, some actual harm, from some harm that threatens or hangs over. What sort of harm does immigration authority act against? In a small minority of cases, United States immigration authority responds to harm that is not simply threatened but actual. In one such case, current federal law places restrictions on those who have been convicted of "aggravated felonies."[162] Those guilty of committing murder, exacting a ransom, or running a prostitution business, among other offenses, are barred from returning to the United States for twenty years.[163] On top of the punishment that these men and women already receive for their crimes, immigration policy mandates that they leave the United States and stay away for some time. Here, immigration policy protects what is held in common, a freedom from violence, fear, and mistreatment, against a threat that has already occurred. Still, these cases form only a small proportion of the cases that U.S. authorities deal with. The current Department of Homeland Security admits noncitizens to the United States, grants residency, and naturalizes persons much more often than it apprehends and removes individuals convicted of aggravated felonies.[164] In a second case described in Chapter 3, where U.S. immigration

---

[161] The phrase appears, for example, in the Fathers of the Second Vatican Council and Paul VI, *Gaudium et Spes: Pastoral Constitution on the Church in the Modern Word*, 1965, sec. 69, www.vatican.va/archive/hist_councils/ii_vatican_council/documents/vat-ii_cons_19651207_gau dium-et-spes_en.html. It is affirmed in *Rerum Novarum*, 1891, sec. 22, in a quotation from Thomas Aquinas: "Man should not consider his material possessions as his own, but as common to all, so as to share them without hesitation when others are in need."

[162] 8 U.S.C. § 1101(a)(43); An Act: To prevent the manufacturing, distribution, and use of illegal drugs, and for other purposes, Pub. L. No. 100–690, 8 USC. § 1101(a)(43), 102 Stat. 4181 (1988); cf. An Act: Making omnibus consolidated appropriations for the fiscal year ending September 30, 1997, and for other purposes, Pub. L. No. 104–208, 110 Stat. 3009–546 (1996), 3009–627–28.

[163] Immigration and Nationality Act (I.N.A.) § 212(a)(9)(A)(ii)(II)(2013).

[164] As an example, in the 2014 fiscal year, branches of the Department of Homeland Security removed 63,159 individuals convicted of aggravated felonies, "I.C.E. Enforcement and

authorities responded to what was taken to be present harm, Congress placed restrictions on Chinese immigration and naturalization from 1882 onward. The legislature judged that Chinese immigrants were at that time threatening the cohesion of American society, its institutions, language, economy, and morals, and it passed laws to fend off what it took to be harm. Still, the Chinese Exclusion Acts run against the grain of federal immigration law. In no other prominent example has the United States permitted a whole class of persons to enter the country with no time limit but later acted to discourage them from remaining in the United States or to expel them.

These cases of harm committed in the past or the present are worth noting, but they are the exception to the rule. In most cases U.S. immigration policy responds to a *threat* of harm against what is held in common. One example is the exclusion of those who are most impoverished. Colonial authorities sought to exclude paupers, early state laws did the same, and an 1882 federal law forbade "any person unable to take care of himself or herself without becoming a public charge" from landing at a U.S. port.[165] The ban on those "liable to become a public charge" continues in federal law.[166] This exclusion may or may not be just, but it serves as a helpful example. When a U.S. citizen's French husband is not granted permanent residency in the United States because the American earns a low income, the Frenchman is not excluded because he has harmed or is harming the United States. Rather, the concern is that if he comes, he will depend on government funds to live, and his presence will drain federal funds or detract from the life of the local community. The harm here is not actual, but threatened. This is the sort of harm that much of U.S. immigration law guards against. Newcomers are not admitted without sufficient wealth, an adequately paid job, or support from a family member because Congress has judged that the presence of those who lack a way to support themselves is detrimental to society.

In a second example, federal law currently places numerical caps on how many can immigrate from any given country.[167] Only so many nationals of the Philippines

Removal Operations Report" (United States Department of Homeland Security; Immigration and Customs Enforcement, Fiscal Year 2014), www.ice.gov/doclib/about/offices/ero/pdf/2014-ice-immigration-removals.pdf. In the same fiscal year, the branches of the Department granted 1,016,518 individuals lawful permanent resident status, 653,416 were naturalized, 69,975 refugees arrived, 180,500,000 individuals were admitted in temporary, nonimmigrant categories, and 223,253 were determined inadmissible, "Yearbook of Immigration Statistics" (Office of Immigration Statistics, United States Department of Homeland Security, Fiscal Year 2014), www.dhs.gov/yearbook-immigration-statistics. The Yearbook does not distinguish aggravated felonies from other types of crime, but it notes that 167,740 individuals with prior criminal convictions for all sorts of crimes were removed in 2014.

[165] For example, the Massachusetts Poor Laws enabled the deportation of paupers of foreign origin, Zolberg, *A Nation by Design*, 75; An act to regulate Immigration, 22 Stat. 214 (1882), 214.

[166] 8 U.S.C. § 1182(a)(4).

[167] Quotas first went into place in 1921 for countries in the Eastern Hemisphere and then in 1965 for the Western Hemisphere, An Act: To limit the immigration of aliens into the United

are granted visas to settle in the United States each year, and these limits are not qualitative, based on some injury to the common good, but quantitative. What such laws imply is that if too many men, women, and children arrived from the Philippines in the next few years, their presence would harm the common good of the United States. The availability of jobs or housing, the capacity of present U.S. residents to include these newcomers as members of society, or the resilience of a common language might be under threat. Once again, it is not clear whether these concerns are warranted or just. What is clear is that immigration law does not protect against some actual damage that those hoping to immigrate have done. Instead, the legislature has made a judgment about the future injury that immigrants will cause to the common good if too many enter the United States. Even if this judgment about the future finds backing from past evidence, it is an uncertain judgment. The legislature cannot know in advance what will happen if more Filipinos settle in the United States next year. While in some cases, immigration authority responds to *actual* harm, *most of the time*, immigration authority responds to *threatened* harm, as in this case.

Third, Leo XIII speaks of *detrimentum*, harm, injury, or detriment. Leo's definition encompasses many types of harm that civil authority is tasked with countering, harms that might include *wrongs*. In some rare cases, immigration authority responds to wrongs, or threats of wrongs. In the case of aggravated felonies above, these usually involve some wrong, something for which a person can be held guilty. Intentional acts of violence, coercion with words, and forcible exaction of property: these are types of acts for which someone is morally culpable. In some cases, immigration authority responds to wrongs already committed, or it responds to wrongs that might happen in the future. For example, the Immigration Act of 1891 excluded from admission into the United States "persons who have been convicted of a felony or other infamous crime or misdemeanor involving moral turpitude."[168] It appears that lawmakers were concerned that an immigrant might continue a pattern of immoral criminal activity once in the United States. This law was concerned about future *wrong*, but this concern forms the exception to the rule.

Most of the time, immigration authority deals not with wrong but with *harm*, some act that though injurious to the common good does not entail moral guilt.

States, Pub. L. No. 67–5, 42 Stat. 5 (1921); An Act: To amend the Immigration and Nationality Act, and for other purposes, Pub. L. No. 89–236, 79 Stat. 911 (1965). See pp. 149–78 for more on numerical limits.

[168] An act in amendment to the various acts relative to immigration and the importation of aliens under contract or agreement to perform labor, 26 Stat. 1084 (1891), 1084. As recently as 2013, the term "turpitude" still confronted those applying to enter the United States: "Have you ever been arrested or convicted for an offense or crime involving moral turpitude …?" "Electronic System for Travel Authorization – Application," accessed December 19, 2013, https://esta.cbp.dhs.gov/esta/application.html?execution=e1s1. The phrase "moral turpitude" had been removed a few years later, "Official E.S.T.A. Application Website, U.S. Customs and Border Protection," accessed June 20, 2016, https://esta.cbp.dhs.gov/esta/application.html?execution=e1s1.

When the Johnson-Reed Act of 1924 severely restricted immigration from countries like Poland and Italy, what the lawmakers primarily had in view was not "moral turpitude."[169] Congress acted on an assessment of recent immigrants as dirty, physically deficient, disease-ridden, socialist, Jewish, or unable to assimilate into the Nordic race, on Peter Schrag's telling.[170] The likes of Congressman Albert Johnson blamed immigrants for not integrating, for not becoming part of "white" American society, for bringing disease or dangerous ideas, but they did not focus their criticisms on immorality or crime. The concern was that new immigrants would be part of larger trends that would detract from what Americans shared over time. New immigrants would join separate societies and fail to contribute to the health, strength, wealth, and democratic ideals of the United States, those behind the Johnson-Reed Act alleged. Senators and Congressmen might have thought that the presence of many more Greeks or Ukrainians would cause some future damage to social bonds, to the goods that American citizens share. Above all, these immigrants would sully the country's Northern European gene pool.

The way lawmakers and writers characterized immigrants at this time was rancorous and racist, but they still only alleged *harm* rather than *wrong*. They did not blame individuals for specific wrongs, but instead they were concerned that new immigrants would contribute to broad trends that would detract from common life. The contemporary tenor of American discussions of immigration policy may be more civil, but their allegations are of a similar type. When some say that immigrants will take jobs from American citizens or that they will fail to learn English, the allegations are analogous to those made around 1924. Those who voice these concerns do not blame immigrants for moral wrongs; instead, they predict that the arrival of a large number of women and men from, say, Mexico will contribute to economic and social trends that detract from what Americans share. In conclusion, immigration authority by and large responds to these sorts of *harm* rather than wrong, harm not due to specifiable immoral acts, but harm when one person contributes to trends whose cumulative effects damage common possessions.

In three steps, then, Leo XIII's statement on civil authority paves the way for a definition of immigration authority: *In most cases, authority over immigration responds to a threat of harm against what is held in common.* The rule frames, directs, and limits the use of immigration authority without dictating its use. Questions of judgment remain open in each case: What is it that is held in common? Common practices, ways of speaking, a tract of land, or a marketplace? Will new arrivals threaten this community or bring it new life? As those in authority seek to answer these questions with honesty and justice, Pope Leo's comments about limits to authority serve as a concluding warning. His encyclical states that if there is

---

[169] An Act: To limit the immigration of aliens into the United States, and for other purposes, Pub. L. No. 68–139, 43 Stat. 153 (1924).

[170] Peter Schrag, *Not Fit for Our Society: Nativism and Immigration* (Berkeley: University of California Press, 2010), 115–22.

no other way to prevent harm, then civil authority must meet that threat. He stresses that the law must act within limits, doing no more than it must to bring restoration to some unfavorable circumstance or avert some danger.[171] In the case of immigration, then, government must restrict entry and residence if there remains no other way to fend off some trouble. Still, the government may only act if other less formal or less coercive approaches cannot preclude harm. In the case of nineteenth-century Chinese immigration to the West Coast, perhaps some way could have been found to resolve difficulties without recourse to legal restrictions on entry and residence. Perhaps peace would have come about through the efforts of neighbors to get to know one another, or through meetings and negotiations between community groups. Proper limits to immigration authority are worth observing.

WRONG ONLY BECAUSE PROHIBITED: BLACKSTONE AND IMMIGRATION OFFENSES

Given this framework for the proper functioning of immigration authority, how should an immigration offense and its punishment be understood? *Most immigration offenses are not* mala in se, *wrong in themselves, but* mala prohibitum, *wrong because prohibited.* This conclusion will arise through a reading of eighteenth-century English legal scholar William Blackstone's statement on two types of *malum*, types still in current usage among lawyers.[172]

In the introduction to his authoritative *Commentaries on the Laws of England*, Blackstone makes a distinction between *malum in se* and *malum prohibitum*. The distinction arises out of a discussion on the nature of law that begins with the creation of the world. Blackstone writes that when the "supreme being" created the universe, "he impressed certain principles upon that matter, from which it can never depart."[173] "God . . . created man" too as "entirely a dependent being."[174] God gave human beings "freewill" but established "certain immutable laws of human nature" as limits that direct them to right and away from wrong.[175] God also gave human beings "reason" so that they could search out those laws, but according to

---

[171] *Videlicet non plura suscipienda legibus, nec ultra progrendiendum, quam incommodorum sanatio, vel periculi depulsio requirat,* author's paraphrase, with reference to *O.L.D.,* 521, 872, 1342, 1686.

[172] Thanks to Lisa Lorish for suggesting that this legal distinction would help reveal the nature of immigration offenses. An early, brief example of this sort of distinction comes from Aristotle's distinction between that part of the politically just that is natural (φυσικόν, *phusikon*) and that part that is legal or conventional (νομικόν, *nomikon*), Aristotle, *Nicomachean Ethics,* trans. H. Rackham, rev. edn., Loeb Classical Library 73 (Cambridge, Mass.: Harvard University Press, 1934), V.vii.1; Aristotle, *Nicomachean Ethics,* trans. Terence Irwin, 2nd edn. (Indianapolis: Hackett Publishing, 1999), 1134b19.

[173] William Blackstone, *Commentaries on the Laws of England,* vol. 1 (Oxford: Clarendon Press, 1765), 38, from the Lillian Goldman Library at the Yale Law School, "The Avalon Project: Documents in Law, History, and Diplomacy," 2008, http://avalon.law.yale.edu/default.asp.

[174] Blackstone, *Commentaries on the Laws of England,* 1765, 1:39.

[175] Ibid., 1:39–40.

Blackstone, human reason is "corrupt, ... full of ignorance and error."[176] Thus, to guide humanity to the knowledge of the natural law, at different times and in different places, God provided "an immediate and direct revelation ... the revealed or divine law ... found only in the holy scriptures."[177]

On these two sources, the law of nature and the law of revelation, depend the "municipal or civil law," the law that governs communities.[178] Much of human law merely declares what is already made plain from nature and the Scriptures. Along these lines, when municipal law declares that certain acts are crimes and misdemeanors, the inferior, earthly legislature "acts only ... in subordination to the great lawgiver, transcribing and publishing his precepts."[179] These kinds of acts are *mala in se*," wrong in themselves.[180] Blackstone cites murder, theft, and perjury as examples of wrongs already forbidden by the "superior laws," wrongs that "contract no additional turpitude from being declared unlawful by the inferior legislature."[181] Since human beings are already bound by superior laws, they are bound in conscience not to commit those offenses that are *mala in se*.[182] When the municipal law declares something to be a crime, it does not make them any more wrong than they already were.

According to Blackstone, there are other sorts of wrongs that are not *mala in se* but "*mala prohibita*," wrong because they are prohibited.[183] The law of nature and the law of revelation command and forbid certain actions, but there remain a number of "indifferent points" on which municipal law restrains action to benefit society.[184] These indifferent matters, writes Blackstone, "become either right or wrong, just or unjust, duties or misdemesnors [*sic*], according as the municipal legislator sees proper, for promoting the welfare of the society, and more effectually carrying on the purposes of civil life."[185] Monopolies serve as one of Blackstone's examples of *mala prohibita*: these are not wrong by nature, but municipal law declares them wrong to protect civil society.[186] Following Blackstone's logic, when in 1984 the United States Department of Justice broke up A.T.&T.'s longstanding monopoly on telephone services, it did this not because the company had done something wrong in itself but because it judged that A.T.&T.'s monopoly was damaging to the public welfare.[187] Without competitors, the monopoly might command too high a price for

176 Ibid., 1:41.
177 Ibid., 1:42.
178 Ibid., 1:42, 44.
179 Ibid., 1:54.
180 Ibid.
181 Ibid.
182 Ibid., 1:57.
183 Ibid.
184 Ibid., 1:42.
185 Ibid., 1:55.
186 Ibid.
187 "Excerpts from Text of a Decree Signed by A.T.&T. and U.S.," *The New York Times*, January 9, 1982, sec. Business, www.nytimes.com/1982/01/09/business/excerpts-from-text-of-a-decree-signed-by-at-t-and-us.html.

its services, supply substandard services, or prevent the innovation that competitors could bring. Legislatures ban such monopolies to protect common goods, and holding a monopoly becomes an offense not wrong in itself but wrong because prohibited, *malum prohibitum.*

Blackstone goes on to indicate how *malum prohibitum* differs from *malum in se* in its relation to the conscience. For offenses that are *mala in se*, he writes, the conscience is bound before there are human laws, but for offenses that are *mala prohibita*, the conscience is only bound to submit to the penalty given for breaking the law.[188] In these cases, he writes, the main strength and force of the law comes not from what is God-given but from the penalty that the legislator gives for the law.[189] Blackstone, then, shows that civil authorities do not only forbid and punish what natural and divine law indicate is wrong. Rather, civil authorities prohibit a range of actions in the interest of securing common goods, and an offense against laws in these cases is not an offense against what is wrong by nature, but an offense against what is wrong because the authorities have prohibited it.

The distinction between *malum in se* and *malum prohibitum* raises some difficulties. In many cases, its application is not clear: Theft might appear to be *malum in se*, but there are good reasons to think that stealing to help someone in dire need is not wrong in itself. Blackstone's sources require interpretation: Even if someone trusts the Christian Scriptures to clarify the created moral order, the Scriptures do not make plain what of that order is rightfully enshrined in civil law. Blackstone's account of law that funds his distinction has its issues, too. When Blackstone says that we need nothing more to prompt us toward justice than "our own self-love, the universal principle of action," and when he offers "the one paternal precept, that man should pursue his own happiness" as the foundation of ethics or natural law, his system remains impoverished in the same way as Vattel's and Hobbes'.[190] Furthermore, Blackstone's confidence about the law of nature and the law of revelation will be greeted with doubt outside of and after Christendom, where the natural is contested and where the Christian Scriptures are not taken as divinely given. Though the distinction between types of wrong can be difficult to apply, and though the conception of law that lies behind it leaves unresolved questions, the distinction is still in currency in legal discourse. This distinction remains a useful, if blunt, tool for understanding types of wrong. In what follows, his distinction enables a clearer understanding of immigration offenses and the punishment of those offenses.[191]

---

[188] Blackstone, *Commentaries on the Laws of England*, 1765, 1:57–58.

[189] Ibid., 1:57.

[190] Ibid., 1:40, 41. Internal quotation marks are omitted. See pp. 88–94.

[191] In vol. 4 of the *Commentaries*, Blackstone discusses the power of civil magistrates to punish, saying that the punishment of offenses that are *mala prohibita* depends on the consent of those who gather to form a political community, *Commentaries on the Laws of England*, vol. 4 (Oxford: Clarendon Press, 1769), 8–10, from the Lillian Goldman Library at the Yale Law School, "Avalon Project."

What is an immigration offense? A Mexican national who walks across the Sonoran Desert from Mexico into the United States breaks federal law and commits an immigration offense. Likewise, someone from Brazil who receives a tourist visa, flies to New York, and stays longer than the visa allows, commits an immigration offense. At times, immigration authorities take into account sorts of crimes that are not immigration offenses when they issue a visa or deport someone, like in the example of aggravated felonies above. Burglary, for example, does not violate immigration laws even though it violates other laws. Only when someone is ordered to leave the country because he has committed a burglary and he goes into hiding, or when after being deported he reenters the country without permission, does he commit an immigration offense.

Where do immigration offenses fall in Blackstone's two types? Someone who enters a country on a visa for a fixed time in effect promises to leave that country, and if that person overstays the visa, the person breaks a promise. This is *malum in se*, though it is not as serious as theft or murder. What about entering a country's territory without permission: Is this *malum in se*? Some would say yes, but to qualify as *malum in se*, it would have to be obvious where one country's territory ends and another's begins. In the mountains of the Sonoran Desert where there is no border wall, it is not clear where Mexican territory ends and U.S. territory begins; the border is a line drawn on a map in the Gadsden Purchase of 1853, and it has no relation to features of the land. Even where the Mexico-U.S. border coincides with a geographical feature like the Rio Grande, this division is neither natural nor divinely established. Luther prompts this analysis: Mexico and the United States may govern the territories in their possession under divine government, but it took the U.S.-Mexican War of 1846–48 and the Treaty of Guadalupe Hidalgo to establish the river as the border. This border is fixed by custom, war, and treaty between peoples and governments over which God presides, not fixed by nature or revelation. It is not wrong in itself to be on one side of a river rather than another, and thus immigration offenses are *mala prohibita*.

Some might object that once the authorities have ruled on the matter, many *mala prohibita* offenses are gravely immoral. For example, whether someone drives on the right or the left side of the road is a morally indifferent matter. But once the custom is set, or once an authority declares which side to drive on, it is a grave offense to drive on the wrong side of the road, since doing so endangers others on the road. This offense is criminal, and illegal entry is likewise immoral and criminal, some might argue.[192] But in the case of driving on the wrong side of the street, this act presents an immediate danger to fellow drivers and cyclists, a danger that is obvious to the driver in question – except, perhaps, when the street is deserted and visibility extends far off into the distance. Driving on the wrong side of the road threatens the life and health of fellow human beings, but crossing a border or overstaying a visa

[192] Thanks to Nigel Biggar for suggesting this example.

does not present such an immediate threat. The threat that illegal entry presents tends to be distant and indirect, and the person who commits this act cannot see the potential for harm in the same way as the driver can. This *malum prohibitum* act causes no immediate injury.

In conclusion, overstaying a visa constitutes a *malum in se*, though a minor one. Most immigration offenses are *mala prohibita*, and most of these in turn present only a future potential for harm.

A FITTING PUNISHMENT? SEVEN CASES
OF IMMIGRATION OFFENSES

If most immigration offenses are wrong because the legislature has declared them to be wrong to protect the wellbeing of society, and if they inflict no immediate harm, what punishment suits these offenses? To answer this question, here are seven plausible examples of immigration offenses in the United States and the penalties these offenses are subject to under federal law:

(1) A man and a woman from Vancouver, British Columbia, set off to hike a section of the Pacific Crest Trail from its northern end in Canada into Washington State. They know they are not allowed to cross into the United States on the trail since they will not cross by an official port of entry, but they want to hike the trail, and they have heard that they should not run into any trouble. What is more, as Canadian passport holders they would be eligible to enter the United States as tourists without applying in advance for a visa. As they hike into the United States, Customs and Border Protection (C.B.P.) agents meet them. In a federal court, the pair is charged with failing to present themselves at a border crossing point when arriving other than by conveyance. They are fined $1000 each in civil penalties, and because they knowingly violated the law, they are also fined $1000 each in criminal penalties. The authorities "remove" or deport them to Canada, where they return to their university studies.[193]

(2) A Mexican national hides in a truck and crosses into the United States from Nuevo Laredo, Tamaulipas, to Laredo, Texas. At the border,

---

[193] In 2010, the C.B.P. warned the Pacific Crest Trail Association that hikers could not hike south into the United States on the trail without being liable for prosecution for a federal crime, K. C. Mehaffey, "Feds Warn Pacific Crest Trail Hikers About Crossing Border," *The Seattle Times*, July 1, 2010, www.seattletimes.com/seattle-news/feds-warn-pacific-crest-trail-hikers-about-crossing-border/. The hikers are each liable for criminal penalties of up to one year in jail and a $5,000 fine and an additional $5,000 fine as a civil penalty, 19 U.S.C. § 1459. The Association's website still advises hikers of this at the time of writing, and it notes that it is possible to hike from the United States into Canada with an entry permit from the Canadian government, "Entering the U.S. from Canada," *Pacific Crest Trail Association*, accessed June 21, 2016, www.pcta.org/discover-the-trail/permits/entering-the-u-s-from-canada-on-the-pct/.

officials find and arrest him. They discover that he was previously removed from the United States after being convicted of a violent crime, a felony. The man is tried and convicted in a federal court for the felony of illegal reentry, he is imprisoned for a year, and then he is removed by plane to Mexico City. Tired of trying to return to the United States, he returns to live with family members and looks for a job.[194]

(3) A young man from Chihuahua, Mexico, paddles across the Rio Grande into Texas to look for work and escape the lawlessness of his home town, now dominated by a drug cartel. A day later, he is found walking through the countryside, arrested, and taken before a federal judge under the mass prosecution program Operation Streamline. He is told to plead guilty to the misdemeanor of illegal entry if he wants to avoid further time in jail. The judge sentences him to the time he has already served in jail, and he is removed to the border town of Manuel Ojinaga. He considers trying to enter again.[195]

(4) A woman is arrested for using falsified documents to cross into the United States from Ciudad Juárez, Chihuahua, to El Paso, Texas. She has traveled to visit her ailing mother in the town where she was born in Sinaloa, Mexico, and she is attempting to return to her partner and her two young U.S. citizen children along with her job as a housekeeper in Kansas, where she has lived for eight years without proper documents. Tried and convicted for the misdemeanor of attempting to enter the United States by a willingly false representation, the woman is found to have a clean criminal record, and she is imprisoned for thirty days in El Paso and then removed to Ciudad Juárez. She is now ineligible to receive a visa to enter the United States for ten years, but she is determined to return to her family.[196]

(5) Border Patrol agents find a man by a road north of Sasabe, Arizona, thirsty and hungry, sunburned with torn clothes. Originally from El Salvador, he has made the grueling journey north, riding freight trains through Mexico, and fending off threats from gangs and police.[197]

---

[194] One who commits illegal reentry is liable for fines and imprisonment of up to two years, for up to ten years if the person has committed a felony, and for up to twenty years if that felony is an aggravated felony, 8 U.S.C. § 1326.

[195] One who commits illegal entry is liable to be fined and imprisoned for up to six months, 8 U.S.C. § 1325.

[196] The woman is liable for the same penalties as in the case of illegal entry, and because she is removed by an immigration judge, she is "inadmissible" for ten years, I.N.A. § 212(a)(9)(A)(ii), instituted 110 Stat. 3009–546, 3009–576.

[197] Sonia Nazario, *Enrique's Journey* (New York: Random House, 2006), depicts the often-fatal dangers of the migrant trail through Mexico in a moving account of a boy's journey from Guatemala to join his mother in North Carolina.

The man paid a *coyote* to lead him across the border into the United States, and once there the *coyote* told him and his companions to keep walking north. He had intended to return as he has each year to work on a California farm and send money to support his wife and five children. With a charge of illegal entry already on his record, he is convicted in federal court of the felony of illegal reentry, imprisoned for ninety days, and removed to San Salvador. He begins the journey north once more.

(6) Police officers in Birmingham, Alabama, stop a man for driving a car with a broken taillight. He lacks a driver's license, and they suspect he might lack authorization to be in the country. When pressed, he cannot prove his immigration status, and they hand him over to federal agents. He tells them his parents brought him to the United States from Guatemala at age two, he grew up in Alabama, and now at age eighteen he has just graduated from high school. Customs and Border Protection grants the man "voluntary removal" and flies him to Guatemala City. Since he is not guilty of a criminal offense, he is eligible to apply for a visa to go to the United States immediately, but he is unlikely to receive a visa since he lacks a U.S. citizen spouse, he has reached the age of majority, and he has no offer of a highly skilled job. The man speaks very little Spanish and ends up living on the streets.[198]

(7) An elderly man from the United Kingdom visits his son in New Jersey along with his wife. While there, she gets sick, is hospitalized, and eventually dies in hospice care. He petitions U.S. Citizenship and Immigration Services (U.S.C.I.S.) to extend his stay so that he can live near his son, but because he has now overstayed his ninety-day visitor's visa, he is told that he needs to return to his home country to apply for a new visa. At the U.S. Embassy in London, the man hears that because of his overstay, he is barred from entering the United States for ten years. This means that he will not be able to live near his son until he is ninety-nine years old. After pressing for a review of his case, the Department of Homeland Security and the State Department eventually reduce the delay, awarding him a conditional parole that can be renewed every two years. This is due to extraordinary circumstances: He otherwise would spend the end of his life far from close family members. He moves to New Jersey to live with his son and his son's fiancée.[199]

---

[198] Rep. Spencer Bachus cited a similar case, "Speech to Constituents" (Gardendale Civic Center, Gardendale, Ala., August 21, 2013), www.dropbox.com/sh/lwo6835cvqrzofc/-xwvCTxas9.

[199] This is based on the story of John Oliver in Mark Di Ionno, "U.S. Immigration Policy Puts Ailing W.W. II Vet in Limbo," *The Star-Ledger*, September 4, 2015, www.nj.com/news/index.ssf/2015/09/us_immigration_policy_puts_ailing_wwii_vet_in_limb.html; Mark Di Ionno, "U.S. Immigration Finally Allows W.W. II Vet 'Home,'" *The Star-Ledger*, June 1, 2016,

These examples represent typical cases of immigration offenses in the United States today, except for the case of the Canadians (1). The hikers could be convicted for crossing into the United States, but such convictions are either rare or nonexistent. The cases of entering, reentering, or residing in the United States without author-ization represent common kinds of convictions.[200] Most of these cases involve criminal penalties on top of civil penalties and removal from the country. The Immigration and Nationality Act of 1952 first called immigration offenses criminal offenses, making illegal entry a misdemeanor and illegal reentry a felony and leaving those who commit these offenses liable to be fined and imprisoned.[201] Since then, Congress has increased the maximum periods for which offenders can be imprisoned, up to twenty years in a case like case (2), where someone illegally reenters after being removed for an aggravated felony.[202] The twenty-first century has seen a significant increase in convictions for illegal entry and reentry, with illegal reentry emerging as the top criminal charge brought before federal courts, far ahead of cases involving drugs, violent crime, and white-collar crime.[203] Along with a rising probability of receiving a criminal conviction and being fined and imprisoned, those found guilty of immigration offenses may also be subject to fines as civil penalties.[204] Those found guilty are typically returned to their country of citizenship, either through voluntary return, through expedited removal, or through court-ordered removal. Even those who do not receive jail sentences can face

---

www.nj.com/news/index.ssf/2016/06/us_immigration_finally_allows_wwii_vet_home_di_ion .html. The regulation of visa overstays came into effect in 110 Stat. 3009–546, 3009–701; this caused updates of I.N.A. § 222(g) and 8 U.S.C. § 1202.

[200] By far the lead type of charge in April 2016 for an immigration offense was 8 U.S.C. § 1326, reentry of deported alien. This conviction held the lead for the past five years, and far behind this charge were the second and third most frequent charges, also consistent from 2011 to 2016. In second place was 8 U.S.C. § 1324, bringing in and harboring certain aliens, and in third place, 18 U.S.C. § 1546, fraud and misuse of visas, permits, and other documents, "Immigration Convictions for April 2016" (Transactional Records Access Clearinghouse, Syracuse University, June 10, 2016), http://trac.syr.edu/tracreports/bulletins/immigration/monthlyapr16/gui/.

[201] An Act: To revise the laws relating to immigration, naturalization, and nationality; and for other purposes, Pub. L. No. 82–414, 66 Stat. 163 (1952), 229.

[202] 110 Stat. 3009–546, 3009–576.

[203] Two sources differ in the numbers they offer for illegal entry and illegal reentry, but both sources cite a very large increase of both across the 2000s and early 2010s, "Turning Migrants into Criminals: The Harmful Impact of U.S. Border Prosecutions" (Human Rights Watch, May 22, 2013), 13, www.hrw.org/reports/2013/05/22/turning-migrants-criminals; "Despite Rise in Felony Charges, Most Immigration Convictions Remain Misdemeanors" (Transactional Records Access Clearinghouse, Syracuse University, June 26, 2014), http://trac.syr.edu/immigra tion/reports/356/. Illegal reentry became the top criminal charge brought by federal prosecutors in fiscal year 2011, "Illegal Reentry Becomes Top Criminal Charge" (Transactional Records Access Clearinghouse, Syracuse University, June 10, 2011), http://trac.syr.edu/immigration/ reports/251/; see also "Turning Migrants into Criminals," 14. These trends happen against the backdrop of a marked increase in the use of prison sentences and an attendant increase in prison population that began in the 1970s, subjected to trenchant critique by William J. Stuntz, *The Collapse of American Criminal Justice* (Cambridge, Mass.: Belknap Press of Harvard University Press, 2011), 5.

[204] 8 U.S.C. § 1325, 1326; both refer to 18 U.S.C. § 3571–74.

months in detention while they wait for their cases to be processed or while they wait to be removed from the country.[205]

Do the punishments fit the wrongs committed in these cases? As Oliver O'Donovan demonstrates with reference to Hegel, punishments cannot repay wrongs, but only represent them.[206] The first step in representing wrongs is to state the truth about them. Punishment begins by enacting a judgment, in O'Donovan's account: The judge declares that something is an unlawful act.[207] If acts run against the law, then it is important to name them as against the law so that the offender and the community may know they are unlawful. Offenders deserve to hear the truth about their offense, and society deserves being told what counts as breaking the law.[208] So long as individuals break immigration laws, it is right to declare their acts unlawful.

How then should infractions of immigration laws be named? Should they be considered criminal offenses? Here further distinctions from Blackstone point to an answer. Blackstone distinguishes private wrongs from public wrongs, or civil injuries from crimes and misdemeanors, writing that

> private, or civil injuries, are an infringement or privation of the civil rights which belong to individuals, considered merely as individuals; wrongs, or crime and misdemesnors [sic], are breach and violation of the public rights and duties, due to the whole community, considered as community, in it's [sic] social aggregate capacity.[209]

Blackstone's examples are these: Using someone else's field is a civil injury against an individual, not a crime, but treason, murder, and robbery are crimes "since, besides the injury done to individuals, they strike at the very being of society."[210] Now misdemeanors, properly speaking, are a variety of crime, since they infringe against society, but Blackstone accepts the common usage that crimes are "deeper and more atrocious" while misdemeanors have "less consequence."[211] In a later section, Blackstone deals with felonies, which he says involve some forfeiture, though they are not necessarily capital offenses deserving death. Blackstone does not make clear how felonies and crimes relate, but it seems that he does not think that all crimes other than misdemeanors are felonies.[212]

---

[205] On detention conditions, see Julie Sullivan, "Prisons: Conditions Severe Even for Jails," *The Oregonian*, December 10, 2000, www.pulitzer.org/archives/6511; Stephanie J. Silverman, "Immigration Detention in America: A History of Its Expansion and a Study of Its Signifi-cance" (Centre on Migration, Policy, and Society, 2010).

[206] O'Donovan, *The Ways of Judgment*, 110; O'Donovan cites Georg Wilhelm Friedrich Hegel, Philosophy of Right, trans. T. M. Knox (Oxford: Oxford University Press, 1952), around secs. 93–100.

[207] O'Donovan, *The Ways of Judgment*, 107, 109, 114.

[208] Again, following O'Donovan, ibid., 115–18.

[209] *Commentaries on the Laws of England*, 1769, 4:5.

[210] Ibid.

[211] Ibid.

[212] Ibid., 4:94–98.

Putting Blackstone's categories to work, immigration offenses strike against the public good rather than against individuals, and thus they are crimes or misdemeanors. Excluding the rare cases of illegal entry by those intending to kill, or visa overstay by those convicted of some other crime, immigration offenses are banned because of projected rather than actual wrongs, such as the harm an immigrant might cause to a citizen's job prospects. These offenses tend to be of a sort that is not wrong in itself. For these reasons, it seems right to class immigration offenses not as grave crimes or felonies, or as crimes in the common sense, but as misdemeanors. As misdemeanors, Blackstone suggests they can be understood as a minor variety of crime or as no crime at all.

If it is right to class immigration offenses as misdemeanors, is imprisonment an appropriate punishment? In case (4) above, for example, the woman determined to return to her partner and children will face prison time that will keep her away from her family for a longer time and keep her from working to support them. Time in prison will cause the same harm for the father and migrant worker in case (5). For these two, criminal prosecutions name unlawful acts that are not morally grave, but imprisonment prevents these two individuals from achieving the substantial goods of living with their families, working, and supporting themselves and their families. Further, time in prison will induce those who commit immigration offenses to spend time among more serious offenders, where they may be subject to abuse or encouraged to consider committing offenses of a graver sort.[213] Thus, judges do well not to use the full extent of the criminal penalties available to them under federal law, keeping those who commit these misdemeanors out of prison.

If someone's first immigration offense is a misdemeanor, should a repeat offense be classed as a felony? In case (4), if the mother tries to return to her family and is apprehended, she may be sentenced with a felony, making legal reunion with her family less and less possible. In case (5), the migrant farm worker's only wrong is entering and residing illegally, and so long as he does not commit an offense that is *malum in se*, a repeat offense need not be called a felony. On their own, it appears that immigration offenses should not be considered felonies.

Having concluded that immigration offenses are best called misdemeanors, it is time to move beyond labels to concrete punishments. What punishments rightly correspond to infractions against immigration laws? Federal United States law has its own set of conventions, its own language of punishment: Is this set of conventions truthful and proportionate?[214]

What of civil penalties? Fines may be an appropriate way to penalize those a government wants to keep from entering its territory in an irregular manner. In case (1), fines may be a good way to make sure that everyone, even hikers, enter the United States at an official port of entry. Hikers are likely to be Internet-savvy, and

---

[213] See the ethnographic evidence offered by Daniel Martinez and Jeremy Slack, "What Part of 'Illegal' Don't You Understand? The Social Consequences of Criminalizing Unauthorized Mexican Migrants in the United States," *Social & Legal Studies* 22, no. 4 (2013): 535–51.

[214] The notion of penal languages or dialects follows O'Donovan, *The Ways of Judgment*, 120–22.

other hikers would likely hear of a conviction in case (1) and avoid walking south along the Pacific Coast Trail from Canada to the United States. In cases (2) to (5) and (7), if fines had been levied, perhaps they would serve as a deterrent and allow some of the costs to the enforcement agencies to be recouped.

Is removal or deportation a fitting punishment for an immigration offense? In one sense, removal proves a fitting response to the wrong in question. A noncitizen enters or resides in the country without permission, and the authorities act to remove that person from the country. On the face of it, there is a simple correspondence between act and punishment, but things are not so simple. If the only wrong committed by the person is failing to comply with government regulations, and if they have not done something *malum in se*, then other goods must be taken into account. To tell if removal fits an immigration offense, the goods that immigration law is thought to protect must be weighed against the goods that the person breaking that law seeks to gain or preserve.

Of the seven cases above, it is easiest to argue that removal is appropriate in the first two. In case (1), perhaps the conviction of the pair of Canadian hikers sends a message to other hikers that everyone who wants to enter United States territory should do so in the proper, legal way. The conviction promotes a federal effort to keep track of every person who enters the country. If the pair had only planned to hike a short part of the trail and then return to Canada, they might have bought food and supplies in the United States. If they had hiked a longer part of the trail, they might have worked odd jobs in exchange for food or cash, work that a U.S. citizen might have performed. For them, removal might be frightening, but they have studies and homes to return to in Canada. In this case, removal promotes the federal government's efforts to certify every entry into U.S. lands, but it seems heavy-handed, since there is only a small possibility that the pair's presence will harm the common possessions of U.S. society. The removal of the Mexican national in case (2) is easier to support. Since the man has already been convicted of a violent crime in the United States, he has forfeited grounds for remaining in the United States as a noncitizen. His removal might keep the country free of someone who could commit another crime. Still, his prosecution does not give him an opportunity to demonstrate that he has amended his way of life since being convicted, leaving no room for mercy. At the same time, as in the first case, there are reasons to argue that removal fits his offense.

In the rest of the cases, it is harder to argue that removal fits the wrong done, and it is difficult to see that what removal does for U.S. society is worth the damage done to the individuals who are deported. In case (3), if the man from Chihuahua remains in the United States, some would say he would take away a job that a citizen could do, but others would say that he would do work that citizens are not willing to do or that he might start a business and create work for others. On the other hand, there are good reasons to be suspicious of attempts to measure the worth of an immigrant based on his contribution to the cash economy of the United States. If the man returns to his home state in Mexico, he will return to a place overrun by drug cartels and killings.[215] The uncertain effects of his presence in the United States balance unevenly with a difficult life for him at home. If this case (3) is modified, would removal be more fitting? If the man came from the state of Guanajuato and had a chance to study engineering and work in the automobile industry, perhaps removal would do no great injury to him. Then again, he would be less likely to attempt to cross into the United States in the first instance. What if the man in case (3) lacked these opportunities but came from a different village, safer than the town in Chihuahua but impoverished? Removal might prevent the man from finding decent food and shelter that he could find in the neighboring country to the north, and his effect on the common possessions of U.S. citizens remains undetermined. Only if case (3) is modified to place the man in a safe hometown with work opportunities could removal be fitting, but in that case the man would not be likely to enter the United States illegally.

In case (4), it is harder to justify removal. Were the woman in case (4) to remain in the United States, she would do so against the federal government's authority over the admission of noncitizens. She would add to a community of men and women living in the United States without permission, a community living in fear and prevented from contributing to her Kansas community by that fear. Those interested in an economic calculus would raise concerns about her taking work from U.S. citizens, and those who think culture is best preserved by limiting immigration would ask how well she would integrate into U.S. culture. On the other hand, the woman's regular work over eight years creates a bond between the woman and the Kansas residents who employ her. If the woman is removed, her children will be without a mother and her partner without her company, and she will be left alone. Administrative regularity matters, and some will think that protecting businesses and culture through immigration restrictions is worthwhile. Still, to remove her would be to ignore the bond she has formed with her Kansas community during eight years of work and residence. Also, to remove her would require that the state and the nation matter more than the woman's family. When children are left without a mother, federal intervention on a *malum prohibitum* matter appears unjustified.

Similar considerations come into play in case (5). The man from El Salvador has been offered regular work on California farms, participating in longstanding cyclical migration patterns. It is likely that he has provided steady, hard work for farm owners who have paid him less than the legal minimum wage and who might have avoided paying taxes related to his labor. As an undocumented worker, the man has been afraid to complain if his employers leave him to breathe fumes from pesticides or strain his back. He has been without medical insurance, and perhaps he has nursed

---

[215] The man might be eligible for asylum, but interviews indicate that in recent years, officials who apprehend individuals near the border are not in the habit of advising Mexican nationals of their opportunities to apply for asylum, "Turning Migrants into Criminals," 65.

injuries sustained on the job. The farm owners have passed on the benefits of his cheap labor to consumers who buy their produce at low cost. Still, the man's low pay helps his family survive, and they depend on his work in the United States. Some would express concerns about the rule of law, economics, and culture like in case (4) above, but to remove him is to fail to recognize the relationship the man has built with farm owners and consumers in the United States. Removing him also endangers the wellbeing of his wife and five children in El Salvador. Once again, it is hard to argue that removing the man is a fitting punishment for the *malum prohibitum* he has committed by reentering illegally.

In case (6), it is difficult to make an argument that removal fits the wrong done. The man's parents brought him from Guatemala to the United States as a boy, and he is largely enculturated, possessing little knowledge of Spanish. Removing him to Guatemala sentences him to life in an unfamiliar country for which he is not prepared. In this case, removal punishes the man for his parents' illegal act when he is not responsible for that act. Some might say that allowing the man to stay would encourage other parents to do the same with their children, but a stronger argument is that the direct harms done to this man by deporting him outweigh the value of preventing possible future harm to what U.S. citizens share.

In case (7), the government's demands that the man return to the UK and wait for even two years seem excessive. The cause of the man's overstaying his visa was the ill health and death of his wife. After her death, he merits being allowed to stay in the United States as an elderly man whose only close relative lives there. Eventually, the Department of Homeland Security sees fit to approve this. Still, the man would not have caused the United States any significant harm had he stayed with his son in New Jersey while his case was considered. Behind these circumstances lies another feature of case (7): The man has overstayed a visa that granted him a limited amount of time in the United States. Visa overstay ties together a wide variety of cases, some more intentional, as when someone enters as a tourist but stays to work in the United States. Here, a moral fact arises that does not arise in the other cases: The person enters into a written agreement to leave the United States within a certain amount of time, but that person does not keep their word. This is a broken promise: something that is *malum in se*.[216] Still, this untruth is not a grave matter like a violent crime. Perhaps a fine would be appropriate for the case, and otherwise, removal would depend on the other circumstances of the case. Requiring the elderly man to leave the country does not seem necessary. There might be more reason to remove someone who entered the country with plans to overstay a visa and work. Still, the damage done to common possessions does not seem great. The longer the person stays in the United States, establishing local ties and contributing to a community, the more that reasons to remove the person would diminish.

---

[216] Thanks to Joshua Hordern for posing this example of a *malum in se*.

Removal as a punishment far exceeds what most immigration offenses deserve: This is the conclusion to which these considerations lead. Perhaps in cases where noncitizens have committed other offenses that are *mala in se*, and perhaps where no substantial harm is done to these persons could removal be an acceptable punishment, proportionate to the offense. However, removal is a powerful and potentially life-changing act by government, and when it does damage to goods more substantial than national sovereignty, it is not justified. As ties to the host country grow, as a migrant contributes labor, as a newcomer builds a life and a home, it becomes more difficult to justify removal to punish the *mala prohibita* of falsifying immigration documents, illegally entering, overstaying a visa, and related offenses. When removal breaks up families or consigns them to poverty, what it does in the name of common possessions goes too far. When lawlessness and despotism threaten in the immigrant's country of origin, removal does more harm than is needed.

This argument against removal in the case of most immigration offenses resembles the right of domicile that the dissenting justices in *Fong Yue Ting v. United States* favored. There, they said that an alien who is lawfully admitted and who establishes a place of residence and builds ties gains a right of domicile, a right not to be displaced from home. If a government does otherwise, these justices argued, it becomes tyrannical and despotic.[217] This section argues for something slightly different, since it deals with noncitizens who are not lawfully admitted. Still, those who establish a home and build ties to a community, who do not commit crimes that are *mala in se*, deserve to be left in place. A government that displaces settled people who do not commit serious crimes is a government that goes beyond its remit, holding an excess of power over the persons in its lands.[218]

If immigration offenses are not wrong in themselves but wrong because they are prohibited, then their immediate harm lies in failing to respect the sovereignty of the country in question, sovereignty that protects goods that a society holds in common against future harm. This section has argued that it is right for governments to state when wrong is done: to provide a "sentence" in the simplest sense. Civil penalties may be appropriate in the case of these wrongs, but they should be considered misdemeanors rather than felonies. The standard punishment for immigration offenses, removal or deportation, usually far outstrips the wrong done in breaking the law. Sovereignty cannot be taken as the overarching good in these cases, and other moral goods must come into account. Alongside protecting the society of

---

[217] Fong Yue Ting v. United States, Wong Quan v. United States, Lee Joe v. United States, 149 U.S. 698 (1893).

[218] Joseph H. Carens makes a similar argument in a pair of articles, arguing that the longer migrants stay in a country, the stronger their claims to membership become, "Live-in Domestics, Seasonal Workers, and Others Hard to Locate on the Map of Democracy," *Journal of Political Philosophy* 16, no. 4 (2008): 419–45; "The Case for Amnesty," *Boston Review*, 2009, www.bostonreview.net/forum/case-amnesty-joseph-carens.

those already within the land, civil authorities have responsibilities to preserve other goods, to protect family life, to ensure good relationships between employers and laborers, to defend the most vulnerable from destitution, and to seek good relations with other nations. Other works argue that immigration law needs to protect families and those in poverty, and Part III will indicate how immigration law shows more respect for relationships with neighboring countries.[219]

—

Bad news for immigrants in the last chapter prompted a search for good news in Christian theology in this chapter. Martin Luther and other trusted interpreters guided a reading of what the Bible suggests about immigration authority. On this reading, Christian teaching agrees on the need to guard places, but it subjects that guarding to God's guarding. Defending territories against threats by those from outside is a feature of divine providence for this era before the open gates of the New Jerusalem, but it remains subject to God. Under divine judgment, human judgment is obligated to protect vulnerable migrants and to respect limits to its powers. By failing in these obligations, federal United States law arrogates to itself sovereign powers reserved for God. Still, so long as they seek power for power's sake, those in authority must be aware that it is within God's powers to displace and dispossess them, something this chapter found affirmed in Scripture. But now is the time for repentance: The God revealed in Jesus Christ will forgive.

Within this broader frame, resources from the Christian tradition pointed toward a more exacting account of what immigration authority rightly does and what punishment is appropriate for those who go against it. On this reading, the guarding of places under God's guarding is best expressed as a protection on human life, preventing unjust killing and vengeance. It is less clear that places may be guarded for other reasons – to protect jobs for citizens or to preserve a culture, for example. Indeed, forbidding immigration for such reasons places authorities in a bind, since with restrictions comes a commitment to enforcement through detention and deportation. Especially when an immigrant has established a residence in a new country, the diffuse harm that that person threatens to bring against an economy or a culture is rarely or ever commensurate with the standard punishment for illegal entry or overstay: removal from the country. These considerations and others suggest that the authority over immigration is best understood modestly and best practiced mercifully.

---

[219] Victor Carmona, "Neither Slave nor Free: A Critique of U.S. Immigration Policy in Light of the Work of David Hollenbach, Gustavo Gutiérrez, and Thomas Aquinas" (Ph.D. Dissertation, University of Notre Dame, 2014), deals with the family and poverty in immigration preferences.

PART III

An Unlawfully Present Alien from a Neighboring Country?

5

How Nationals of Neighboring Countries
Became Illegal Aliens

Nondiscrimination, Mexican Migration,
and Federal Immigration Law

On October 3, 1965, United States President Lyndon B. Johnson stood before the Statue of Liberty in New York Harbor, signed a new immigration Act and declared, "This bill . . . repair[s] a very deep and painful flaw in the fabric of American justice. It corrects a cruel and enduring wrong in the conduct of the American Nation . . . For over four decades," he explained, "the immigration policy of the United States has been twisted and . . . distorted by the harsh injustice of the national origins quota system. Under that system," Johnson said, "the ability of new immigrants to come to America depended on the country of their birth. Only three countries were allowed to supply seventy percent of all the immigrants . . . Men . . . were denied entrance because they came from southern or eastern Europe or from one of the developing continents." The old system, the President said, "violated the basic principle of American democracy – the principle that values and rewards each man on the basis of his merit as a man." The bill he was signing into law, he told the crowd on Liberty Island, said "simply that from this day forth those wishing to immigrate to America shall be admitted on the basis of their skills and their close relationship to those already here."[1]

The law Johnson signed that day was the Immigration Act of 1965. This new Congressional legislation made this promise: "No person shall receive any preference or priority or be discriminated against in the issuance of an immigrant visa because of his race, sex, nationality, place of birth, or place of residence"[2] Few would be inclined to oppose such language, to suggest that it would be good to discriminate against persons based on their country of origin, or to say that

---

[1] Lyndon B. Johnson, "Remarks at the Signing of the Immigration Bill, Liberty Island, New York, October 3, 1965," in *Public Papers of the Presidents of the United States: Lyndon B. Johnson, 1965*, vol. 2 (Washington, D.C.: Government Printing Office, 1965), 1037–40, www.lbjlib.utexas.edu/johnson/archives.hom/speeches.hom/651003.asp.

[2] An Act: To amend the Immigration and Nationality Act, and for other purposes, Pub. L. No. 89-236, 79 Stat. 911 (1965), 911.

government should not treat human beings equally. Yet behind Johnson's talk of "reward[ing] each man on the basis of his merit as a man" and the law's promise to end discrimination lay other shifts that proved more problematic. The national origins quota system in place from 1924 to 1965 had severely limited immigration from places like Italy and Romania, but it placed no limit on countries in the Western Hemisphere. As the framers of the 1965 Act worked to end discrimination against Southern and Eastern Europeans, they placed every nation on an equal footing, whether from the Eastern Hemisphere or the Western Hemisphere. Besides special allowances for family members and sought-after workers, by 1976, each country in the world received the same number of visas per year.

This shift would have significant implications for the United States' southern neighbor, Mexico. The federal government had long encouraged Mexicans to come north to provide labor on American farms, and the most recent policy to encourage this, the Bracero Program, had ended just a year before, in 1964. Under the new immigration regime, if Mexicans were to migrate into the United States at the same rate they had before, most of them would have to come without legal permission. After the 1965 law went into effect in 1968, Mexicans continued to migrate to the United States in similar numbers, but most immigrated illegally. Half a century later, some eleven million immigrants live in the United States without permission, and just over half come from Mexico.[3] What is now a permanent and predominant feature of American political life, the alien unlawfully present, likely to be a native of Mexico, was made possible in part by the Immigration and Nationality Act of 1965. A move to end discrimination produced a shadowy existence for the many who remain neither slave nor free.

How did it come about that so many millions today could be considered illegal aliens under United States law? Part I examined the rise of the alien in law and provided a Christian alternative in creation and the church. Part II discovered how aliens became illegal in U.S. law and qualified that shift through a theology of political authority. Part III looks at a third innovation that enabled many men, women, and children from neighboring countries to be classed as illegal aliens, and it suggests a picture of justice for neighbors that points a way out of the dilemma of illegal immigration.

This chapter will argue that although the 1965 change in immigration law to end discrimination based on national origins made great forward strides, it proved unneighborly. In it, the United States Congress chose an abstract, universal ethic without recognizing U.S. debts to neighboring Mexico. The chapter will explore the context of the 1965 Act and the moral arguments that brought it about, and it will

---

[3] Some 11.1 million people lived in the United States without permission as of 2014. An estimated 5.8 million of those, or 52 percent, came from Mexico, Jeffrey S. Passel and D'Vera Cohn, "Overall Number of U.S. Unauthorized Immigrants Holds Steady Since 2009" (Washington, D.C.: Pew Research Center, September 20, 2016), 3, www.pewhispanic.org/2016/09/20/overall-number-of-u-s-unauthorized-immigrants-holds-steady-since-2009/. See p. 4 note 6.

survey the longstanding ties between Mexico and the United States. An internal critique of the 1965 statute will indicate that in jettisoning discrimination, the federal government failed to recognize near neighbors and left them open to an oppressive sort of discrimination. The account will circle around the wordings of legislation and the speeches and letters of political actors. Contemporary American and Mexican historians and social scientists, particularly Daniel J. Tichenor, Mae M. Ngai, Aristide E. Zolberg, Douglas S. Massey, Jorge Durand, and Nolan J. Malone, will assist in rounding out the account. This will leave an opportunity for the next chapter to review this history and propose a better way forward, drawing on philosophy and theology.

ENDING FAVOR FOR NEIGHBORS: FEDERAL IMMIGRATION LAW, 1921 TO 1990

Scientific Racism and Cultural Preservation: The National Origins Quota System of 1924

In his speech at the Statue of Liberty, Lyndon B. Johnson declared the triumph of American democratic principles in immigration law. The bill he signed into law overturned a pattern that had been fixed since the Immigration Act of 1924, with a precursor in 1921.

What was the pattern that the 1965 Act overturned? As Daniel Tichenor tells the story, the Progressives of the early twentieth century had a penchant for expertise that was scientific and exacting, and this scientism turned its gaze to anthropology, positing distinct races among human beings.[4] In federal immigration law, both the Chinese and the Japanese were excluded, classed as unassimilable races, but scientific attention to race did not stop with Asia.[5] The scientists of race turned their attention to Europe, splitting the peoples of the continent into different types. A 1907 Congressional commission on immigration produced volumes that coalesced around a contrast between the longer-standing immigrant stocks from northern and western Europe and the newer arrivals from southern and eastern Europe, who were said to imperil the nation.[6] The commission's lengthy "Dictionary of Races" parroted William Ripley's 1899 typology of three distinct European races, the Teutonic, the Alpine or Celtic, and the Mediterranean, with the last judged inferior to the others.[7] Though immigrant associations and some intellectuals

[4] Daniel J. Tichenor, *Dividing Lines: The Politics of Immigration Control in America* (Princeton: Princeton University Press, 2002), 114–15, 128.
[5] Ibid., 123. On the Gentleman's Agreement, see pp. 70 note 24.
[6] Tichenor, *Dividing Lines*, 129.
[7] Ibid., 129–31; Daniel Folkmar and Elnora C. Folkmar, "Dictionary of Races or Peoples, Presented by Mr. Dillingham, Dec. 5, 1910," Reports of the Immigration Commission (Washington, D.C.: Government Printing Office, 1911), 5, 31; William Z. Ripley, *The Races of Europe: A Sociological Study Accompanied by a Supplementary Bibliography of the*

envisioned a pluralist America, the tide swung in favor of Progressive, scientific racism. The movement achieved its first victory in the realm of immigration law in 1917, with a literacy test and further restrictions on immigrants.[8] Its second victory came in 1921, when under President Warren G. Harding and his America First nationalism, Congress enacted "emergency quotas" on immigration from the Eastern Hemisphere.[9]

The movement to restrict immigration gained steam in the following three years while the quotas were renewed. The head of the House immigration committee, Albert Johnson, enlisted a eugenics expert who argued that the belief in the equality of all men should not blind Americans from "natural inborn hereditary mental and moral differences."[10] Johnson also maintained regular contact with Madison Grant, who thought the Nordic race, the "Great Race," was being diluted in the United States through immigration, in part because Christianity, "the religion of the slave, the meek, and the lowly" had broken down race distinctions.[11] Others who joined in the movement for racist immigration laws did not stress racial superiority so much as the idea that different races had better not mix.[12] Historian Otis Graham, favorable to this milder account of race, suggests that a better grasp of the writings of the time results from substituting "culture" or "nationality" for "race," capturing the often nonbiological account of race present when, for example, Theodore Roosevelt spoke of the "American race."[13] Beyond commitments to racism or cultural separation, other factors pushed Congress toward a restrictive immigration regime: isolationism after the war, a desire to protect domestic workers from competition that would drive down wages, concerns about political subversives, and a sense that too many newcomers of whatever national origin would destroy social unity.[14]

Anthropology and Ethnology of Europe, 2 vols. (New York: Appleton, 1899); references are drawn from *The Races of Europe: A Sociological Study* (London: Kegan Paul, Trench, Trübner & Co., 1900), 121.

[8] An Act: To regulate the immigration of aliens to, and the residence of aliens in, the United States, Pub. L. No. 64-301, 39 Stat. 874 (1917), 875, 877.

[9] An Act: To limit the immigration of aliens into the United States, Pub. L. No. 67-5, 42 Stat. 5 (1921), 5; Tichenor, *Dividing Lines*, 129.

[10] Harry H. Laughlin, in Oscar Handlin, *Immigration as a Factor in American History* (Englewood Cliffs, N.J.: Prentice-Hall, 1959), 132; cited in Tichenor, *Dividing Lines*, 144.

[11] Madison Grant, *The Passing of the Great Race; Or, the Racial Basis of European History* (New York: C. Scribner, 1916); references are drawn from *The Passing of the Great Race; Or, the Racial Basis of European History*, 4th rev. edn. with a documentary supplement (New York: C. Scribner, 1936), 167, 175, 222, 231.

[12] For example, Edward R. Lewis, *America: Nation or Confusion?* (New York: Harper & Brothers, 1928), in Roger Daniels and Otis L. Graham, eds., *Debating American Immigration, 1882-Present* (Lanham, Md.: Rowman & Littlefield Publishers, 2001), 194–97; Mae M. Ngai, *Impossible Subjects: Illegal Aliens and the Making of Modern America* (Princeton: Princeton University Press, 2004), 25.

[13] Otis L. Graham, "The Unfinished Reform: Regulating Immigration in the National Interest," in *Debating American Immigration, 1882-Present*, ed. Roger Daniels and Otis L. Graham (Lanham, Md.: Rowman & Littlefield Publishers, 2001), 109.

[14] John F. Kennedy, *A Nation of Immigrants*, rev. and enl. edn. (London: Hamish Hamilton, 1964), 75–76.

Senator David Reed signaled his assessment of public opinion to a Senate sub-committee: "I think the American people want us to discriminate; and I don't think discrimination in itself is unfair ... We have got to discriminate."[15]

Congress acted in the Immigration Act of 1924, known by the name of its sponsors, Johnson and Reed. The Johnson-Reed Act enacted the discriminations that Reed had proposed, at first limiting yearly immigration from each country to 2 percent of foreign-born people from that country represented in the 1890 U.S. census. In a second quota system that was not implemented until 1929, immigrants of each nationality were admitted in a number that bore that same ratio to 150,000 as the number of U.S. citizens of that national origin bore to the total number of U.S. inhabitants in 1920.[16] The first plan reproduced a long-past foreign-born population, while the second plan indexed a more recent figure of those who were full citizens, either by birth or naturalization. The second plan held until the Act of 1965 went into effect in 1968, and it continued to enforce a replication of the society of 1920. The national origins calculus effected a severe drop in the overall numbers of immigrants, with northern and western Europe allowed a much greater number than southern and eastern Europe. Alongside quotas for most of the Eastern Hemisphere, the Johnson-Reed Act perpetuated the thorough-going 1917 ban on immigration from most of Asia.[17] Still, the Act maintained an exception for the Western Hemisphere. Along with the children and wives of citizens, immigrants previously admitted but returning from a trip abroad, ministers, professors, and students, the Act listed those who were born in independent countries of the Americas as nonquota immigrants. Addressing males, it admitted an immigrant's wife and his unmarried children under eighteen years of age. Nevertheless, the Act counted those in Western Hemisphere colonies within the quotas of their respective colonizing powers.[18]

By 1929, then, only those races thought to be superior could join American society – or at least only those peoples that resembled Americans of years gone by. There remained a glaring exception: Those from the Western Hemisphere were exempt from restriction, even if they were classed outside of the desired Nordic or Teutonic races. The invisibility and small proportion of Western Hemisphere immigrants who tended to work on farms, a push by Southern and Western legislators to keep the border open to these workers,[19] and a sense of neighborhood each contributed to keep the Western Hemisphere free of numerical quotas.

---

[15] Quoted in President's Commission on Immigration and Naturalization, "Whom We Shall Welcome" (Washington, D.C.: Government Printing Office, 1953), 89.

[16] An Act: To limit the immigration of aliens into the United States, and for other purposes, Pub. L. No. 68–139, 43 Stat. 153 (1924), 159; Tichenor, *Dividing Lines*, 144–45.

[17] 39 Stat. 874, 876.

[18] The Act reads, "the term 'non-quota immigrant' means ... (c) An immigrant who was born in the Dominion of Canada, Newfoundland, the Republic of Mexico, the Republic of Cuba, the Republic of Haiti, the Dominican Republic, the Canal Zone, or an independent country of Central or South America, and his wife, and his unmarried children under 18 years of age, if accompanying or following to join him," 43 Stat. 153, 155.

[19] Tichenor, *Dividing Lines*, 146.

Good Neighbors and Discrimination: Toward Reform

The national origins quotas of the 1924 Act did not come under serious threat of reform until the early 1950s. Those on both sides of the debate were troubled by past theories of superior races, and the role such dogmas played among the Nazis further doomed racist theories. The report of a 1950 Congressional commission, the McCarran Report, for example, repudiated "any theory of Nordic superiority" while arguing that the 1924 Act's proponents were "fully justified in determining that ... further immigration would not only be restricted but directed to admit immigrants considered to be more readily assimilable because of the similarity of their cultural background to those of the principal components of our population."[20] A magazine article from the time by Robert C. Alexander sounded a similar theme: "Our national origins quota system is like a mirror held up before the American people," allowing immigration in a way that reflects the national origins of the United States. Alexander reasoned, "Those who object to our national origins quota system obviously disapprove the national origins of our people."[21]

An incipient reform movement was not strong enough to resist a repetition of the national origins quotas under a new guise in the Immigration and Nationality Act of 1952, known as the McCarran-Walter Act.[22] The law served primarily to introduce a new bureaucracy for immigration admissions, while maintaining the quotas that allowed admission to immigrants in proportion to the contribution a country made to the U.S. citizenry in 1920, altering the formula to one sixth of 1 percent of the 1920 figure.[23] The quotas saw only cosmetic changes, with one hundred visas annually for the previously barred Asia-Pacific triangle as well as for Western Hemisphere colonies.[24] The Act also left in place the exception for the Western Hemisphere, placing no quota on independent countries in the Americas.[25] Within the quotas, a new pattern of "preferences" for those with occupational skills and family connections guided the allocation of visas.[26] Naturalization law underwent a more

[20] "Immigration and Naturalization Systems of the United States: Report of the Committee on the Judiciary Pursuant to S. Res. 137 (80th Congress, 1st Session, as Amended), a Resolution to Make an Investigation of the Immigration System (McCarran Report)," Senate Report 1515 (Washington, D.C.: Government Printing Office, 1950), 455.

[21] Robert C. Alexander, "Our National Origins Quota System: The Mirror of America," *The American Legion Magazine*, September 1956, 52, quoted in Daniels and Graham, *Debating American Immigration, 1882-Present*, 198.

[22] Tichenor, *Dividing Lines*, 187, 189.

[23] An Act: To revise the laws relating to immigration, naturalization, and nationality; and for other purposes, Pub. L. No. 82-414, 66 Stat. 163 (1952), 175; see Aristide R. Zolberg, *A Nation by Design: Immigration Policy in the Fashioning of America* (Cambridge, Mass.: Harvard University Press, 2006), 318, and Ngai, *Impossible Subjects*, 249–50.

[24] Moving the colonies from the unrestricted category to this quota was widely interpreted as an effort to prevent Afro-Caribbeans from immigrating to the United States, 66 Stat. 163, 177–78; Zolberg, *A Nation by Design*, 312, 316–17.

[25] 66 Stat. 163, 169.

[26] 66 Stat. 163, 178.

significant shift than immigration law did when Congress declared that race was no longer a barrier to naturalization.[27]

Why did the McCarran-Walter Act of 1952 maintain only qualitative restrictions on Western Hemisphere immigration, imposing no numerical caps on independent countries? Just before the Act, the McCarran Report gave this rationale: "The blanket nonquota status in the case of Western Hemisphere aliens rests chiefly upon considerations arising from geographical proximity of Western Hemisphere countries and considerations of friendly relations among them." The report also said that quota restrictions on the Western Hemisphere would not be "compatible with our good-neighbor policy."[28]

As applied to the Western Hemisphere, this Good Neighbor Policy was President Franklin D. Roosevelt's response to decades of distrust in response to the United States' readiness to intervene in Latin America. Earlier patterns of intervention by the United States in the Americas caused Roosevelt to proceed with the policies of nonintervention of his recent predecessors Calvin Coolidge and Herbert Hoover.[29] In 1933, at his first inauguration, Franklin Roosevelt said,

> In the field of world policy I would dedicate this Nation to the policy of the good neighbor – the neighbor who resolutely respects himself and, because he does so, respects the rights of others – the neighbor who respects his obligations and respects the sanctity of his agreements in and with a world of neighbors.[30]

Roosevelt elaborated on the neighborliness of respect and obligation in a speech to the Pan-American Union a month later. He stressed the interdependence of nations, particularly in the Western Hemisphere, calling for a "Pan Americanism." Roosevelt called for "fraternal cooperation" and "friendship among nations," bound by "mutual . . . responsibilities." He went on to say, "The essential qualities of a true Pan Americanism must be the same as those which constitute a good neighbor, namely, mutual understanding, and, through such understanding, a sympathetic appreciation of the other's point of view." Roosevelt stressed that the hemisphere would defend itself; he opposed wars within the hemisphere, and he sought to abolish barriers to trade in the Americas.[31]

In the years of his presidency, Roosevelt took concrete steps toward becoming a good neighbor, or at least a better neighbor. He was the first president to discuss U.S. foreign policy with Latin American diplomats and the first to visit

[27] 66 Stat. 163, 239.
[28] "McCarran Report," 473.
[29] Fredrick B. Pike, *F.D.R.'s Good Neighbor Policy: Sixty Years of Generally Gentle Chaos* (Austin: University of Texas Press, 1995), 171.
[30] Franklin D. Roosevelt, "Presidential Inaugural Address" (Washington, D.C., March 4, 1933), www.inaugural.senate.gov/swearing-in/address/address-by-franklin-d-roosevelt-1933.
[31] Franklin D. Roosevelt, "Address on the Occasion of the Celebration of Pan-American Day" (Washington, D.C., April 12, 1933), www.presidency.ucsb.edu/ws/index.php?pid=14615.

South America.[32] His administration took steps, too, offering a policy of non-intervention at the Montevideo Pan-American Conference, giving up most of its special privileges in Cuba, withdrawing troops from Haiti, and not intervening when Mexico nationalized American-owned oil industries.[33] One historian, Frederick B. Pike, interprets the Good Neighbor Policy as disingenuous, arguing that the United States defined whatever it was doing at the moment as nonintervention while continuing to intervene in Latin America, at least through economic measures and diplomatic encouragements or threats.[34] Pike raises further objections, writing that as Roosevelt faced Latin America, his outlook was European, and he romanticized the primitive "Other" of the Americas and constructed a mystical affinity for the hemisphere.[35] Nevertheless, Roosevelt succeeded in securing hemispheric unity against the Axis powers during the Second World War, but soon after and against talk of being a good neighbor, the United States picked up the pace of its Western Hemisphere interventions. Still, the notion of the Good Neighbor remained available for matters of Latin American relations in immigration law.

Along with the Good Neighbor Policy, a second reason that the Western Hemisphere was placed under no numerical restrictions in the McCarran-Walter Act had to do with a duplicitous truce with the illegal immigration of laborers. The McCarran Report stated, "The extensive Canadian and Mexican borders make it almost impossible to protect land borders from illegal entries."[36] Such a statement acknowledged the futility of policing land borders, and it tacitly allowed the illegal movement of migrant workers across the southern border. Senator Pat McCarran himself expressed a desire to allow such movement in testimony to a Senate subcommittee, saying that illegal labor was better than *bracero* or contract labor. "A farmer can get a wetback and he does not have to go through that red tape," he stated. "We might just as well face this thing realistically. The agricultural people, the farmers . . . want this help. They want this farm labor. They just cannot get along without it."[37] This framer of the 1952 Act made plain that he did not want to discourage the illegal immigration of farm workers, citing the "reality" that farmers want and need these workers. The next section will reveal more about this truce with illegal immigration.[38]

[32] Robert Dallek, *Franklin D. Roosevelt and American Foreign Policy, 1932–1945* (New York: Oxford University Press, 1995), 63, 87.

[33] Ibid., 66, 86, 87, 128, 175–76.

[34] Pike, *F.D.R.'s Good Neighbor Policy*, 164, 166.

[35] Ibid., 211, 212.

[36] "McCarran Report," 473.

[37] Hearings before the Subcommittee of the Senate Committee on Appropriations on H.R. 4974, 83rd Congress, 1st Session (1953), 245–246, quoted in Eleanor Hadley, "A Critical Analysis of the Wetback Problem," *Law and Contemporary Problems* 21 (1956): 336, 337.

[38] See pp. 163–77.

In the years that followed, agitation continued against the national origins quotas and the discrimination that the 1924 Act's sponsor, Senator Reed, had said they represented. The reformers took aim at discrimination based on race or nationality. *Whom We Shall Welcome*, the 1953 report of a commission Truman authorized while he was still in office in 1952, served as the manifesto of the movement. The report declared immigration law to be the sign of "whether Americans today believe in the essential worth and dignity of the individual human being," in "unalienable rights," in the notion that people are "the children of God."[39] The report judged that the national origins quotas system failed to uphold American ideals before other nations. "We cannot be true to the democratic faith of our own Declaration of Independence in the equality of all men, and at the same time pass immigration laws which discriminate against people because of national origin, race, color, or creed," the Commission stated.[40] The Commission acknowledged that immigration laws needed to protect and preserve America from danger and disease, but it expressed "that full security can be achieved only with a positive immigration policy based not on fears but on faith in people and in the future of a democratic and free United States."[41] The Report called for faith: faith in the value of every human being, and faith that newcomers would aid in the continuing formation of a democratic America.

Whom We Shall Welcome linked immigration reform to another reform movement of the time when it said, "We cannot defend civil rights in principle, and deny them in our immigration laws and practice."[42] The matter of equality for African Americans was different from immigration law, as it concerned residents and citizens of the United States, yet the arguments were strikingly similar. As an example, two major provisions in the Civil Rights Act of 1964 used language that paralleled the campaign against discrimination in immigration law. In terms it reiterated for matters of employment, the Civil Rights Act declared, "All persons shall be entitled to the full and equal enjoyment of the goods [and] services ... of any place of public accommodation ... without discrimination or segregation on the ground of race, color, religion, or national origin."[43] The power of these arguments was persuasive, and the immigration reform movement made use of a parallel discourse.

---

[39] "Whom We Shall Welcome," xii.
[40] Ibid., xiv.
[41] Ibid.
[42] Ibid., xv.
[43] An Act: To enforce the constitutional right to vote, to confer jurisdiction upon the district courts of the United States to provide injunctive relief against discrimination in public accommodations, to authorize the Attorney General to institute suits to protect constitutional rights in public facilities and public education, to extend the Commission on Civil Rights, to prevent discrimination in federally assisted programs, to establish a Commission on Equal Employment Opportunity, and for other purposes, Pub. L. No. 88–352, 78 Stat. 241 (1964), 243, 255; see also Brown v. Board of Education of Topeka, 349 U.S. 294 (1954).

Despite support from each president in the 1950s and considerable support from both parties in Congress, it was not until the 1960s that promises of immigration reform came true. The man elected as president in 1960, John F. Kennedy, had published a book setting out the case for immigration reform while a Senator, arguing that the national origins quota system was irrational and undemocratic.[44] In 1963, Kennedy commended immigration legislation to the House and the Senate, leveling the charge that the existing system was irrational, without national or international purpose, and "an anachronism, for it discriminates among applicants for admission into the United States on the basis of accident of birth." Kennedy reiterated the themes of *Whom We Shall Welcome*, of equality and human dignity, of a nation made strong by immigrants, of "traditions of welcome."[45] Still, it would not be until after his assassination that an immigration reform bill would pass in 1965. Through the skillful maneuvering of President Lyndon B. Johnson, Congress passed the bill with the support of representatives from the urban Northeast and Midwest, despite the opposition of many from the South and Southwest. It was this Act that Johnson eulogized under the Statue of Liberty in New York harbor, proclaiming, "it does repair a very deep and painful flaw in the fabric of American justice."[46]

The End of Discrimination and the Rise of Numerical Limits on the Western Hemisphere: The Immigration Act of 1965

The Immigration Act of 1965 ushered in a new era for immigration law, both opening and restricting. Known by the names of its sponsors, Philip A. Hart in the Senate and longsuffering reformer Emanuel Celler in the House, the Act produced a great leveling. It provided opportunities for immigration for many Eastern Hemisphere countries, while at the same time establishing a global system of immigration restrictions that would touch countries even in the Western Hemisphere. The Act dislodged national origins quotas, forbidding discrimination in the issuing of visas based on race, sex, or nationality.[47] At the same time, the Act retained the categories of the McCarran-Walter Act that gave priority to family members of citizens and legal residents, professionals, and desired workers.[48] In the language of the

---

[44] John F. Kennedy, *A Nation of Immigrants* (New York: Anti-Defamation League of B'nai B'rith, 1959).

[45] John F. Kennedy, "Letter to the President of the Senate and to the Speaker of the House on Revision of the Immigration Laws, July 23, 1963," in *Public Papers of the Presidents of the United States: Containing the Public Messages, Speeches, and Statements of the President, January 1 to November 22, 1963* (Washington, D.C.: Government Printing Office, 1964), 594–97.

[46] Tichenor, *Dividing Lines*, 212–13; Ngai, *Impossible Subjects*, 258; Johnson, "Remarks at the Signing of the Immigration Bill."

[47] 79 Stat. 911, 911.

[48] 66 Stat. 163, 169, 178; 79 Stat. 911, 912.

legislation, there was no "discrimination," but there were "special immigrants" and "preferences." For nonpreference immigrants, the Hart-Celler Act allotted 170,000 places each year to the Eastern Hemisphere, and within this each country could take up twenty thousand places per year. No longer was Ireland preferred over Greece, Britain over Nigeria, or Germany over China; each country in the Eastern Hemisphere had been equalized. Beyond unlimited classes of family members and workers, every country was subject to a system that limited immigrants not by identifying some fault, lack, or threat they posed to the United States, but by simply allowing a certain number every year.

The changes did not stop there: For the first time, the Act of 1965 subjected the Western Hemisphere to a cap. Previous immigration reform bills from 1955 to 1965 had exempted the Western Hemisphere from numerical restrictions.[49] But as the House bill came to the Senate immigration subcommittee, Senators Sam Ervin and Everett Dirksen introduced an amendment, adding a cap on the Western Hemisphere. A result of a deal the Johnson administration made with those who were resisting reform, the amendment was included in the Act.[50] As approved, the legislation placed the Western Hemisphere under an overall cap of 120,000 per year with no per-country caps. Maintaining no per-country caps would allow nearest neighbors Mexico and Canada to continue to occupy the lion's share of the overall cap, which went into place in 1968.[51]

In the years to come, the logic of nondiscrimination soldiered on. An amendment in 1976 extended the cap of twenty thousand for each foreign state from the Eastern Hemisphere to the Western Hemisphere, going into effect in 1977.[52] No longer could Mexico and Canada take up a large portion of the Western Hemisphere cap of 120,000 per year, and so immigration from Mexico and Canada would have to drop measurably if it was to remain legal. An amendment in 1978 united the two hemispheric caps into one global cap of 290,000, so that the Western Hemisphere no longer had proportionally more visas than the Eastern.[53] The move to

[49] Ngai, *Impossible Subjects*, 255–57. Ibid., 256n95, lists these as S. 1206, 84th Congress, 1st Session, 1955 (Lehman); H.R. 3364, 85th Congress, 1st Session, 1957 (Celler); S. 3043, 87th Congress, 2d Session, 1962 (Hart); S. 747, 88th Congress, 1st Session, 1963 (Hart); S. 1932/ H.R. 7700, 88th Congress, 1st Session, 1963 (Hart-Celler, Kennedy administration bill); S. 500/ H.R. 2580, 89th Congress, 1st Session, 1965 (Hart-Celler, Johnson administration bill).

[50] Ngai, *Impossible Subjects*, 257–58; Zolberg, *A Nation by Design*, 332. Zolberg reports a deal between Dirksen and Attorney General Nicolas Katzenbach, ibid., 332n120.

[51] The 1965 Act limited to 120,000 those "special immigrants" born in the Western Hemisphere and their spouses and children in Section 101(a)(27)(A) of the 1952 Immigration and Nationality Act, 79 Stat. 911, 916, 921.

[52] The 1976 Act eliminated those born in the Western Hemisphere from the "special immigrant category" and instituted a cap of twenty thousand per year for every single foreign state and six hundred per year for every colony or dependent area, An Act: To amend the Immigration and Nationality Act, and for other purposes, Pub. L. No. 94–571, 90 Stat. 2703 (1976), 2704, 2076. See Ngai, *Impossible Subjects*, 261.

[53] An Act: To amend section 201(a), 202(c) and 203(a) of the Immigration and Nationality Act, as amended, and to establish a Select Commission on Immigration and Refugee Policy, Pub. L. No. 95–412, 92 Stat. 907 (1978), 907.

limit numbers also continued, with a decreased global cap of 270,000 in 1980. 1990 legislation that would go into effect in 1994 introduced a cap of 675,000 on all sorts of immigrants, including family-sponsored and employment-based immigrants.[54] The moves to equalize all countries and to limit the numbers of all immigrants were complete.

What was the source of the unprecedented 1965 move to place the Western Hemisphere under numerical limits? These limits had not come in Acts that sought to protect American racial and cultural uniformity, the Acts of 1924 and 1952, and thus the more moderate supporters of national origins quotas had not supported Western Hemisphere quotas. Only the fringe elements of the movement had pushed to cap immigration from the Americas. The idea of protecting American society from the peoples of Latin America gained a sense of urgency when growing populations in Latin America in the fifties and sixties led to predictions of increased migration to the United States.[55] Still, the liberal reform camp by and large eschewed Western Hemisphere quotas, and reformers Lehman, Hart, Celler, Kennedy, and Johnson did not include such quotas in their bills from 1955 to 1965.[56] Nevertheless, the earliest proposal to reform the McCarran-Walter Act did include Western Hemisphere quotas. Though *Whom We Shall Welcome* advocated keeping the hemisphere out of the quotas in 1953, the proposal Senator Herbert Lehman made along with freshman Senator John F. Kennedy and others, and the proposal that Celler and Peter Rodino made in the House, included Western Hemisphere quotas.[57] Here were the early signs that the reform movement was open to applying numbers across the entire globe.

Logically, Western Hemisphere quotas were consistent with the liberal aims of the reform movement. If reforms were to end discrimination based on race or nationality in immigration admissions, and if that was to be achieved by distributing visas equally, then it made no sense for Canadians, Mexicans, or Dominicans to be favored over Indians, Filipinos, or Chinese. Mae Ngai finds an early instance of this logic in a letter by historian of immigration Oscar Handlin to Senator Lehman's executive assistant, Julius Edelstein, writing in 1953,

[54] An Act: To amend the Immigration and Nationality Act to revise the procedures for the admission of refugees, to amend the Migration and Refugee Assistance Act of 1962 to establish a more uniform basis for the provision of assistance to refugees, and for other purposes, Pub. L. No. 96–212, 94 Stat. 102 (1980), 106–7; An Act: To amend the Immigration and Nationality Act to change the level, and preference system for admission, of immigrants to the United States, and to provide for administrative naturalization, and for other purposes, Pub. L. No. 101–649, 104 Stat. 4978 (1990), 4982.

[55] Ngai, *Impossible Subjects*, 256.

[56] See p. 159 note 49.

[57] Ngai, *Impossible Subjects*, 255; Zolberg, *A Nation by Design*, 318–19. The Senate bill was S. 2585, 83rd Congress, 1st Session, 1953 (Lehman), according to Ngai, *Impossible Subjects*, 256n95; Zolberg, *A Nation by Design*, 319n85.

Elimination of the Western Hemisphere [exemption from quota restriction] would be desirable. The argument of consistency, from our point of view, is so strong that none of the objections I have heard raised seem to me to have weight against it.[58]

Even if Western Hemisphere quotas cohered with Eastern Hemisphere quotas, what was the logic in allotting equal numbers of visas to countries that differed so widely in population? Why did China and Mongolia receive the same quota? Ngai chalks it up to a commitment to formal equality. She says that the motivations of the reform movement depended in part on the Cold War demand that the United States represent democracy to the rest of the world.[59] To be a democratic nation that believed in human equality required placing citizens on an equal footing, and what was true for civil rights extended to immigration law. In Ngai's analysis, citing Oscar Handlin, the national origins quotas sent a message about those already present in the United States.[60] The quotas indicated that the descendants of immigrants from Poland, Italy, and Russia were less worthy to be Americans than the descendants of immigrants from Germany, Ireland, or England. Immigration reform was not so much needed because the United States had to treat other nations fairly, but because it needed to signal to current Americans citizens that they were of equal value, regardless of their national origin. For the reformers, the solution was to institute a "formal equality" between these groups, on Ngai's account.[61] They chose only one possible solution among many, giving equal numbers of visas to countries with unequal populations. This solution maintained a symbolic equality between nationalities.

Those who stood for formal equality tended to be from the Northeast and urban Midwest of the United States, with only distant acquaintance with migration of migrant laborers across the U.S.-Mexico border. Philip Hart was from Detroit, Michigan; Emmanuel Celler and Herbert Lehman were from New York; Peter Rodino was from New Jersey; and Kennedy was from Massachusetts.[62] Lyndon B. Johnson was the exception, hailing from Texas, but he was a latecomer to the cause of immigration reform, embracing it just a year before the 1965 Act's passage.[63] Ngai cites Handlin and Kennedy's writings on immigration as evidence that for these parochial universalists, the descendants of immigrants were primarily European-Americans.[64] Asian, African, and Latin American immigration did not figure

---

[58] Letter, Oscar Handlin to Julius Edelstein, July 17, 1953, file C76–18, Legislative files, Papers of Herbert H. Lehman, quoted in Ngai, *Impossible Subjects*, 255.

[59] Ngai, *Impossible Subjects*, 243.

[60] Oscar Handlin, "The Immigration Flight Has Just Begun," *Commentary* 14 (July 1952): 6; in Ngai, *Impossible Subjects*, 245.

[61] Ngai, *Impossible Subjects*, 245.

[62] Tichenor, *Dividing Lines*, 159, 163, 191.

[63] Ibid., 213.

[64] Ngai, *Impossible Subjects*, 246. Ngai points out that Kennedy's celebration of America as *A Nation of Immigrants* only spends two paragraphs on Asian and Latin American immigrants, *A Nation of Immigrants*, 1964, 62–63.

prominently in their stories of immigration. Likewise, for these liberals, racism among immigrant groups was a primarily intra-European problem for the descendants of the likes of the English, the Italians, or the Russians. The reformers admitted equal treatment for those from the majority world, but what they promised conservatives, and what they seemed to believe, was that opening immigration from the Asia-Pacific Triangle would bring only a small increase in Asian immigration.[65]

On the occasion when the reformers did deal with Western Hemisphere policy, a strong commitment to the territorial nation-state was revealed. Against this backdrop, Lehman in 1954 decried the McCarran-Walter Act's continued openness to immigration from the Americas as allowing "'undesirable aliens' by the thousands to stream across the Mexican and Canadian borders."[66] In the same year, Edelstein bemoaned the fact that

> in 1953, 1,500,000 illegal immigrants – mostly wetbacks – streamed across the Mexican border, without so much as a How-do-you-do to an American immigration inspector. We stand triple guard, at the front door, bayonets at the ready, to repel legal immigration, while illegal immigration swarms in at the back door and through the windows.[67]

The comments of these seminal figures in the reform movement, Lehman and Edelstein, permit an explanation for how the reformers were able to support Western Hemisphere quotas when conservatives demanded them in 1965. The reformers held to a universalism that was formal, demanding equal treatment of groups. That universalism was birthed in the Northeast, a region far from the site of migration through the back door, the migration of laborers from Mexico. The reformers expressed a strong attachment to territorial sovereignty, not taking into account the special nature of the United States' land borders or the links between farms, industries, and migrant workers in the American West.

With numerical limits in place on Western Hemisphere immigration, the reach of immigration controls was complete. Now firmly in place was the assumption that immigration policy needed to restrict immigration from every country numerically, that every part of the globe needed constraint within a set of figures. The reformers of the 1950s and 60s did not counter what they saw as discriminatory laws by lifting numerical restrictions and returning to only qualitative restrictions that would evaluate visa applicants for health or job skills or family connections. Instead, they extended the numerical restrictions that had first come into place in the 1920s.

---

[65] Ngai, *Impossible Subjects*, 246; Tichenor, *Dividing Lines*, 218. See Johnson, "Remarks at the Signing of the Immigration Bill."

[66] Letter, Herbert Lehman to Norman R. Sturgis, Jr., March 5, 1954, file C75–34, Legislative files, Papers of Herbert H. Lehman, quoted in Ngai, *Impossible Subjects*, 247.

[67] Transcript of Remarks by Julius Edelstein before National Federation of Settlements, March 1, 1954, file C75–34, Legislative files, Papers of Herbert H. Lehman, quoted in Ngai, *Impossible Subjects*, 247.

The reformers were not opposed to the restrictionists; they were restrictionists.[68] When they briefly justified their agreement on overall limits on immigration, Presidents Kennedy and Johnson sounded much like conservative Senator Robert C. Byrd. Kennedy said that the United States no longer needed settlers for virgin lands, and he said that the economy was growing more slowly than it had.[69] Byrd, who opposed these presidents' reform bills, said that since the nation had expanded to use the resources available, it was time for the United States to stop seeking immigrants.[70] Johnson declared in front of the Statue of Liberty, "The days of unlimited immigration are past."[71]

—

On the face of it, the reforms enacted in 1965 accomplished a laudable aim: removing the vestiges of racism from the law. Once the Hart-Celler Act was passed, Americans would no longer look at immigration law and feel that they were more or less worthy of membership than someone else. Still, the reforms further ensconced a tendency of the 1920s legislation and agreed to something new. By 1976, the global reach of immigration controls that began in 1921 was complete: Immigration from each region of the world was fixed by numbers. At the same time, a push to replace quotas that favored northwestern Europe with color- and culture-blind admissions brought about numerical caps on Western Hemisphere immigration. If done in the name of ending discrimination, it was fair to subject the Eastern Hemisphere to formal equality, and it was fair to do the same to the Western Hemisphere. The move ignored the greater proximity of some countries than others, and the United States tried to treat Mexico like any other country. Led by universalists from the Northeast, the move prized the abstract nation-state over land, farm, industry, and neighborhood. Forgetting its aspirations to be a good neighbor, the United States turned out to be an indifferent neighbor and an oppressive neighbor, as the next section will demonstrate.

THE MAKING OF AN UNDERCLASS: MIGRATION BETWEEN MEXICO AND THE UNITED STATES, 1810-PRESENT

The move to end discrimination based on national origin had particular import for the United States' neighbor to the south, Mexico. Sharing a long land border that now runs to nearly two thousand miles, the two countries are linked not only by geography but by war, trade, and migration. The following offers an

---

[68] Ngai, *Impossible Subjects*, 227–28, 248–49; Zolberg, *A Nation by Design*, 293.
[69] Kennedy, *A Nation of Immigrants*, 1964, 80.
[70] Robert C. Byrd, in *Congressional Record – Senate*, vol. 111, 1965, 23793–95, quoted in Daniels and Graham, *Debating American Immigration, 1882-Present*, 201, 202.
[71] Johnson, "Remarks at the Signing of the Immigration Bill."

analysis of Mexican-U.S. relations that highlights territorial claims and migration. What emerges is a pattern of Mexicans migrating to the United States who, in the words of American voices from the time, provided backs and arms to serve American brains. Immigrating as contract laborers and increasingly as undocumented workers, these would form an enduring class of those who are "neither slave nor free," in the words of a historian.[72] This was a direct result of reforms that sought to end discrimination based on nationality while ignoring that the United States has neighbors.

American Migration to Mexico: Insurrection, War, and Land-Grabbing in the Early Nineteenth Century

The tale begins with two federal republics, recently independent from European colonial powers and only recently sharing a land border. As Mexico declared independence from Spain in 1810, as Spain recognized that independence in 1821, and as Mexico instituted a republican constitution in 1823, the new country held approximately twice as much territory as it does today. Mexico included its current lands from Chiapas to Baja California along with the states of Texas, New Mexico, and Alta California, as far north as the border with Oregon. Most of the former British colonies to the north had declared independence in 1776, which Britain acknowledged in 1782 and 1783, and the new federation approved a lasting constitution in 1789. The United States of America controlled land from the Atlantic to the Mississippi River, and an 1803 purchase from France doubled its territories, adding lands west of the Mississippi River to the Rocky Mountains and north to the British Canadas. The year 1819 saw the United States acquire lands from Spain, the Floridas, and in 1846 lands from Great Britain, the Oregon territory to the forty-ninth parallel. Both sides had gained their territories from a multitude of native peoples. As new confederations, los Estados Unidos Mexicanos and the United States of America came to abut one another along a line winding from Louisiana northwest along the mountainous continental divide.

The relations of these new neighbors started off with a bang. Mexico's northern lands were sparsely populated, and in this period some twenty to thirty thousand United States citizens moved into Texas on the invitation of the Mexican government. After Mexico halted further immigration in 1830 and introduced measures to give the capital more control over the Mexican states, American immigrants sought to throw off what they saw as harsh control. They declared Texas independent in

---

[72] Zolberg, *A Nation by Design*, 181. Thanks to Victor Carmona for pointing out Zolberg's phrase, which forms a focus of Carmona's critique of U.S. immigration preferences in "Neither Slave nor Free: A Critique of U.S. Immigration Policy in Light of the Work of David Hollenbach, Gustavo Gutiérrez, and Thomas Aquinas" (Ph.D. Dissertation, University of Notre Dame, 2014).

1836, and after a famous loss at the Alamo, Texans of American and Mexican descent defeated the federal Mexican forces. After most of a decade as an independent republic, Texas became a U.S. state in 1845, with a southern border at the Nueces River. One writer famously stated that other nations working against this annexation were "checking the fulfillment of our manifest destiny to overspread the continent allotted by Providence for the free development of our yearly multiplying millions."[73] Having come to power on a platform of annexing Mexican lands, U.S. President James K. Polk claimed that Texas extended farther south to the Rio Grande, also known as the Río Bravo del Norte. When Mexico rebuffed Polk's efforts to buy the land between the rivers, Polk commanded troops to move into the disputed area in 1846. Two months later, Mexican forces attacked American troops in a war they saw themselves forced into, and Polk cited this as provocation for war, failing to honor requests by the young Congressman Abraham Lincoln for clarification about whether these attacks took place on American soil.[74]

Though Whigs alleged that the war was a way to seize land illegitimately,[75] the majority in the U.S. Congress supported the war, with Democrats in the South leading the way. A declaration of war ensued, and after some months of fighting, Mexico also declared war. Mexico proved too disunited at home to wage an effective war, and during the war it experienced antagonism between federalists and centralists, rioting in Mexico City, and multiple coups that finally saw Antonio López de Santa Anna serve as general.[76] After victories in Upper California and New Mexico, U.S. forces under Winfield Scott took Mexico City in 1848. In the settlement that ended the war, the Treaty of Guadalupe Hidalgo, the United States gained land north of the Rio Grande as well as lands north of a line that ran from the western fringes of the river to the Pacific Ocean. What it gained would become part or all of eight U.S. states, Arizona, California, Colorado, Nevada, New Mexico, Oklahoma, Utah, and Wyoming.[77] In what might have been a gesture of remorse, the United States paid Mexico fifteen million dollars for these lands and assumed millions more

---

[73] John O'Sullivan, "Annexation," *United States Magazine and Democratic Review* 17, no. 1 (1845): 5–10, in Christopher Conway, ed., *The U.S.-Mexican War: A Binational Reader* (Indianapolis: Hackett Publishing Company, 2010), 51–54.

[74] James K. Polk, "War Message," May 11, 1846, in Conway, *The U.S.-Mexican War*, 58–61; among Lincoln's protestations was the Spot Resolution, December 22, 1847, in Conway, *The U.S.-Mexican War*, 122–24; Christopher Conway, "Introduction," in *The U.S.-Mexican War*, xii–xxi; Orlando Martínez, *The Great Landgrab: The Mexican-American War, 1846–1848* (London: Quartet Books, 1975), 7.

[75] Representative Joshua Giddings of Ohio, May 12, 1846, in Conway, *The U.S.-Mexican War*, 108–9.

[76] Conway, "Introduction," in *The U.S.-Mexican War*, xix–xxi; Timothy J. Henderson, *A Glorious Defeat: Mexico and Its War with the United States* (New York: Hill and Wang, 2007), xviii.

[77] "Treaty of Guadalupe Hidalgo (February 2, 1848)," in *Treaties and Conventions between the United States of America and Other Powers Since July 4, 1776* (Washington, D.C.: Government Printing Office, 1871), http://avalon.law.yale.edu/19th_century/guadhida.asp, art. 5.

in claims that U.S. citizens had made against Mexico.[78] For the Mexican nationals that lived in these newly acquired lands, the Treaty stipulated that if they remained, they could either remain Mexican citizens or become citizens of the United States.[79] Despite the protestations of some in its legislature, Mexico begrudgingly accepted the terms of the treaty, and no more than fifty thousand Mexicans became U.S. citizens through its provisions.[80] Five years later, in the Gadsden Treaty of 1853, the United States bought a southerly strip of land south of the Gila River from Mexico for ten million dollars for the purpose of building another transcontinental rail link.

—

Armed rebellion by American immigrants to Mexico, war, and American seizures of land characterized the early decades of relations between two newly independent colonies, Mexico and the United States. U.S. citizens moved into Mexican lands and fought to be an independent country; the United States acquired that country and much more under questionable circumstances. As a result, those Mexicans who did not move south found that the border crossed them, that all of a sudden they were in the United States with the opportunity to become naturalized citizens. On the one hand, very few Mexicans lived in the northern territories that became U.S. possessions. It appears that Mexico was too divided to populate and govern these northern lands, while Americans were ready to begin settling Texas and beyond. On the other hand, President Polk jumped at an excuse to go to war with Mexico and to claim new lands, in an era when the ideology of Manifest Destiny ruled and the United States saw itself as destined to gain lands "from sea to shining sea."

Though many Americans gathered around the war effort against Mexico, there were protesters, among them Lincoln, who said that "the blood of this war, like the blood of Abel, is crying out against it."[81] In the years following the war, opinion did not look so favorably on the war. Ulysses S. Grant, who served in the war before leading the Union forces in the United States Civil War and serving as the nation's president, said in 1879, "I do not think there was ever a more wicked war than that waged by the United States on Mexico. I thought so at the time, when I was a youngster, only I had not the moral courage enough to resign."[82] The war did much

[78] Ibid., art. 12–15; Otis A. Singletary, *The Mexican War* (Chicago: University of Chicago Press, 1960), 5.

[79] "Treaty of Guadalupe Hidalgo," art. 8.

[80] Conway, "Introduction," in *The U.S.-Mexican War*; Douglas S. Massey, Jorge Durand, and Nolan J. Malone, *Beyond Smoke and Mirrors: Mexican Immigration in an Era of Free Trade* (New York: Russell Sage Foundation, 2002), 25.

[81] Robert W. Johannsen, *To the Halls of the Montezumas: The Mexican War in the American Imagination* (New York: Oxford University Press, 1985), chaps. 3–5; Martínez, *The Great Landgrab*, 8.

[82] Grant to a journalist, quoted in Amy S. Greenberg, *A Wicked War: Polk, Clay, Lincoln, and the 1846 U.S. Invasion of Mexico* (New York: Alfred A. Knopf, 2012), 274.

more than resolve the dispute about the southern border of Texas: It brought in vast new western lands to the United States. The war transferred lands to a country more capable of fending off attacks from Comanches, Navajos, Apaches, and other indigenous peoples who had first settled the region, and the United States soon managed to contain on reservations what the Treaty of Guadalupe Hidalgo called "savage tribes."[83] In the Texan revolt and again in the U.S.-Mexican War, United States citizens proved the aggressors, violating Mexican sovereignty and dispossessing it of half of its lands. Today Americans think little on the war, but *la Guerra de 47* or *la invasión norteamericana* remains in the collective Mexican memory as a national failure and reason for suspicion of their northern neighbor.[84]

It is to this triangle of land the United States wrested from Mexico that most Mexican immigrants to the United States have come.[85] The new border crossed Mexicans, and from the early twentieth century, many more Mexicans crossed the border. In the United States, those who began to immigrate from Mexico were in a state of limbo since at the time, naturalization law only enabled persons who were white or of African descent or nativity to become citizens.[86] As a *mestizo* people descended from Spanish colonizers and indigenous peoples, Mexicans were seen as racially ambiguous. The eligibility of Mexicans for citizenship was tested in 1897, when a federal court considered whether Ricardo Rodríguez could become a citizen. A native of Mexico, Rodríguez lived in San Antonio, Texas, for ten years, and a district court judge classed him "with the copper-colored or red men." The judge decided that he was not an Indian, since he "knows nothing of the Aztecs or Toltecs."[87] In the final case, the judge admitted that though Rodríguez might not strictly be classed as white, the Texas constitution, the Treaty of Guadalupe Hidalgo,

---

[83] Brian DeLay, *War of a Thousand Deserts: Indian Raids and the U.S.-Mexican War* (New Haven: Yale University Press, 2008), xv, xxi; "Treaty of Guadalupe Hidalgo," art. 11.

[84] "The War of '47," "The North American Invasion," Michael Van Wagenen, *Remembering the Forgotten War: The Enduring Legacies of the U.S.-Mexican War* (Amherst: University of Massachusetts Press, 2012), xv; Martínez, *The Great Landgrab*, 2.

[85] In 2010, 58 percent of Mexican-born immigrants to the United States lived in California, while in 2000, 63 percent lived in California and Texas, Jeffrey S. Passel, D'Vera Cohn, and Ana Gonzalez-Barrera, "Net Migration from Mexico Falls to Zero – and Perhaps Less" (Washington, D.C.: Pew Research Center, April 23, 2012), 36–38, 44, www.pewhispanic.org/2012/04/23/net-migration-from-mexico-falls-to-zero-and-perhaps-less/.

[86] An Act to establish an uniform Rule of Naturalization, 1 Stat. 103 (1790), 103, stated that only a "free white person" was eligible for citizenship. In 1868, the Fourteenth Amendment to the United States Constitution declared that all those born in the United States were citizens, allowing former slaves and their descendants to become citizens. Two years later, An Act to amend the Naturalization Acts and to punish Crimes against the same, and for other Purposes, 16 Stat. 254 (1870), 256, stated that "naturalization laws are hereby extended to aliens of African nativity and to persons of African descent." Only with 66 Stat. 163, 239, did the law state that race could not be a factor in determining eligibility for naturalization.

[87] In re Rodríguez, 81 F. 337 (W. D. Tex. 1897).

the Gadsden Treaty, and other agreements gave citizenship to Mexicans or allowed for their naturalization without reference to color.[88] Because testimony indicated that Rodríguez was "a very good man, peaceable and industrious, of good moral character, and law-abiding 'to a remarkable degree,'" the judge allowed him to be naturalized.[89] The case established that Mexicans could seek naturalization, but their status remained ambiguous. Even as Euro-Americans in the new Southwest intermarried with Mexican-Americans, rhetoric against Mexicans grew, alleging criminality, lack of health, mental disability, and a liability to become a public charge.[90]

From the end of the U.S.-Mexican War until the 1920s, the new U.S.-Mexico border existed in law and on maps, but it hardly existed as a physical reality. This was especially the case west of the Rio Grande, where the border was little more than a line drawn on a map accompanied by a few piles of stones and markers laid down by representatives of the two countries. A series of events began to make the border more significant, from civil conflicts to contraband trade. In the U.S. Civil War of 1861 to 1865, trade bypassed a Union naval blockade, moving through Mexico to supply the Confederate states. During the Mexican Revolution of 1910 to 1917, U.S. border towns proved places for combatants to seek refuge, assemble, and secure weapons. These towns were sources of banned goods and entertainment, especially during the United States' era of prohibition on alcohol, and the border limited each country's authorities from pursuing both native peoples and criminals. With the founding of the U.S. Border Patrol in 1924, policing made the border a more tangible reality.[91]

Mexican Migration to the United States: Backs and Arms in the Early Twentieth Century

While in the late nineteenth century, only about thirteen thousand Mexicans had migrated to the new U.S. lands, the pace increased at the turn of the century.[92] The latter years of the presidency of Porfirio Díaz in Mexico (1876–1910) brought privatization, growth in rail and mining, the fencing and consolidation of lands, and the mechanization of agriculture. By the end of the Porfiriato, some 95 percent of rural households were landless, and there was little rural work.[93] Crossing a border that was only minimally policed, Mexicans began to move north to work on the farms of the American Southwest.[94] There, few U.S. citizens wanted to work in

[88] 81 F. at 348, 350, 354–55.
[89] 81 F. at 355.
[90] Ngai, *Impossible Subjects*, 52–53.
[91] Massey, Durand, and Malone, *Beyond Smoke and Mirrors*, 25–26.
[92] Ibid., 26, 31.
[93] Ibid., 29–30.
[94] Tichenor, *Dividing Lines*, 168.

the heat, where with only occasional dwellings in the large fields, workers spent harvest seasons in temporary accommodations.[95] After the migration of workers from China and then Japan was halted, Western farmers and industrialists desired more laborers, and private labor contractors began to recruit men from Mexico. In what was called *el enganche* or "the hook," recruiters told Mexicans of riches to be made in the United States and advanced them the money to travel north. On arrival, they were bound to repay the *enganchadores* while facing low wages, high interest rates, and poor working conditions.[96] The only large movement of refugees in the history of migration from Mexico to the United States came around the same time, during the violent final years of the Mexican Revolution.[97]

The U.S. Immigration Act of 1917 placed a hold on free movement so that Mexican nationals could not only be excluded from the United States because they were liable to become a public charge, but also because they failed to pass a literacy test or pay an increased head tax of eight dollars.[98] But such a hold did not stand: In the same year, as the United States fought in the First World War, Secretary of Labor William B. Wilson used a proviso of the Act to waive these requirements for laborers coming to the United States from Mexico. Along with the Immigration Bureau, the Labor Department enabled thousands of Mexicans to work as contract laborers while U.S. citizens fought abroad, and the 1917 restrictions continued to be waived beyond the war's ending in 1918 until 1921.[99] Many others avoided the legal requirement that they bathe, be deloused, have their baggage fumigated, shave their heads, and walk naked before medical inspectors, and many migrated illegally to work in the United States.[100]

In 1921, when the first national quotas were set in place, an exemption of the Western Hemisphere from the quotas enabled laborers to continue to come north. Though nativists feared the results of intermarriage between Mexicans and Anglo-Saxons, farm lobbies and Southern and Western lawmakers pushed for continuing exemption for the Western Hemisphere from the quota system. Many nativists came to see Mexicans on labor contracts in the United States as no threat to white civilization, since in Tichenor's words they were "by definition temporary, powerless, and easily expelled."[101] In the end, Congress exempted immigrants from the Western Hemisphere from quotas in the Johnson-Reed Act of 1924.

---

[95] Timothy J. Henderson, *Beyond Borders: A History of Mexican Migration to the United States* (Malden, Mass.: Wiley-Blackwell, 2011).

[96] Massey, Durand, and Malone, *Beyond Smoke and Mirrors*, 27–28.

[97] Ibid., 30.

[98] 39 Stat. 874, 875, 877.

[99] Tichenor, *Dividing Lines*, 169–70; see 39 Stat. 874, 878. Restrictions were lifted first on agricultural workers in 1917 and then on mining, rail, factory, and construction workers in 1918, Henderson, *Beyond Borders*, 31.

[100] Henderson, *Beyond Borders*, 35.

[101] Tichenor, *Dividing Lines*, 170, 172.

The demand for migrant laborers from Mexico was made clear in testimony before a House committee two years later. Representing thousands of sugar beet farmers in Colorado, Fred Cummings declared that ten years before, farm help had come from Russia or Germany, but now many of those men and women owned or rented farms. The farmers looked to help from Mexicans, whom he said produced more sugar beets per acre than the remaining Russian or German workers.[102] Cummings testified,

> there is not a white man of any intelligence in our country that will work an acre of beets ... I want to say that I do not want to see the condition arise again when white men who are reared and educated in our schools have got to bend their backs and skin their fingers to pull those little beets ... If you are going to make the young men of America do this back-breaking work, shoveling manure to fertilize the ground, and shoveling beets, you are going to drive them away from agriculture. I will tell you, you have got to give us a class of labor that will do this back-breaking work, and we have the brains and ability to supervise and handle the business part of it. There is no danger of that class of labor taking over the supervising work.[103]

The lines were clear: white, educated, with brains, unwilling to pull beets on the one side, and a laboring class, skinning their fingers, bending and breaking their backs, on the other side.

The coming of the Depression changed the tenor of the debate, and the American Federation of Labor (A.F.L.) spoke out against the some two million Mexicans whom they believed were in the United States.[104] The Immigration Bureau responded with a 1929 campaign that combined a few deportations of undocumented Mexican workers with prominent publicity that prompted hundreds of thousands more to return to Mexico.[105] At the same time in Mexico, the new *mestizo* class that came to power after the Revolution enacted a redistribution of land that came to fruition in the 1930s, dividing up rural estates and providing opportunities that reduced the push for the rural poor to migrate to the United States.[106] In the same decade, the A.F.L. continued to campaign for Western Hemisphere quotas, but soon another war changed the game. As U.S. citizens once again left to fight in the Second World War, Western growers asked for Mexican workers. The Roosevelt administration responded in 1942, negotiating a treaty with Mexico to bring what would be called *braceros* to lend their *brazos* or arms to work in the fields. In the treaty, the United States promised fair wages,

[102] *Seasonal Agricultural Laborers from Mexico: Hearings before the Committee on Immigration and Naturalization, House of Representatives, 69th Congress, 1st Session, January 28 and 29, February 2, 9, 11, and 23, 1926, on H.R. 6741, H.R. 7559, H.R. 9036* (Washington, D.C.: Government Printing Office, 1926), 61.

[103] Ibid., 62, 66.

[104] Tichenor, *Dividing Lines*, 172.

[105] Ibid., 173.

[106] Massey, Durand, and Malone, *Beyond Smoke and Mirrors*, 30–31.

good living and working conditions, no discriminatory acts, and no military service for *braceros*, and the Mexican government would oversee their recruitment and contracting. The Bracero Program brought hundreds of thousands from Mexico to the United States to work over the course of two decades, but neither the federal U.S. administrators nor the employers kept to the terms of the agreement. *Braceros* were regularly paid less than citizens, their living and working conditions were poor, and employers were allowed to recruit *braceros* right at the border. Many more Mexicans circumvented the terms of the Bracero Program to immigrate illegally, and those that swam across the Rio Grande earned these migrants the name *mojados* or wetbacks.[107]

In the 1950s, as *braceros* continued to work in the United States without receiving the protections they had been promised, and as other Mexican nationals came to work illegally, the federal government struggled over how best to proceed. One response was to "dry out wetbacks"; the Border Patrol rounded up men who were unlawfully present, taking them to recruitment centers on the Mexican border, where they were legalized under the Bracero Program and "paroled" to American employers who had wide authority over them.[108] A second response was to avoid enforcing measures against illegal immigration in an effort to protect crops. Under pressure from farm groups, the Immigration and Naturalization Service (I.N.S.) periodically avoided deporting those illegally present and allowed them to work the fields.[109] A third response came in a convoluted section of the McCarran-Walter Act of 1952, which placed a ban on helping to enter, transporting, harboring, or concealing an alien not lawfully admitted, while declaring that employment did not constitute harboring. This provision made a show of cracking down on illegal entry but protected those who employed unauthorized workers in what was called the "Texas proviso."[110]

A fourth response came in the same Act of 1952, where deportation of long-term residents of good moral character could be stayed and they could be given permanent residence if deportation would cause them or their families severe hardship. Those from contiguous countries – Mexicans – were excluded from this ban on deportations, making it more difficult for them to join a path to citizenship.[111] A fifth response was the first large deportation campaign in years, Operation Wetback of 1954. The I.N.S. recruited a military general who rounded up over a million illegal aliens who worked in Southwestern farms and Midwestern factories in what the then Attorney General called a "wetback invasion." Though the I.N.S. declared that it had secured the border, this was an empty boast. What Tichenor calls an

[107] Tichenor, *Dividing Lines*, 173–74; Zolberg, *A Nation by Design*, 308–11.
[108] Zolberg, *A Nation by Design*, 309; Henderson, *Beyond Borders*, 73–74.
[109] Tichenor, *Dividing Lines*, 174, 201.
[110] 66 Stat. 163, 228–29; Tichenor, *Dividing Lines*, 194; Zolberg, *A Nation by Design*, 310.
[111] 66 Stat. 163, 214–16; Zolberg, *A Nation by Design*, 313.

"iron triangle" of growers, Congressional subcommittee chairs, and I.N.S. bureaucrats protected a continuing stream of temporary Mexican laborers.[112]

Despite talk from the time of the Mexican Revolution of the "Mexican family" with the government as patriarch, Mexicans continued to move north to the United States. In one instance in 1952, when the United States and Mexico failed to come to an agreement and Mexico forbade its people from crossing into the United States, Mexican immigrants rushed the border against an opposing force of U.S. border guards.[113] Those who made their way north were met by American business owners, who willingly hired both those who came legally and those who came illegally, not only on farms, but in mining, construction, and railroads. Alongside the many *braceros* came an increasing number of legal immigrants from Mexico, though *braceros* far outnumbered them. During the Bracero Program of 1943 to 1964, numbers of both peaked in 1956, when there were over 445,000 *braceros* and over sixty-five thousand legal immigrants who were granted permanent residence.[114] In this year, Mexico emerged as the largest source of legal immigrants to the United States, and it would remain so from 1956 on through the turn of the century.[115] Still, at this point most Mexicans coming to the United States came as temporary workers, and the Mexican immigrant became identified in the minds of Americans with the manual laborer who lacked a path to citizenship.

—

Amid the seeming incoherence of the policies in the *bracero* era there emerged a marked coherence. As arms of the federal government sometimes deported but often ignored illegal entry, as legal guest workers were underpaid for work in poor conditions while those who worked illegally experienced much the same, patterns became firmly established. Mexican migration to the United States became frequent and circular, and many returned after short stays as *braceros* or without lawful admission across a little-policed land border.[116] First Southwestern growers, and then employers in other industries, became "addicted to Mexican labor."[117] And those who came to the United States from Mexico were understood primarily as labor or as workers, but not as persons. As testimony from the Great Western Sugar Company indicated, Mexicans provided backs for the breaking and fingers for the skinning to complement American brains. Those who came through the Bracero Program were valued for their arms, their *brazos*. Women and men from Mexico formed a class of bodies to work for American businesses.

[112] Tichenor, *Dividing Lines*, 202.

[113] Henderson, *Beyond Borders*, 71, 75.

[114] Data from I.N.S., Annual Report, 1943–1964 (Washington, D.C.: Government Printing Office, 1944–1965), cited in Tichenor, *Dividing Lines*, 210, table 7.9.

[115] Zolberg, *A Nation by Design*, 321.

[116] Henderson, *Beyond Borders*, 87.

[117] Roger Daniels, *Guarding the Golden Door: American Immigration Policy and Immigrants Since 1882* (New York: Hill and Wang, 2004), 142.

This is the class of those who are "neither slave nor free," on Aristide Zolberg's interpretation, a long-running class of contract laborers and unauthorized workers who have entered through a "revolving back door" of United States immigration policy.[118] As Federal policies authorized yet restrained the enforcement of immigration laws at the border, and as they forbade the harboring of unauthorized workers but exempted employers from prosecution, disparate federal policies conspired to maintain a class of men and women from Mexico in a liminal state. As Congress promised that *braceros* would be well treated but broke the agreement, and as it encouraged Mexicans to come for a short time but prevented them from seeking permanent residence, the legislature colluded to foster the growth of this suspended class. These women and men remained in limbo between free and slave, between legal and illegal, between dominated and self-determined. They would be present in American communities, but they would move on soon enough; they would work willingly but not supervise others in work. In another of Zolberg's phrases, they were "wanted but not welcome."[119]

This era reached its denouement soon enough when Congress failed to renew the Bracero Program in 1964, as it had been under attack from 1961 onward. Religious groups and welfare organizations denounced the Bracero arrangement for keeping men and women in poor conditions.[120] Representative Henry B. González, Democrat of Texas, emerged as a voice for Latino civil rights, arguing that Latinos should be welcomed as legal immigrants who could become citizens of the United States.[121] The united A.F.L.-C.I.O. argued that the program caused problems not only for *braceros* but also for U.S. citizen farmworkers.[122] Other factors like the increased mechanization of cotton picking in Texas also played a part.[123] Protests from agricultural lobbies kept the program afloat for a time, but it expired in 1964.

Illegal Immigration and a Permanent Underclass in the Late Twentieth Century

This was the moment of the arrival of the Immigration and Nationality Act of 1965, described in the previous section. As U.S. farmers and businesspeople came to count on temporary Mexican laborers, both legal contract workers and undocumented workers, the legal route for menial laborers came to a halt. Labor markets had adapted to this source of labor, and a structural demand for migrant labor remained

---

[118] Zolberg, *A Nation by Design*, 10, 181. Zolberg traces the origins of this class to the Chinese laborers who came to California from 1848 onward, ibid., 181.

[119] Zolberg, *A Nation by Design*, 313.

[120] Tichenor, *Dividing Lines*, 209.

[121] Ibid., 211n116, n117, cites *Congressional Record*, Sept. 18, 1963, pp. 16438–39, and an interview with González.

[122] Tichenor, *Dividing Lines*, 209, 211.

[123] Zolberg, *A Nation by Design*, 321–22.

after the Bracero Program was gone.[124] In the latter years of the contract labor schemes and until the 1965 Act went into effect in 1968, a smaller but still significant number of Mexicans received visas for permanent residency. In 1968, when Mexican immigration came under the Western Hemisphere cap, prospective immigrants had to compete with other countries from the Americas for space within the 120,000 limit. The favoring of Cuban immigrants in the aftermath of the 1959 Revolution resulted in a successful class-action lawsuit by Refugio Silva, who alleged that Mexican immigrants were disadvantaged by Washington's political stance against the communist regime in Cuba. As a result, during a brief window from 1977 to 1981, Mexicans received nearly 150,000 extra visas.[125]

But soon, legal immigration from Mexico was subject to the stricter caps of 1976 Congressional legislation that allowed Mexico only twenty thousand non-preference slots and erected barriers to family reunification by preventing citizens under twenty-one years of age from petitioning for visas for a parent.[126] Though visas for close family members and desirable workers were not under numerical restrictions, by the early 1980s, the scene had changed drastically. While in 1956, over 450,000 per year received *bracero* permits and over 65,000 received permanent residency visas from Mexico, legal Mexican immigration dropped to 45,000 in 1977, surged to 101,000 in 1981 with the Silva program, and settled at around 55,000 to 60,000 in the early 1980s.[127] In the space of three decades, legal immigration from Mexico was a tenth of what it had been. This same period saw population growth and economic decline in Mexico. The habitual, ingrained patterns of Mexican migration to the United States did not go away, and as Massey, Durand, and Malone put it, "only one outcome was possible: the explosion of undocumented migration."[128]

This explosion of illegal immigration came, first with a mobile class of short-term migrants, and after 1986, with a growing class of settled migrants. Substantiating such a claim with numbers requires delving into what one article in demography calls "a count of the uncountable" in a search that reveals as much about the limits of statistical analysis as it does about what it is like to migrate without authorization.[129] Before 1965, the available statistics count deportations, which are only tenuously related to the number of those who migrate temporarily or permanently.[130] For the period from 1965 to 1986, demographers offer figures of high rates of entry and exit, with a comparatively small number that remain in the United States.

[124] Massey, Durand, and Malone, *Beyond Smoke and Mirrors*, 41.

[125] Ibid., 43.

[126] 90 Stat. 2703, 2704, 2705.

[127] Massey, Durand, and Malone, *Beyond Smoke and Mirrors*, 43–44.

[128] Ibid., 44.

[129] Robert Warren and Jeffrey S. Passel, "A Count of the Uncountable: Estimates of Undocumented Aliens Counted in the 1980 United States Census," *Demography* 24, no. 3 (1987): 375–93.

[130] See, for example, Parker Frisbie, "Illegal Migration from Mexico to the United States: A Longitudinal Analysis," *International Migration Review* 9, no. 1 (1975): 5.

Heer estimated in 1979 that from 1970 to 1975, the net flow of those into the country unlawfully was anywhere from 82,000 to 232,000 per year.[131] In 1986, Passel adjusted U.S. Census data to estimate that in 1980, there were between 2.5 and 3.5 million at any one time who were unlawfully present, with approximately two thirds of these from Mexico.[132] In 1995, Massey and Singer drew on surveys from Mexican communities to estimate that from 1965 to 1986, 28.0 million Mexicans entered the United States unlawfully, though only 4.6 million of those stayed.[133] During the same period, there were a mere 1.3 million legal immigrants and forty-six thousand contract workers from Mexico.[134] Thus, during these two decades, Mexican migrants to the United States tended to immigrate illegally and stay only temporarily before returning to Mexico. For the young men who made up most of these temporary workers, the United States in effect operated a temporary guest worker program, though this time without legal approval or the protections that the law might afford.

This community in the shadows changed shape after the Immigration Reform and Control Act of 1986, briefly shrinking in size, but soon growing rapidly and becoming more permanent. The 1986 legislation allowed two categories of those unlawfully present to gain legal status – those present since 1982 as well as Special Agricultural Workers – and by 1992 some 2.7 million had been legalized.[135]After a brief drop in numbers, studies indicate that the population of those illegally present began to grow again from 1990 at the latest, when the numbers were about 3.5 million. The population rose every year until 2007, when it reached a peak of 12.2 million, and then it dropped to 11.3 million in 2009 where it has stabilized.[136] A steady increase in border enforcement from the 1986 Act onward discouraged circular migration, and those who came to the United States more often stayed, fearful that if they returned to their home countries, they would not be able to return

---

[131] David M. Heer, "What Is the Annual Net Flow of Undocumented Mexican Immigrants to the United States?," *Demography* 16, no. 3 (1979): 421.

[132] Jeffrey S. Passel, "Undocumented Immigration," *Annals of the American Academy of Political and Social Science* 487 (September 1986): 188, draws his figures from the 1980 Census, adjusting for estimates of what percentage of those unlawfully present the Census successfully counted. Kenneth Hill, "Illegal Aliens: An Assessment," in *Immigration Statistics: A Story of Neglect*, ed. Daniel B. Levine, Kenneth Hill, and Robert Warren (Washington, D.C.: National Academies Press, 1985), 243, estimates a population of 1.5 to 3.5 million.

[133] Douglas S. Massey and Audrey Singer, "New Estimates of Undocumented Mexican Migration and the Probability of Apprehension," *Demography* 32, no. 2 (1995): 210.

[134] Massey, Durand, and Malone, *Beyond Smoke and Mirrors*, 45.

[135] An Act: To amend the Immigration and Nationality Act to revise and reform the immigration laws, and for other purposes, Pub. L. No. 99–603, 100 Stat. 3359 (1986), 3394ff, 3417ff; Zolberg, *A Nation by Design*, 372.

[136] The estimates for 1990 are drawn from Robert Warren and John Robert Warren, "Unauthorized Immigration to the United States: Annual Estimates and Components of Change, by State, 1990 to 2010," *International Migration Review* 47, no. 2 (2013): 315; with figures current as of 2014, the rest of the estimates come from Passel and Cohn, "Overall Number of U.S. Unauthorized Immigrants Holds Steady Since 2009." Warren and Warren's closely mirror those of Passel and Cohn. Warren and Warren point to 2008 as the peak year for the unauthorized immigrant population, at 12.0 million, and they see a drop to 11.7 million in the last year of their estimates, 2010, when Passel et al. offer an estimate of 11.4 million.

to work, family, and homes in the United States.[137] The 1986 Act also forbade businesses from hiring those unlawfully present, reversing the Texas proviso and creating a new locus of enforcement, the workplace.[138]

While laws further restricted migrant labor, within a few years, Mexico, the United States, and Canada reached an agreement that lifted restrictions on the movement of goods between the three countries. When the North American Free Trade Agreement (N.A.F.T.A.) went into effect in 1994, the three countries opened trade and business across their borders, and Mexico agreed to alter its protective land policies that had allowed subsistence farmers to remain on their land. Though these farmers were now on the move, the movement of human persons across national borders remained highly restricted.[139] In effect, a move toward the free trade of goods was paired with continuing restrictions on the movement of labor so that workers could not legally work in another country. Still, women as well as men moved in ever larger numbers from Mexico to the United States to work without proper documentation. From 1986 onward, what had been an unofficial program for temporary guest workers turned into an unofficial program for permanent guest workers. This population established themselves in and among American communities, but without the controls and benefits that the rule of law would provide.

Along with ties through neighborhood, friendship, and worship, the labor of those unlawfully present continues to tie them to U.S. citizen and legal resident consumers. In 2014, about eight million immigrants worked without documents, forming 5 percent of the U.S. workforce. These workers were clustered in particular industries, so that a quarter of all farmworkers, over one in ten construction workers, and just under one in ten production and service workers lacked permission to be in the country. In specific professions, those lacking documents formed a larger proportion of workers: between twenty-five and thirty one percent of drywall installers, miscellaneous agricultural workers, roofers, construction painters, and brick masons lacked documentation to work.[140] In the early twenty-first century, then, American citizens and legal residents depend on unauthorized laborers to pick fruit, install drywalls, lay brick, roof buildings, and paint them. Those with legal permission to work in the United States are implicated in this unofficial guest worker program that keeps men, women, and children in the shadows, with low pay, poor conditions, an uncertain future, and fear of deportation.

The farcical film *A Day Without a Mexican* presents a California where Mexicans have suddenly disappeared, and the state is disabled by their absence.[141] Something

---

[137] 100 Stat. 3359, 3381ff.

[138] 100 Stat. 3359, 3360ff.

[139] Zolberg, *A Nation by Design*, 383; Massey, Durand, and Malone, *Beyond Smoke and Mirrors*, 48–49.

[140] Jeffrey S. Passel and D'Vera Cohn, "Size of U.S. Unauthorized Immigrant Workforce Stable After the Great Recession" (Washington, D.C.: Pew Research Center, November 3, 2016), 4, 5, 14, 15, 30, www.pewhispanic.org/2016/11/03/size-of-u-s-unauthorized-immigrant-workforce-stable-after-the-great-recession/.

[141] Sergio Arau, *A Day Without a Mexican* (Santa Monica, Calif.: Xenon Pictures, 2004).

like this happened in Alabama in 2011, after the state legislature passed House Bill 56, a bill that, according to the sponsoring Representative Micky Hammon, "attacks every aspect of an illegal alien's life."[142] The bill enabled police to stop and search those suspected of unlawful presence, added penalties for hiring and transporting aliens, and required record keeping on illegal aliens at schools. It also forbade contracts made between illegal aliens and the state, including for the provision of water or power.[143] Though judges struck down most of the bill within a year of its going into effect, the bill served its intended purpose of attrition through enforcement, intimidating many into leaving the state.[144] A report from Albertville, Ala., told of a chicken factory that lost many of its workers when Mexican immigrants fled the state, while the managers found it difficult to recruit citizens and legal residents to spend their days standing in a cool, wet factory and cutting the heads off chickens. The article also told of a tomato farmer who lost his entire crew and struggled to find workers to bend over in the heat, picking tomatoes for two dollars for a large box.[145] Though only a small proportion of the Alabama population either originates from Mexico or lacks legal status, many businesses found themselves crippled without unauthorized laborers.[146] With the current size of the undocumented population, with its close involvement in a variety of industries, Americans with legal status are implicated in the lives of those who butcher their chickens, pick their tomatoes, and live down the road.

—

Over the course of the twentieth century, a solution to one problem created another problem. Bringing an end to racist, protectionist immigration laws led the United States Congress to disregard neighboring Mexico, enabling a settled, servile underclass of undocumented workers to grow. The mid-century was an era of national

[142] Kim Chandler, "Alabama House Passes Arizona-Style Immigration Law," *AL.com*, April 5, 2011, http://blog.al.com/spotnews/2011/04/alabama_house_passes_arizona-s.html.

[143] Beason-Hammon Alabama Taxpayer and Citizen Protection Act, Alabama House Bill (H.B.) 56 (2011).

[144] Brian Lawson, "Much of Alabama's Far-Reaching Immigration Law Permanently Blocked in Final Settlement of Lawsuits," *AL.com*, November 25, 2013, http://blog.al.com/breaking/2013/11/final_settlement_reached_block.html; see Jessica M. Vaughan, "Attrition Through Enforcement: A Cost-Effective Strategy to Shrink the Illegal Population," Backgrounder (Washington, D.C.: Center for Immigration Studies, April 2006), http://cis.org/articles/2006/back406.html.

[145] Pamela Constable, "Alabama Law Drives Out Illegal Immigrants but Also Has Unexpected Consequences," *The Washington Post*, June 18, 2012, sec. Local, www.washingtonpost.com/local/alabama-law-drives-out-illegal-immigrants-but-also-has-unexpected-consequences/2012/06/17/gJQA3RmojV_story.html.

[146] Warren and Warren, "Unauthorized Immigration to the United States," 318, 319, estimate that in January 2010, a year before the passage of H.B. 56, Alabama had ninety-five thousand unauthorized immigrants. Alabama ranked number twenty-five out of fifty states in numbers of unauthorized immigrants, much fewer than states like California (with 2,934,000) and Texas (1,068,000) and fewer than neighboring Georgia (397,000). Still, Alabama was the state with the fastest growing population of unauthorized immigrants between 1990 and 2010, better explaining the state's harsh legislative response.

origins quotas that were alternately defended as allowing only superior races or those like Americans to immigrate. At the same time, Congress maintained a lack of quotas on the Americas, whether seeking to be a good neighbor or enabling farm workers to come and go from Mexico. These came through the Bracero Program or crossed illegally, providing arms and backs to serve American brains, in the language of one farmer.

As a reform movement gained steam, its leaders announced that discrimination based on nationality had to end, and they sought to signal racial and cultural equality through a policy of formal equality. After categories for close family members and needed workers, each nation would get an equal number of visa slots. Those who trumpeted democratic values of equality and dignity landed on an abstract universalism nurtured in the Northeast, and those leaders had little acquaintance with migration from Mexico across the Southwestern border. An opposition to discrimination meant that immigration law could not take into account the place, neighborhood, and historical relations of the United States. This was the aleatory, denatured liberalism that John Kennedy expressed when he said that the United States should stop considering the "accident of birth."[147]

In tandem with patterns of migration between the United States and Mexico, the ideology of equality worked to foster the growth of an underclass, against the better instincts of its adherents. The twentieth century saw growing migration from Mexico to the United States, with contract laborers and undocumented workers migrating back and forth between the countries from the turn of the century through the 1960s. From the sixties to the eighties, workers kept coming and going, but most were unlawfully present, due to the 1965 and 1976 Acts that sought to end discrimination and give Mexico the same number of visas as Mauritania or Mongolia. From the eighties, women and men came from Mexico, often to work, but they came and stayed. A temporary underclass of migrant workers who would return to Mexico was replaced by a permanent underclass of migrant workers who remained in the United States. By the early twenty-first century, some eleven million of these were present without permission, and they provided unskilled labor in a variety of industries. The citizens and legal residents of the United States continue to be bound up with these women, men, and children. So far as Americans participate in the economy, and so far as they depend on bodies to do the hard work they would rather not do, they are tied to those who work on the black market. Americans do not keep slaves anymore, but they have something close. Across town or next door live members of a settled underclass that is neither slave nor free.

---

[147] Kennedy, "Letter on Revision of the Immigration Laws."

6

Justice and Mercy Among Neighbors

A move to end discrimination in federal U.S. immigration law made the United States a bad neighbor to Mexico. This move turned largely legal migration streams from Mexico to the United States into illegal ones, facilitating the creation of a servile underclass that would build houses, mow grass, and pick apples. The move against discrimination based on nationality, a shift from national origins quotas to equal allotments in U.S. immigration law was consistent with placing new numerical caps on migration from the Western Hemisphere. These shifts described in the last chapter were interwoven with moral arguments. These arguments focused on race and culture, on economy and work, and on democracy and equality. The arguments leave open lines of inquiry that could point a way out of the conundrum of the alien unlawfully present in the United States.

This chapter will deal with two elements of the discussions surrounding immigration law in the twentieth century. The first section will interrogate the talk of discrimination, using Aristotle and Grotius' twofold patterns of justice to analyze the history of U.S. immigration admissions and point toward a more appropriate kind of justice. This justice recognizes that legal status is owed to immigrants who are already enmeshed in life in their new country. This justice also attributes visas to the fitting, among them to nearby neighbors. Justice in immigration admissions might go so far as to defer to international society between countries sharing a land border by protecting longstanding migration corridors. In the second section, talk of a Good Neighbor Policy on the part of the United States raises the question of what it means to be a neighbor. Jesus creates the notion of the neighbor in the Parable of the Good Samaritan from the Gospel According to Luke. The chapter interprets this parable in response to laws that give Americans an excuse to neglect their neighbors and in response to laws that make the United States a bad neighbor to Mexico. This reading points toward a special consideration of Mexico that will make way for neighborly assistance in everyday life.

IMMIGRATION ADMISSIONS FOR NEIGHBORS: ARISTOTLE,
GROTIUS, AND JUSTICE AS CORRECTION AND ATTRIBUTION

Different sorts of goods require different notions of justice. Most would agree that
some goods should be distributed equally, goods like treatment in emergency
medical care or fair hearings before a judge. Some would go farther to name other
goods that should be distributed equally, from education to health care to wealth.
But this justice of equal distribution does not fit immigration admissions. The
1965 and 1976 United States moves to distribute visas in equal numbers to every
independent country are a misapplication of distributive justice. In what follows,
Aristotle will offer a classic account of justice as corrective and distributive, and
Hugo Grotius will reconfigure these as expletive and attributive justice. In an
analysis indebted to Oliver O'Donovan, a philosopher will have his system modified
by an early modern jurist and theologian.[1] Employing these accounts of justice, an
analysis of immigration admissions will indicate what is owed to immigrants who
lack legal status but who establish residence and contribute to a community through
labor or otherwise. This analysis will also indicate what is fairly given to prospective
immigrants from nearby Mexico.

Aristotle: Corrective and Distributive Justice

What is justice, and what is injustice? In Book Five of the *Nicomachean Ethics*,
Aristotle considers general justice, the virtue of the just person, and then a part of
that justice, the way that judgment is carried out in a community.[2] The philosopher
of the fourth century B.C. proposes that there are two species of special justice: a
justice of distribution and a justice of rectification in transactions. The first species
of special justice, he writes, "is found in the distributions of honors or wealth or
anything else that can be divided among members of a community who share in a
political system."[3] He also describes this as "the just in distributing what is held in
common."[4] Since "the unjust is unfair," he reasons, "the just is fair."[5] Or, translating

---

[1] Oliver O'Donovan, "The Justice of Assignment and Subjective Rights in Grotius," in *Bonds of
Imperfection: Christian Politics, Past and Present*, ed. Oliver O'Donovan and Joan Lockwood
O'Donovan (Grand Rapids, Mich.: Eerdmans, 2004), 167–203; Oliver O'Donovan, *The Ways
of Judgment* (Grand Rapids, Mich.: Eerdmans, 2005), 31–51.

[2] Aristotle explores justice, δικαιοσύνη, *dikaoisunē*, injustice, ἀδικία, *adikia*, and a part, μέρος,
meros, of each, Aristotle, *Nicomachean Ethics (E.N.)*, trans. H. Rackham, rev. edn., Loeb
Classical Library 73 (Cambridge, Mass.: Harvard University Press, 1934), 1130a15.

[3] Aristotle, *Nicomachean Ethics (E.N.)*, trans. Terence Irwin, 2nd edn. (Indianapolis: Hackett
Publishing, 1999), 1130b30; Henry George Liddell et al., eds., *A Greek-English Lexicon*, 9th
edn. (Oxford: Clarendon Press, 1940), 405. "Distributions" = διανομαῖς, *dianomais*.

[4] τὸ...διανεμητικὸν δίκαιον τῶν κοινῶν, *to...dianemētikon dikaion tōn koinōn*, author's
translation, Aristotle, *E.N.*, 1934, 1131b29.

[5] *E.N.*, 1999, 1131a13.

this claim differently: "If the unjust is unequal, the just is equal." Crucially, Aristotle's Greek term τὸ ἴσον, *to ison*, can be translated as "the fair" or "the equal."[6] This kind of justice, Aristotle argues, involves apportioning an amount that is neither too little nor too much, but in the middle – the mean or the intermediate. The relation between the goods apportioned is the same as the relation between the persons involved. So, argues Aristotle, those who are equal should receive equal shares, and the unequal, unequal shares, or else there will be quarrels.[7] Along these lines, he describes the proportions of distributive justice as geometrical, so that the proportion between two people matches the proportion of the two goods that are allotted to them.[8] From there, he says, distribution proceeds κατ' ἀξίαν, *kat' axian*, in accordance with worth, dignity, merit, or desert.[9] What marks those worthy of receiving some common good: Is it citizenship? Wealth? Good birth? Virtue? It all depends on what conception of political justice someone has, says Aristotle. He expresses this kind of justice in another way: it is ἀνάλογον, *analogon*, according to, *ana*, a due *logon* or rationality.[10] *Analogon* is often translated as a "proportion": Goods are allotted proportionately to the worth of the recipient.

There is another type of special justice, on Aristotle's analysis. This kind of justice happens in συναλλάγμα, *sunallagma*, the transactions or dealings between people, in interchange, covenant, or contract.[11] This second kind of justice corrects; it sets straight, it restores to order, reconciles, or rectifies.[12] While the other kind of justice gives out what is held in common, this kind of justice steps in when someone's gain has meant someone else's loss. When one person steals from another, when one person kills another, rectificatory justice seeks to bring the situation back to a state of equality.[13] Again, when one person takes too much in a transaction, corrective justice ensures that this profit is returned to the one who has lost.[14] Often called commutative justice, this justice does not require what distributive justice required, a geometrical proportion, where the ratio of the merit of two people matches the ratio between the goods allotted. Instead, says Aristotle, it requires a numerical or arithmetical proportion.[15] In these cases, it does not matter if one person is more worthy than the other; the two are treated as equals.[16] The calculation here only

---

[6] Ibid., 230, 325–26; *E.N.*, 1934, 256; *Liddell-Scott*, 839. Thanks to Stuart Ramsay for drawing attention to the dual meaning of *ison*.

[7] *E.N.*, 1999, 1131a23.

[8] Ibid., 1131b13.

[9] *E.N.*, 1934, 1131a25; *Liddell-Scott*, 170, 171.

[10] Aristotle, *E.N.*, 1934, 1131a15–30.

[11] Ibid., 1135b25; *Liddell-Scott*, 1694.

[12] Aristotle uses two terms to mean corrective or rectificatory, διορθωτικός, *diorthōtikos*, and ἐπανορθωτικός *epanorthōtikos*, *E.N.*, 1934, 1131b25, 1132a19; *Liddell-Scott*, 434, 609.

[13] *E.N.*, 1999, 1132a7.

[14] Ibid., 1132b13.

[15] Ibid., 1132a2.

[16] Ibid., 1132a1–6.

concerns the profit and loss of the two equals, and this justice requires that the amount wrongly taken is restored.[17] Here justice requires a judge or a mediator.[18]

Stepping back to get a view of these two types of special justice, distributive and corrective, Aristotle's arrangement seems both discerning and adaptable.[19] The distinction between the two serves to make justice appropriately complex: There might be different ways of being just that fit different scenarios. But Aristotle's notions are troubled in one significant way. At every level, he foregrounds the mathematical, suggesting that to some degree harm can be calculated in terms of loss and profit, or that to some degree the worth and merit of individuals can be quantified. As such, even distributive justice involves certain demands to give what the recipient is due. His conception of justice suggests a scarcity of goods in a closed system: that the goods held in common must be distributed proportionately. He does not leave room for the justice of giving out of abundance, beyond the goods that are rightfully due to a person.

Grotius: Expletive and Attributive Justice

Gratuity is what Grotius allows for in his adaptation of Aristotle's system. Hugh de Groot, seventeenth-century jurist, theologian, and diplomat for Sweden, reconfigures Aristotle's two types of justice at the start of *The Right of War and Peace*.[20] Unlike Aristotle, he does not deal with justice within the virtues but within

[17] Ibid., 1132a25–1132b10.

[18] Ibid., 1132a20–24.

[19] This account does not consider Aristotle's further thoughts about reciprocity in exchange, which first appears to fall under rectificatory justice as another sort of transaction, and then is said to fit neither kind of justice, ibid., 1131b25, 1132b11–20, 1132b25.

[20] The work was first published in Latin as *De Iure Belli ac Pacis: In quibus ius naturae & Gentium: item iuris publici praecipua explicantur* (Paris: Nicolas Buon, 1625). Latin citations here come from *De Iure Belli ac Pacis: In quibus ius naturae & Gentium: item iuris publici praecipua explicantur (I.B.P.)*, Ed. 2a emendatior & multis locis auctior (Amsterdam: Guilielmum Blaeuw, 1631). There is no faithful, complete, contemporary English translation of the work. This section relies on the excerpts translated by the O'Donovans, who pay close attention to the translation of *ius* as Right, right, or law, Oliver O'Donovan and Joan Lockwood O'Donovan, eds., *From Irenaeus to Grotius: A Sourcebook in Christian Political Thought 100–1625 (I.G.)* (Grand Rapids, Mich.: Eerdmans, 1999), 792–815. These excerpts are based on a new Latin edition, *De Iure Belli ac Pacis: In quibus ius naturae & Gentium: item iuris publici praecipua explicantur*, ed. B. J. A. de Kanter-van Hettinga Tromp et al., 1939 ed. based on the 1631 edn. with new annotations (Aalen: Scientia Verlag, 1993). This section also refers to a translation that is less careful in translating *ius*, *On the Law of War and Peace*, trans. Francis W. Kelsey (Oxford: Clarendon Press, 1925). Kelsey's translation is based on *De Iure Belli ac Pacis: In quibus ius naturae & Gentium: item iuris publici praecipua explicantur*, Editio nova, cum annotatis auctoris, ex postrema ejus ante obitum cura multo nunc auctior (Amsterdam: Iohannem Blaeu, 1646). As he introduces his abridged version of Kelsey's translation, Neff says that the 1646 edition includes new material from contemporary events but represents no substantial changes on the 1631 edition, *On the Law of War and Peace*, ed. Stephen C. Neff, student edn. (Cambridge: Cambridge University Press, 2012), xxxvi. The only full English edition in print today relies on Morrice's 1738 English translation of Barbeyrac's 1715 French

an account of *ius* or Right, marking his place at the tail end of a long interaction between Christian theology and Roman law. In the Prolegomena and in Book I, Grotius outlines natural Right, which he argues flows from the desire for society that is a feature of every human being.[21] The inclination to society implies two senses of Right that correspond to Aristotle's two kinds of justice, says Grotius. The distinction between the two kinds of justice comes not between public and private or between types of proportion, writes Grotius, but between two kinds of right that attach to a subject. By right, Grotius means "a moral quality attaching to a subject enabling the subject to have something or do something justly."[22] One kind of right Grotius calls a "real" or "perfect right," "a right in the strict sense," or a *facultas*, best translated as faculty, power, or entitlement.[23] This kind of right has to do with the classic rule of *suum cuique*, to each his own, and is in effect when someone has power, dominion, or ownership, or when someone owes something under contract.[24] This is like Aristotle's corrective justice, and Grotius calls it *justitia Expletrix*, or expletive justice, justice that satisfies the demands of rights that someone already possesses.[25] The word *Expletrix* suggests this justice responds to rights already in place by filling them, carrying them to completion, satisfying their demands, or making good.[26] As examples, Grotius mentions keeping promises, repaying losses, deserving punishment, and restoring someone's property along with the profit gained from it.[27] Expletive justice has to do with "letting someone keep, or have, what is already his," says Grotius.[28]

The second kind of justice parallels Aristotle's distributive justice, but here Grotius makes more decisive shifts. While expletive justice metes out what is owed to someone due to an entitlement, this second kind of justice responds to a less perfect right, an *aptitudo*. Grotius appropriates Aristotle's *axia*, or worth, and replaces it with this term *aptitudo*, saying that it has to do with something that is fitting or suitable (*convenit*).[29] To this fitness corresponds what Grotius prefers to

---

edition, *The Rights of War and Peace*, ed. Richard Tuck and Jean Barbeyrac, trans. John Morrice (Indianapolis: Liberty Fund, 2005).

[21] I.B.P., 1631, Prolegomena, 6, 16, in I.G., 793, 795. See also pp. 92–4.

[22] I.B.P., 1631, I.10, in I.G., 797.

[23] I.B.P., 1631, I.4, 5, in *Kelsey*, 35, and I.G., 797–98; R. E. Latham, ed., *Revised Medieval Latin Word-List from British and Irish Sources* (London: Published for the British Academy by the Oxford University Press, 1965), 184; P. G. W. Glare, ed., *Oxford Latin Dictionary* (O.L.D.) (Oxford: Clarendon Press, 1982), 670–71; see O'Donovan, "The Justice of Assignment and Subjective Rights in Grotius," 180.

[24] Grotius' words for these three types of right in the strict sense are *Potestas*, *Dominium*, and *creditum*, I.B.P., 1631, I.5.

[25] Ibid., I.8, in I.G., 790, 798.

[26] From *explere*, J. F. Niermeyer, *Mediae Latinitatis Lexicon Minus: A Medieval Latin-French/ English Dictionary*, 2nd edn. (Leiden: Brill, 1993), 398; O.L.D., 650.

[27] I.B.P., 1631, Prol.8, in *Kelsey*, 12–13, and I.G., 793.

[28] I.B.P., 1631, Prol.10, in I.G., 794.

[29] I.B.P., 1631, I.7, in I.G., 797–98; O.L.D., 155.

call not distributive justice but *justitia Attributrix*, attributive justice.[30] This kind of justice no longer has to do with righting wrongs or awarding what is due by right; it has to do with virtues like "liberality, compassion, and prudent government."[31] Nor does Grotius take on Aristotle's suggestion that this justice is about distributing what is already common property to those who are owed it. Rather, this kind of justice has to do with attributing, assigning, or granting goods to fitting recipients.

Grotius announces attributive justice as a wider sort of justice, one that enlarges and elaborates: "To this belongs the prudent allocation of resources in *adding* to what individuals and collectives own."[32] The term that the O'Donovans paraphrase as "adding," *elargiendis*, speaks of enlarging or increasing, from the older Latin word *largior*, meaning to give generously or lavishly.[33] In a legal sense, it seems to refer to grants. Grotius suggests that beyond the expletive justice that gives out what is owed, within this kind of justice it is right to show preference to those most fit to receive the good in question: "Sometimes a wiser person is favored over someone less wise, sometimes a neighbor receives preferential treatment over a foreigner, sometimes a poor man is treated more generously than a rich man."[34] The example that Grotius uses to explode Aristotle's notion that justice always enacts a proportion between at least two people is this: If an opening for a public office only has one suitable candidate, then by attributive justice that person assumes the office. This is just even if there are no competitors.[35] Thus attributive justice, on Grotius' reckoning, shows preference when it is fitting, "depending on what is being done in each case and what the business in hand requires."[36]

Grotius' account of Right goes further, but in reapportioning Aristotle's two kinds of justice, he gives an insight into how good judgment operates.[37] Grotius' arrangement of justice into expletive and attributive justice is capable and supple, leaving room both for justice that rights wrongs and justice that promotes future welfare. There is a kind of justice that responds to what is due and what is owed, that rights

---

[30] *I.B.P.*, 1631, I.8, in *Kelsey*, 37, and *I.G.*, 798.

[31] *Liberalitatis, misericordiae, providentiae rectricis, I.B.P.*, 1631, I.8, in *I.G.*, 798.

[32] *Atque huc etiam pertinet in his quae cuique homini aut coetui propria sunt elargiendis prudens dispensatio, I.B.P.*, 1631, Prol.10, in *I.G.*, 793–94, emphasis translators'. In translating this phrase, an issue arises. How can there be an enlarging, *elargiendis*, of what someone owns, *quae ... propria sunt*? Kelsey subsumes *elargiendis* with *dispensatio* as "allotment" (13). Tuck's version of Morrice keeps *elargiendis* as "gratuitous Distribution," but he takes this to be distribution "of Things that properly belong to each particular Person or Society" (87). The O'Donovans interpret Grotius as talking about grants that enlarge by giving things that become what someone owns, and they paraphrase *elargiendis* as "adding." Thanks to Oliver O'Donovan for comments on the translation in private communication.

[33] *Mediae Latinitatis Lexicon Minus*, 367; *Revised Medieval Latin Word-List*, 162; *O.L.D.*, 1003.

[34] *I.B.P.*, 1631, Prol.10, in *I.G.*, 794.

[35] *I.B.P.*, 1631, I.8, in *I.G.*, 798.

[36] *I.B.P.*, 1631, Prol.10, in *I.G.*, 794.

[37] This analysis leaves behind Grotius' third sense of natural Right as legal obligation, as well as his sources of Right in the will of God, in agreements, and in the practice of nations, *I.B.P.*, 1631, Prol.12, 15, 17; I.9, in *I.G.*, 794, 795, 799.

inequalities when those inequalities are hurtful or harmful. But there is also a kind of justice that responds to diversity, that gives what fits the particular character of the recipient. So, there is a time for justice to punish wrongs, to return what has been gained wrongfully, but there is also a time for justice to give out honors and opportunities, to give opportunity to talent, to strengthen bonds of family or community. This is why Oliver O'Donovan praises Grotius' attributive justice: It "elaborates differences," enhancing healthy differentiation in social life.[38] He goes further, claiming that Grotius' is "the best Christian revision of Aristotle's theory."[39] His praise for Grotius indicates why he thinks Grotius' system is right, but he does not make clear what makes it Christian.

If Grotius' rearrangement of Aristotle is a particularly Christian one, then this is because it leaves room in justice for gift and overflow. If distributive justice was still beholden to the idea of proportional distribution of what the recipients had some right to, attributive justice allows for the recognition of something more within justice. Beyond the justice that corrects wrongs, that rewards to individuals what is already theirs, there is a side to justice that gives more than is owed or needed. In the private life of one who has more than they need, in the prudential reasoning of a government official who looks to promote the future welfare of his people, then there are times to give out more than what is required. There is a prudence, a right judgment, that goes beyond rights and duties to include giving and enabling.

Justice in Immigration Admissions:
Undocumented Workers and Neighboring Countries

What does this conversation reveal about justice in immigration admissions? The discussion between Aristotle and Grotius about types of justice produces a matrix for evaluating the justice of the different regimes the United States has maintained for granting visas. What follows analyzes the two primary regimes of immigration admissions as mistaken forms of distributive justice. It points toward what is owed to those already present in the United States and when it is fitting to grant admission to newcomers, especially near neighbors. The analysis also explores whether admissions policies owe something to longstanding patterns of migration between two countries.

The national origins quotas of the 1920s were an assertion that immigration admissions are a form of distribution. When Congress acted to restrict the number of immigrants admitted, it chose to work with proportions. The first set of proportions matched the nationalities of new immigrants to the nationalities of immigrants already present, admitting newcomers as a small percentage of those who had already arrived. The second set of proportions matched the nationalities of new

---

[38] O'Donovan, *The Ways of Judgment*, 42.
[39] Ibid., 38.

immigrants to the national origins of citizens, admitting the first as a fraction of the second. Immigration admissions were not equal, but they were fair under a certain logic, distributing to each nation of origin visas in a way that reflected that nation's contribution to current United States residents or citizens.

There were exceptions to this logic: Close family members, those born in the Western Hemisphere, and members of professions were exempted from the quotas. Though these exceptions can be seen as a form of attributive justice, recognizing those fitted for admission, it appears better to interpret them as expletive justice. The federal government recognized spheres of Right that already obtain. It was right that husbands and wives, parents and children remain together and have privileges within their own sphere, not primarily because government thinks it in its interest to maintain that integrity but because these relationships were created alongside ordered civil society. Likewise, the 1924 legislation recognized that it was right for certain professions to have the privilege of drawing their members from other nations. Finally, the federal government recognized that it was right to allow migration within the Western Hemisphere to continue with little hindrance, fostering a society of societies lying close to one another. Sadly, in an under-handed way, the federal government also recognized that it was right that an unfair and oppressive system of migrant labor continue. As Western Hemisphere migrants were given special recognition, they were like family – or like household servants.

The equal allotment of visas from the 1960s and 70s onward represented a new understanding of distribution where each nation was treated equally. The new legislation treated each independent nation as a unit, rather than considering its population. Nationalities were now treated symbolically, so that each independent nation received an equal number of visas each year. This way of understanding distributive justice tied admissions more strongly to what was owed to each country. The logic of the system seemed to be that each nation was owed equal treatment, and so this distributive justice kept to the rule of *suum cuique*, to each his own. Indeed, it borrowed the logic of a different movement for justice in the United States, the civil rights movement. This movement worked to rectify injustices between American residents of different nationalities, giving to each person what was owed them, acknowledging rights to equal treatment and equal access to public schools and accommodations. The reform movement in immigration applied this form of corrective or expletive justice to foreign affairs, treating each foreign country as a person that ought to be given equal opportunity and equal treatment. The system of the late twentieth century continued to recognize spheres of Right beyond the federal government, enacting expletive justice by expanding categories for family members and for skilled workers. But in keeping with the steamrolling logic of equality, Western Hemisphere immigrants no longer received special recognition. There was no special community between the American republics, and these immigrants were owed the same treatment as immigrants from any other country. While the legislation simply assumed that reducing visas for the Western Hemisphere would reduce immigration from that hemisphere, the movement back and forth between Mexico and the United States in particular carried on, without legal permission.

The reform movement that produced the shifts of the 1960s and 70s fought against what was rightly called injustice, but the reforms furthered another sort of injustice. The scientific racism that some invoked as a rationale for national origins quotas was unfair: It either posited some groups within humanity as superior, or at least it posited different groups that should not intermarry. The milder understanding of the quotas as a mirror of American society was also unfair, since it mirrored a society long-past, making the Anglo-American feel a worthier American than the Greek-American by favoring British immigrants over Greek immigrants. The system took scarcity for granted, counting human beings as equal units and implying that American society could take in only about one sixth of 1 percent of its population as new immigrants each year. It evaluated these new immigrants not in terms of their abilities or their promise but in terms of their sheer numbers. Still, at the same time family members and skilled workers were given special recognition, and so were those in special need of a country under separate legislation concerning refugees.

The reforms of the sixties and seventies shared this assumption of scarcity: America could only take so many at a time. It up-ended the racism and the vicious side of the inequalities of the national origins quotas, but it adopted a strange new kind of justice. To end discrimination, the new system admitted immigrants in proportion to units of sovereignty. One nation that could claim the right to conduct its own affairs without interference was given visas for twenty thousand persons. The system ignored the difference between a unit of sovereignty and an immigrant: Some independent nations have many more people than others, and some have more that apply for visas than others. So long as they do no great injustice, China and Nepal are both independent nations, but China has a much greater population than Nepal. The Netherlands and the Dominican Republic both deserve to have their territories respected, but the Dominican Republic has many more men and women who hope to immigrate to the United States than the Netherlands. The 1965 and 1976 system landed on a type of proportionality that did not fit the matter at hand.

—

In the twenty-first century, the United States Congress has the opportunity to mollify the injustices built into its immigration policy with advances in both expletive and attributive justice. In the area of expletive justice, new immigration legislation ought to recognize those immigrants who are already present in the United States, though present illegally. For these millions of men, women, and children who have broken the law, as they establish a residence and a domicile, it is right that they are allowed to remain in their new country. Their stability is more significant than upholding the laws that forbade their immigration in the first place. As they work for employers willing to hire them, perhaps immigrating because they knew they would be hired, they become part of the economy that federal law elsewhere recognizes as having certain privileges to enable its workers to move across borders. Justice in this area is not a matter of attributing visas for some future immigrants; instead, justice responds to relationships that are already in place and obligations that already obtain between newcomers and an established community. The law ought to recognize the unauthorized work that so many contribute by authorizing it and giving it the benefits and protection that legal recognition affords. Immigration law must also do more to recognize not only professional work but also manual work as valuable and essential to American society.

What does justice look like for future immigrants? Beyond visas for family members and workers, it seems right to think of immigration admissions as a matter of attributive justice. The United States is in the position to give out visas to the most suitable, recognizing fitness. Federal law already works this way for refugees, giving visas to those who would most benefit because it would free them from persecution and danger. Federal law also gives visas to those who would bring some gift to the United States. Whether because of their health, wealth, or strength, immigrants qualify over the unhealthy and the impoverished. These sets of priorities deserve further evaluation, but that is not our business here.

Within the logic of attributive justice, as visas are attributed to the fitting, immigration law ought to recognize members of closely tied countries as fit to be admitted. Mexico qualifies on a number of counts. Its people lived on lands the United States took unjustly, and Mexicans have continued to come and go regularly for a century, forming a sizeable community in the United States. More recently, Mexico has proved an ally, top officials from the two countries tend to be on friendly terms, and Mexico is one of the primary trade partners of the United States. Most importantly, the country shares a land border with the United States that is nearly two thousand miles long. The militarization of the border since the 1990s by the United States has made migration more difficult, but those who have the desire still get across. To stop the flow altogether would require an increase in fencing, guards, and weapons at many times the current level.

These same qualifiers might also establish Canada, Guatemala, Cuba, the Dominican Republic, and others in the Western Hemisphere as fit for visas, and to a lesser degree they would qualify allies like Great Britain, sites of warfare like Iraq, and trading partners like China for special consideration. The primary aim here, however, is to establish Mexican citizens as having an aptitude to be admitted into the United States. Their fitness qualifies them for special dispensation as the federal government gives out visas, as it attributes the gift of legal immigration. This could happen through an increased numerical cap for Mexico or the removal of the cap altogether, while retaining some of the qualitative restrictions on all immigrants. A notion of attributive justice indicates that the United States need not hold on to its attachment to mathematical proportions, instead admitting or denying entry on more substantial grounds. When immigration visas are a matter of surplus, Mexicans are recipients suited to carrying forward a beneficial relationship with the United States.

Are Mexicans simply fit to be admitted, or are they owed admission? The argument has already been made that the 1924 immigration system recognized that it was right for social interchange between Western Hemisphere republics to continue through migration that was unhindered by numerical limits. It did so by classing immigrants born in the Western Hemisphere with family and the professions as deserving recognition. It is possible to argue for more extensive allowances for Mexico on the basis of attributive justice, based on Mexicans' fit with the surplus good of visas. But could justice demand more? Perhaps this is a matter not just of attributive justice but also of expletive or corrective justice. Established patterns of migration, not only for family members but also for communities and nationalities, deserve the law's recognition and respect. When one country's people are accustomed to traveling by land to the neighboring country to work and live, when they are used to coming and going in large numbers, it is simply not feasible to stop this process with a piece of legislation. The caps on Mexican immigration that went into place from the sixties did not stop Mexican immigration; they merely pushed it underground. The inability of a powerful country like the United States to halt immigration from its neighboring country proves that flows of migrants are not amenable to quick shifts of policy. They have a momentum to them. Migration carries on largely unheeded, though migrants may take different land routes or require a *coyote*'s guidance rather than a stamp on a passport.

Perhaps it is right that patterns of migration be allowed to continue. These patterns mark out special relations between countries, types of society that sovereign power ought to defer to when its efforts to stop them require large outlays of weapons and guards. On these grounds, then, the federal government has a place in watching over the migration process between Mexico and the United States, guarding those involved and keeping the process free of danger and exploitation. Its most immediate task would be to end the reign of death in the Sonora Desert, where thousands of migrants have died in this century while crossing into the United States. The nation-state must defer to long-established patterns of land migration; the United States must defer to more than a century of unstoppable migration from Mexico. Coming to terms with this will make it easier to resolve the other issues of expletive justice, exploitation, and low pay in the workplace, when migrant labor is seen for what it is, a normal feature of life in the United States today.

Is it right to maintain the numerical caps that were the product of twentieth-century immigration legislation? Limits on immigration might rightfully help the United States keep the arrival of newcomers to a manageable pace, allowing time for them to get accustomed to a new setting. Still, the numbering of human persons is troublesome when, beyond a certain number of thousands, an extra person is deemed damaging to the country. It is possible to imagine a system that protects the country from harm without using numbers, instead focusing on qualitative measures that restrict the likes of convicted felons from entering. Grotius' account of attributive justice suggests that immigration admissions might not only operate as a response to need in a closed system. Rather, admitting immigrants might be an expression of overflow, meting out the abundance of a country to those who wish to join it. Even if this suggestion is correct, that numerical limits need not stand, the preceding analysis of immigration admissions still applies if the current orthodoxy about numerical limits remains in place. Though it is not the purpose of this work to justify numerical limits on immigration, the work nevertheless seeks justice in the way that those limits are applied.

In the end, legal reforms through the twentieth century moved from one form of injustice to another. It is within the powers of Congress to ameliorate this situation. It is right to give legal recognition to migrants who are well-established and have contributed to American businesses. It is right that immigration admissions be given to nearby neighbors as fitting recipients. Perhaps it is also right for the federal government to defer to migration patterns that continue unheeded by laws and policing, protecting those who migrate rather than escalating enforcement.

In a setting where notions of justice have rectified errors of racism in U.S. immigration law while neglecting duties toward neighboring countries, philosophy with a theological twist has suggested a suppler understanding of justice toward neighboring countries. What more does Christian theology have to say about just relationships with neighbors? This question motivates the next section.

MERCY RECEIVED AND GIVEN: THE ILLEGAL NEIGHBOR AND THE PARABLE OF THE GOOD SAMARITAN

"And who is my neighbor?" This is the question that a legal scholar puts to Jesus of Nazareth, prompting him to tell the Parable of the Merciful Samaritan in Luke's Gospel (10:25–37). Known as the Parable of the Good Samaritan, this is the parable that invents the Christian concept of the neighbor. It is the inspiration for Franklin D. Roosevelt's Good Neighbor Policy, the stance sometimes thought to account for a special dispensation for the Western Hemisphere in U.S. immigration law.[40] This section will return to the source, letting the story come alive as a story about receiving and giving mercy. Reading it in relation to the question of the alien unlawfully present in the United States, the parable speaks to those who live in the United States, whether settled or newly arrived. The over-confident judgment that some U.S. residents are illegal, it will be argued, gives Americans an excuse not to recognize the love shown by their neighbors or to return that love. The next question taken up will be this: Can the United States of America, its land, its society, and government, become a neighbor? With reservations about the degree to which

---

[40] On Roosevelt's Good Neighbor Policy, see pp. 155–6

a country can be a neighbor in the Christian sense, in a modest way it is right for the United States to periodically reassess its relationships with other nation-states so as to recognize its neighbors and become a neighbor.

The Parable

The story runs like this: A legal scholar stood to challenge Jesus. He knew the Mosaic law well, but something in this upstart teacher Jesus goaded him on and prompted a question: What kind of action brings the kind of life that lasts forever? Jesus turned the question back on him, asking how he reads the law, and he responded, "You shall love the Lord your God with all your heart and with all your soul and with all your strength and with all your mind, and your *friend* as yourself."[41] The lawyer drew together two strands from the Torah, a command to love God from Deuteronomy 6 that follows a declaration of who Yhwh is, and a command to love the friend, companion, fellow country-man, or fellow covenant member from the Holiness Code of Leviticus 19. As Jeremias, Fichtner, and Greeven suggest, the lawyer would not have meant "love your neighbor" in the way subsequent generations might imagine it, since it is this very parable that creates the neighbor in the Christian sense.[42] Using the word πλησίον, *plēsion* in Luke's Greek, the scholar would have meant what רֵעַ, *rēa'* means in Leviticus 19, a "brother or sister," one of "the children of your own people" to be loved as oneself.[43] The legal scholar would have thought he was commanded and promised to love a fellow member of Israel. Later in the same passage from Leviticus, Yhwh issued a separate command through Moses to love as yourself the stranger who sojourns with you, the migrant who comes to stay, the גֵּר, *gēr* (19:33–34), but it is clear this is different from the *rēa'* that the scholar mentioned, who is a fellow participant in the covenant with Yhwh.[44] The man found at the center of the Mosaic law the love of Yhwh and the love of the friend or compatriot. And Jesus commended him: You have answered rightly; if you do this, you will live life to the full.

The lawyer did not stop there; it was not enough to stand and challenge this Jesus. The man wished to prove himself right, to justify himself. He asked a question that sidestepped the first half of the command. He assumed that he knew how to love Yhwh, and he thought that if there is a dispute, it was about the second half: "And who is my friend?" Who am I responsible for? The man would have been enmeshed in a discussion about who counted as a true worshipper of Adonai, about who was

---

[41] Luke 10:27, author's translation.
[42] Joachim Jeremias, *The Parables of Jesus*, trans. S. H. Hooke, 3rd rev. edn. (London: S.C.M. Press, 1972), 202n53; Heinrich Greeven and Johannes Fichtner, "πλησίον plēsion," in *The Theological Dictionary of the New Testament*, ed. Gerhard Friedrich and Geoffrey W. Bromiley, trans. Geoffrey W. Bromiley, vol. 6 (Grand Rapids, Mich.: Eerdmans, 1968), 314, 317.
[43] Lev. 19:17–18, author's translation.
[44] On the *gēr*, see pp. xiii–xv

in the covenant community. Among the sects of the day, Pharisees thought that love need only extend to Pharisees, Essenes thought love need not extend to the "sons of darkness," and a rabbinical judgment demanded that apostates and rebels be allowed to die.[45] In Matthew's Gospel, Jesus quoted a contemporary saying, "You shall love your friend and hate your personal enemy."[46] Some were in and some were out.

Jesus resisted this line of thinking in a story that answered the question, "Who is my friend?" A man, a man perhaps like you, traveled a lonely mountain road from Jerusalem to Jericho. Robbers fell upon him, and they stripped him and beat him, probably because he resisted them. They left him half dead. By coincidence, a priest came down the road, likely a priest from the central temple of Jerusalem.[47] Seeing him, he moved over to pass by the bloodied man on the other side of the road.[48] To get closer would have risked ritual uncleanness, uncleanness that would have kept him from completing his duties in the temple for a time, eating the food due to him and his family, or participating in giving to the poor. Or, if he risked approaching the altar in an unclean state, the Mishnah would require that his brain be smashed with clubs.[49] A secondary minister in the temple also passed by, and he acted like the priest, moving to the other side of the road. This Levite had less to risk, but contact with a dead or wounded man would also have made him unclean.[50]

A third man came along the road, and the listening law expert suspected he will be a Jewish layperson, but no: the man was a Samaritan. The scholar had nothing but contempt for such a man. One of the prophets, the Nevi'im, tells him that the Samaritans were a mix of five peoples that the king of Assyria brought in from around his empire to settle in the north of Israel (2 Kings 17:24–41). When Yhwh punished them with marauding lions for their failure to worship Yhwh, the Assyrian king sent Israelite priests to teach them how to worship. "So they feared the Lord but also served their own gods," he would have heard (v. 33a, E.S.V.) The Samaritans failed to recognize the covenant that Yhwh had made with the children of Jacob called Israel, as the legal scholar saw it. They were mired in a hopeless compromise. The law expert would have heard the prophet in the present tense: "To this day they do according to the former manner" (v. 34a). They continued to get many of the key points of Jewish worship wrong, worshipping on Mount Gerizim rather than Mount Zion, taking only the first five books of the Hebrew Scriptures to

---

[45] Jeremias, *The Parables of Jesus*, 202–3.

[46] Matt. 5:43, author's translation.

[47] By coincidence, συγκυρίαν, *sugkurian*, Walter Bauer, *A Greek-English Lexicon of the New Testament and Other Early Christian Literature*, ed. Frederick W. Danker, 3rd edn. (Chicago: University of Chicago Press, 2000), 953.

[48] Seeing him, ἰδὼν αὐτὸν, *idōn auton*.

[49] Kenneth E. Bailey, *Jesus through Middle Eastern Eyes: Cultural Studies in the Gospels* (London: S.P.C.K., 2008), 293.

[50] Jeremias thinks it less clear that the Levite avoids the man to maintain cleanness, *The Parables of Jesus*, 203–4.

be speech from God, and reading even those in a version that differed from Israel's text at thousands of points. Just a couple of decades beforehand, Samaritans had entered the Jerusalem temple by night and scattered human bones across the floor, an outrage to those who worshipped there.[51]

But Jesus told his interlocutor that the Samaritan is unlike the clerics who "seeing" him decided that the fallen man lay beyond who counts as their friend, their *rēaʿ* or *plēsion*. As he came to where the man was, the Samaritan was moved with compassion. Seeing him, he was hit in the heart.[52] Though this word had come to mean the seat of emotion and eventually of compassion, its earlier connotations were of the organs of the heart, lungs, liver, and kidneys.[53] His insides were moved immediately upon seeing the man; in the words of Bernd Wannenwetsch, his "heart was 'in' the eye."[54] He treated and bandaged the man's wounds, placed him on his horse, and took him to an inn to be cared for. The Samaritan spent the night, likely endangering his life if he went down to the hostile Judean town of Jericho.[55] The next day, he promised the innkeeper that he would come back and pay the bill for the man's stay, saving the wounded man from the risk of being sold into slavery as a debtor.[56]

The legal expert had started by asking whom he had to love, by asking how far his responsibilities extended. But Jesus concluded his story by flipping the question around: "Who became, who turned out to be, who proved to be a friend, a neighbor to the man in need?"[57] Here the verb γεγονέναι, *gegonenai*, emphasizes not being but becoming, a change of state to arrive at being a neighbor.[58] And here the Greek permits Jesus in Luke's hands to reveal something the Hebrew does not. Though the etymology of the Hebrew *rēaʿ* implies a friend, spouse, or fellow shepherd, the term for neighbor in Luke's Greek contains a root indicating a coming near,

---

[51] Joachim Jeremias, "Σαμαρεια Samareia, Σαμαρίτης Samaritēs, Σαμαρῖτις Samaritis," in *The Theological Dictionary of the New Testament*, ed. Gerhard Friedrich and Geoffrey W. Bromiley, trans. Geoffrey W. Bromiley, vol. 7 (Grand Rapids, Mich.: Eerdmans, 1971), 89, 90.

[52] ἰδὼν ἐσπλαγχνίσθη, *idōn esplanchnisthē*.

[53] Helmut Köster, "σπλάγχνον splanchnon, σπλαγχνίζομαι splanchnizomai, εὔσπλαγχνος eusplanchnos, ἄσπλαγχνος asplangchnos," in *The Theological Dictionary of the New Testament*, ed. Gerhard Friedrich and Geoffrey W. Bromiley, trans. Geoffrey W. Bromiley, vol. 7 (Grand Rapids, Mich.: Eerdmans, 1971), 548–53.

[54] Bernd Wannenwetsch, "The Fourfold Pattern of Christian Moral Reasoning According to the New Testament," in *Scripture's Doctrine and Theology's Bible: How the New Testament Shapes Christian Dogmatics*, ed. Markus Bockmuehl and Alan J. Torrance (Grand Rapids, Mich.: Baker Academic, 2008), 183.

[55] Bailey believes that the Samaritan risked his life by going to the inn and staying the night in the hostile Jewish town of Jericho, *Jesus through Middle Eastern Eyes*, 295. Jeremias, on the other hand, thinks the Samaritan regularly traveled the road as a merchant because he had at least one animal with him, knew the way, and promised to return soon, *The Parables of Jesus*, 204–5. If Jeremias is right, it is harder to imagine that the Samaritan is in grave danger.

[56] Bailey, *Jesus Through Middle Eastern Eyes*, 296.

[57] Luke 10:36, author's translation.

[58] See p. 55 note 48 on the verb γίνομαι, *ginomai*.

pela- or *plā-* in *plēsion*.[59] This nearness the Latin *proximus* indicates, as do terms in modern languages like the Spanish *prójimo*, the German *Nächster*, and *nigh* in the English "neighbor."[60] The Greek is a seed that turns the love command into something other than love for friend or compatriot. "Love the one nearby you as yourself," the command becomes. Who became a neighbor, who en-neighbored himself? Jesus asked the law expert. Unwilling to let the word "Samaritan" pass through his lips, the man told Jesus, "The one who showed him mercy." With ἔλεος, *eleos*, this man expressed love in other terms, as mercy, kindness, or concern for someone in need. He used the word that in Greek literature denotes an affection kindled by meeting someone who is afflicted without deserving it. This is the word the Septuagint version of the Hebrew Scriptures uses to translate חֶסֶד, *ḥeseḏ*, the free binding of one to another that characterizes Yhwh's self-giving in covenant with his people.[61] As the man admitted that the Samaritan has become a neighbor, Jesus drew the encounter to a close: "Go and act in the same way."[62]

Interpreting the Parable

Again, "who is my neighbor?" As Jesus in Luke's Gospel created the notion of the neighbor, four points stand out. These come to the fore through a reading of the parable alongside the trustworthy interpreters who have guided past chapters, Karl Barth and Oliver O'Donovan, along with Ben Daniel. First, the parable's polemics push and push again against any confidence that mercy is only for the in-group. To "love your neighbor as yourself" does not just extend to brothers and sisters, to co-religionists, or to co-nationals like in the first command in Leviticus. It does not stop with the resident alien, the immigrant who settles, like in the second command in Leviticus. The Samaritan and the wounded man met on the road, in transit, with no more context than that. In addition, the Samaritan was not just a foreigner passing through, a member of some group from far away. He was a member of a group that is too close for comfort, who worshipped the same God as the Judeans but committed sacrilege by worshipping in the wrong place and reading from corrupted Scriptures. To the law expert, these heretics from just north of Judea were worthy of hate if anyone was. Yet it was one of these apostates that, without calculating the

[59] D. Kellermann, "רֵעַ rēaʿ; רָעָה rāʿâ; רֵעֶה rēʿeh; מֵרֵעַ mērēaʿ; רֵעָה rēʿâ; רַעְיָה raʿyâ; רְעוּת rᵉʿûṯ," in *The Theological Dictionary of the Old Testament*, ed. G. Johannes Botterweck, Helmer Ringgren, and Heinz-Josef Fabry, trans. David E. Green, vol. 13 (Grand Rapids, Mich.: Eerdmans, 2004), 523–24; Greeven and Fichtner, "πλησίον plēsion," 312n1.

[60] "Neighbour | Neighbor, N. and Adj.," *Oxford English Dictionary Online* (Oxford University Press), accessed July 8, 2016, www.oed.com/view/Entry/125923.

[61] Bauer, *Greek-English Lexicon*, 316; Rudolf Bultmann, "ἔλεος eleos, ἐλεέω eleeō, ἐλεήμων eleēmōn, ἐλεημοσύνη eleēmosunē, ἀνέλεος aneleos, ἀνελεήμων aneleēmōn," in *The Theological Dictionary of the New Testament*, ed. Gerhard Friedrich and Geoffrey W. Bromiley, trans. Geoffrey W. Bromiley, vol. 2 (Grand Rapids, Mich.: Eerdmans, 1964), 477–87.

[62] Luke 10:37, author's translation.

extent of his responsibility and without hesitating, went to the wounded man and bound his wounds. It is this idolater and syncretist who became a neighbor. The parable critiques love that only extends to insiders, to friends, family, race, class, nation, or religious community. It prepares the hearer to be ready to help anyone.

Second, the parable highlights an encounter with one who by chance comes near. This Oliver O'Donovan makes clear. By chance, by coincidence, as it happened – the priest went down the road, and the same circumstances brought the Levite and the Samaritan down the same road. Though each was tied to some who were near them by affinity, the Samaritan responded to a different kind of nearness: the nearness of encounter and of contingency.[63] The parable militates against what Oliver O'Donovan calls an abstract universalism, a love in principle for all humankind that can turn complacent and translate into very little love for anyone in particular.[64] O'Donovan warns against instances when love for neighbor becomes mere respect for persons or equal regard, since this neglects proximity.[65] It is one thing to send money or food to someone far away, and it is another to receive and extend mercy to those close by who are easy to hate. The parable raises a challenge to receive love from those nearby with their smelly food, loud music, distorted religion, or dubious standing before the law. This O'Donovan calls a concrete universalism: Giving and receiving mercy may happen anywhere, but it will happen in a particular place, with the one we run into.[66] Even the road, where we pass through, becomes a place of encounter. This is the sort of universalism Jesus' parable draws attention to: love anywhere, but especially here, in this encounter.

Third, the parable puts the power to act in the hated stranger's hands. Those who discover what it means to "love your neighbor" do not start by imagining themselves as the moneyed Samaritan traveler, as the actor who shows mercy. Rather, they start by identifying with the one who is beaten and left half-dead, the one who is passive and helpless. There they imagine the person they most hate coming along and showing them mercy. Identifying the neighbor means a shift toward receiving mercy from someone who has become a neighbor. As Ben Daniel writes,

> when we ask "who is my neighbor?" the answer is not so much a person who may benefit from our charity (though charity is good and often needed) or from a change in public policy (something we also need), but rather the person

---

[63] Oliver O'Donovan, *Resurrection and Moral Order: An Outline for Evangelical Ethics* (Leicester: Inter-Varsity, 1986), 240.

[64] "The Loss of a Sense of Place," in *Bonds of Imperfection: Christian Politics, Past and Present*, ed. Oliver O'Donovan and Joan Lockwood O'Donovan (Grand Rapids, Mich.: Eerdmans, 2004), 316, 317.

[65] *Resurrection and Moral Order*, 240.

[66] "The Loss of a Sense of Place," 317–18. Karl Barth drives home a similar point: Neighbor love does not consist in mercy for all humanity, as John Calvin argues, but in receiving mercy from a particular person who has become a neighbor, *Church Dogmatics (C.D.)*, ed. G. W. Bromiley and T. F. Torrance, trans. G. T. Thomson and Harold Knight, vol. I/2, *The Doctrine of the Word of God* (Edinburgh: T. & T. Clark, 1956), 420.

from outside our community who saves and blesses us despite the walls erected by long-held hostility.[67]

To hear Jesus' parting command, "go and do likewise," begins not with doing like the Samaritan but with doing like the fallen man. The legal expert's task was first to receive mercy from a distasteful neighbor. Only then could he go and do like the Samaritan, becoming a neighbor to someone he disliked. Only after receiving mercy could he show mercy.

Fourth, the parable situates the love of neighbor within the love of God, in an encounter with Jesus Christ. Karl Barth points to this reading, following Origen, Clement of Alexandria, Ambrose, and Augustine.[68] The expert on the law answered the question about eternal life by saying that it comes through the love of God and the love of the friend, but he chose to ask a question about who counts as the friend. The man assumed he knew what it means to love God, but Jesus' telling of the parable begged the question of what it is to love God. Here was the strange rabble-rouser, come as a man to deliver the helpless at the cost of his life: The Good Samaritan represented Jesus. On Barth's reading, the story does not operate as the kind of sign of Jesus' saving work that allows the listener to forget the human encounter in the story. Rather, as the Samaritan acted as a "benefactor" to the man fallen among the thieves, as he showed mercy, the Samaritan bore divine mercy to the man.[69] Those who receive mercy and give mercy to one another are drawn into receiving God's mercy and in return offering God the praise God is due. Barth turns to the passage in Matthew 25 about the sheep and the goats, where Jesus spoke to those who have fed the hungry and clothed the naked. Confused, they hear the news that Jesus encountered them in the hungry and the naked that they served. Likewise in the parable, for Barth, "the afflicted fellow-man ... is actually the representative of Jesus Christ." Barth continues, "As such he is actually the bearer and representative of the divine compassion. As such he actually directs us to the right praise of God."[70] Both Samaritan benefactor and afflicted fellow-human represent Jesus, each in their own way.

Is the neighbor actually Christ? Barth's claims about what is actual do not go quite that far. Barth says that mercy from the neighbor refers him to the order in which he offers the praise that is acceptable to God.[71] The neighbor is not the same thing as

---

[67] Ben Daniel, *Neighbor: Christian Encounters with "Illegal" Immigration* (Louisville, Ky.: Westminster John Knox Press, 2010), xix.

[68] Barth, *C.D.*, I/2:419; O'Donovan, *Resurrection and Moral Order*, 241; Arthur A. Just, ed., *Luke*, Ancient Christian Commentary on Scripture, New Testament III (Downers Grove, Ill.: InterVarsity Press, 2003), 178–81.

[69] *C.D.*, I/2:416, 420.

[70] Ibid., I/2:429.

[71] "Through my neighbor I am referred to the order in which I can and should offer to God, whom I love because He first loved me, the absolutely necessary praise which is meet and acceptable to Him," ibid., I/2:420.

divine compassion: rather, the neighbor bears and represents divine compassion.[72] The one who recognizes the neighbor comes before Christ, says Barth. Barth flirts with identifying the neighbor with Christ in his brief treatment of the last judgment from Matthew 25, where he says that Jesus is not only seen in the least, but "actually declares Himself to us in solidarity, indeed in identity with them."[73] But Barth does not press this point. Though he does not speak of the neighbor as an icon, an Eastern Orthodox understanding of the icon captures what Barth conveys: the neighbor as fleshy reality draws one into the divine. And though Barth does not speak of this as a mystery, mystery it is: somehow, beyond understanding, someone who recognizes a neighbor is drawn into the divine life. Those who "see and have a neighbor," in Barth's words, are actually brought before Christ.[74]

Becoming Neighbors in the United States

The neighbor is a familiar trope in debates about immigration: President Franklin D. Roosevelt claimed that the United States should be a "good neighbor" to countries in the Americas, and a Congressional report claimed this as a reason for keeping Western Hemisphere immigration to the United States free of a numerical cap. Having spent time with the parable of Jesus that created the notion of the neighbor, what would it look like to be a good neighbor in contemporary America? When so many millions are unlawfully present in the United States, and when federal law restricts the immigration of more from Latin America, what could it mean to become a neighbor? The question of whether the United States as a nation-state can become a neighbor will be left for later. For now, in a time of illegal immigration, what does it mean for women and men in the United States, for churches, families, or communities, to become neighbors?

First, the Parable of the Good Samaritan combats a notion that mercy is only due to an in-group. Today, someone who identifies another person as Mexican or American, as Cuban or Guatemalan, as white or brown or black, can keep them from becoming a neighbor and from letting that person become a neighbor to them. Does the parable say more, drawing into question distinctions between legal and illegal residents? In one sense, one group is right, following the law, while the other is wrong. And yet the lawfully present community is bound up with those among it who employ those who are unlawfully present, and this employment represents an invitation to immigrate illegally, to do something that is not wrong in itself but wrong because prohibited. These legal distinctions are legitimate, but they are linked with market demands that draw many into living without the full privileges and responsibilities of lawfully present persons.

---

[72] Ibid., I/2:416, 429.
[73] Ibid., I/2:429.
[74] Ibid., I/2:419.

Much like identifying someone as a Samaritan, identifying someone as an illegal alien can serve as an excuse not to be a neighbor. To place someone not only in a different ethnic group but in a group that defies the law allows Americans to expect that an undocumented worker will not be an exemplary neighbor. The more firmly Americans believe that distinctions between legal and illegal immigration are just, the more they are tempted to discount unauthorized immigrants as neighbors. Even for those who have experienced the love of God through their neighbors and who desire to love their neighbors, "illegals" hardly count. They should not be here. They are illegal neighbors. But the Parable of the Good Samaritan opens up new possibilities. In the eyes of the Jewish legal expert, the Samaritan was a heretic, a lawbreaker, and an unwanted neighbor. Yet this Israelite pretender, outside the law, is the one who gave him mercy and the one who showed him how to extend mercy.

Second, the Parable of the Good Samaritan draws attention to the encounter with the neighbor. Its hearers cannot be content with the aspirations of the Immigration Act of 1965, seeking to measure out their mercy and distribute it equally on all occasions. If they want to experience the life that goes on forever, they should be ready to extend mercy, but to extend mercy to those they actually encounter. They are to extend mercy to those they meet by chance and seek out ways to bring about these happenstances, becoming neighbors to those they might not otherwise meet.

What kind of encounters happen in early twenty-first century America? As some three or four of every hundred have immigrated illegally, citizens and legal residents regularly run into those who are unlawfully present. They live in the same neighborhood, they meet at the grocery store or the movie theater, they go to school together, they worship together, or they play soccer together. There are other encounters that happen through buying and selling when the landscapers, the tomato pickers, the dishwashers at the restaurant, or the cleaners at the office are unlawfully present. The parable invites those in the United States to set their sights close by, beginning with those they run into. The story invites those with and without legal status to recognize one another as neighbors. Each hearing of the parable invites a reassessment: Who is my neighbor? Who am I ignoring who actually is my neighbor?

Third, the Parable of the Good Samaritan lets the hated stranger set the example for being a neighbor. The initiative is not in the hands of the majority culture, nor does the parable start with charity as philanthropy. It tells the story of an abhorred outsider who leads the way in becoming a neighbor, in loving and extending mercy. In the United States today, then, discovering neighborhood will start by looking to those men and women without legal status to demonstrate what it is to be a neighbor.

Ben Daniel illuminates this theme with a story of how a member of his community who lacks legal status becomes a neighbor to him. María Teresa is the mother of a girl in his daughter's third-grade class at a charter school in inner-city East San José, California. Daniel is an American citizen and a Presbyterian minister, and María Teresa is originally from Mexico and in the United States without permission. The two families trade cooking lessons, making pesto and enchiladas. María Teresa takes the opportunities the charter school provides to contribute by speaking to teachers about homework and offering her opinions on the direction of the school. Daniel attributes to María Teresa and mothers like her much of the success of the school, which so exceeds the expectations for schools in its area that its test scores are among the best in the state. Who is Daniel's neighbor? "The teaching of Jesus ... suggests that a person's neighbor is the marginalized foreigner who blesses him or her," he writes. "If that's the case, if Jesus is correct, then María Teresa, an undocumented, unemployed, single mother from Mexico is my neighbor."[75]

This is a pleasant story of someone who lacks legal status becoming a neighbor, but there are unpleasant stories too. When those without legal status dig the ditches or slaughter the chickens or lay the brick that those with legal status would rather not do, when they do so for little pay under conditions that they cannot complain about, they are showing mercy. So long as their work goes on unseen, unappreciated, and inadequately remunerated, their en-neighboring is not met on the side of the settled community with recognition. The fullness of being neighbors does not come about here.[76]

Fourth, the Parable of the Good Samaritan suggests that those who become neighbors are summoned into the praise of God. Receiving and extending mercy, becoming neighbors, draws those actors into praising Christ through whom they have received mercy. In modern America, the divide between legal and illegal residents has a power akin to the divide between Jew and Samaritan in the parable. When women and men move across this divide to become neighbors, overcoming aversion and judgment, they are drawn into worshipping God. When men and women allow this divide to stand and avoid becoming neighbors, they neglect an opportunity to bring honor to Jesus Christ. Even those who care little for Jesus or believe in no god may find that an experience of becoming a neighbor speaks of something beyond the ordinary.

The Country as Neighbor

Could a country become a neighbor as it receives immigrants? It is clear that individuals and communities in the United States are drawn into new ways of being

---

[75] Daniel, *Neighbor*, 144.
[76] T. C. Boyle's novel *The Tortilla Curtain* (London: Bloomsbury, 2004) offers another story of mercy from the immigrant who is unlawfully present, a story that closely reflects the parable of the Good Samaritan. Delaney the middle-class white man, who lives in a gated community in southern California, hunts for Candido the Mexican man who lacks legal status. Delaney believes Candido has caused him a great deal of trouble, but in the end, Delaney is swept away in a flash flood only to be saved by a hand that reaches down from a bridge, the hand of Candido.

neighbors when it comes to immigration and illegal immigration. But can a land with its people and its government become a neighbor? The following section will explore how a country can and cannot be a neighbor, beginning with Franklin D. Roosevelt's speeches, progressing through the writings of Michael Walzer, Oliver O'Donovan, Justo L. González, and Luke Bretherton, and concluding with the etymology of the word "country."

The idea that the United States could be a neighbor arose in Franklin D. Roosevelt's Good Neighbor Policy, discussed in the previous chapter. In an inaugural address, he announced this as a policy for foreign relations with all countries, but he soon elaborated on it at a meeting of the Pan-American Union.[77] On the first occasion, Roosevelt's picture of a good neighbor circled around respect, respect first of oneself and then of the rights of others. Respect, he surmised, consisted in upholding obligations and keeping agreements. On the second occasion, when he spoke to representatives of the countries of the Americas, he said more, indicating that to be a good neighbor involved "a sympathy which recognizes only equality and fraternity." It was something mutual, a friendship that began with understanding another's point of view and appreciating it. He did not apologize for behavior that the other republics would readily identify as disrespectful, but one area he identified for improvement was the area that the others would identify as the United States' primary wrong: Roosevelt praised recognizing the independence of the other republics and not seizing territory at the expense of a neighbor, against a long-running domineering role by the United States in the Americas. Roosevelt's select concrete suggestions indicated something else of what it meant to be a neighbor: He supported mutual self-defense for the hemisphere, opposed war between its nations, and proposed open trade. He also professed a belief in the "spiritual unity of the Americas."

Though there is much to appreciate in Roosevelt's sketch of the nation as good neighbor, there is also much that falls short of what the Parable of the Good Samaritan proposes as a neighbor. Insofar as countries recognize one another through diplomacy, by meeting and talking with one another, and by understanding one another, they operate as corporate persons in ways that approach the neighbors of the parable. When countries defend one another from attack, aid another, and keep peace with another, they move further toward the risky love of the Samaritan. When they give and receive by trading, they do something like giving and receiving mercy, though trade involves reciprocal gifts. Roosevelt's insinuation that the United States has not respected other nations' independence indicates a willingness to move beyond his cousin President Theodore Roosevelt's Corollary of 1905 and its assertion that the United States will intervene when its interests are threatened, though a further move to explicit confession would have been better.

---

[77] Franklin D. Roosevelt, "Presidential Inaugural Address" (Washington, D.C., March 4, 1933), www.inaugural.senate.gov/swearing-in/address/address-by-franklin-d-roosevelt-1933; Franklin D. Roosevelt, "Address on the Occasion of the Celebration of Pan-American Day" (Washington, D.C., April 12, 1933), www.presidency.ucsb.edu/ws/index.php?pid=14615; see pp. 155–6.

Roosevelt's attention to respect troubles his account of neighborhood: The parable does not dwell on any sort of self-respect or self-understanding as a starting point for the Samaritan's action; he merely acts when he sees the bloodied man. When Roosevelt speaks of friendship and fraternity, he turns the good neighbor into something better established and less occasional than the neighborhood of the parable. These images move the neighbor into a realm of longstanding agreements and treaties, something more comfortable and bourgeois than the stark and joyous appeal of the parable to be ready to help anyone who comes along. Still, insofar as he unfolds the Good Neighbor Policy before the representatives of nearby nations, his speech to the Pan-American Union allows the biblical reference a polemical edge. He implies: We are close to one another, and closely tied; let us learn to treat one another better. Finally, his gesture toward spiritual unity is, on one level, sentimental slop and idolatrous civil religion: Some spirits of unity are allied with Christ, but some international agreements prove devilish. At another level, though, Roosevelt leaves open hemispheric relations to some trust beyond contracts, a trust that speaks of divine faithfulness. Roosevelt's sketch looks more or less like the liberal ideal of an autonomous actor who respects the autonomy of others, though his appeal for Pan-American neighborhood carries those actors a step further. Though flawed and limited in what it can accomplish, Roosevelt's aspiration to become a Good Neighbor opens up Pan-American relations to salutary influences through its gesture toward the biblical source of the notion of the neighbor.

Another attempt to treat countries like neighbors makes more explicit reference to the Parable of the Good Samaritan. As he spells out a principle of mutual aid between countries within a discussion of the distribution of national membership, political philosopher Michael Walzer speaks of two strangers meeting by the side of the road as in the Good Samaritan story. He writes that one individual ought to stop and help the other, regardless of group membership. Still, he qualifies this obligation in two ways, saying that help is only called for if the risks and costs of helping are "relatively low."[78] He wishes to capture the parable's sense of occasion, where help is required without regard to the strangers' attachments. But his proviso blunts the force of the parable, since he calls for assistance only when the actor does not have to risk very much. The Samaritan went beyond cleaning up the man and calling for help, carrying him to a town and staying the night in a place where he was likely in great danger.

Having gotten part of the way there but muting the parable's demands, Walzer writes that what applies to individuals also applies to collectives: "Groups of people ought to help necessitous strangers whom they somehow discover in their midst or on their path."[79] Here Walzer moves with the grain of the parable. His groups of people do not just learn respect, but they also discover strangers they must help.

[78] Michael Walzer, *Spheres of Justice: A Defense of Pluralism and Equality* (New York: Basic Books, 1983), 33.
[79] Ibid.

He brings up this story in the process of addressing immigration admissions, and there his telling of the story is evocative. On a country's path, Walzer's terse phrase suggests, perhaps in the course of trading or warring, that country meets necessitous strangers and in an ad hoc way admits them as refugees. In the country's midst, too, a country discovers necessitous strangers. This phrase of Walzer's speaks to our question of women and men who lack legal permission to be in the country. Though the authority under which their presence is illegal deserves consideration, the sort of consideration paid in Chapter 3, what matters is that they are in the country's midst. Once again, Walzer returns to his proviso: A group need not take on too much risk or cost in providing aid. "My life cannot be shaped and determined by such chance encounters," Walzer writes.[80] Here Walzer goes astray again from the parable, but his suggestion that a people may discover necessitous strangers in their midst or on their path carries a reading of the parable a step forward.

A further treatment of the political community as a neighbor comes from Oliver O'Donovan when he casts a vision of a plural international system within divine providence. His attention is on the territorial border, which divides not only to set a limit to a people. He says the border also forms "a horizon which will stimulate neighborly relations between the people and other peoples. It defines a 'You' in relation to which the people acts as a corporate 'I.'"[81] In his idiosyncratic use of the word "horizon," O'Donovan sees the border as not just a stopping point, but also an opportunity to relate and interact. Again, he writes, "Localities have boundaries that also form horizons. If bounded locality fosters neighborly responsibility within the society's compass, horizoned locality makes the society itself into a neighbor."[82] O'Donovan suggests a line of thought about how a land border can make countries into neighbors. A related thought, that being a people requires having neighbors, gets his picture of international relations off to a start, and how he develops this thought sounds much like Roosevelt. Imagining peoples as actors, he speaks of "respect and letting-be," of "a truly universal common good of reciprocal acting and being acted open."[83] O'Donovan makes a step beyond Roosevelt through the Parable of the Good Samaritan. Instead of the perspective of empire that foreigners are enemies until they are brought into unity with us, O'Donovan commends not only recognition but welcome, friendship, hospitality, and love for the stranger met on the road.[84] In short-hand, he alludes to something more than Roosevelt's respect, but he does not reveal what it looks like for peoples to welcome and to love.

---

[80] Ibid.

[81] O'Donovan, *The Ways of Judgment*, 151.

[82] Ibid., 257. On this, see the author's "Philosophical and Theological Reflections on the U.S.-Mexico Border, with Special Reference to Joseph Carens, Michael Walzer, and Oliver O'Donovan" (M.Phil. Thesis, Faculty of Theology, University of Oxford, 2010), 63–70.

[83] O'Donovan, *The Ways of Judgment*, 152.

[84] "Xenophilia is commanded us: the neighbor whom we are to love is the foreigner whom we encounter on the road," Oliver O'Donovan, *The Desire of the Nations: Rediscovering the Roots of Political Theology* (Cambridge: Cambridge University Press, 1996), 268.

O'Donovan's thought that borders make neighbors finds echoes and elaborations in the writings of two other theologians. Theologian Justo L. González reflects on how the Spanish *frontera* can be translated either as "frontier" or as "border" in English. He suggests that while a frontier only moves forward, bringing light to darkness, a border is a place where two realities and two cultures meet. The U.S.-Mexico border, he writes, expanded as an unstoppable frontier under the American ideology of Manifest Destiny and through "the most unjustifiable, unjust, and despicable war this nation has ever waged," speaking of the United States' war on Mexico.[85] González thinks that the Hispanic experience of being *mestizo*, mixed-breed, lends particular insight on the border as a place of encounter.[86] A border, says González, works not like armor but like skin:

> Our skin does set a limit to where our body begins and where it ends. Our skin also sets certain limits to our give-and-take with our environment, keeping out certain germs, helping us to select that in our environment which we are ready to absorb. But if we ever close up our skin, we die.[87]

Such a picture captures something of what it is to be a well-functioning border, providing protection but allowing movement if it is not to stifle the life within.

Another theologian offers an image of a border that draws out the reciprocal character of neighborhood. Theologian interprets the border not as a filter or fence but as a face. The border serves as the face a nation presents to the world, displaying whether it is hospitable or hostile, Bretherton writes. "A face says that I am somebody who deserves respect, I am not simply a piece of land to be bought and sold or a thing made use of for a time." Bretherton goes on: "I have a personality and a history and a way of doing things, but I am made for relationship, and without coming into relationship with others who are different from me, then I do not grow." Here Bretherton achieves what Roosevelt did: A face indicates a worthiness of respect, and it indicates a desire and need for relationship. But in a theological twist on the face, Bretherton considers it destined for God:

> Ultimately, I am a face who seeks to look upon the face of God and who finds the face of God reflected not in the faces of the strong and powerful, the skilled and the economically capable but in the face of the orphan, the widow and the refugee – and this is who God bids me be hospitable to.[88]

---

[85] Justo L. González, *Santa Biblia: The Bible through Hispanic Eyes* (Nashville: Abingdon Press, 1996), 86.

[86] Ibid., 77.

[87] Ibid., 86–87.

[88] Luke Bretherton, "Filters, Fences or Faces? The Moral Status of Borders" ("Strangers No More" Conference organized by the University of Notre Dame, Citizens Organizing Foundation, and the Von Hügel Institute, Cambridge University, London, April 20, 2007); also available as "Filters, Fences or Faces? Asylum Seekers and the Moral Status of Borders," *Australian Broadcasting Corporation*, June 28, 2012, Online edition, sec. Religion and Ethics,

That a face is destined to see the face of God, Bretherton argues, means that a face is on its way to its intended end when it encounters the face of the widow, the orphan, and the immigrant who presents God's face. Insofar as a faced nation becomes a neighbor only to the strong, it has a face that is not on its way to God, a face that is hardened. This is a face that is headed toward death rather than eternal life, recalling the interchange that frames the Parable of the Good Samaritan. But as a people faces the weak, as it becomes a neighbor to the weak, it sets its face toward Christ and toward the never-ending life that comes in encountering him. Like Walzer's adaptation of the parable, Bretherton's explication of the border as a face lends neighborliness a direction beyond mutual respect: It implies aid for the powerless.

A final way of understanding the country as a neighbor comes from the etymology of the word "country." The English term first appears as a word for a region or district, and it is derived from the Old French *cuntrée*, from the late Latin *contrāta*, referring to a region or urban district.[89] This in turn comes from the Latin *contrā*, meaning in its most basic sense what lies in front of one or opposite one. From there, *contrā* may signify facing the enemy, or it may simply signify toward, up to a person, to meet a person, or face to face.[90] Indeed, this is the same root as in the English "counter" or "encounter," at the heart of what it means to become a neighbor. One source suggests that the term was applied to a region from the perspective of one in the city who viewed the country opposite.[91] Then again, letting the etymological possibilities lie open, the term is suggestive. The country is the land that presents itself to the gaze, across from the viewer. It takes shape in relation to a viewer and to a distinct country. A people becomes defined by its land and its land fosters its growth. Here the term "country" holds together informal society, formal government, and the land in which a society dwells and in which government has authority.[92] A country has the potential to stand against another country, indifferent, unhelpful, oppressive, or ready for war. Then again, it might present its face in an opening to another country. That encounter is an opening to Christ the neighbor, an opening in which to receive mercy and extend mercy.

Can a country be a neighbor in the sense revealed by the Parable of the Good Samaritan? The picture that President Roosevelt and these theologians offer of an agent respectful of other agents gets part of the way there. When countries treat one another as free and independent, their achievement of this liberal ideal

---

www.abc.net.au/religion/articles/2012/06/28/3535073.htm; see also Heimburger, "Reflections on the U.S.-Mexico Border," 78.

[89] *Oxford English Dictionary*, compact edition, vol. 1 (Oxford: Clarendon Press, 1971), 580; *Mediae Latinitatis Lexicon Minus*, 67.

[90] O.L.D., 432–33; see also Heimburger, "Reflections on the U.S.-Mexico Border."

[91] *Mediae Latinitatis Lexicon Minus*, 67.

[92] "Country" is Michael Walzer's favorite term, e.g., in *Spheres of Justice*, 44.

is no small achievement. Seeing a neighboring country not as a country to be used, exploited, or conquered leaves room for more considerate relationships. Roosevelt's appeal to countries in the Western Hemisphere moves a step closer to the neighborhood of the parable: Certain countries encounter one another simply because they are located nearer one another. As the theologians call countries to aid one another in times of need, they take another step toward the parable. Defending one another from attack, granting funds to avert a financial crisis, receiving refugees when strife threatens the members of another country: these seem good examples of becoming a neighbor.

At other points, it is harder to imagine a country as a neighbor. Walzer thinks that chance occurrences are easy to come by, but more often those who govern peoples move slowly in becoming neighbors. When they act through legislative acts, they cannot be hit in the heart and act in mutual aid as quickly as an individual can, though perhaps executive action allows for quicker, less reflective action. By and large, through treaties and agreements, countries relate in a lethargic way, setting up longstanding arrangements without the "by chance" of the Samaritan passing the injured man. Borders rarely change, and so geographical neighbors do not often shift. Still, Walzer's suggestion bears a repeated hearing: Groups of people do somehow discover necessitous strangers in their path and among them. Perhaps a people can be a neighbor if its leaders stop regularly to ask, "who are our neighbors?" This could be an occasion to reassess their current position and the state of the countries around them, asking who has come into their path through their diplomatic efforts, their development goals, their peacekeeping operations, or their trading.

The United States as Neighbor

Such a suggestion draws attention back to the United States. The United States cannot be as flexible as an individual can in becoming a neighbor, yet it still has opportunities to become a neighbor. Still, those in authority can regularly ask, "Who is my neighbor?" This question could open up Congress and executive branches of the federal government to receiving mercy and giving mercy. In the early twenty-first century, the United States regularly encounters certain countries through its longstanding ties, its land borders, through shipping and travel, and through migration. Chief among these is Mexico: Mexicans are among the foreigners that the United States encounters on its path, and many Mexican citizens live within United States territory and form part of U.S. communities. These women, men, and children are already acting as neighbors, contributing to the wellbeing of the United States through their presence, activity, and labor. The U.S. government ought to recognize the many ways these men and women offer help to American communities and act to deliver them from their subjugation. Those from Mexico should not be used and exploited, but they should be received as neighbors.

Here are three ways that the United States government can become a neighbor to Mexico and to its people. First, Congress ought to act to recognize those who have lived peaceably in the United States without legal status for a length of time. This recognition should include an opportunity for these residents to admit that they have broken the law by entering the country or remaining in the country without permission. This recognition should include an offer of legal residence, allowing these men, women, and children to come out of the shadows. After a further length of time, legal residence should lead to citizenship for those who desire it. This move toward legal status and citizenship is in keeping with democratic faith in the equality of every human being, but it goes further. When unlawful presence leaves someone in a subservient and exploitable state, the good news of liberation from slavery demands that those in this status be offered a way to achieve legal residence.

The second way that the United States government can become a neighbor to Mexico and its people is to reform its laws so that future generations of Mexicans will not become illegal aliens in such large numbers. If the United States will carry on heavily restricting immigration, then it should face up to the problems caused by a policy that applies the same numerical limit to immigration from Mexico as from every other country. Lawmakers should not hold to a principle of nondiscrimination in immigration admissions that proves indifferent and harmful to a nearby neighbor, ignoring place and contingency in the name of an abstract goal. Instead, the federal government should look to its limits and its place, to Mexico its neighbor, and to the people from that nation who come to live in it. It is time to relinquish such a small numerical cap for Mexico, either expanding the numerical limit or giving it up in favor of only substantial, qualitative limits. It is time to receive the mercy that the Mexican people continue to extend to the United States, contributing to American prosperity in a way that Americans too easily dismiss as illegal.[93]

The third way that the United States government can be a neighbor is to seek opportunities for cooperation across its border with Mexico. Immigration laws could be drawn up in conversation with officials from Mexico and other nearby countries. Law enforcement agencies could work together more closely. Such cooperation tends not to go well because of leaks in Mexican agencies that allow information to flow to smugglers and drug cartels.[94] There are further opportunities for the United States to assist Mexico in preventing the forces that uproot Mexicans and cause them to move north. Promoting education for women as well as men, providing reliable and secure banking, and promoting small business initiatives would enable the most

---

[93] Theologian Dana W. Wilbanks agrees, arguing that the U.S. immigration policy should involve a "principle of proximity" that favors the "neighbor close at hand," *Re-Creating America: The Ethics of U.S. Immigration and Refugee Policy in a Christian Perspective* (Nashville: Abingdon Press, 1996), 160.

[94] Julia Preston, "Officers on Border Team Up to Quell Violence," *The New York Times*, March 25, 2010, sec. World/Americas, www.nytimes.com/2010/03/26/world/americas/26border.html. Here, there are questions to ask about how authorities on both sides of the border conceive of and respond to the drug trade.

disadvantaged regions of Mexico to allow for a better life for their people so that they do not have to leave for the United States.[95] Greater cooperation at the border, in the interior, and between the Distrito Federal and the District of Columbia would be steps toward neighborhood.

The best a government can do is to become a neighbor so that women and men can become neighbors. These reforms of federal U.S. law would remove barriers for members of different communities, Americans and Mexicans, to become neighbors. Legal reform, if successful, will foster everyday acts of receiving mercy and giving mercy. Reform will enable a new openness to those who are different that is no longer prevented through legal penalties for transporting or employing these neighbors: that no longer keeps men and women in their houses out of fear of being apprehended. Reformed laws will enable a new recognition of neighbors in the public square and in the public forum that is the church. The real business of becoming neighbors lies with ordinary Mexicans, Americans, and Mexican-Americans. As they receive mercy and extend mercy, they must keep in mind the promise that the neighbor represents the face of Christ. They should take courage that becoming a neighbor is the way to eternal life; indeed, it is already a taste of the life that goes on forever.

—

The first two parts of the book explained how someone could become an alien and an illegal alien under U.S. law. Part III explained what made it possible for so many immigrants from countries neighboring the United States to qualify as an illegal alien. What at first seems a quirk of logic made it possible, as an effort to overcome racism and discrimination in immigration admissions led to equalizing the number of visas for each country annually. In this system, Mexico and other nearby countries were placed on a par with countries farther away, but rather than heeding the severe drop in allowances for legal immigration, Mexicans kept migrating to the United States, primarily through illegal channels. One problem created another, though the fix was consistent with a certain American commitment to abstract equality. This attempt at equality proceeded without acknowledging the United States' history with Mexico, especially its dependence on Mexicans to do much of its manual work. Under the new regime, more and more of these workers went through life without visas, breaking immigration laws, living a precarious existence, and compromising the rule of law in the United States.

This chapter looked for ways of thinking through the laws that make nearby neighbors into illegal aliens through discussion on justice from philosophy and theology. An analysis of types of justice revealed that federal law in its current form

---

[95] Sonia Nazario makes this argument in "The Heartache of an Immigrant Family," *The New York Times*, October 14, 2013, sec. Opinion, www.nytimes.com/2013/10/15/opinion/the-heart ache-of-an-immigrant-family.html.

fails to right the wrongs done to the unlawfully present and fails to offer visas to suitable nearby neighbors. This analysis suggested a possible step farther, an argument that justice requires recognizing ongoing patterns of migration and protecting those who migrate between Mexico and the United States. Talk of the United States as a good neighbor pointed to a second way of evaluating these laws and the lives they engender, the parable of Jesus that produces this notion of a neighbor. Reading this parable suggested that the laws under which so many in the United States are unlawfully present erect barriers to acts of love and mercy. This reading led to an invitation to recognize mercy shown from illegal neighbors and to become a neighbor, a process that draws the neighbor into the worship of God. The next step was to discern how the United States could become a neighbor, first by recognizing its role as an indifferent and oppressive neighbor to Mexico. Legal reform would allow the country to become a neighbor in modest ways that start by acknowledging the mercy it receives from Mexican immigrants.

Conclusion

A vulnerable and exploited underclass forms part of American society, an underclass living under the moniker of the "illegal alien." Given the demands of this subject, what has this book added to a theological discussion about illegal immigration in the United States? A review of Christian responses to the issue found issues unresolved. Rejecting territorial government completely in the name of the body of Christ seemed wrong, but it also seemed wrong to acquiesce to a political arrangement under which exploitation and law-breaking are the norm. Those who agreed in rejecting these extremes were left with conflicts: between following the law and welcoming the stranger, in the case of evangelical biblical interpreters, or between a right to migrate when work is lacking and a right of sovereign nations to control their borders, in the case of Catholic Social Teaching. Scholarly works in Christian ethics have carried the conversation forward, but to respond to illegal immigration, two areas needed further exploration: legal history and a theology of politics. Rather than treating government as monolithic and timeless, how did federal U.S. immigration laws develop so that it would be possible for so many people to break them? So far as Americans assume what the law tells them, where did these legal assumptions come from? Once this is clear, how might the Christian tradition analyze and qualify the government of immigration? What do biblical narratives and resources from the tradition say about authority over who comes into and out of U.S. territory?

Encountering the history of U.S. immigration law, both legislative and judicial, it became clear that things have not always been as they are today. It was not always clear that those from far away were aliens, but this characterization emerged out of a late medieval and early modern hardening of bonds between subjects and sovereigns. Only in the late nineteenth century was it clear that the federal government had authority over immigration, and that authority was deeply contested by Supreme Court justices. Only since the late twentieth century did the United States limit immigration from nearby countries to a specific number. What many

Americans assume has not always been the same. These concepts have developed in a certain way, and they could be otherwise.

As this work traced the development of U.S. immigration law, it revealed how the courts and the legislature developed powerful and harsh conceptual instruments to protect a land where civil rights for all were growing. While provisions for those already inside increased, the law depended on classifying some persons as aliens who could make no rightful claim against the federal government's power to exclude and expel them. A country that professed liberty and justice for all made it clear that those privileges were for citizens, not aliens, since practically no norms of justice constrained the executive powers to deny entry, detain, and deport aliens. Particularly against the claimed power to expel aliens lawfully residing in the country, judges protested that the federal government was turning despotic and lawless, but those who advocated such extensive authority over immigration prevailed. These moves by the Supreme Court bore affinities to assertions by jurists and philosophers in past centuries that international justice rested on national self-preservation and nothing greater.

This book also observed that a high-minded campaign to end legal discrimination based on nationality reversed a pattern of special allowances for neighboring countries. As recently as the 1960s, the United States placed no numerical limits on immigration from Mexico and other Western Hemisphere countries, and many of those countries' citizens came to the United States under contract labor programs. Only in recent history did numerical limits come into place on immigration from Mexico and other nearby countries. The contours of Mexico-U.S. relations over the past century revealed that Congress was playing a game, requiring visas but letting illegal entry carry on, drawing contract laborers and then undocumented workers to do the work Americans did not want to do. In effect, Congress and businesses collaborated to enable continued migration while classing it as illegal, using and exploiting Mexican workers.

Illegal immigration is not what it seems, then. It only became possible in the United States through terms that cast suspicion on those from afar, through claims of government power over immigration with little reference to justice, and through a flawed admissions policy that maintained a class of migrant workers who were neither slave nor free.

Having seen that the possibility of illegal immigration rests on legal discourses about aliens, immigration authority, and justice, this book uncovered ways that the Christian tradition understands those features of life during this age. Peoples or nations came to be seen as fluid distinctions, given both to bless human beings as they fill the earth and to judge human beings for their self-worship. These far-flung conglomerations of language, land, and history are best understood as opportunities to draw near to one another, a process that is complete in the people of God, in Israel and the church. The apostolic character of God's people means that they are sent out across national distinctions so that those of every tribe can share in the fullness of life that comes through Christ's death and resurrection. If nations find their end in drawing near, then calling those from elsewhere "aliens" cannot sit well with those who take on this narrative as their own. A Christian narrative of the healing of the nations stands at odds with treating those from other nations like aliens.

After discovering a Christian unease with the notion of the alien, the book looked for a way that Christian theology might qualify the guarding of places. The keeping of places emerged as a task given to human creatures, a task that transformed into the guarding of places against fellow human beings when the threat of murder arose. This guarding, the Scriptures affirmed, takes place only under God's guarding, and it is subject to God's direction that guards judge fairly and shield those under their care, including migrants. Characterizations of government from the Christian tradition indicated what immigration authority ought to do: that it primarily fends off threats of harm to what a society shares. Those who defy this authority do something that is not wrong in itself but wrong because it is prohibited, and so the punishment of such wrongs ought not exceed the wrong done. On this reading, the Christian tradition would cast immigration authority not as a strong expression of sovereignty by which a nation protects its life in the way it chooses, but as a ministry of the sovereign God who uses it to preserve human life.

Moving on from a chastened description of immigration authority, this work found ways that the Christian tradition describes the ways of justice for migrants and the ways of mercy for neighbors. Justice is not only about equal distribution of goods like visas, but it rights wrongs and attributes gifts to the fitting. On this analysis, immigration admissions ought to give up equal treatment for Mexico and recognize American debts to Mexican migrant workers. Further, future admissions should be given to those nearby as among the most fitting, and perhaps patterns of migration deserve recognition and protection by government. New insights emerged about what it means to be a neighbor, whether for individuals and communities in the United States or for the country as a whole. A fresh hearing of the Parable of the Good Samaritan brought attention to encounter, an encounter with someone from a hated group who shows mercy and teaches the recipient how to show mercy. An overly strong interpretation of the category of the illegal alien proved an excuse not to be a neighbor, to turn a blind eye. The work concluded that it is time that U.S. residents receive mercy from the neighbors they dislike. It is time too for the United States as a whole to recognize the mercy it receives from its neighbor Mexico and to respond with mercy.

—

Is this book too stuck in the past to be relevant to today's issues surrounding illegal immigration? Since this work takes 1965 as the last date that a significant shift happened to make persons into illegal aliens, hasn't more happened in decades since? No: From 1965, all the ingredients for the creation of a large community of people without legal status were in place. Changes since then have mostly served to reinforce the terms of federal law that make for the rise of the illegal alien as a form of life. The illegal alien has been taken as a notion that is here to stay, and as the main problem for immigration law to deal with, setting aside refugee law.

While the Supreme Court has offered some tweaks, opening the way for U.S. citizens to hold dual citizenship, since 1965 Congress has primarily acted to intensify enforcement of the regime that creates the illegal alien.[1] The Immigration Reform and Control Act of 1986 provided notable changes within that regime, releasing nearly three million from unlawful status and creating a new focus of enforcement at the workplace.[2] In 1996, the Illegal Immigration Reform and Immigrant Responsibility Act increased the policing of borders and made it easier to detain and deport migrants.[3] The Secure Fence Act of 2006 aimed to achieve "operational control" of all U.S. borders, introducing increased surveillance and fencing sections of the U.S.-Mexico border.[4] Both Republican President George W. Bush in 2006–7 and Democratic President Barack Obama in 2013–14 sought to enact comprehensive immigration reform that would combine heavier policing of the border with a path to citizenship for those without legal status, but at each point Congress failed to reach a consensus. Early in his presidency, Republican Donald Trump sought to strengthen the current terms of immigration law, and he promised to increase the deportation of immigrants lacking legal status and complete a wall along the Mexican border. While policing of immigration laws rises and falls in intensity, over the last half century this policing has reinforced the terms that make it possible for so many people to live in the United States without permission.

The community of irregular migrants has changed since 1965. In earlier decades, unauthorized migrants from Mexico came and went in a circular pattern.[5] In the 1990s and 2000s a settled community grew, in part because rising enforcement deterred Mexicans from traveling to Mexico, as they knew they might not be able to return to the United States. In a change that coincided with the Great Recession, the number of those without legal status peaked in 2007, declined, and then stabilized from 2009 onward. The unauthorized population from Mexico continued to decline through the last year for which records were available, 2014, while numbers from Guatemala, India, and Honduras grew in the same period. Adults among irregular migrants had lived in the United States for a median of

---

[1]   Two rulings enabled Congress and the State Department to make dual citizenship possible, Afroyim v. Rusk, 387 U.S. 253 (1967), and Vance v. Terrazas, 444 U.S. 252 (1980).

[2]   An Act: To amend the Immigration and Nationality Act to revise and reform the immigration laws, and for other purposes, Pub. L. No. 99–603, 100 Stat. 3359 (1986).

[3]   An Act: Making omnibus consolidated appropriations for the fiscal year ending September 30, 1997, and for other purposes, Pub. L. No. 104–208, 110 Stat. 3009–546 (1996).

[4]   An Act: To establish operational control over the international land and maritime borders of the United States, Pub. L. No. 109–367, 120 Stat. 2638 (2006).

[5]   Douglas S. Massey and Audrey Singer, "New Estimates of Undocumented Mexican Migration and the Probability of Apprehension," *Demography* 32, no. 2 (1995): 210.

more than thirteen years in 2014, when in 2008 the median was eight years.[6] These changes have implications. Stopping people from entering is not so much of an issue. Instead, there is a large, stable community without legal status. What future will these men, women, and children have in the United States? Then again, if forces push and pull new immigrants to the United States by crossing illegally or overstaying visas, immigration law is still in a position to cast these newcomers as illegal aliens.

Within the regime that makes possible unauthorized immigration in large numbers, the 1986 Act deserves more reflection. When Republican President Ronald Reagan signed this Act into law, it was the first legislation to identify the "illegal alien" and the "unauthorized alien" as problematic figures.[7] The Act sought to reduce both the unlawful presence and the unauthorized work that the Immigration and Nationality Act of 1965 enabled, adjusting the status of about 2.7 million women, men, and children from unlawful to lawful.[8] At the same time, the Act made it unlawful to hire an "unauthorized alien," placing a new emphasis on the local business as a venue for enforcement.[9] This Act, then, raises questions of what happens after someone lacks legal status and what makes for good work. Should adjustment of status be interpreted as amnesty and as a forgetting of wrongs, like in recent debates in Washington? Or, do the working conditions of these women and men mean that it should be thought of as release from servitude? If, as Chapter 6 argues, U.S. legislators, businesspeople, and consumers have fostered the existence of a permanent underclass lacking in freedom, perhaps talk of amnesty for wrong needs to be replaced by talk of release from slavery. And, if the 1986 Act makes activities of working and offering work a new place for enforcement, there is a need for the reshaping of employment as just, properly paid, and meaningful.

Along these lines, there remains a question about the history told in Chapter 5: What has kept so many U.S. residents in a class that is neither slave nor free? Behind the racism against Africans that perpetuated slavery in the United States, Wendell Berry finds a problem Americans have with their own condition. He says that as Americans, we have an "ordinate desire to be superior – not to some inferior or subject people, though this desire leads to the subjection of people – but to our condition." He continues: "We wish to rise above the sweat and bother of taking

---

[6] An estimated 11.1 million people resided in the United States without permission as of 2014, down from 12.2 million in 2007 and not far from 11.3 million in 2009. In 2014, an estimated 5.8 million of those, or 52 percent, came from Mexico, a decline from a 2007 peak of 6.9 million from Mexico, Jeffrey S. Passel and D'Vera Cohn, "Overall Number of U.S. Unauthorized Immigrants Holds Steady Since 2009" (Washington, D.C.: Pew Research Center, September 20, 2016), 3, 4, 14, www.pewhispanic.org/2016/09/20/overall-number-of-u-s-unauthorized-immi grants-holds-steady-since-2009/.

[7] 100 Stat. 3359, 3360.

[8] 100 Stat. 3359, 3394–95.

[9] 100 Stat. 3359, 3360.

care of anything – of ourselves, of each other, or of our country."[10] Berry thinks that
the history of slavery reveals a desire to cast some work as "'nigger work' ... that is,
fundamental, necessary, and inferior."[11] That Americans wish to get beyond necessary work and to ignore the messes they make requires that they subjugate people
and ruin places with their waste, says Berry.[12] Perhaps this is why American society
has perpetuated a class of contract laborers and undocumented workers to do
the dirty work it would rather ignore. Perhaps this is why calls for legal reform still
focus on expanding the immigration of professionals without recognizing that
immigrants do a significant portion of the United States' manual work. A response
to this disavowal of the flesh requires a new valuation of the body and of work.

The book leaves other questions unexamined. In Chapter 1, exploring the roots of
immigration law in the notion of the alien raised a question: When legal systems cast
persons as aliens, do they at the same time require an allegiance beyond what a
political community should require? The earliest U.S. naturalization laws suggest
that the answer is yes. These required that to be admitted as a citizen, an alien had
"to renounce for ever all allegiance and fidelity to any foreign prince, potentate, state
or sovereignty whatever, and particularly, by name, the prince, potentate, state or
sovereignty whereof such alien may, at the time, be a citizen or subject."[13] This
renunciation can be read as operating simply on the level of earthly politics and not
excluding allegiance and fidelity to the Lord Jesus. But two centuries before, Queen
Elizabeth I of England instituted an Oath of Supremacy with very similar wording,
an oath that went further than previous oaths. Like the American oath, the Oath of
Supremacy not only required a subject to promise faithfulness to the monarch but
to renounce allegiances to other powers. The Oath of Supremacy also included a
declaration that the Queen was "the only supreme governor of this realm, ... as well
in all spiritual or ecclesiastical things or causes, as temporal."[14] During the sixteenth
century, the Crown may have pared back a Roman church that claimed too much
temporal power, but it answered that distortion by claiming too much authority
for the Queen over churches in England. The oath that distinguishes an English
subject from an alien in 1559 and the oath or affirmation that distinguishes a United
States citizen from an alien in 1802 promises allegiance that excludes other allegiances. This appears to be an allegiance that is not limited by an allegiance to
Christ or to his church, a body not governed by civil authorities.

The discussion about the church as a migrant community in Chapter 2 raises
the question of what churches are doing. When it comes to irregular migration
in the United States, how are members of the body of Christ migrating, and how

---

[10] *The Hidden Wound*, new edn. (San Francisco: North Point Press, 1989), 112.

[11] Ibid., 113.

[12] Ibid., 123.

[13] An act to establish an uniform rule of naturalization; and to repeal the acts heretofore passed on
      that subject, 2 Stat. 153 (1802), 153.

[14] 1 Elizabeth, cap. 1: *Statutes of the Realm*, 4, pt. 1. 350. [G. and H. 79], cited in Henry Scowcroft
      Bettenson and Chris Maunder, eds., *Documents of the Christian Church*, 3rd edn. (Oxford:
      Oxford University Press, 1999), 261.

are they responding to migrants? Documentary works contribute to the picture: Leah Sarat describes a Pentecostal community in Mexico as it prepares to send its members north, and Jacqueline Maria Hagan depicts the role of faith in the journey of the undocumented. Pierrette Hondagneu-Sotelo describes religious activists defending immigrants, and Ananda Rose captures opposing approaches to the U.S.-Mexico border that both come from faith communities. Grace Yukich illustrates the New Sanctuary Movement as its members protect men and women from unjust deportation.[15] As they migrate and respond to migrants, Christian communities merit more of this sort of attention.

There is room too for practical theology that advises and exhorts churches to live out their migrant character. Many Christians in the United States fail to reflect on the witness of the Christian tradition on migration, holding to a law-and-order response to illegal immigration. Leaders of evangelical, mainline Protestant, and Roman Catholic denominations and parachurch organizations continue to call for faithful witness and legal reform, but many laypeople are a step behind. Christians provide healthcare and legal advice, and churches blossom in migrant communities or include migrants in their midst. Some, like the Sanctuary Movement, take more radical measures, hosting women and men in houses of worship to protect them from unjust deportation. Much is going on, but there remains room for imaginative responses from churches in the United States.

There is also room for imaginative responses from women and men in authority. This book has made several suggestions that are ready to be filled out by those involved in the government of immigration. How can judges move beyond treating immigrants as classes to consider the individual, the family, and the effect of sentencing on them? How can legislators recognize undocumented neighbors who have shown mercy to citizens and legal residents? How can laws be reformed to prevent the creation of new generations of immigrants living in the shadows? How can the policing of immigration be limited and redirected toward its proper purposes? How can the United States cooperate with Mexico and other countries in the region rather than work in opposition?

—

I reestablished contact with Miguel Villanueva two years after we first met. Miguel was still in Mexico, it turned out. After I had spoken with him in Nogales, Mexico, he slept on its streets for about a month before a relative sent him money to take a bus back to stay with his mother. Since then, Miguel has been enrolled in a

---

[15] Leah Sarat, *Fire in the Canyon: Religion, Migration, and the Mexican Dream* (New York: New York University Press, 2013); Jacqueline Maria Hagan, *Migration Miracle: Faith, Hope, and the Undocumented Journey* (Cambridge, Mass.: Harvard University Press, 2008); Pierrette Hondagneu-Sotelo, *God's Heart Has No Borders: How Religious Activists Are Working for Immigrant Rights* (Berkeley: University of California Press, 2008); Ananda Rose, *Showdown in the Sonoran Desert: Religion, Law, and the Immigration Controversy* (New York: Oxford University Press, 2012); Grace Yukich, *One Family Under God: Immigration Politics and Progressive Religion in America* (New York: Oxford University Press, 2013).

local university. He once tried again to cross into the United States, this time in Texas, but border agents caught him. He expected a judge to charge him with a felony, but instead the judge charged him with a misdemeanor and sentenced him to several days in jail. After that, Miguel was deported to Mexico. He told me he did not want to try to enter the United States again. He did not want to go to jail again, and he wanted to prevent his record from becoming irredeemable. A lawyer told Miguel that the United States might reform its immigration laws, and Miguel hoped that this might allow him to return north. In the meantime, Miguel said that his wife did not contact him anymore. He was not able to return to her and their daughter, and so his wife was now with another man.

A year later, Miguel related another twist in his story. He said he had spoken to his ex-wife in the United States – no, his ex-girlfriend, he self-corrected. She told him that he was not the father of her daughter. A mutual friend told Miguel the same thing: that someone else was the girl's father. In the end, Miguel believed them. After years of thinking about his daughter every day and regretting not being with her, this news allowed him to get on with life in Mexico with his girlfriend and his studies.

The 146th Psalm offers words for those who are troubled by migrating illegally or troubled on behalf of those who do. There the psalmist praises the Lord, declaring earthly rulers to be unworthy of trust, unable to deliver, and headed toward the grave. The God of Jacob is not so, for this God made heaven and earth and keeps trust forever. This Yhwh executes judgment for the oppressed, feeds the hungry, frees the prisoner, and upholds the widow and the orphan. "The LORD watches over the sojourners," or better: "Yhwh keeps the migrants" (v. 9a). The psalmist concludes: "Yhwh will reign forever ... Praise Yhwh!" (v. 10).

Works Cited

Ahn, Ilsup. *Religious Ethics and Migration: Doing Justice to Undocumented Workers.* New York: Routledge, 2014.

Ahn, John J. *Exile as Forced Migrations: A Sociological, Literary, and Theological Approach on the Displacement and Resettlement of the Southern Kingdom of Judah.* Beihefte zur Zeitschrift für die alttestamentliche Wissenschaft 417. Berlin: De Gruyter, 2011.

Alexander, Robert C. "Our National Origins Quota System: The Mirror of America." *The American Legion Magazine*, September 1956.

Anderson, Benedict. *Imagined Communities: Reflections on the Origin and Spread of Nationalism.* London: Verso, 1983.

Anonymous. "The Epistle to Diognetus." In *Early Christian Writings: The Apostolic Fathers,* edited by Andrew Louth, translated by Maxwell Staniforth and Andrew Louth, 142–51. Harmondsworth: Penguin, 1987.

Anzaldúa, Gloria. *Borderlands/La Frontera: The New Mestiza.* San Francisco: Aunt Lute, 1987.

Aquino, María Pilar, Daisy L. Machado, and Jeanette Rodríguez, eds. *A Reader in Latina Feminist Theology: Religion and Justice.* Austin, Tex.: University of Texas Press, 2002.

Arau, Sergio. *A Day without a Mexican.* Santa Monica, Calif.: Xenon Pictures, 2004.

Aristotle. *Nicomachean Ethics.* Translated by H. Rackham. Rev. edn. Loeb Classical Library 73. Cambridge, Mass.: Harvard University Press, 1934.

Nicomachean Ethics. Translated by Terence Irwin. 2nd edn. Indianapolis: Hackett Publishing, 1999.

Politics. Translated by H. Rackham. Rev. edn. Loeb Classical Library 264. Cambridge, Mass.: Harvard University Press, 1944.

Arnold, Bill T. *Genesis.* New Cambridge Bible Commentary. Cambridge: Cambridge University Press, 2009.

Augustine. *The City of God against the Pagans.* Edited and translated by R. W. Dyson. Cambridge: Cambridge University Press, 1998.

Awabdy, Mark A. *Immigrants and Innovative Law: Deuteronomy's Theological and Social Vision for the Gēr.* Tübingen: Mohr Siebeck, 2014.

Azaransky, Sarah, ed. *Religion and Politics in America's Borderlands.* Lanham, Md.: Lexington Books, 2013.

Bachus III, Rep. Spencer. "Speech to Constituents." Gardendale Civic Center, Gardendale, Ala., August 21, 2013. www.dropbox.com/sh/lwo6835cvqrzofc/-xwvCTxas9. Accessed January 2, 2014.

Bailey, Kenneth E. *Jesus through Middle Eastern Eyes: Cultural Studies in the Gospels.* London: S.P.C.K., 2008.

Bar, Ludwig von. *Das internationale Privat- und Strafrecht.* Hannover: Hahn'sche Hofbuchhandlung, 1862.

———. *International Law: Private and Criminal.* Translated by G. R. Gillespie. Edinburgh: W. Green, 1883.

Barrett, C. K. *A Commentary on the First Epistle to the Corinthians.* London: Adam & Charles Black, 1968.

Barth, Karl. *Church and State.* Translated by G. Ronald Howe. London: Student Christian Movement Press, 1939.

———. *Church Dogmatics.* Edited by G. W. Bromiley and T. F. Torrance. Translated by A. T. Mackay, T. H. L. Parker, H. Knight, H. A. Kennedy, and J. Marks. Vol. III/4. The Doctrine of Creation. Edinburgh: T. & T. Clark, 1961.

———. *Church Dogmatics.* Edited by G. W. Bromiley and T. F. Torrance. Translated by G. T. Thomson and Harold Knight. Vol. I/2. The Doctrine of the Word of God. Edinburgh: T. & T. Clark, 1956.

———. *Church Dogmatics.* Edited by Geoffrey W. Bromiley and T. F. Torrance. Translated by Harold Knight, Geoffrey W. Bromiley, J. K. S. Reid, and R. H. Fuller. Vol. III/2. The Doctrine of Creation. Edinburgh: T. & T. Clark, 1960.

———. *Die kirchliche Dogmatik.* Vol. III/4. Die Lehre von der Schöpfung. Zürich: Theologischer Verlag Zürich, 1980.

———. *Ethics.* Edited by Dietrich Braun. Translated by Geoffrey W. Bromiley. Edinburgh: T. & T. Clark, 1981.

Bauer, Walter. *A Greek-English Lexicon of the New Testament and Other Early Christian Literature.* Edited by Frederick W. Danker. 3rd edn. Chicago: University of Chicago Press, 2000.

Bayer, Oswald. *Martin Luther's Theology: A Contemporary Interpretation.* Grand Rapids, Mich.: Eerdmans, 2008.

Becker Sweeden, Nell. *Church on the Way: Hospitality and Migration.* Eugene, Ore.: Pickwick, 2015.

Benedict XVI. "Message for the World Day of Migrants and Refugees (2013)." October 12, 2012. https://w2.vatican.va/content/benedict-xvi/en/messages/migration/documents/hf_ben-xvi_mes_20121012_world-migrants-day.html. Accessed September 17, 2016.

Bennett, Harold V. *Injustice Made Legal: Deuteronomic Law and the Plight of Widows, Strangers, and Orphans in Ancient Israel.* Grand Rapids, Mich.: Eerdmans, 2002.

Berry, Wendell. *The Hidden Wound.* New edn. San Francisco: North Point Press, 1989.

Bettenson, Henry Scowcroft, and Chris Maunder, eds. *Documents of the Christian Church.* 3rd edn. Oxford: Oxford University Press, 1999.

Biggar, Nigel. "The Value of Limited Loyalty: Christianity, the Nation, and Territorial Boundaries." In *Boundaries and Justice: Diverse Ethical Perspectives,* edited by David Miller and Sohail H. Hashmi, 38–54. Princeton: Princeton University Press, 2001.

Blackstone, William. *Commentaries on the Laws of England.* 4 vols. Oxford: Clarendon Press, 1765–69.

Blume S.V.D., Michael A. *Migration and the Social Doctrine of the Church.* Pontifical Council for the Pastoral Care of Migrants and Itinerant People, 2002. www.vatican.va/roman_curia/pontifical_councils/migrants/pom2002_88_90/rc_pc_migrants_pom88-89_blume.htm. Accessed September 17, 2016.

Boyer, Allen D., ed. "Introduction." In *Law, Liberty, and Parliament: Selected Essays on the Writings of Sir Edward Coke,* vii–xiv. Indianapolis: Liberty Fund, 2004.

Boyle, T. C. *The Tortilla Curtain*. London: Bloomsbury, 2004.

Bracton, Henry de. *Bracton's Note Book: A Collection of Cases Decided in the King's Courts during the Reign of Henry the Third*. Edited by Frederic William Maitland. London: C. J. Clay & Sons, 1887.

De legibus et consuetudinibus Angliæ. Edited by George E. Woodbine. Vol. 2. New Haven: Yale University Press; London: Humphrey Milford; Oxford: Oxford University Press, 1922.

On the Laws and Customs of England. Edited by George E. Woodbine. Translated by Samuel E. Thorne. Vol. 2. Cambridge, Mass.: The Belknap Press of Harvard University Press, 1968.

Bretherton, Luke. *Christianity and Contemporary Politics: The Conditions and Possibilities of Faithful Witness*. Oxford: Wiley-Blackwell, 2010.

"Filters, Fences or Faces? Asylum Seekers and the Moral Status of Borders." *Australian Broadcasting Corporation*, June 28, 2012, Online edition, sec. Religion and Ethics. www.abc.net.au/religion/articles/2012/06/28/3535073.htm. Accessed July 11, 2012.

"Filters, Fences or Faces? The Moral Status of Borders." Presented at the "Strangers No More" Conference organized by the University of Notre Dame, Citizens Organizing Foundation, and the Von Hügel Institute, Cambridge University, London, April 20, 2007.

Hospitality as Holiness: Christian Witness Amid Moral Diversity. Aldershot: Ashgate, 2006.

Brock, Brian, and Bernd Wannenwetsch. *The Malady of the Christian Body: A Theological Exposition of Paul's First Letter to the Corinthians*. Vol. 1. 2 vols. Eugene, Ore.: Cascade, 2016.

Brueggemann, Walter. "'Exodus' in the Plural (Amos 9:7)." In *Many Voices, One God: Being Faithful in a Pluralistic World*, edited by Walter Brueggemann and George W. Stroup, 15–34. Louisville, Ky.: Westminster John Knox Press, 1998.

Deuteronomy. Abingdon Old Testament Commentaries. Nashville: Abingdon Press, 2001.

Genesis. Interpretation. Atlanta: John Knox Press, 1982.

The Land: Place as Gift, Promise, and Challenge in Biblical Faith. 2nd edn. Philadelphia: Fortress Press, 2002.

Brunner, Emil, and Karl Barth. *Natural Theology: Comprising "Nature and Grace" by Emil Brunner and the Reply "No!" by Karl Barth*. Translated by Peter Fraenkel. London: Geoffrey Bles, The Centenary Press, 1946.

Bultmann, Christoph. *Der Fremde im antiken Juda: eine Untersuchung zum sozialen Typenbegriff gēr und seinem Bedeutungswandel in der alttestamentlichen Gesetzgebung*. Göttingen: Vandenhoeck & Ruprecht, 1992.

Bultmann, Rudolf. "ἔλεος eleos, ἐλεέω eleeō, ἐλεήμων eleēmōn, ἐλεημοσύνη eleēmosunē, ἀνέλεος aneleos, ἀνελεήμων aneleēmōn." In *The Theological Dictionary of the New Testament*, edited by Gerhard Friedrich and Geoffrey W. Bromiley, translated by Geoffrey W. Bromiley, 2:477–87. Grand Rapids, Mich.: Eerdmans, 1964.

Campese, Gioacchino. *Hacia una teología desde la realidad de las migraciones: método y desafíos*. Guadalajara: Cátedra Eusebio Francisco Kino SJ, 2008.

Carens, Joseph H. "The Case for Amnesty." *Boston Review*, 2009. www.bostonreview.net/forum/case-amnesty-joseph-carens. Accessed March 3, 2014.

"Live-in Domestics, Seasonal Workers, and Others Hard to Locate on the Map of Democracy." *Journal of Political Philosophy* 16, no. 4 (2008): 419–445.

Carmona, Victor. "Neither Slave nor Free: A Critique of U.S. Immigration Policy in Light of the Work of David Hollenbach, Gustavo Gutiérrez, and Thomas Aquinas." Ph.D. Dissertation, University of Notre Dame, 2014.

Carroll R., M. Daniel, and Leopoldo A. Sánchez M., eds. *Immigrant Neighbors Among Us: Immigration Across Theological Traditions*. Eugene, Ore.: Pickwick, 2015.

Carroll R., M. Daniel. "Review: James K. Hoffmeier, The Immigration Crisis: Immigrants, Aliens, and the Bible." *Denver Journal* 13 (2010). www.denverseminary.edu/article/the-immigration-crisis-immigrants-aliens-and-the-bible/. Accessed September 14, 2016.

———. *Christians at the Border: Immigration, the Church, and the Bible*. Grand Rapids, Mich.: Baker Academic, 2008.

———. *Christians at the Border: Immigration, the Church, and the Bible*. 2nd edn. Grand Rapids, Mich.: Brazos Press, 2013.

Chandler, Kim. "Alabama House Passes Arizona-Style Immigration Law." *AL.com*, April 5, 2011. http://blog.al.com/spotnews/2011/04/alabama_house_passes_arizona-s.html. Accessed January 28, 2014.

Chavez, Leo R. *Shadowed Lives: Undocumented Immigrants in American Society*. Fort Worth: Harcourt Brace Jovanovich, 1992.

Chin, Gabriel J. "Chae Chan Ping and Fong Yue Ting: The Origins of Plenary Power." In *Immigration Stories*, edited by David A. Martin and Peter H. Schuck, 7–29. New York: Foundation Press and Thomson/West, 2005.

———. "Is There a Plenary Power Doctrine? A Tentative Apology and Prediction for Our Strange but Unexceptional Constitutional Immigration Law." *Georgetown Immigration Law Journal* 14 (2000): 257–87.

Cisneros, Sandra. *Caramelo: Or Puro Cuento*. New York: Alfred A. Knopf, 2002.

Cobbett, William, Thomas Bayly Howell, Thomas Jones Howell, and David Jardine, eds. *Cobbett's Complete Collection of State Trials and Proceedings for High Treason and Other Crimes and Misdemeanors from the Earliest Period to the Present Time*. Vol. 2. London: R. Bagshaw, 1809.

Cochrane, Arthur C. *The Church's Confession under Hitler*. Philadelphia: Westminster Press, 1962.

Coke, Sir Edward. "Calvin's Case, or the Case of the Postnati." In *Selected Writings of Sir Edward Coke*, edited by Steve Sheppard, Vol. 1. Indianapolis: Liberty Fund, 2003. http://oll.libertyfund.org/title/911/106337. Accessed November 21, 2012.

Coke, Edward. *The First Part of the Institutes of the Laws of England, or, a Commentary upon Littleton (Coke on Littleton)*. Edited by Francis Hargrave, Charles Butler, and Charles Butler. 18th edn., Corrected. Vol. 1. 2 vols. London: J. & W. T. Clarke, R. Pheney, and S. Brooke, 1823.

Colford, Paul. "'Illegal Immigrant' No More." *The Associated Press: The Definitive Source*. April 2, 2013. http://blog.ap.org/2013/04/02/illegal-immigrant-no-more/. Accessed April 3, 2013.

Conferencia del Episcopado Mexicano, and United States Conference of Catholic Bishops. *Strangers No Longer: Together on the Journey of Hope: A Pastoral Letter Concerning Migration from the Catholic Bishops of Mexico and the United States*. Washington, D.C.: United States Conference of Catholic Bishops, 2003.

Constable, Pamela. "Alabama Law Drives Out Illegal Immigrants but Also Has Unexpected Consequences." *The Washington Post*, June 18, 2012, sec. Local. www.washingtonpost.com/local/alabama-law-drives-out-illegal-immigrants-but-also-has-unexpected-consequences/2012/06/17/gJQA3RmojV_story.html. Accessed March 21, 2014.

Conway, Christopher, ed. *The U.S.-Mexican War: A Binational Reader*. Indianapolis: Hackett Publishing Company, 2010.

Conzelmann, Hans. *1 Corinthians: A Commentary on the First Epistle to the Corinthians*. Edited by George W. MacRae. Translated by James W. Leitch. Philadelphia: Fortress Press, 1975.

Corbett, Jim. *The Sanctuary Church.* Wallingford, Pa.: Pendle Hill Publications, 1986.

Crittenden, Ann. *Sanctuary: A Story of American Conscience and the Law in Collision.* New York: Weidenfeld & Nicolson, 1988.

Crocker, Deputy Special Agent in Charge, I.C.E., Southern Arizona, Richard, and Rudy Bustamante, Community Relations Officer. "Immigration and Customs Enforcement in Southern Arizona." Borderlinks, Tucson, Ariz., July 28, 2011.

Cruz, Gemma Tulud. *An Intercultural Theology of Migration: Pilgrims in the Wilderness.* Leiden: Brill, 2010.

 Toward a Theology of Migration: Social Justice and Religious Experience. Basingstoke: Palgrave Macmillan, 2014.

Cuéllar, Gregory Lee. *Voices of Marginality: Exile and Return in Second Isaiah 40–55 and the Mexican Immigrant Experience.* 2nd edn. New York: Peter Lang, 2008.

Dallek, Robert. *Franklin D. Roosevelt and American Foreign Policy, 1932–1945.* New York: Oxford University Press, 1995.

Daniel, Ben. *Neighbor: Christian Encounters with "Illegal" Immigration.* Louisville, Ky.: Westminster John Knox Press, 2010.

Daniels, Roger, and Otis L. Graham, eds. *Debating American Immigration, 1882-Present.* Lanham, Md.: Rowman & Littlefield Publishers, 2001.

Daniels, Roger. *Guarding the Golden Door: American Immigration Policy and Immigrants Since 1882.* New York: Hill and Wang, 2004.

Davidson, A. B. *Davidson's Introductory Hebrew Grammar: Syntax.* 4th edn. Edinburgh: T. & T. Clark, 1994.

De La Torre, Miguel A. *Trails of Hope and Terror: Testimonies on Immigration.* Maryknoll, N.Y.: Orbis Books, 2009.

DeLay, Brian. *War of a Thousand Deserts: Indian Raids and the U.S.-Mexican War.* New Haven: Yale University Press, 2008.

"Despite Rise in Felony Charges, Most Immigration Convictions Remain Misdemeanors." Transactional Records Access Clearinghouse, Syracuse University, June 26, 2014. http://trac.syr.edu/immigration/reports/356/. Accessed June 21, 2016.

Di Ionno, Mark. "U.S. Immigration Finally Allows W.W. II Vet 'Home.'" *The Star-Ledger,* June 1, 2016. www.nj.com/news/index.ssf/2016/06/us_immigration_finally_allows_wwii_ vet_home_di_ion.html. Accessed June 22, 2016.

 "U.S. Immigration Policy Puts Ailing W.W. II Vet in Limbo." *The Star-Ledger,* September 4, 2015. www.nj.com/news/index.ssf/2015/09/us_immigration_policy_puts_ailing_wwii_ vet_in_limb.html. Accessed June 22, 2016.

Driver, S. R. *A Treatise on the Use of the Tenses in Hebrew.* 3rd rev. edn. Oxford: Clarendon Press, 1892.

Eliot, George. *Silas Marner.* London: Penguin, 1994.

Elizondo, Virgilio P. *Galilean Journey: The Mexican-American Promise.* 2nd rev. edn. Maryknoll, N.Y.: Orbis Books, 2000.

 Galilean Journey: The Mexican-American Promise. Maryknoll, N.Y.: Orbis Books, 1983.

 The Future Is Mestizo: Life Where Cultures Meet. New York: Crossroad, 1992.

Elliott, John H. *1 Peter: A New Translation with Introduction and Commentary.* Anchor Bible 37B. New York: Doubleday, 2000.

 A Home for the Homeless: A Sociological Exegesis of 1 Peter, Its Situation and Strategy. Philadelphia: Fortress Press, 1981.

Ellul, Jacques. *The Meaning of the City.* Translated by Dennis Pardee. Grand Rapids, Mich.: Eerdmans, 1970.

 Sans feu ni lieu : signification biblique de la grande ville. 2nd edn. Paris: Table Ronde, 2003.

Espín, Orlando O., ed. *Building Bridges, Doing Justice: Constructing a Latino/a Ecumenical Theology.* Maryknoll, N.Y.: Orbis Books, 2009.

———. ed. *The Wiley Blackwell Companion to Latino/a Theology.* Wiley Blackwell Companions to Religion. Chichester, West Sussex: Wiley Blackwell, 2015.

"Excerpts from Text of a Decree Signed by A.T.&T. and U.S." *The New York Times,* January 9, 1982, sec. Business. www.nytimes.com/1982/01/09/business/excerpts-from-text-of-a-decree-signed-by-at-t-and-us.html. Accessed April 26, 2014.

Fife, John. "The Sanctuary Movement." Borderlinks, Tucson, Ariz., July 28, 2011.

Folkmar, Daniel, and Elnora C. Folkmar. "Dictionary of Races or Peoples, Presented by Mr. Dillingham, Dec. 5, 1910." Reports of the Immigration Commission. Washington, D.C.: Government Printing Office, 1911.

Fortescue, John. "In Praise of the Laws of England." In *On the Laws and Governance of England,* edited by Shelley Lockwood, translated by S. B. Chrimes, 1–80. Cambridge: Cambridge University Press, 1997.

———. *De Laudibus Legum Anglie.* Translated by S. B. Chrimes. Cambridge: Cambridge University Press, 1942.

Francis. "Homily." Presented at the Holy Mass, Apostolic Journey to Mexico, Ciudad Juárez Fairgrounds, February 17, 2016. https://w2.vatican.va/content/francesco/en/homilies/2016/documents/papa-francesco_20160217_omelia-messico-ciudad-jaurez.html. Accessed September 13, 2016.

———. "Press Conference." Presented at the Apostolic Journey to Mexico, Flight from Mexico to Rome, February 17, 2016. https://w2.vatican.va/content/francesco/en/speeches/2016/february/documents/papa-francesco_20160217_messico-conferenza-stampa.html. Accessed September 13, 2016.

Francisco. "Conferencia de prensa." Presented at the Viaje apostólico a México, Vuelo de México a Roma, February 17, 2016. https://w2.vatican.va/content/francesco/es/speeches/2016/february/documents/papa-francesco_20160217_messico-conferenza-stampa.html. Accessed September 13, 2016.

Frisbie, Parker. "Illegal Migration from Mexico to the United States: A Longitudinal Analysis." *International Migration Review* 9, no. 1 (1975): 3–13.

Gaius. *The Institutes of Gaius and Rules of Ulpian: The Former from Studemund's Apograph of the Verona Codex.* Edited and translated by James Muirhead. Edinburgh: T. & T. Clark, 1880.

García López, F. "שָׁמַר šāmar; אַשְׁמֶרֶת/אַשְׁמוּרָה ʾašmûrâ/ʾašmōreṭ; מִשְׁמָר mišmār; שָׁמְרָה šōmrâ; שְׁמֻרָה šᵉmurâ; שִׁמֻּרִים šimmurîm; שֶׁמֶר šemer." In *The Theological Dictionary of the Old Testament,* edited by G. Johannes Botterweck, Helmer Ringgren, and Heinz-Josef Fabry, translated by David E. Green, 15:279–305. Grand Rapids, Mich.: Eerdmans, 2006.

Glanville, Mark. "Immigration, Refugees, and the Old Testament." *Comment: Public Theology for the Common Good,* December 12, 2011. www.cardus.ca/comment/article/3015/immigration-refugees-and-the-old-testament/. Accessed November 30, 2012.

———. "The *Gēr* in Deuteronomy: An Ethic of Inclusivism?" Ph.D. Thesis, Trinity College Bristol, forthcoming.

Glare, P. G. W., ed. *Oxford Latin Dictionary.* Oxford: Clarendon Press, 1982.

Goebel, Ulrich, Anja Lobenstein-Reichmann, and Oskar Reichmann, eds. *Frühneuhochdeutsches Wörterbuch.* Vol. 8. Berlin: de Gruyter, 2013.

———. eds. *Frühneuhochdeutsches Wörterbuch.* Vol. 5: Lfg. 2. Berlin: de Gruyter, 2014.

González, Justo L. *Santa Biblia: The Bible through Hispanic Eyes.* Nashville: Abingdon Press, 1996.

Gorospe, Athena, Paul Tyson, Calvin Chong, Stephen Pardue, Timoteo Gener, Rei Lemuel Crizaldo, and Charles Ringma, eds. *God at the Borders: Globalization, Migration, and Diaspora.* A.T.S. Theological Forum. Manila: O.M.F. Literature and Asian Theological Seminary, 2015.

Gorringe, Timothy. *Karl Barth: Against Hegemony.* Oxford: Oxford University Press, 1999.

Graham, Otis L. "The Unfinished Reform: Regulating Immigration in the National Interest." In *Debating American Immigration, 1882–Present,* edited by Roger Daniels and Otis L. Graham, 89–185. Lanham, Md.: Rowman & Littlefield Publishers, 2001.

Grant, Madison. *The Passing of the Great Race; or, the Racial Basis of European History.* New York: C. Scribner, 1916.

The Passing of the Great Race; or, the Racial Basis of European History. 4th rev. edn. with a documentary supplement. New York: C. Scribner, 1936.

Greenberg, Amy S. *A Wicked War: Polk, Clay, Lincoln, and the 1846 U.S. Invasion of Mexico.* New York: Alfred A. Knopf, 2012.

Greeven, Heinrich, and Johannes Fichtner. "πλησίον plēsion." In *The Theological Dictionary of the New Testament,* edited by Gerhard Friedrich and Geoffrey W. Bromiley, translated by Geoffrey W. Bromiley, 6:311–18. Grand Rapids, Mich.: Eerdmans, 1968.

Griffin, Mark, and Theron Walker. *Living on the Borders: What the Church Can Learn from Ethnic Immigrant Cultures.* Grand Rapids, Mich.: Brazos Press, 2004.

Groody, Daniel G. *Border of Death, Valley of Life: An Immigrant Journey of Heart and Spirit.* Celebrating Faith. Lanham, Md.: Rowman & Littlefield, 2002.

Groody, Daniel G., and Gioacchino Campese, eds. *A Promised Land, a Perilous Journey: Theological Perspectives on Migration.* Notre Dame: University of Notre Dame Press, 2008.

Grotius, Hugo. *Commentary on the Law of Prize and Booty.* Edited by Martine Julia van Ittersum and Gwladys L. Williams. Indianapolis: Liberty Fund, 2006.

De Iure Belli ac Pacis: In quibus ius naturae & Gentium: item iuris publici praecipua explicantur. Ed. 2a emendatior & Multis locis auctior. Amsterdam: Guilielmum Blaeuw, 1631.

De Iure Belli ac Pacis: In quibus ius naturae & Gentium: item iuris publici praecipua explicantur. Paris: Nicolas Buon, 1625.

De Iure Belli ac Pacis: In quibus ius naturae & Gentium: item iuris publici praecipua explicantur. Editio nova, Cum annotatis auctoris, Ex postrema ejus ante obitum cura multo nunc auctior. Amsterdam: Iohannem Blaeu, 1646.

De Iure Belli ac Pacis: In quibus ius naturae & Gentium: item iuris publici praecipua explicantur. Edited by B. J. A. de Kanter-van Hettinga Tromp, Robert Feenstra, C. E. Persenaire, and E. Arps-de Wilde. 1939 edn. based on the 1631 edn., With new annotations. Aalen: Scientia Verlag, 1993.

De Iure Praedae Commentarius: Commentary on the Law of Prize and Booty. Edited by Gwladys L. Williams and Walter H. Zeydel. 2 vols. Oxford: Clarendon Press, 1950.

On the Law of War and Peace. Translated by Francis W. Kelsey. Oxford: Clarendon Press, 1925.

On the Law of War and Peace. Edited by Stephen C. Neff. Student edn. Cambridge: Cambridge University Press, 2012.

The Rights of War and Peace. Edited by Richard Tuck and Jean Barbeyrac. Translated by John Morrice. Indianapolis: Liberty Fund, 2005.

Habel, Norman C. *The Land Is Mine: Six Biblical Land Ideologies.* Minneapolis: Fortress Press, 1995.

Hadley, Eleanor. "A Critical Analysis of the Wetback Problem." *Law and Contemporary Problems* 21 (1956): 334–57.

Hagan, Jacqueline Maria. *Migration Miracle: Faith, Hope, and the Undocumented Journey.* Cambridge, Mass.: Harvard University Press, 2008.

Hanciles, Jehu. *Beyond Christendom: Globalization, African Migration, and the Transformation of the West.* Maryknoll, N.Y.: Orbis Books, 2008.

Handlin, Oscar. *Immigration as a Factor in American History.* Englewood Cliffs, N.J.: Prentice-Hall, 1959.

"The Immigration Flight Has Just Begun." *Commentary* 14 (July 1952): 1–7.

Hauerwas, Stanley, and William H. Willimon. *Resident Aliens: Life in the Christian Colony.* Nashville: Abingdon Press, 1989.

Hauerwas, Stanley. *With the Grain of the Universe: The Church's Witness and Natural Theology.* London: S.C.M. Press, 2002.

Heer, David M. "What Is the Annual Net Flow of Undocumented Mexican Immigrants to the United States?" *Demography* 16, no. 3 (1979): 417–23.

Hegel, Georg Wilhelm Friedrich. *Philosophy of Right.* Translated by T. M. Knox. Oxford: Oxford University Press, 1952.

Heimburger, Robert W. "Migration through the Eyes of Faith: God's People, National Lands, and Universities." *IFES Word & World*, no. 1 (May 2016): 3–14.

"Philosophical and Theological Reflections on the U.S.-Mexico Border, with Special Reference to Joseph Carens, Michael Walzer, and Oliver O'Donovan." M.Phil. Thesis, Faculty of Theology, University of Oxford, 2010.

Henderson, Timothy J. *A Glorious Defeat: Mexico and Its War with the United States.* New York: Hill and Wang, 2007.

Beyond Borders: A History of Mexican Migration to the United States. Malden, Mass.: Wiley-Blackwell, 2011.

Heyer, Kristin E. *Kinship Across Borders: A Christian Ethic of Immigration.* Washington, D.C.: Georgetown University Press, 2012.

Hill, Kenneth. "Illegal Aliens: An Assessment." In *Immigration Statistics: A Story of Neglect*, edited by Daniel B. Levine, Kenneth Hill, and Robert Warren, 225–50. Washington, D.C.: National Academies Press, 1985.

Hobbes, Thomas. *Leviathan, or, the Matter, Form, and Power of a Common-Wealth Ecclesiastical and Civil.* London: Printed for Andrew Crooke, 1651.

Leviathan. Edited by Richard Tuck. Rev. student edn. Cambridge: Cambridge University Press, 1996.

Hoffmeier, James K. *The Immigration Crisis: Immigrants, Aliens, and the Bible.* Wheaton, Ill.: Crossway, 2009.

Hofreiter, Christian. "Genocide in Deuteronomy and Christian Interpretation." In *Interpreting Deuteronomy: Issues and Approaches*, edited by David G. Firth and Philip S. Johnston, 240–62. Nottingham: Apollos, 2012.

"Reading Herem as Christian Scripture." D.Phil. Thesis, Faculty of Theology and Religion, University of Oxford, 2014.

Hollenbach S. J., David, ed. *Driven from Home: Protecting the Rights of Forced Migrants.* Washington, D.C.: Georgetown University Press, 2010.

ed. *Refugee Rights: Ethics, Advocacy, and Africa.* Washington, D.C.: Georgetown University Press, 2008.

Hondagneu-Sotelo, Pierrette. *God's Heart Has No Borders: How Religious Activists Are Working for Immigrant Rights.* Berkeley: University of California Press, 2008.

Houston, Fleur S. *You Shall Love the Stranger as Yourself: The Bible, Refugees, and Asylum*. London: Routledge, 2015.

Houten, Christiana van. *The Alien in Israelite Law*. Sheffield: J.S.O.T. Press, 1991.

"I.C.E. Enforcement and Removal Operations Report." United States Department of Homeland Security; Immigration and Customs Enforcement, Fiscal Year 2014. www.ice.gov/doclib/about/offices/ero/pdf/2014-ice-immigration-removals.pdf. Accessed June 9, 2016.

"Illegal Reentry Becomes Top Criminal Charge." Transactional Records Access Clearinghouse, Syracuse University, June 10, 2011. http://trac.syr.edu/immigration/reports/251/. Accessed June 21, 2016.

"Immigration and Naturalization Systems of the United States: Report of the Committee on the Judiciary Pursuant to S. Res. 137 (80th Congress, 1st Session, as Amended), a Resolution to Make an Investigation of the Immigration System (McCarran Report)." Senate Report 1515. Washington, D.C.: Government Printing Office, 1950.

"Immigration Convictions for April 2016." Transactional Records Access Clearinghouse, Syracuse University, June 10, 2016. http://trac.syr.edu/tracreports/bulletins/immigration/monthlyapr16/gui/. Accessed June 21, 2016.

Isasi-Díaz, Ada María. *Mujerista Theology: A Theology for the Twenty-First Century*. Maryknoll, N.Y.: Orbis Books, 1996.

Jeremias, Joachim. "Σαμαρεια Samareia, Σαμαρίτης Samaritēs, Σαμαρῖτις Samaritis." In *The Theological Dictionary of the New Testament*, edited by Gerhard Friedrich and Geoffrey W. Bromiley, translated by Geoffrey W. Bromiley, 7:88–94. Grand Rapids, Mich.: Eerdmans, 1971.

The Parables of Jesus. Translated by S. H. Hooke. 3rd rev. edn. London: S.C.M. Press, 1972.

Johannsen, Robert W. *To the Halls of the Montezumas: The Mexican War in the American Imagination*. New York: Oxford University Press, 1985.

John Paul II. *Ecclesia in America: Exhortación apostólica postsinodal sobre el encuentro con Jesucristo vivo, camino para la conversión, la comunión y la solidaridad en América*. 1999. www.vatican.va/holy_father/john_paul_ii/apost_exhortations/documents/hf_jp-ii_exh_22011999_ecclesia-in-america_sp.html. Accessed December 13, 2011.

Ecclesia in America: Post-Synodal Apostolic Exhortation on the on the Encounter with the Living Jesus Christ: The Way to Conversion, Communion and Solidarity in America. 1999. www.vatican.va/holy_father/john_paul_ii/apost_exhortations/documents/hf_jp-ii_exh_22011999_ecclesia-in-america_en.html. Accessed December 13, 2011.

Laborem Exercens: Encyclical on Human Work, 1981. http://w2.vatican.va/content/john-paul-ii/en/encyclicals/documents/hf_jp-ii_enc_14091981_laborem-exercens.html. Accessed September 10, 2016.

John XXIII. *Mater et Magistra: Encyclical on Christianity and Social Progress*, 1961. http://w2.vatican.va/content/john-xxiii/en/encyclicals/documents/hf_j-xxiii_enc_15051961_mater.html. Accessed September 10, 2016.

Pacem in Terris: Encyclical on Establishing Universal Peace in Truth, Justice, Charity, and Liberty, 1963. http://w2.vatican.va/content/john-xxiii/en/encyclicals/documents/hf_j-xxiii_enc_11041963_pacem.html. Accessed November 27, 2015.

Johnson, Lyndon B. "Remarks at the Signing of the Immigration Bill, Liberty Island, New York, October 3, 1965." In *Public Papers of the Presidents of the United States: Lyndon B. Johnson, 1965*, 2:1037–40. Washington, D.C.: Government Printing Office, 1965. www.lbjlib.utexas.edu/johnson/archives.hom/speeches.hom/651003.asp. Accessed August 17, 2012.

Just, Arthur A., ed. *Luke*. Ancient Christian Commentary on Scripture, New Testament III. Downers Grove, Ill.: InterVarsity Press, 2003.

Kellermann, D. "גּוּר gûr; גֵּר gēr; גֵּרוּת gērûth; מְגוּרִים mᵉghûrîm." In *The Theological Dictionary of the Old Testament*, edited by G. Johannes Botterweck and Helmer Ringgren, translated by J. T. Willis, 2:439–49. Grand Rapids, Mich.: Eerdmans, 1975.

"רֵעַ rēaʿ; רָעָה rāʿâ; רֵעֶה rēʿeh; מֵרֵעַ mērēaʿ; רֵעֶה rēʿâ; רַעְיָה raʿyâ; רְעוּת rᵉʿût." In *The Theological Dictionary of the Old Testament*, edited by G. Johannes Botterweck, Helmer Ringgren, and Heinz-Josef Fabry, translated by David E. Green, 13:522–32. Grand Rapids, Mich.: Eerdmans, 2004.

Kelly, J. N. D. *Early Christian Creeds*. 3rd edn. London: Longman, 1972.

Kennedy, John F. "Letter to the President of the Senate and to the Speaker of the House on Revision of the Immigration Laws, July 23, 1963." In *Public Papers of the Presidents of the United States: Containing the Public Messages, Speeches, and Statements of the President, January 1 to November 22, 1963*, 594–97. Washington, D.C.: Government Printing Office, 1964.

Kennedy, John F. *A Nation of Immigrants*. New York: Anti-Defamation League of B'nai B'rith, 1959.

A Nation of Immigrants. Rev. and enl. edn. London: Hamish Hamilton, 1964.

Kim, Keechang. *Aliens in Medieval Law: The Origins of Modern Citizenship*. Cambridge: Cambridge University Press, 2000.

Köhler, Ludwig, and Walter Baumgartner. *The Hebrew and Aramaic Lexicon of the Old Testament*. Translated by M. E. J. Richardson. 5 vols. Leiden: Brill, 1994.

Köster, Helmut. "σπλάγχνον splanchnon, σπλαγχνίζομαι splanchnizomai, εὔσπλαγχνος eusplanchnos, ἄσπλαγχνος asplangchnos." In *The Theological Dictionary of the New Testament*, edited by Gerhard Friedrich and Geoffrey W. Bromiley, translated by Geoffrey W. Bromiley, 7:311–18. Grand Rapids, Mich.: Eerdmans, 1971.

Lang, B., and Helmer Ringgren. "נכר nkr; נֵכָר nēkār; נָכְרִי nokrî." In *The Theological Dictionary of the Old Testament*, edited by G. Johannes Botterweck, Helmer Ringgren, and Heinz-Josef Fabry, translated by David E. Green, Rev. edn., 9:423–32. Grand Rapids, Mich.: Eerdmans, 1998.

Langenscheidt Muret-Sanders Grosswörterbuch Englisch. Völlige Neubearbeitung. Vol. 2. Berlin: Langenscheidt, 2004.

Latham, R. E., ed. *Revised Medieval Latin Word-List from British and Irish Sources*. London: Published for the British Academy by the Oxford University Press, 1965.

Lawson, Brian. "Much of Alabama's Far-Reaching Immigration Law Permanently Blocked in Final Settlement of Lawsuits." *AL.com*, November 25, 2013. http://blog.al.com/breaking/2013/11/final_settlement_reached_block.html. Accessed April 21, 2017.

Leo XIII. *Rerum Novarum: Encyclical on Capital and Labor*, 1891. www.vatican.va/holy_father/leo_xiii/encyclicals/documents/hf_l-xiii_enc_15051891_rerum-novarum_en.html. Accessed November 19, 2013.

Rerum Novarum: Litterae Encylicae de Conditione Opificum, 1891. http://w2.vatican.va/content/leo-xiii/la/encyclicals/documents/hf_l-xiii_enc_15051891_rerum-novarum.html. Accessed February 9, 2016.

Lewis, Edward R. *America: Nation or Confusion?* New York: Harper & Brothers, 1928.

Liddell, Henry George, Robert Scott, Henry Stuart Jones, and Roderick McKenzie, eds. *A Greek-English Lexicon*. 9th edn. Oxford: Clarendon Press, 1940.

Lohfink, Norbert. "יָרַשׁ yāraš; יְרֵשָׁה yᵉrēšâ; יְרֻשָּׁה yᵉruššâ; מוֹרָשׁ môrāš; מוֹרָשָׁה môrāšâ." In *The Theological Dictionary of the Old Testament*, edited by G. Johannes Botterweck and

Helmer Ringgren, translated by David E. Green, 6:368–96. Grand Rapids, Mich.: Eerdmans, 1990.

Lorish, Philip A. "Subjected to the Spirit: An Investigation of Luther's Political Ethics." M.Phil. Thesis, Faculty of Theology, University of Oxford, 2010.

Los Tigres del Norte. *Jaula de Oro*. Jaula de Oro. Fonovisa, 1984.

Luther, Martin. *Christians in Society II*. Edited by Walter I. Brandt. American edn. Luther's Works 45. Philadelphia: Fortress Press, 1962.

   Genesisvorlesung (cap. 1–17) 1535/38. D. Martin Luthers Werke: Kritische Gesamtausgabe 42. Weimar: Hermann Böhlaus Nachfolger, 1911.

   Lectures on Genesis Chapters 1–5 (1535/1538). Translated by George V. Schick. American edn. Luther's Works 1. St. Louis: Concordia, 1958.

   Predigten und Schriften 1524. D. Martin Luthers Werke: Kritische Gesamtausgabe 15. Weimar: Hermann Böhlaus Nachfolger, 1899.

   Psalmenauslegungen 1529/32. D. Martin Luthers Werke: Kritische Gesamtausgabe 31. Weimar: Hermann Böhlaus Nachfolger, 1913.

   Selected Psalms II. American edn. Luther's Works 13. St. Louis: Concordia, 1956.

Martinez, Daniel, and Jeremy Slack. "What Part of 'Illegal' Don't You Understand? The Social Consequences of Criminalizing Unauthorized Mexican Migrants in the United States." *Social & Legal Studies* 22, no. 4 (2013): 535–51.

Martínez, Orlando. *The Great Landgrab: The Mexican-American War, 1846–1848*. London: Quartet Books, 1975.

Massey, Douglas S., and Audrey Singer. "New Estimates of Undocumented Mexican Migration and the Probability of Apprehension." *Demography* 32, no. 2 (1995): 203–13.

Massey, Douglas S., Jorge Durand, and Nolan J. Malone. *Beyond Smoke and Mirrors: Mexican Immigration in an Era of Free Trade*. New York: Russell Sage Foundation, 2002.

McConville, J. G. *Deuteronomy*. Apollos Old Testament Commentary 5. Leicester, England: Apollos; Downers Grove, Ill.: InterVarsity Press, 2002.

   Law and Theology in Deuteronomy. Journal for the Study of the Old Testament Supplement Series 33. Sheffield: J.S.O.T., 1984.

Mehaffey, K. C. "Feds Warn Pacific Crest Trail Hikers a About Crossing Border." *The Seattle Times*, July 1, 2010. www.seattletimes.com/seattle-news/feds-warn-pacific-crest-trail-hikers-about-crossing-border/. Accessed June 21, 2016.

Meilaender, Peter C. *Toward a Theory of Immigration*. Basingstoke: Palgrave, 2001.

Moseley, Carys. *Nations and Nationalism in the Theology of Karl Barth*. Oxford: Oxford University Press, 2013.

Moucarry, Georges Chawkat. "The Alien According to the Torah." Translated by Joye Smith. *Themelios* 14 (1988): 17–20.

Moulton, James Hope. *A Grammar of New Testament Greek*. Vol. 3. Edinburgh: T. & T. Clark, 1976.

Myers, Ched, and Matthew Colwell. *Our God Is Undocumented: Biblical Faith and Immigrant Justice*. Maryknoll, N.Y.: Orbis Books, 2012.

Nanko-Fernández, Carmen. *Theologizing En Espanglish: Context, Community, and Ministry*. Maryknoll, N.Y.: Orbis Books, 2010.

Nazario, Sonia. *Enrique's Journey*. New York: Random House, 2006.

   "The Heartache of an Immigrant Family." *The New York Times*, October 14, 2013, sec. Opinion. www.nytimes.com/2013/10/15/opinion/the-heartache-of-an-immigrant-family.html. Accessed October 15, 2013.

Ngai, Mae M. *Impossible Subjects: Illegal Aliens and the Making of Modern America.* Princeton: Princeton University Press, 2004.

Nguyen, VanThanh, and John Prior, eds. *God's People on the Move: Biblical and Global Perspectives on Migration and Mission*, Eugene, Ore: Pickwick Publications, 2014.

Niermeyer, J. F. *Mediae Latinitatis Lexicon Minus: A Medieval Latin-French/English Dictionary.* 2nd edn. Leiden: Brill, 1993.

O'Brien, David J., and Thomas A. Shannon, eds. *Catholic Social Thought: The Documentary Heritage.* Maryknoll, N.Y.: Orbis Books, 1992.

O'Donovan, Oliver, and Joan Lockwood O'Donovan, eds. *From Irenaeus to Grotius: A Sourcebook in Christian Political Thought 100–1625.* Grand Rapids, Mich.: Eerdmans, 1999.

O'Donovan, Oliver. *The Desire of the Nations: Rediscovering the Roots of Political Theology.* Cambridge: Cambridge University Press, 1996.

"Judgment, Tradition, and Reason: A Response." *Political Theology* 9, no. 3 (2008): 395–414.

"The Justice of Assignment and Subjective Rights in Grotius." In *Bonds of Imperfection: Christian Politics, Past and Present*, edited by Oliver O'Donovan and Joan Lockwood O'Donovan, 167–203. Grand Rapids, Mich.: Eerdmans, 2004.

"The Loss of a Sense of Place." In *Bonds of Imperfection: Christian Politics, Past and Present*, edited by Oliver O'Donovan and Joan Lockwood O'Donovan, 296–320. Grand Rapids, Mich.: Eerdmans, 2004.

Resurrection and Moral Order: An Outline for Evangelical Ethics. Leicester: Inter-Varsity, 1986.

"Romulus's City: The Republic without Justice in Augustine's Political Thought." Unpublished manuscript used with permission, 2009.

The Ways of Judgment. Grand Rapids, Mich.: Eerdmans, 2005.

O'Sullivan, John. "Annexation." *United States Magazine and Democratic Review* 17, no. 1 (1845): 5–10.

Oberman, Kieran. "What Is Wrong with Permanent Alienage?" Oxford, October 29, 2012. http://podcasts.ox.ac.uk/what-wrong-permanent-alienage. Accessed March 12, 2014.

Ortolan, Théodore. *Règles internationales et diplomatie de la mer.* 4th edn. 2 vols. Paris: Henri Plon, 1864.

Otto, E. "עִיר ʿîr." In *The Theological Dictionary of the Old Testament*, edited by G. Johannes Botterweck, Helmer Ringgren, and Heinz-Josef Fabry, translated by David E. Green, 11:51–67. Grand Rapids, Mich.: Eerdmans, 1997.

Ottosson, Magnus. "גְּבוּל gᵉbûl; גָּבַל gābal; גְּבוּלָה gᵉbûlâ." In *The Theological Dictionary of the Old Testament*, edited by G. Johannes Botterweck and Helmer Ringgren, translated by J. T. Willis, 2:361–66. Grand Rapids, Mich.: Eerdmans, 1975.

Oxford English Dictionary. Compact edition. Vol. 1. 2 vols. Oxford: Clarendon Press, 1971.

Padilla, Alvin, Roberto S. Goizueta, Eldin Villafañe, and Justo L. González, eds. *Hispanic Christian Thought at the Dawn of the 21st Century: Apuntes in Honor of Justo L. González.* Nashville: Abingdon Press, 2005.

Padilla, Elaine, and Peter C. Phan, eds. *Contemporary Issues of Migration and Theology.* Christianities of the World. Basingstoke: Palgrave Macmillan, 2013.

eds. *Theology of Migration in the Abrahamic Religions.* Christianities of the World. Basingstoke: Palgrave Macmillan, 2014.

Palmer, R. R. *The Age of the Democratic Revolution: A Political History of Europe and America, 1760–1800.* Vol. 1. 2 vols. Princeton: Princeton University Press, 1959.

Pantoja, Jr., Luis, Sadiri Joy B. Tira, and Enoch Wan. *Scattered: The Filipino Global Presence*. Manila: Lifechange Publishing, 2004.

Passel, Jeffrey S. "Undocumented Immigration." *Annals of the American Academy of Political and Social Science* 487 (September 1986): 181–200.

Passel, Jeffrey S., and D'Vera Cohn. "Overall Number of U.S. Unauthorized Immigrants Holds Steady since 2009." Washington, D.C.: Pew Research Center, September 20, 2016. www.pewhispanic.org/2016/09/20/overall-number-of-u-s-unauthorized-immigrants-holds-steady-since-2009/. Accessed April 7, 2017.

"Size of U.S. Unauthorized Immigrant Workforce Stable after the Great Recession." Washington, D.C.: Pew Research Center, November 3, 2016. www.pewhispanic.org/2016/11/03/size-of-u-s-unauthorized-immigrant-workforce-stable-after-the-great-recession/. Accessed April 7, 2017.

Passel, Jeffrey S., D'Vera Cohn, and Ana Gonzalez-Barrera. "Net Migration from Mexico Falls to Zero – and Perhaps Less." Washington, D.C.: Pew Research Center, April 23, 2012. www.pewhispanic.org/2012/04/23/net-migration-from-mexico-falls-to-zero-and-perhaps-less/. Accessed September 19, 2012.

Paul VI. *Populorum Progressio: Encyclical on the Development of Peoples*, 1967. http://w2.vatican.va/content/paul-vi/en/encyclicals/documents/hf_p-vi_enc_26031967_populorum.html. Accessed September 10, 2016.

Phillimore, Robert. *Commentaries upon International Law*. 3rd edn. Vol. 1. 4 vols. London: Butterworths, 1879.

Pike, Fredrick B. *F.D.R.'s Good Neighbor Policy: Sixty Years of Generally Gentle Chaos*. Austin: University of Texas Press, 1995.

Pohl, Christine D. *Making Room: Recovering Hospitality as a Christian Tradition*. Grand Rapids, Mich.: Eerdmans, 1999.

Pollock, Frederick, and Frederic William Maitland. *The History of English Law before the Time of Edward I*. Vol. 1. 2 vols. Cambridge: Cambridge University Press, 1895.

Pontifical Council for the Pastoral Care of Migrants and Itinerant People. *Erga Migrantes Caritas Christi: The Love of Christ Towards Migrants*. London: Catholic Truth Society, 2004.

President's Commission on Immigration and Naturalization. *"Whom We Shall Welcome."* Washington, D.C.: Government Printing Office, 1953.

Preston, Julia. "Officers on Border Team Up to Quell Violence." *The New York Times*, March 25, 2010, sec. World/Americas. www.nytimes.com/2010/03/26/world/americas/26border.html. Accessed May 9, 2012.

Price, Polly J. "Natural Law and Birthright Citizenship in Calvin's Case (1608)." *Yale Journal of Law & the Humanities* 9, no. 1 (1997): 73–146.

Rad, Gerhard von. *Deuteronomy: A Commentary*. Translated by Dorothea M. Barton. London: S.C.M., 1966.

Ramírez Kidd, José E. *Alterity and Identity in Israel: The Gēr in the Old Testament*. Berlin: De Gruyter, 1999.

Ringgren, Helmer, U. Rüterswörden, and H. Simian-Yofre. "עָבַד ʿābad; עֶבֶד ʿebed; עֲבֹדָה ʿᵃbōdâ." In *The Theological Dictionary of the Old Testament*, edited by G. Johannes Botterweck, Helmer Ringgren, and Heinz-Josef Fabry, translated by Douglas W. Stott, 10:376–405. Grand Rapids, Mich.: Eerdmans, 1999.

Ripley, William Z. *The Races of Europe: A Sociological Study Accompanied by a Supplementary Bibliography of the Anthropology and Ethnology of Europe*. 2 vols. New York: Appleton, 1899.

The Races of Europe: A Sociological Study. London: Kegan Paul, Trench, Trübner & Co., 1900.

Roosevelt, Franklin D. "Address on the Occasion of the Celebration of Pan-American Day." Washington, D.C., April 12, 1933. www.presidency.ucsb.edu/ws/index.php?pid=14615. Accessed April 2, 2014.

"Presidential Inaugural Address." Washington, D.C., March 4, 1933. www.inaugural.senate .gov/swearing-in/address/address-by-franklin-d-roosevelt-1933. Accessed March 31, 2014.

Rose, Ananda. *Showdown in the Sonoran Desert: Religion, Law, and the Immigration Controversy*. New York: Oxford University Press, 2012.

Ruiz, Jean-Pierre. *Readings from the Edges: The Bible and People on the Move*. Maryknoll, N.Y.: Orbis Books, 2011.

Sarat, Leah. *Fire in the Canyon: Religion, Migration, and the Mexican Dream*. New York: New York University Press, 2013.

Sargent, Greg. "A Conservative Christian in a Deep Red District Makes Case for Immigration Reform." *Washington Post*, August 23, 2013. www.washingtonpost.com/blogs/plum-line/ wp/2013/08/23/a-conservative-christian-in-a-deep-red-district-makes-case-for-immigration-reform/. Accessed January 2, 2014.

Schrag, Peter. *Not Fit for Our Society: Nativism and Immigration*. Berkeley: University of California Press, 2010.

Second Vatican Council. *Ad Gentes: Decree on the Mission Activity of the Church*, 1965.

Segovia, Fernando F. *Decolonizing Biblical Studies: A View from the Margins*. Maryknoll, N.Y.: Orbis Books, 2000.

Interpreting Beyond Borders. Sheffield: Sheffield Academic Press, 2000.

Silverman, Stephanie J. "Immigration Detention in America: A History of Its Expansion and a Study of Its Significance." Centre on Migration, Policy, and Society, 2010.

Singletary, Otis A. *The Mexican War*. Chicago: University of Chicago Press, 1960.

Snyder, Susanna. *Asylum-Seeking, Migration, and Church*. Farnham, Surrey: Ashgate, 2012.

Spina, Frank Anthony. "Israelites as *Gērîm*, 'Sojourners,' in Social and Historical Context." In *The Word of the Lord Shall Go Forth: Essays in Honor of David Noel Freedman in Celebration of His Sixtieth Birthday*, edited by Carol L. Meyers and Michael Patrick O'Connor, 321–35. Winona Lake, Ind.: Eisenbrauns, 1983.

Stuntz, William J. *The Collapse of American Criminal Justice*. Cambridge, Mass.: Belknap Press of Harvard University Press, 2011.

Sullivan, Julie. "Prisons: Conditions Severe Even for Jails." *The Oregonian*, December 10, 2000. www.pulitzer.org/archives/6511. Accessed October 2, 2012.

The Fathers of the Second Vatican Council, and Paul VI. *Gaudium et Spes: Pastoral Constitution on the Church in the Modern Word*, 1965. www.vatican.va/archive/hist_ councils/ii_vatican_council/documents/vat-ii_cons_19651207_gaudium-et-spes_en.html. Accessed November 30, 2015.

Tichenor, Daniel J. *Dividing Lines: The Politics of Immigration Control in America*. Princeton: Princeton University Press, 2002.

"Treaty of Guadalupe Hidalgo (February 2, 1848)." In *Treaties and Conventions between the United States of America and Other Powers Since July 4, 1776*. Washington, D.C.: Government Printing Office, 1871. http://avalon.law.yale.edu/19th_century/guadhida.asp. Accessed August 21, 2012.

Turner, Laurence A. *Genesis*. 2nd edn. Readings. Sheffield: Sheffield Phoenix Press, 2009.

"Turning Migrants into Criminals: The Harmful Impact of U.S. Border Prosecutions." Human Rights Watch, May 22, 2013. www.hrw.org/reports/2013/05/22/turning-migrants-criminals. Accessed May 28, 2013.

U.S. Census. "American Community Survey Demographic and Housing Estimates: 2014 1-Year Estimates." U.S. Census Bureau, 2014. https://factfinder.census.gov/faces/table services/jsf/pages/productview.xhtml?pid=ACS_14_1YR_DP05&prodType=table. Accessed June 29, 2016.

Van Wagenen, Michael. *Remembering the Forgotten War: The Enduring Legacies of the U.S.-Mexican War*. Amherst: University of Massachusetts Press, 2012.

Vattel, Emer de. *Le Droit des Gens, ou, Principes de la Loi naturelle appliqués à la conduite et aux affaires des Nations et des Souverains*. 2 vols. London, 1758.

The Law of Nations: Or Principles of the Law of Nature Applied to the Conduct of Nations and Sovereigns*. London: G. G. and J. Robinson, 1797.

The Law of Nations: Or Principles of the Law of Nature Applied to the Conduct of Nations and Sovereigns*. Edited by Béla Kapossy and Richard Whatmore. Indianapolis: Liberty Fund, 2008.

Vaughan, Jessica M. "Attrition through Enforcement: A Cost-Effective Strategy to Shrink the Illegal Population." Backgrounder. Washington, D.C.: Center for Immigration Studies, April 2006. http://cis.org/articles/2006/back406.html.

Vitoria, Francisco de. *Political Writings*. Translated by Anthony Pagden and Jeremy Lawrance. Cambridge: Cambridge University Press, 1991.

Wallace, Daniel B. *Greek Grammar beyond the Basics: An Exegetical Syntax of the New Testament with Scripture, Subject, and Greek Word Indexes*. Grand Rapids, Mich.: Zondervan, 1996.

Waltke, Bruce K. *An Old Testament Theology: An Exegetical, Canonical, and Thematic Approach*. Grand Rapids, Mich.: Zondervan, 2007.

Walzer, Michael. *Spheres of Justice: A Defense of Pluralism and Equality*. New York: Basic Books, 1983.

Wannenwetsch, Bernd. "'Becoming All Things to All People': The Migration of the Gospel and the Kenotic Travelling of the Migrant Missionary." Presented at the Societas Ethica, Sibiu, Romania, August 24, 2012.

"'For in Its Welfare You Will Find Your Welfare': Political Realism and the Limits of the Augustinian Framework." *Political Theology* 12, no. 3 (2011): 457–65.

"The Fourfold Pattern of Christian Moral Reasoning According to the New Testament." In *Scripture's Doctrine and Theology's Bible: How the New Testament Shapes Christian Dogmatics*, edited by Markus Bockmuehl and Alan J. Torrance, 177–90. Grand Rapids, Mich.: Baker Academic, 2008.

Warren, Robert, and Jeffrey S. Passel. "A Count of the Uncountable: Estimates of Undocumented Aliens Counted in the 1980 United States Census." *Demography* 24, no. 3 (1987): 375–93.

Warren, Robert, and John Robert Warren. "Unauthorized Immigration to the United States: Annual Estimates and Components of Change, by State, 1990 to 2010." *International Migration Review* 47, no. 2 (2013): 296–329.

Weinfeld, Moshe. *Deuteronomy 1–11: A New Translation with Introduction and Commentary*. Anchor Bible 5. New York: Doubleday, 1991.

Deuteronomy and the Deuteronomic School. Oxford: Clarendon Press, 1972.

Weingreen, J. *A Practical Grammar for Classical Hebrew*. 2nd edn. Oxford: Clarendon Press, 1959.

Westermann, Claus. *Genesis 1–11: A Commentary*. Translated by John Scullion S.J. London: S.P.C.K., 1984.

Wharton, Francis, ed. *A Digest of the International Law of the United States: Taken from Documents Issued by Presidents and Secretaries of State, and from Decisions of Federal*

Courts and Opinions of Attorneys-General. 2nd. edn. 3 vols. Washington: Government Printing Office, 1887.

Wilbanks, Dana W. *Re-Creating America: The Ethics of U.S. Immigration and Refugee Policy in a Christian Perspective*. Nashville: Abingdon Press, 1996.

Williams, Michael C. "Hobbes and International Relations: A Reconsideration." *International Organization* 50, no. 2 (1996): 213–36.

Woods, Paul. *Theologizing Migration: Otherness and Liminality in East Asia*. Oxford: Regnum Books International, 2015.

"Yearbook of Immigration Statistics." Office of Immigration Statistics, United States Department of Homeland Security, Fiscal Year 2014. www.dhs.gov/yearbook-immigration-statistics. Accessed June 9, 2016.

Yardley, Jim, and Azam Ahmed. "Pope Francis Wades Into U.S. Immigration Morass With Border Trip." *The New York Times*, February 17, 2016. www.nytimes.com/2016/02/18/world/americas/pope-francis-ciudad-juarez.html?emc=edit_ee_20160218&nl=todaysheadlines-europe&nlid=56985746. Accessed September 13, 2016.

Yukich, Grace. *One Family under God: Immigration Politics and Progressive Religion in America*. New York: Oxford University Press, 2013.

Zolberg, Aristide R. *A Nation by Design: Immigration Policy in the Fashioning of America*. Cambridge, Mass.: Harvard University Press, 2006.

CASES

Afroyim v. Rusk, 387 U.S. 253 (1967).

Brown v. Board of Education of Topeka, 349 U.S. 294 (1954).

Calvin v. Smith, 77 Eng. Rep. 377 (1608).

Chae Chan Ping v. United States, 130 U.S. 581 (1889).

Chew Heong v. United States, 112 U.S. 536 (1884).

Chy Lung v. Freeman, 92 U.S. 275 (1875).

Fong Yue Ting v. United States, Wong Quan v. United States, Lee Joe v. United States, 149 U.S. 698 (1893).

Head Money Cases: Edye and Another v. Robinson, Collector; Cunard Steamship Company v. Same; Same v. Same, 112 U.S. 580 (1884).

Henderson v. Mayor of City of New York, 92 U.S. 259 (1875).

Ho Ah Kow v. Nunan, 5 Sawyer 552 (C.C.D. California 1879).

In re Rodríguez, 81 F. 337 (W. D. Tex. 1897).

John Inglis v. Trustees of the Sailor's Snug Harbor, 28 U.S. 99 (1830).

Nishimura Ekiu v. United States, 142 U.S. 651 (1891).

Passenger Cases: George Smith v. William Turner, Health Commissioner of the Port of New York; James Norris v. The City of Boston, 48 U.S. 283 (1849).

Shaughnessy v. United States ex rel. Mezei, 345 U.S. 206 (1953).

The Schooner Exchange v. McFaddon & Others, 11 U.S. 116 (1812).

United States ex rel. Knauff v. Shaughnessy, 338 U.S. 537 (1950).

United States v. Aguilar, 883 F.2d 662 (9th Cir. 1989).

United States v. Jung Ah Lung, 124 U.S. 621 (1887).

United States v. Wong Kim Ark, 169 U.S. 649 (1898).

Vance v. Terrazas, 444 U.S. 252 (1980).

Yick Wo v. Hopkins, Sheriff and Wo Lee v. Hopkins, 118 U.S. 356 (1886).

Zadvydas v. Davis, 533 U.S. 678 (2001).

ACTS, BILLS, AND EXECUTIVE ORDERS

Additional Articles to the Treaty between the United States and China, June 18, 1858, 16 Stat. 739 (1868).

An Act a supplement to an act entitled "An act to execute certain treaty stipulations relating to Chinese," approved the sixth day of May eighteen hundred and eighty-two, 25 Stat. 504 (1888).

An Act concerning Aliens, 1 Stat. 570 (1798).

An Act in addition to the act intituled, "An act to establish an uniform rule of naturalization; and to repeal the acts heretofore passed on that subject," 2 Stat. 292 (1804).

An act in amendment to the various acts relative to immigration and the importation of aliens under contract or agreement to perform labor, 26 Stat. 1084 (1891).

An Act in further addition to "An act to establish an uniform rule of naturalization; and to repeal the acts heretofore passed on that subject," 4 Stat. 69 (1824).

An Act: Making omnibus consolidated appropriations for the fiscal year ending September 30, 1997, and for other purposes., Pub. L. No. 104–208, 110 Stat. 3009–546 (1996).

An act regulating passenger ships and vessels, 3 Stat. 488 (1819).

An Act relative to evidence in cases of naturalization, 3 Stat. 258 (1816).

An Act respecting Alien Enemies, 1 Stat. 577 (1798).

An Act supplementary to and to amend the act, intituled "An act to establish an uniform rule of naturalization; and to repeal the act heretofore passed on that subject," 1 Stat. 566 (1798).

An Act supplementary to the acts heretofore passed on the subject of an uniform rule of naturalization, 3 Stat. 53 (1813).

An act supplementary to the acts in relation to immigration, 18 Stat. 477 (1875).

An Act to amend an act entitled "An act to execute certain treaty stipulations relating to Chinese approved May sixth eighteen hundred and eighty-two," 23 Stat. 115 (1884).

An Act: To amend section 201 (a), 202(c) and 203(a) of the Immigration and Nationality Act, as amended, and to establish a Select Commission on Immigration and Refugee Policy, Pub. L. No. 95–412, 92 Stat. 907 (1978).

An Act to amend the acts concerning naturalization, 4 Stat. 310 (1828).

An Act: To amend the Immigration and Nationality Act to change the level, and preference system for admission, of immigrants to the United States, and to provide for administrative naturalization, and for other purposes, Pub. L. No. 101–649, 104 Stat. 4978 (1990).

An Act: To amend the Immigration and Nationality Act to revise and reform the immigration laws, and for other purposes, Pub. L. No. 99–603, 100 Stat. 3359 (1986).

An Act: To amend the Immigration and Nationality Act to revise the procedures for the admission of refugees, to amend the Migration and Refugee Assistance Act of 1962 to establish a more uniform basis for the provision of assistance to refugees, and for other purposes, Pub. L. No. 96–212, 94 Stat. 102 (1980).

An Act: To amend the Immigration and Nationality Act, and for other purposes, Pub. L. No. 89–236, 79 Stat. 911 (1965).

An Act: To amend the Immigration and Nationality Act, and for other purposes, Pub. L. No. 94–571, 90 Stat. 2703 (1976).

An Act to amend the Naturalization Acts and to punish Crimes against the same, and for other Purposes, 16 Stat. 254 (1870).

An Act to encourage Immigration, 13 Stat. 385 (1864).

An Act: To enforce the constitutional right to vote, to confer jurisdiction upon the district courts of the United States to provide injunctive relief against discrimination in public accommodations, to authorize the Attorney General to institute suits to protect constitutional rights in public facilities and public education, to extend the Commission on Civil Rights, to prevent discrimination in federally assisted programs, to establish a Commission on Equal Employment Opportunity, and for other purposes, Pub. L. No. 88–352, 78 Stat. 241 (1964).

An Act to establish an uniform Rule of Naturalization, 1 Stat. 103 (1790).

An act to establish an uniform rule of naturalization; and to repeal the act heretofore passed on that subject, 1 Stat. 414 (1795).

An act to establish an uniform rule of naturalization; and to repeal the acts heretofore passed on that subject, 2 Stat. 153 (1802).

An Act: To establish operational control over the international land and maritime borders of the United States, Pub. L. No. 109–367, 120 Stat. 2638 (2006).

An act to execute certain treaty stipulations relating to Chinese, 22 Stat. 58 (1882).

An Act: To limit the immigration of aliens into the United States, Pub. L. No. 67–5, 42 Stat. 5 (1921).

An Act: To limit the immigration of aliens into the United States, and for other purposes, Pub. L. No. 68–139, 43 Stat. 153 (1924).

An Act: To prevent the manufacturing, distribution, and use of illegal drugs, and for other purposes, Pub. L. No. 100–690, 8 U.S.C. § 1101 (a) (43) 102 Stat. 4181 (1988).

An Act to prohibit the "Coolie Trade" by American Citizens in American Vessels, 12 Stat. 340 (1862).

An act to prohibit the coming of Chinese persons into the United States, 27 Stat. 25 (1892).

An act to prohibit the importation and migration of foreigners and aliens under contract or agreement to perform labor in the United States, its Territories, and the District of Columbia, 23 Stat. 322 (1885).

An Act to prohibit the importation of Slaves into any port or place within the jurisdiction of the United States, from and after the first day of January, in the year of our Lord one thousand eight hundred and eight, 2 Stat. 426 (1807).

An act to regulate Immigration, 22 Stat. 214 (1882).

An act to regulate the Carriage of Passengers in Merchant Vessels, 9 Stat. 127 (1847).

An Act to Regulate the Carriage of Passengers in Steamships and other Vessels, 10 Stat. 715 (1855).

An Act: To regulate the immigration of aliens into the United States, Pub. L. No. 57–162, 32 Stat. 1213 (1903).

An Act: To regulate the immigration of aliens to, and the residence of aliens in, the United States, Pub. L. No. 64–301, 39 Stat. 874 (1917).

An Act: To revise the laws relating to immigration, naturalization, and nationality; and for other purposes, Pub. L. No. 82–414, 66 Stat. 163 (1952).

Beason-Hammon Alabama Taxpayer and Citizen Protection Act, Alabama House Bill (H.B.) 56 (2011).

Border Security, Economic Opportunity, and Immigration Modernization Act, U.S. Senate Bill S. 744 (2013).

Gentleman's Agreement, Executive Order no. 589 (1907).

Support Our Law Enforcement and Safe Neighborhoods Act, Arizona Senate Bill (S.B.) 1070 (2010).

Index